T0314302

PRECISION RETAILING

Behaviourally Informed
Organizations

BEHAVIOURALLY INFORMED ORGANIZATIONS

To date, there has been a lack of practical advice for organizations based on behavioral research. The Behaviourally Informed Organizations series fills this knowledge gap with a strategic perspective on how governments, businesses, and other organizations have embedded behavioral insights into their operations. The series is rooted in work by academics and practitioners co-creating knowledge via the Behaviourally Informed Organizations Partnership (www.biorgpartnership.com), and is written in a highly accessible style to highlight key ideas, pragmatic frameworks, and prescriptive outcomes based on illustrative case studies.

Also in the series:

The Behaviorally Informed Organization, edited by Dilip Soman and Catherine Yeung

Behavioral Science in the Wild, edited by Nina Mažar and Dilip Soman

Cash Transfers for Inclusive Societies: A Behavioral Lens, edited by Jiaying Zhao, Saugato Datta, and Dilip Soman

Precision Retailing

Driving Results with Behavioral Insights and Data Analytics

EDITED BY LAURETTE DUBÉ, MAXIME C. COHEN,
NATHAN YANG, AND BASSEM MONLA

UNIVERSITY OF TORONTO PRESS
Toronto Buffalo London

Rotman-UTP Publishing
An imprint of University of Toronto Press
© University of Toronto Press 2024
Toronto Buffalo London
utorontopress.com

Library and Archives Canada Cataloguing in Publication

Title: Precision retailing : driving results with behavioral insights and data analytics / edited by Laurette Dubé, Maxime C. Cohen, Nathan Yang, and Bassem Monla.
Names: Dubé, Laurette, editor. | Cohen, Maxime C., editor. | Yang, Nathan, editor. | Monla, Bassem, editor.
Description: Series statement: Behaviourally informed organizations | Includes bibliographical references.
Identifiers: Canadiana (print) 20230568963 | Canadiana (ebook) 2023056903X | ISBN 9781487542719 (cloth) | ISBN 9781487542733 (PDF) | ISBN 9781487542726 (EPUB)
Subjects: LCSH: Consumer behavior – Research. | LCSH: Consumers – Decision making – Research. | LCSH: Marketing – Research. | LCSH: Economics – Psychological aspects.
Classification: LCC HF5415.32 .P74 2024 | DDC 658.8/342 – dc23

ISBN 978-1-4875-4271-9 (cloth)   ISBN 978-1-4875-4272-6 (EPUB)
                                      ISBN 978-1-4875-4273-3 (PDF)

Jacket design: Regina Starace

We wish to acknowledge the land on which the University of Toronto Press operates. This land is the traditional territory of the Wendat, the Anishnaabeg, the Haudenosaunee, the Métis, and the Mississaugas of the Credit First Nation.

University of Toronto Press acknowledges the financial support of the Government of Canada and the Ontario Arts Council, an agency of the Government of Ontario, for its publishing activities.

Canada Council for the Arts
Conseil des Arts du Canada

ONTARIO ARTS COUNCIL
CONSEIL DES ARTS DE L'ONTARIO
an Ontario government agency
un organisme du gouvernement de l'Ontario

Funded by the Government of Canada
Financé par le gouvernement du Canada

Canadä

Contents

Preface

Without a doubt, the COVID-19 era has forced the retail sector to rethink the way it conducts business. Customer experience has largely shifted into the digital realm, and questions have emerged about how to best optimize digital and physical business operations considering this change in everyday life. In such an algorithmically infused society, measurements to support personal and business operation, investment, policy, and retail occupy more than ever a central position in helping enterprises in value chains, industry, and society as a whole to thrive in the digital and physical world. It does not just come down to having a strong online presence. Rather, success comes down to having a sophisticated understanding of how to map customer journeys and realizing that the digital and physical realms of customer experience constantly fuse into an interactive experiential landscape. Oftentimes, consumers conduct their background research about a service or product in one channel, while shifting to another to make their final decisions. The way we understand and handle this complex customer journey will not just have a bearing on how retail evolves but also shape how business meets its future on a sustainable growth trajectory, which is the inevitable continuation of the digital transition of science, business, and society.

Building upon earlier books in the Behaviourally Informed Organization series, the precision retailing approach featured here stands on the shoulder of behavioral economics, decision neurosciences, and management disciplines to progressively bridge on the one hand, what we know of the neurobiology of real-time and long-term human decision-making in real-world contexts and, on the other hand, the most recent advances in artificial intelligence, big data analytics, and other facets of the Industry 4.0 digital transformation, with the objective to support *adaptive real-world behaviors and contexts* – what is now called precision convergence. Such knowledge is to be integrated in as real time as possible into innovation, communication, professional practice, organizational design, and policy to create adaptive real-world contexts that are economically, socially, and environmentally sustainable for individuals, businesses, and society.

The book takes a broad perspective of precision retailing, "retail" here meaning the interaction point between individuals (with their biology, brain, and life trajectories and aspirations) and the professions, organizations, institutions, systems, and policies that support them in ever-changing contexts. Businesses are one of the keys intermediaries between individuals and society, with digitization now enabling finer-grained linkages between human behavior components and the dynamic and interconnected real-world contexts created in real time by innovation pipelines, delivery systems, supply chains, and markets. Precision retailing (PR) enriches the traditional view of retail as adaptive to human behavior/biology at a large scale. Consequently, PR is an interdisciplinary concept, leveraging innovations from precision medicine, neuroinformatics, and analytics (behavioral, business, and systems), as well as other disciplines that have integrated AI and other digital technologies to improve commercial, social, environmental, and health outcomes at the same time. By integrating this wide scope of disciplines, PR can help make retail a powerful catalyst in creating such a convergence economy.

In line with the objectives of the Behaviourally Informed Organizations series, the goal of this book is to assemble key precision retailing concepts, methods, and tools to complement existing behavioral research and decision-support tools that help managers better capture in real time the multiscale drivers of consumer behavior and integrate these in transaction-level and long-term navigation of dynamic real-world complexity to support adaptive contexts for all. Real-world adaptive contexts power convergence of economic, social, environmental, and health outcomes for individuals, organizations, and institutions along supply chains and systems. The core focus is on consumer-facing retailing and marketing practices, with backend linkages to keep a human-centered approach throughout business-to-business processes along supply chains and market systems, weaving AI and analytics within on-the-ground innovation, operations, and transformation.

The book is organized in four parts. Part One, *From Behavioral Insights to Precision Consumer Research*, sketches the journey of individual-level research and its linkages to enterprise- and aggregate-level outcome, be it in terms of economic, human health, or environmental performance. Chapter 1 paves the way for journey maps – core tools of behavioral economic research since its onset three decades ago – to evolve from a singular expectation of the customer journey to one that leverages insights from behavioral economics' approaches and theories to reflect how decisions and behavior happen in the real world and provide useful case studies. Chapter 2 introduces genetics as a neurobiological factor impacting real-time choices as well as long-term predisposition and behavior, addressing challenges and possibilities for better targeted and more precise offering, accounting for privacy and other ethical considerations. In turn, Chapter 3 expands to neuroscience methods and contexts, introducing neuroforecasting as a method to extrapolate results from experimental protocols that trace neurobehavioral responses from communications and contexts to their real-world individual and market-level impact. Chapter 4 adapts and assembles methods from linguistics, semiotics, and evidence-based behavioral modeling, unlocking unconscious facets of consumer motivations and behaviors to inform corporate strategy and brand. Chapter 5 comes back on another early pillar of behavioral economic research, namely human-centric design, to reflect upon the challenges and the possibility of precision consumers with both machines and humans as data sources.

In Part Two, *Weaving Behavioral and Precision Consumer Research into Marketing and Retail Strategy*, we advance the precision retailing journey proper by examining key strategic facets of marketing and retail as they are designed, deployed, and monitored in diverse and changing contexts, be these physical or digital. In Chapter 6, the state-of-practice and the state-of-theory of personalized retailing are studied as the core, evolving pillars in the journey from behaviorally informed organization to precision retailing. Advancing insights on such structural and dynamic transformation in a resource scarcity context, Chapter 7 delves into the COVID-19 pandemic period to present a framework and generous illustrative example of how consumer response to different marketing strategies can be reliably anticipated. Chapter 8 zooms in on how evolving (real-time and long-term) behavior and precision research can be integrated specifically in consumer-facing design, be it in shaping the atmospherics and category placement in physical stores or guiding as adaptive navigation in online commerce. Chapter 9 advances further the operational specifications of precision retailing by reviewing key parameters of current practice and research of retail analytics and providing a transformative road map.

Part Three, *Data Analytics and Machine Learning for Decision Support to Retail Strategies*, gets at the core of data science and artificial pillars of precision retailing, providing managers, professionals, and non-data scientists in organizations or in academia with some sophisticated understanding of explanatory or predictive algorithms, with a special focus on enterprise-level real-time decision support. Chapter 10 discusses a prescriptive, analytic approach to solving a joint markdown pricing and inventory allocation optimization problem under demand parameter uncertainty. Chapter 11 shifts to sales promotions and presents a markdown optimization model under demand uncertainty. The model is designed to help retailers undertake sales promotions while considering both direct and indirect effects of price promotions on consumers, and as a result, on demand. Chapter 12 addresses omnichannel pricing challenges through choice models that enable censored demand estimation. Chapter 13 considers the context of finance retail services and presents a pricing model to optimize customer lifetime value.

Part Four, *Retail Channels as Part of Business and Society Ecosystem in Moving towards Adaptive Behavior and Context*, moves from enterprise-level decision-making to those that entail multiple actors in one or another form of ecosystem. Chapter 14 investigates the seller's perspective in examining risk, reward, and uncertainty, and how that guides decision-making about poster prices and auctions in sequential buyer-seller transactions. Chapter 15 examines a second channel decision-making in B2B markets, namely participative pricing. Chapter 16 considers the whole retail supply chain, offering a framework to enhance efficiency, visibility, transparency, and trust at the digital-physical B2B interface through standard harmonization and digital transformation of innovation pipelines, supply chains, and market systems. Chapter 17 offers new models of digital-physical interfaces in retail processes to create and capture business and stakeholder value. Chapter 18 moves to businesses as a key catalyst in the transformation of their own and society's complex and dynamic ecosystems in charting a course towards the mainstream convergence of economic, social, health, and environmental outcomes and processes for a better future for the world.

Weaving a common thread through the book, each chapter is followed by a "Managerial Insights Brief," prepared, in collaboration with the authors, by coeditor Bassem Monla, who co-created with lead editor Laurette Dubé, a new-to-the-world MBA precision retailing course in spring 2020. Bringing to bear more than thirty-five years of professional experience in IT business and consultancy and now an AI subject matter expert at IBM and a leader of the AI practice there, he regularly engages with companies who want to deploy AI and advanced analytics solutions. These briefs provide insights on successful human-centric digital transformation for adaptive real-world behavior by the consumer and sustainable pathways to growth for businesses, placing ethical consideration at the center of both transformations, progressively developing for the reader an AI/digital toolbox. Altogether, this precision retailing book displays how all actors throughout society can not only compete with but also productively complement each other so that nature, human, and machine can co-evolve towards a better future.

Laurette Dubé, Maxime C. Cohen,
Nathan Yang, and Bassem Monla

Acknowledgments

The editorial team and contributors want to acknowledge the financial support of the Social Sciences and Humanities Research Council (Grant #CIHR/Guelph 02083-000, Sub-Award #SSHRC 895-2019-1011, Sub-Award #SSHRC 435-2020-1136) to the book series, and that of the 3-Council SMART training platform (Grant #02083-000) for support to trainees who collaborated in a highly valuable manner to various facets of the production of this manuscript, namely Alexandra Demos, Jenny Yu, Doga Ozkaya and, most importantly, Krishiv Shah (now graduated and a digital consulting analyst at Huron Consulting Group) who assembled the different versions of the manuscript. Special thanks also go to Katheryne Murphy, MCCHE executive assistant.

From Behavioral Insights to Precision Consumer Research

PART ONE

From Behavioral Intention to
Precision Consumer Research

CHAPTER ONE

Evolving Traditional Journey Maps

Kelly Peters

SUMMARY OF CHAPTER

The chapter provides thought leadership for modernizing the journey map to accommodate the need for precision retailing as well as social influences. The modernization of journey mapping requires sophisticated, scientific insights and technologies and not only intuition.

MANAGERIAL IMPLICATIONS (GENERAL)
- Managers in retail business will find in this chapter important and innovative thought leadership that potentially transforms the way journey maps are elaborated.
- Marketers, working in multidisciplinary teams using advanced technology tools, are invited to experiment with social influences when designing their customer experience.

MANAGERIAL IMPLICATIONS (ORGANIZATIONAL)
- From the organizational perspective, managers need to rethink the practice of customer experience and the tools they are using to creating a tight collaboration between this practice and that of advanced analytics.
- An effective way to reach this tight collaboration is to create a "center of excellence in AI & analytics" that is multidisciplinary

and cross-departmental. The center would have the responsibility of designing, developing, deploying, and monitoring such types of advanced analytics and optimization models.

- This center of excellence would feed marketers with insights from social media for designing the customer experience or journey map.

MANAGERIAL IMPLICATIONS (STRATEGIC, TACTICAL, AND OPERATIONAL)

- The managerial decisions are mostly tactical in nature when it comes to transforming the practice of customer experience and the tools used. This also applies to decisions like creating a "center of excellence in AI & analytics," provisioning a data platform, and sourcing the right skills (internally and or externally) to extract insights from social data.

MANAGERIAL IMPLICATIONS (RISK ASSESSMENT)

- Experimenting with the innovative thoughts presented in this chapter can be carried out with a low-risk approach as managers and marketers can proceed iteratively and incrementally to gain experience and validate the concepts discovered.

1. INTRODUCTION

The smallest of bumps in the road can trip up an entire journey. Imagine if during the tedious process of purchasing health insurance through an insurer's website, having completed detailed surveys about your health, your medical history, and other personal information, you arrive at a web page that contains an image of a large red STOP sign prominent in the center of the screen above the "buy now" purchase button, with large, bold text demanding that you "verify that the information you have provided was accurate and true, under penalty of law." From the insurance company's point of view, this page is helpful. They want to call attention to the possibility of the form being incorrectly filled to minimize the potential problems that misspelling a name, for example, might cause. They also need to put a potentially fraudulent applicant on notice. But for the honest customer who had just completed a tedious and complex process and worried they may have made an innocent typo or overlooked some relevant personal information, would they feel confident in proceeding?

This experience was based on a real case at management consulting firm BEworks. Tasked with understanding why online enrollment was lower than the purchase rates of in-person and telephone-based channels at a large insurance company, the team started by creating a journey map through process flow diagrams that detailed each step of the customer's experience. Analysis of web traffic data revealed that the STOP sign page was a major drop-off point where a significant number of prospective customers exited the process without completing the purchase. Note that this shopping cart abandonment happened after a customer had spent an average of thirty minutes inputting the information.

The journey map – with the screenshot of the final STOP sign page – was presented to company executives who immediately recognized the obvious roadblock in the customer's path. The request for accuracy was presented in such a way as to practically intimidate customers into being afraid of consequences of an error. This step in the journey was removed, and along with the implementation of other behaviorally informed interventions, led to a 33 per cent (from 18.9 to 25 per cent) increase in client acquisition, as well as a 40 per cent increase in premiums per customer ($451 to $633). Without seeing the customer's journey with their own eyes, it can be difficult for organizational leaders to understand the customer's experience. Journey maps that capture the operational process and layer on relevant data can provide a path to quick, impactful wins.

2. JOURNEY MAPPING – ASSESSING WHERE WE ARE AT

Examples such as the one above illustrate that journey mapping can be a key tool in improving the customer experience. In a world that has become increasingly complex for consumers to navigate, many organizations are having to work harder to get a better understanding of their client's experience. Journey mapping ought to be considered an essential tool to help with that mandate.

So, what is a journey map? In its essence, it is a schematic representation of the interactions a customer has with a firm, step-by-step, from their welcome, to the close of a sale, and beyond into servicing and the steps required to maintain a relationship. Journey maps at their core are seen as "relatively simple"; they provide "a visual depiction of the sequence of events through which customers may interact with a service organization during an entire purchase process."[1] The process of creating a journey map might include cataloging the touchpoints and channels that a customer might use to interact with the company. The benefits include making it easy or in some cases even possible to create holistic institutional knowledge about what it is like for customers to interact with the company. Because this exercise is often aimed at capturing the operational touchpoints between a firm and its clients, this map can be called an "operational journey map." It can provide a visual representation of the tangible touchpoints between the company and the customer. An operational journey map is to managers what a blueprint is to architects or what a floorplan is for homebuyers. Its sole purpose is to show the entire schematic of how customer touchpoints are placed and connected to one another. Maps are functional and utilitarian: while direct experiences are beneficial to an organization, not every manager can go and buy their firm's insurance, or car, or whatever it is they are selling, to get a line of sight on their customer's experience. Investing in journey mapping allows managers and their teams to gain valuable insight by making the intangible tangible.

While operational journey maps are useful tools, we join others[2] in arguing that there is an urgent need to go further than the typical operational schemata. An operational journey map, as is typically used in many organizations, is necessary but not sufficient to give us a full picture of what the real customer experience looks like. Instead of helping with precision retailing, this kind of journey map can yield an inaccurate or perhaps merely shallow view of the actual experience. Practitioners should apply the depth of scholarly research on human psychology and behavior to maximize the insights that can be derived from this exercise. Such an updated journey map ought to enable the generation of hypotheses regarding how customers feel, think, and behave. Further, to make the journey maps reflect the reality, not only do we need the descriptive "what and how" but the "why" of the customer experience. To achieve this, we need to make a distinction between operational journey maps and psychological journey maps, a separate exercise layered on top of the operational map to capture psychological insights.

3. OPERATIONAL JOURNEY MAPS HAVE SHORTCOMINGS

Though shortcomings of operational journey maps have been previously explored, we ought to address a few more for as clean a distinction as possible between operational journey maps and psychological journey maps. The first is the lack of realism about how people make decisions; people are not unboundedly rational agents, nor are they homogeneous decision makers. The second is the assumption of people making decisions alone; traditional journey maps lack the accounting for social influences. The third shortcoming is the missing acknowledgment of the impact that technology itself has on moderating a customer's choice. Finally, we need to incorporate actual data as par for the course in the mapping exercise.

3.1. An Unrealistic View of How People Make Decisions

People are not "rational agents." An assumption implicitly embedded within journey maps is the idea of the so-called "rational" customer. This rational agent or "economic man" is "assumed to have knowledge of the relevant aspects of his environment which, if not absolutely complete, is at least impressively clear and voluminous" and "is assumed also to have a well-organized and stable system of preferences and a skill in computation that enables him to calculate, for the alternative courses of action that are available to him, which of these will permit him to reach the highest attainable point on his preference scale."[3]

Journey maps often reflect a design that assumes that buyers are this "economic man": unboundedly rational agents who adhere to normative models of search optimization. In other words, it means assuming and expecting that customers approach each purchasing decision with dedication and an unlimited amount of energy to exhaustively identify all the options, to carefully weigh all the costs and benefits, and to make decisions that perfectly meet their short- and long-term needs and wants. However, in the same way that pedestrians will cut corners instead of following the 90-degree angles of carefully planned sidewalks, consumers don't follow normatively outlined operational journey maps.

People are not all the same. One shortcut many journey mappers take is to design as if the map will be followed by just one person. Bradley et al. (2021)[4] demonstrated in their research on mapping the customer experience with railway trains that it is not enough to "average" people's experiences. The public is diverse, and while the steps traversed by most may be reflected in one journey map, some crucial stakeholders' experiences are not reflected. In the real world, those overlooked by these "averaged" experiences may be the disenfranchised, who become even further disenfranchised from systems intended to serve them. Based on their research on the use of a single persona in journey maps of a train system, they warned that "the overall system might suffer in terms of operability and functionality" (Bradley et al., 2021, p. 11). The good news is, as Bradley et al. advise, that the disadvantages of averaging can simply be avoided by incorporating fundamentally distinct personas in the journey mapping exercise. Each persona will reveal its necessarily unique path for the manager to see and act on accordingly.

3.2. No One Walks Alone: Missing Social Influences

Another shortcoming of traditional operational journey mapping is to assume people make decisions alone. Hamilton et al. (2020)[5] point out that "traveling companions" play a vital role in influencing the real-life decision maker. One of the most obvious examples where the traditional approach falls short of reality is the substantial amount of joint purchasing decisions made by couples. But beyond that, both proximal social influences through friends and family, and even distal relationships (e.g., Facebook "friends," interest group members, or even complete strangers on customer review sites) influence decisions. Modern journey maps should account for these local networks of families, friends, and neighborhoods, but also mushroom up and out to cover other, relevant networked resources.

3.3. Technology Is Not a Neutral Influence

One of the key factors overlooked in traditional journey mapping is the quickly evolving nature of technology, especially for precision retailing. There are at least three facets that ought to be considered as they are instrumental for understanding the modern customer experience. The first is that customers often traverse multiple channels as a part of their interaction with an organization. The second is the persuasive nature of technology itself in providing a shaping influence. The third is the most forward-looking in which not only is the precision of retailing strengthened by technology, but technology itself operates as an autonomous agent or decision-maker, pursuing the journey on the customer's behalf. We will explore each of these in turn.

Customer journeys are now multichannel journeys. Operational journey maps often, by design, only capture the customer's progress through a generic, singularly defined channel. In reality, a customer's purchasing journey often begins in one channel and finishes in another, through interactions known as "showrooming," where customers search in bricks-and-mortar locations and buy online; and the inverse, where they shop online then buy in person, known as "webrooming." While multichannel behavior is well-studied, Lemon and Verhoef (2016) argue there is an "urgent need for a meta-analysis on the drivers of channel choice." Bearing in mind a caution from Rosenbaum et al. (2017), who argued for simplicity in the journey mapping process by prioritizing the touchpoints that are strategic and that matter the most to customers (and managers), these cross-channel journeys present meaningful differences in a customer's experience and therefore warrant the more onerous cross-channel mapping approach. Precision retailing requires an understanding of the customer's expectations about a respective channel (e.g., humans but not algorithms can be bargained with) as well as accommodating *the routes* that span across multiple channels.

Technology itself is persuasive. Another shortcoming is assuming that technology is merely a channel for interaction, with no built-in forces for persuasion. The prevalence of internet-enabled devices has made them an integral part of the consumer decision-making process. In addition to impacting how consumers gather information, technology is shaping preferences through the interfaces that people see and touch. One study found that when compared to a mouse and keyboard, the use of a digital-touch interface increased customers' focus on *tangible* aspects of a hotel selection, like "décor and furniture over intangible aspects like WIFI and employee demeanor."[6] Another found that customers "are more likely to be led to welfare-maximizing choices when aided by a product-screening tool"[7] that was calibrated to their own self-weighted preferences. The effects of a technological device's physical properties and haptic interactivity (such as swiping, shaking, tilting) are a nascent but important line of research for understanding technological influences on consumer decisions.

Operational journey maps may acknowledge different touchpoints but typically fall short on recognizing how different channels carry different expectations with respect to authenticity, persuasiveness, and trustworthiness. A message delivered through one platform will not have the same impact as it would being delivered in another. Journey mappers need to keep this in mind as they refine their mapping efforts.

Autonomous agents will travel the journey on the customer's behalf. In the not-too-distant future, autonomous agents, such as Alexa and Siri, will traverse the journey on the consumer's behalf and make purchases based on pre-established habits and preferences. Autonomous shopping systems, as defined by Emanuel de Bellis and Gita V. Johar,[8] are "technology to which consumers can delegate substantial parts of the shopping process, including shopping decisions and tasks" that will reach "a series of conclusions for consumers, such as which and how many items to buy and when to do so, based on input data." In our work on AI with start-ups such as Empatho and Integrate.ai, we are designing and developing operationalizable definitions of human behavior on attributes such as impulsivity, risk-taking (and willingness to try new products), and well-being. These definitions are being used to serve as the mechanisms for better precision retailing experiences on behalf of consumers.

Designing journey maps without consideration for the impact these technologies can have on consumer decisions is a missed opportunity. In keeping with the idea of looking at advances in technology as a practice, journey mapping would benefit from focusing one eye on the future and figuring out where to put the next bridge, not just documenting the current state. Is a map for description or navigation? Journey maps typically stop at being merely descriptive and do not point towards the best path for a given course of action. These demands seem cumbersome, but if we are going to improve the journey mapping exercise by identifying other actors in the decision-making journey, we ought to ensure that we are also watching out for the construction zones that point to a different future soon to come.

3.4. Maps Need Data

Maps should be drawn with more than intuitive observations. The process of journey mapping often starts with managers sitting in a room with a whiteboard or colored sticky notes. The exercise sometimes begins by asking questions that surface the actions that customers engage in, what their first touchpoint is, and what barriers may impede their progress. The example cited at the onset of this chapter illustrates how relevant data, such as customer engagement drop-off at the STOP sign web page of an insurance website, can immediately produce actionable insights. The challenge with these steps is that they provide a limited view of the customer's experience. The steps are constrained by what the managers can see and their intuition about what the barriers are. Transactional data should be gathered to provide an objective lens on the customer experience.

4. JOURNEY MAPPING – WHERE TO GO FROM HERE

Let us make clear the distinction between the operational journey map and the psychological map. The psychological journey map aims to capture the factors that influence how customers arrive at a specific belief or behavior. The job of the operational journey map is to provide managers and retailers with a schemata of the consumer's interaction points with a company; the job of a psychological journey map is to help managers determine what influences exist on the path to purchase. By defining the two types of journey map, the operational and the psychological, we can improve design for the normative flow – the way it ought to be – and capture a more realistic understanding of what and where the influences are that shape the targeted behavior.

We can start by resolving the shortcomings of the operational journey mapping exercise. This means improving journey maps by incorporating social influences, reflecting multiple channels, adding a data layer, and leveraging the influence of technology. Lemon and Verhoef (2016) proposed a process model for the customer journey and experience that identifies the type of touchpoints a customer might experience at each stage of their experience which provides firms with "an organizing framework for understanding potential leverage points in the customer experience." Each organization is unique and should require that their mapping discipline reflect the best of this taxonomy as well as any helpful principles that are being identified here.

4.1. Incorporate Social Influences

People do not make decisions in a vacuum. Let's consider this case study. A client approached BEworks for help in persuading parents that their new type of baby car seat (incorporating groundbreaking technologies) is safe and worth a premium price. The client already had a journey map that went beyond the isolated parent or agent on a single-channel journey. It showed that pregnant mothers usually drive the online research about car seats and the decision to buy, while fathers take care of the post-purchase installation steps. Furthermore, it recognized that some customary steps, like reading the instruction manual, are usually bypassed by parents and replaced with a request for assistance by relatives or professionals. In applying the psychological approach, we discovered that there was further nuance to the decision-making process. For instance, the pre-purchase research was highly dependent on social interactions, online and in real life. Confronted with information and choice overload, parents quickly stopped their exploration of the market options and instead they begin to rely heavily on recommendations by other parents and their immediate social circle. In other words, customers relied on social proof. However, because this product was novel, there was no social proof to influence consumers. As a proxy for the opinion of laypersons, we leveraged endorsements from industry third party insurance professionals, who are reliable in their knowledge of passenger safety data. Furthermore, our analysis of the purchasing decision revealed that when parents evaluated the safety of the car seat, they would typically use the "squish" or depth of the seat cushion as an estimate of the safety. Despite its intuitive appeal, this is not an accurate assessment mechanism for safety. We formulated hypotheses around communication strategies that would overcome these hurdles, and nudge interest and purchase intent. As a result, the client saw a significant increase in purchasing interest and waitlist registration. There are benefits to reap from being more psychologically informed in one's journey mapping; acknowledging the limitations of the "rational man" assumption is sometimes not enough.

4.2. Reflect the Multiple Channels That Consumers Might Travel

One-stop shopping is rare. A project by BEworks supports the belief that the mechanisms underlying multichannel retailing are complex, reveal interesting aspects of human perception, and warrant further study. The task was to optimize the online price quote and purchase process of home insurance. Customers input details about their home and property into a digital quoter, which in turn generated an insurance offer. As outlined in the journey map, customers could then click to purchase. But at the final step required to bind or purchase the policy, a large proportion defected from the website and phoned the call center. This required the customer to reconfirm all the information that they had input to the website with the agent, which was time-consuming.

Our research indicated that there were two reasons for this detour from one channel – the web – where they were nearly done, to another – the call center – where they had to start over. The first is because they had the misperception that their "uniqueness" needed to be assessed by a human.[9] Second, customers had the assumption that insurance was a product that can be *bargained over* with a person but not with a robot or algorithm (e.g., if you ask, you will be given a more competitive offer). Journey maps need to consider where these decision points are.

4.3. Acknowledge and Harness the Persuasiveness of Technology

Retailers have long known that environmental factors matter – and can shape the consumer's experience. Music, scent, and merchandising are traditional tools. But now that influence extends to digital channels. The impact of "channel" was reflected in a case study of a national bank which sought to increase engagement with their multichannel credit card fraud notification system. In this project, BEworks first mapped out the operational journey. Customers would receive contacts from different channels about a potential fraud attempt: an opt-in text message, an alerting email, and finally, a telephone call by an agent. The bank wanted the low-cost text channel to be effective, but clients would feel suspicion or distrust when evaluating the text messages and would not respond to the alerts. To increase the persuasiveness of the messages, we created a journey which combined two touchpoints into one simultaneous touchpoint, that is, receiving both a text message and an email concurrently. The revised approach had a positive impact. Clients that received messages from both channels concurrently were better persuaded to engage with the system than clients that had been using the previously employed stepwise system.

4.4. Add in the Data Layer

The data part is conceptually easy, if and when the data exists. It is simply a matter of taking the data of customer interactions and mapping them to each step. In a project optimizing the online purchases of a consumer-facing data protection company, we mapped the flow of traffic from a landing page through to subsequent product information pages, leading ultimately to the purchase page. Surprisingly, a significant number of prospective customers dropped off at the earliest steps in the process. The company asked for name, address, and billing information before the product selection process. The client did not believe they had an issue with trust – they assumed that if people were showing up on their website, then their biggest concern must be price and product features. We pointed out what the data showed about where the drop-off point existed, and that helped us in turn be able to generate new hypotheses about people's attitudes towards providing personal information. We intuited that consumers would be in a particularly skeptical mindset when interacting with a company that is dedicated to personal data protection. We gathered further data through an intercept survey with prospective customers abandoning the site and asked exploratory questions about their trust attitudes. As predicted, trust was low. With this additional data, we redesigned the landing page to include customer testimonials (adding key details like name and membership duration), added reminders about the product features (like twenty-four-hour support) throughout the enrollment process, and moved the gathering of customer information to later in the journey.

The history of cartography is littered with maps marred by errors, myths, and even intentional deception. In the same way that geographical maps became more accurate with technology, in the modern age, data-driven approaches can yield a better view of the customer's experience. The factors that influence consumer decisions can be quantifiable with the advancements in marketing powered by data science insights. Using data analysis techniques, we can start to account for how much variance in the consumer decision each agent contributes, and in turn, measure the statistical significance versus the practical significance. It might be the case that online reviews contribute to 3 per cent of the decision-making influence, but then an individual's significant other explains 40 per cent of the variability. It may be useful for practitioners to evaluate the weight of each of these sources of influence.

5. DESIGNING PSYCHOLOGICAL JOURNEY MAPS

Behavioral economics has identified an increasing number of psychological processes that have potentially critical roles in consumer decisions, and as such, should play a prominent role in journey maps. These include the formation of different types of attitudes towards products or services based on perceptual information (e.g., advertising) and the generation of consumer intentions based on information processing through distinct cognitive pathways.[10] These processes are evoked under different conditions and can interact in a myriad of ways to impact consumers' processing of marketing communications, the evaluation of product information, and ultimately, purchasing behavior.

Seminal work reflecting the buying journey as "a series of mental and motor steps" was captured in Howard and Sheth's 1969 model that formulated a structure that enabled us to view consumer buying behavior as "a system."[11] The continued efforts of behavioral economics can provide further insight on the extent to which psychological factors, as well as social and technological influences, cause deviations to the steps we expect consumers to take. Behavioral economics as a field was founded on the core insight that exogeneous influences, often subtle, can impact choices. Take the classic research on social proof, for example, which shows that even the subtlest of connections to the thoughts and behaviors of others, such as a notification about the behavior of the preceding guests in a hotel room, can sway the choices of future guests.

The dual processing framework – a way of conceptualizing human cognition that has become widely used in the community of psychologists, behavioral decision theorists, and behavioral economists[12] – can be immensely helpful in teasing these influences apart and crafting a psychological journey map that is predictive of real choices and behaviors. In particular, the framework's juxtaposition between automatic, fast, and non-conscious thinking and controlled, slow, and conscious thinking provides a crucial basis for a new and dualistic way to think about how individuals process their experiences with firms, that is, using a cognitive process punctuated by mutual influences between attitudes and behaviors that are explicit (i.e., self-reported, and reflective of careful calibration and correction by consumers) and implicit (i.e., held by consumers prior to any form of mental correction, and often guided by factors such as social desirability, majority influence, or cognitive dissonance).

The result is a psychological journey map framework with an added layer of realism about the forces ultimately shaping consumer judgments and buying behaviors.[13] Knowing this, we may wish to consider the more "autonomic" and subliminal signals sent by retailers as well as the signals that act on more elaborate decision-making processes. These types of psychological barriers are highly relevant to decision-making and are not uncommon, yet they are completely neglected by operational journey mapping. Engaging in psychological journey mapping helps organizations pick out the psychological or behavioral patterns that so often impede progress along a particular decision path. Diagnosing the barriers that crop up early at the attention and expectation-setting stage in a journey not only helps to optimize that step, but it also provides insights into what may crop up later in the journey to help or hurt the expected course of action.

BEworks employs the psychological journey map and includes in its most basic incarnation the components Attending, Perceiving, Deciding, Action (or Behavior), and Revisiting/Maintenance. These serve as distinct psychological processes meriting sequential analysis. The processes are briefly defined here for practitioners and are followed by a set of questions that can be asked to help identify the factors influencing the consumer's decisions and behaviors at

Figure 1.1. A diagram illustrating the psychological experience of a consumer from pre-purchase to purchase to post-purchase

these points, and which can be modified to suit particular situations. Practitioners who relish tidy categories should not push this model too hard; the distinctions between each component are blurry and more complex than this framework allows. Nonetheless, it is meant to serve as a preliminary framework for bringing the exercise of psychological analysis into the forefront of the evaluation of the consumer experience.

5.1. Building Process

The key is to build a psychological journey map on top of the operational journey map. At each touchpoint or decision point within the operational journey, a customer's mind can be hypothesized to go through multiple steps that are distinct in terms of the speed and psychological mechanisms involved. Constructing a consumer journey provides a useful framework for applying behavioral economics to consumer product choice. In this construct, key behavioral drivers are parsed into three key phases of the product purchasing experience.

- **Pre-purchase:** What consumers know and think about the brand as they step into a retailer
- **Purchase:** How consumers choose and buy products
- **Post-purchase:** How consumers use and evaluate the products

Consumer journey map. In this map, the customer experience is divided into three main stages: pre-purchase, purchase, and post-purchase. Within each stage, the experience is further parsed into its psychological components.

The following section will describe each stage and the corresponding behavioral concept in more detail.

PRE-PURCHASE: WHAT CONSUMERS ATTEND TO AND PERCEIVE

- **Attending:** People do not assess all aspects of information equally. Because of information overload and limited cognitive capacity, people rely on "mental shortcuts" or heuristics to make decisions. These heuristics are designed for efficiency, but they can also lead to irrational choices.
- **Perceiving:** Even when people pay attention to information, the processing of that information is biased. Consumers are constantly interpreting the information provided, and when essential information is not readily available, consumers look to prior experiences and expectations as an interpretive lens to look at brands and products.

PURCHASE: HOW CONSUMERS DECIDE AND PAY

- **Deciding:** How information is presented and the number of choices available affects whether the action will be performed and at what cost.
- **Transacting:** A strong intent to purchase the product can still be thwarted by a mismatch between the price of the product and its perceived value. The perception of value itself is subject to change: it can improve with a better transacting experience.

POST-PURCHASE: HOW CONSUMERS USE THE PRODUCTS

- **Applying:** Long-term motivational drivers are often very different from short-term drivers. Habit formation and appropriately timed reinforcements can help consumers stick to their commitments and goals.
- **Revisiting/Maintaining:** A variety of motivational and cognitive factors keep people from making a satisfactory decision twice or, depending on the context and product set, replenishing.

Outlined here are some of the key steps to getting both the operational and psychological journey mapping process underway: (1) develop an end-to-end operational journey map identifying touchpoints on all channels that are available to customers (physical, digital, etc.); (2) identify the social influences and technological factors that may influence decision-making; (3) gather, identify, and apply relevant data with regard to defined touchpoints, i.e., where customer engagement stops or stalls, where customers leave one channel and pursue another, etc.; (4) determine what behavioral intervention points are of material interest and within the "scope" of the project; (6) layer on the psychological journey map and generate questions about challenges within the Attending, Perceiving, Deciding, Transacting, Applying, and Revisiting concepts related to the touchpoints that are defined as within one's scope; (7) develop strategic hypotheses based on the aforementioned psychological journey map assessment that clearly identify the goal behavior, the challenges to that behavior, and what interventions could be performed to overcome the barriers.

5.2. Psychological Journey Mapping in Action: A Case Study

The remainder of this chapter will show a concrete example of an operational and psychological journey map and the key behavioral barriers during the customer journey. Again, not all maps fit all journeys: this is intended to serve as a basic blueprint to tailor to your own journey.

In this project, a large skincare and cosmetics manufacturer was losing consumer buy-in and satisfaction with their legacy product line. Customers perceived the product to be outdated and out of touch. The operational journey map outlined a temporospatial representation of a typical customer's in-store encounter with their core products. What this revealed was that there was a difference in who approached versus who avoided the product display based on demographics and generational cohorts (i.e., millennials, Gen Z, Gen X, etc.). To better understand the depth and breadth of the barriers to product purchasing behavior as well as uncovering broader opportunities, the BEworks' team layered on the psychological journey map. Indeed, there were challenges across a few of these components: for example, the slogan and the product packaging were related to Attention, while understanding the necessity of purchasing the product bundle fell under Perception and Transacting concepts. Was the slogan insufficient to address the quality of the product? Was the lack of color coordination between products an impediment to buying the bundle? Was the purchasing of a product bundle typical or atypical for a skin cleanser line? And so on.

For illustrative purposes, here is a closer look at the insights from one component of the psychological journey map: Perceiving.

Figure 1.2.

HERE WE ASKED THE QUESTION: *DO CLIENTS HAVE PREFERENCES FOR VISUAL OR VERBAL INFORMATION ABOUT PRODUCTS?*
Our literature review identified key insights such as the visual preference heuristic. That is, clients prefer visual to verbal depictions of information. That means that images which produce greater perceptions of variety are more appealing compared to text. It can, however, result in choice complexity and overload when choice sets are large, and preferences are unknown.
Application to the Challenge: Clients prefer images to words, so the value proposition messaging should be displayed primarily with pictures about the benefits of the products.

HERE WE ASKED THE QUESTION: *WHAT ARE THE FACTORS THAT INFLUENCE A CLIENT'S PERCEPTION OF A PRODUCT'S QUALITY?*

Our literature review examined research on the effects of multiple extrinsic cues on quality perceptions. Intrinsic attributes are those which are integral and inseparable from physical product. Extrinsic attributes (e.g., price, brand name) often serve as cues that affect consumers' quality perceptions. The implications are that when intrinsic information is scarce or not useful, or there is no opportunity to process it, extrinsic cues are more likely to be used to assess product quality. The use of price, brand, and other cues are universal, but they do not examine how global consumers combine multiple cues to arrive at quality judgments. Extrinsic cues are used to reduce the risk associated with product evaluation and choice. When cues are in agreement, they can be averaged or linearly combined to arrive at product evaluations, but the weighting of each piece of information changes when the valence of the cues disagree (more negative cues appears to dominate evaluations). **Application to the Challenge:** Clients prefer images to words, so the value proposition messaging should be displayed with primarily pictures about the benefits of the products.

While this case study is constrained by space, the reader will hopefully see how to explore different aspects of the retailing paradigm using this framework. We hypothesized that we needed to reposition the three products within a mental structure of whole-unit framing.[14] The desire to buy individual units was greater when they were seen as a part of a whole. Second, a unified value proposition that developed trust in the brand worked best across all customer segments. Based on the aforementioned hypotheses that emerged through the journey mapping process, we tested thirteen different experimental conditions and four control conditions in a randomized control trial among over five thousand segmented consumers.[15] The summative effects of changes in the slogan, product conceptualization as a bundle, and shelf positioning with products in very close proximity to each other were a significant increase in intention to purchase which outperformed the control condition by 128 per cent.

Theorists and Practitioners: At a Crossroad. In an effort to go beyond capturing mechanical steps of touchpoints, "empathy maps" are sometimes used to capture insights into what a customer might be thinking and feeling. Questions such as "What would the customer be thinking or feeling? What are some of their worries and aspirations?" are used to transform concrete observations of behavior into explanations of people's emotions, intentions, and desires. This is the process of ordinary personology, by which "ordinary people come to know about each other's temporary states (such as emotions, intentions, and desires) and enduring dispositions (such as beliefs, traits, and abilities)."[16] While these questions are important for managers to ask, these empathy exercises are vulnerable to bias. That is, managers might not realize that they do not see the world objectively, and their evaluation of what a customer might experience may be naïve. A manager's secondhand view of the direct experience of their customers may contrast with a scientific analysis of the perceptions, expectations, and behaviors of customers. This is where behavioral expertise and scientific analysis should be employed to create a new layer and take journey mapping to the next level.

Adding this additional theory-*driven* layer onto journey maps not only benefits practitioners but also theorists who are interested in understanding the *why* because it points to opportunities to collect evidence that can refine the theory in question. While many theories can be tested in a controlled or lab setting, their true value is derived from testing them in an environment closer to the real-world context. This both allows for a better understanding of the theory in the real world and refines the theory of customer behavior itself, creating a cycle of theoretical and interventional refinement.

Threading this all together, practitioners and theorists can begin to ask foundational questions to further advance the utility of journey mapping. For instance, what is the goal of the journey map? How do we best capture the influencers and influences on a consumer's decisions? How do we select which are most important or influential? What is our scope and how many factors are we willing to tolerate from a practical perspective? For example, when building an entire map end to end, would it make sense to limit the number of agents that are built in the model due to the ever-increasing complexity? If the channel for intervention is but one opportunity in that chain, then it makes sense to introduce a multitude of independent agents that act on the targets.

This realization, that the data- and theory-driven journey mapping exercise is beneficial to both practitioners and theorists alike, and that it has potential to answer exponentially more complex questions, suggests that we need to invest in skills that are much more specialized than customer experience teams typically possess. While more challenging, this integration allows us to understand and improve the customer experience in a systematic, clearly defined, and repeatable way. This feature is critical for theory and intervention testing. The experimentation process will lead not only towards identification of effective and ineffective interventions but also to a more robust theory of consumer behavior itself. Tested theories will ultimately help mapmakers and map-users be increasingly successful by including and weighing the mind of the consumer, their *community,* and the other exogenous influences and resources within the map.

Critically, in order to achieve these steps, firms will need not only to take them, but also prioritize behavioral and psychological expertise within their organization. The business world has made long strides in accommodating the need for a deeper understanding of the human experience within the customer journey through its use of journey mapping and empathy mapping. But a bridge needs to be crossed where we bring together the experiences and intuitions of managers with the theoretically rich insights from the disciplines of psychology and behavioral economics. Many organizations resist behavioral approaches[17] but embracing scientific expertise as an important complement to business expertise is crucial for the path to psychological journey mapping.

At the end of the day, what *really* matters in most applications of consumer journey mapping is to help practitioners *drive customer relationships*. And this is where the work of theorists and practitioners meets at a crossroad: practitioners need theoretical insight to expand the horizons of their work; theorists need practical applications to ground it. With the help of psychological journey maps, and the application of the scientific method and testing, we can advance both.

6. CONCLUSION

In this chapter, we explored a position that operational journey maps are insufficient in providing a framework for understanding consumer decisions. Surprisingly few companies have end-to-end journey maps, and yet they have large goals for improving the customer experience. Often in parallel with this lack of foundational tools is a lack of knowing where to start the work. Further, the chapter argues that the reason for the potential failures lies in the biases and assumptions that can be caused by overreliance on an operational map that is intended to serve merely as a blueprint. To overcome this, this chapter offers psychological journey mapping, which enable us to generate both data-driven and theory-driven hypotheses about how people think and feel. The psychological journey map is not intended to replace the operational journey map but rather should augment it. This augmentation is intended not only to complete the mapping process but to help mappers better understand the *what* and *how* and the *why* behind the customers' experiences.

Firms that follow these steps and that commit to embracing psychological journey mapping will gain a significant competitive advantage in their capacity to have better precision in apprehending the needs, wants, and behaviors of their consumers, and the exogenous factors that influence them. Firms that stick with operational journey maps which only capture path logistics will lack a deeper connection to the mind of the consumer. Operational journey maps, although descriptive, are unlikely to lead to strategic solutions found within the minutiae of existing operations. Focusing solely on operational journey maps might even lead the manager astray – they might be prone to sticking with small local insights, when what managers might need are big strategic solutions that TRANSFORM the operational journey. Psychological journey maps SIMPLIFY the process to achieve effective precision marketing. They allow managers to see one level higher and consider the effects of human psychology. It is the critical step needed to help managers identify the STRATEGIC solutions that address the true root causes.

If we want precision retailing, we must delve deeper into the factors that shape consumer preferences. A crucial tool to do this, journey maps, needs updating. This includes distinction between operational journey maps and psychological journey maps. The cost is more time, but this push will result in better insights and a richer understanding of the customer, both which are fundamental to precision. As firms adopt these more advanced methodologies, there exists greater opportunity for the co-creation of empirical advancement and theory-building of journey maps between retailers, managers, researchers, and academics. If we collaborate to mature the process through empirically and systematically constructed journey maps, then we can satisfy business and customer needs as well as advance the scientific knowledge of behavior. Let's walk this road together.

ACKNOWLEDGMENTS

I would like to express my deepest appreciation and respect to my colleagues at BEworks, who have inspired me to push harder on closing the gap between scientific thinking and real-world impact. They led the case studies that are referenced here and the ongoing work on applied methodologies. I would also like to give special thanks to Michelle Hilscher, Ada Le, David Thomson, Jennifer Weeks, Sarah Carpentier, Angela Cooper, Pierre-Jean Malé, Wardah Malek, Erick Roat, Juan Salcedo, Shelbie Sutherland, and Mona Zhu, as well as David Pizarro, Nina Mažar, and Dan Ariely for their insights on the BEworks method, case studies, and their overall efforts in improving this chapter. I want to give further thanks to Kazunaga Matsuki, whose commitment to methodological excellence helped advance this chapter. I am especially grateful to Nathaniel Barr and Bartlomiej Piekarski for their ongoing guidance and nudging. All shortcomings of this paper are the fault of the author.

NOTES

1 Rosenbaum, M.S., Otalora, M.L., & Ramírez, G.C. (2017). How to create a realistic customer journey map. *Business Horizons, 60*(1), 143–50. https://doi.org/10.1016/j.bushor.2016.09.010.

2 Lemon, K.N., & Verhoef, P.C. (2016). Understanding customer experience throughout the customer journey. *Journal of Marketing, 80*(6), 69–96. https://doi.org/10.1509/jm.15.0420.

3 Simon, Herbert A. (1955). A behavioral model of rational choice. *The Quarterly Journal of Economics, 69*(1), 99–118. https://doi.org/10.2307/1884852.

4 Bradley, C., Oliveira, L., Birrell, S., & Cain, R. (2021). A new perspective on personas and customer journey maps: Proposing systemic UX. *International Journal of Human-Computer Studies, 148.* https://doi.org/10.1016/j.ijhcs.2021.102583.

5 Hamilton, R., Ferraro, R., Haws, K.L., & Mukhopadhyay, A. (2020). Traveling with companions: The social customer journey. *Journal of Marketing, 85*(1), 68–92. https://doi.org/10.1177/0022242920908227

6 Melumad, S., Hadi, R. Hildebrand, C., & Ward, A.F. (2020). Technology-augmented choice: How digital innovations are transforming consumer decision processes. *Customer Needs and Solutions, 7*, 90–101. https://doi.org/10.1007/s40547-020-00107-4.

7 Brasel, A.S., & Gips, J. (2015). Interface psychology: Touchscreens change attribute importance, decision criteria, and behavior in online choice. *Cyberpsychology, Behavior, and Social Networking, 18*(9), 535–8. https://doi.org/10.1089/cyber.2014.0546.

8 de Bellis, E., & Venkataramani Johar, G. (2020). Autonomous shopping systems: Identifying and overcoming barriers to consumer adoption. *Journal of Retailing, 96*(1), 74–87. https://doi.org/10.1016/j.jretai.2019.12.004.

9 Tian, K.T., Bearden, W.O., & Hunter, G.L. (2001). Consumers' need for uniqueness: Scale development and validation. *Journal of Consumer Research, 28*(1), 50–66. https://doi.org/10.1086/321947.

10 Samson, A., & Voyer, B.G. (2012). Two minds, three ways: Dual system and dual process models in consumer psychology. *AMS Review, 2*(2–4), 48–71. https://doi.org/10.1007/s13162-012-0030-9.

11 Howard, J.A., & Sheth, J.N. (1969). The theory of buyer behavior. *Journal of the American Statistical Association.* http://dx.doi.org/10.2307/2284311.

12 Evans, J. St. B.T., & Stanovich, K. (2013). Dual-process theories of higher cognition: Advancing the debate. *Perspectives on Psychological Science, 8*(3), 223–41. https://doi.org/10.1177/1745691612460685.

13 Samson & Voyer (2012).

14 Barasz, K., John, L.K., Keenan, E.A., & Norton, M.I. (2017). Pseudo-set framing. *Journal of Experimental Psychology: General, 146*(10), 1460–77. http://dx.doi.org/10.1037/xge0000337.

15 Bendle, N., & Chen, K. (2017). *BEworks: Experimentation in business.* Ivey Publishing. https://hbsp.harvard.edu/product/W17655-PDF-ENG.

16 Gilbert, D.T. (1998). Ordinary personology. In D.T. Gilbert, S.T. Fiske, & G. Lindzey (Eds.), *The handbook of social psychology* (pp. 89–150). McGraw-Hill.

17 O'Malley, S., & Peters, K. (2021). Gut Check: Why organizations that need to be behaviorally informed resist it. In D. Soman & C. Yeung, (Eds.), *The behaviorally informed organization* (pp. 51–70). University of Toronto Press.

CHAPTER TWO

Genetic Data for Precision Retail: Applications and Challenges

Remi Daviet and Gideon Nave

SUMMARY OF CHAPTER

This chapter explores the recent developments in individual-level genetic measures enabled by omics and other big data. These may affect the landscape of retailing over the near future. Possible applications and abuses of genetic data for marketing purposes are discussed.

MANAGERIAL IMPLICATIONS (GENERAL)

From a managerial perspective it is important to:
- Revise the road map of analytics and AI projects to see how genetic data, both in and of itself and in combination with other business and public data, can enable more precise targeting and product/service/communication design, to see where these new types of projects would fit, and to anticipate privacy challenges.
- Start exploring new partnerships with other divisions or external partners to get competitive advantages in the future.

MANAGERIAL IMPLICATIONS (ORGANIZATIONAL)

It is recommended to:

- Have a chief data officer position in place or ensure access to these competencies. If this is not the case, then this should be one of the most important organizational changes to make in order to experiment with new ideas with new data sets.
- Create an analytics and AI center of excellence to govern, manage, operationalize, and monitor analytics and AI models to advance more precise human-centered design.

MANAGERIAL IMPLICATIONS (STRATEGIC, TACTICAL, AND OPERATIONAL)

- From a strategic perspective, managers cannot ignore the possibilities offered by genetic data, and they need to have a road map.
- From a tactical perspective, it might be important to consider a proof of concept project to test the validity, relevance, and performance of the ideas presented in this chapter.

MANAGERIAL IMPLICATIONS (RISK ASSESSMENT)

- Early adoption of these techniques will come with a high risk as omics and other biological human data are tied to strict access, usage, and privacy rules. However, discarding them will also come with its own long-term risk.
- In all cases, a risk mitigation policy must be adopted, and this could be an exploratory experiment with a limited budget in the context of continuous innovations.

1. THE RISE OF CONSUMER GENOMICS

At its core, precision retail involves matching products, promotions, and marketing messages to the right people, at the right time, and in the right place. While consumer behavior is influenced by situational factors – such as time of day, cash on hand, or product availability – some of the variations in consumers' behavior are stable within a given individual across time. Twin studies over the past decades have further shown that many behavioral and demographic (e.g., educational attainment, income) traits are partly heritable, pointing to the contribution of genetic factors to their development.[1]

Until recently, mapping the links between specific genetic variants and consumers profiles and actions was extremely difficult because measuring genetic variation of individuals was remarkably expensive and time-consuming. However, technological advances following the Human Genome Project have enabled cost-effective measurement of the genome across individuals. This development has fueled the exponential growth of the new industry of direct-to-consumer genetic testing (DTC-GT) since the early 2010s. Most sales in this market come from personalized DNA testing kits, which allow consumers to obtain measurements of their own genomes and receive reports about their ancestry and genetic health risks. As of 2020, more than thirty million people have already taken personalized DNA tests (Figure 2.1). In addition to privately-owned endeavors, many governments worldwide have initiated publicly funded efforts to collect genetic variation measures of their citizens at scale. As a result, both private firms and governmental agencies have gained access to massive databases that include individual-level genetic measures.

In this chapter, we explore how these recent developments may affect the landscape of retailing in the near future by discussing possible applications and abuses of genetic data for marketing purposes. Although this chapter could have appeared in a science fiction book just a while ago, usage of genetic data by retailers is already happening in the real world due to commercial partnerships between global online retailers and DTC-GT companies. For example, in September 2018, the music streaming service Spotify announced that all of its users who were also customers of the DTC-GT giant Ancestry could upload their genetic data to the service and create musical playlists that match

Figure 2.1. Size of the direct-to-consumer genetic testing market in the 2010s.

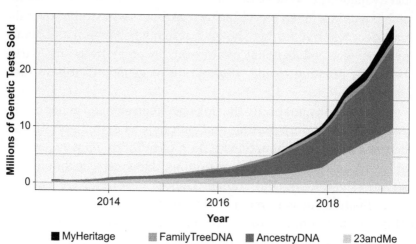

their genetic ancestry. Several months later, the vacation rental platform AirBnB announced a partnership with 23andMe, Ancestry's main competitor – a collaboration that allows AirBnB users who are also 23andMe customers to "connect with their heritage through deeply personal cultural and travel experiences." Thus, it cannot be too early to start evaluating the potential implications of genetic data accumulation on the future of retailing and the well-being of consumers.

As illustrated in the previous examples, one way genetic data may create value is by facilitating development of new products and markets centered around the concepts of "knowing yourself" and "personalization," which were essential in the marketing of genetic test kits themselves. Another potential avenue of value creation resides in opportunities to improve the efficiency of marketing actions that involve segmentation, targeting, and positioning. The usefulness of genetic data for improving efficiency crucially depends on how informative it is about consumer needs, attitudes, and behaviors relative to other easily accessible variables – a topic under active research that we discuss further in this chapter. To date, genetic data has been found to be moderately informative about nearly every behavioral trait.[2] However, this moderate predictive power may be additive to information found in demographic or behavioral data, at least in some cases.[3] The accumulation of larger databases and development of methods exploiting multiple data modalities and their interactions (e.g., genetic, environmental, and behavioral) is expected to greatly raise the attainable predictive performance regarding consumer traits and behaviors.

The remainder of this chapter is organized as follows. We introduce key terms and concepts in genetics and review relevant research, mostly from the fields of behavioral genetics, social genomics, and genealogy, in section 2. We proceed with a conceptual discussion of applications of genetic data for retail, focusing on segmentation, targeting, and positioning, in section 3. We then survey ethical and legal challenges that arise from the potential use of genetic data by marketers in section 4 and conclude in section 5.

2. PRIMER ON HUMAN GENETICS

In this section we introduce basic terms and concepts in human genetics and survey research findings that are relevant for the use of genetic data by retailers. The section is intended for readers without previous acquaintance with genetics and admittedly ignores many biological nuances. For a more detailed exploration of the topic, we invite readers to refer to Lewis's *Human Genetics: The Basics*.[4]

2.1. Measuring the Genome

The human genome is a sequence of about three billion base-pairs. There are four different types of bases or genetic "letters": adenine (A), thymine (T), guanine (G), and cytosine (C). The base-pairs are packaged into structures called *chromosomes*. Every human has 23 pairs of chromosomes, where one chromosome in each pair is inherited from each parent (note that the 23rd pair consists of the sex chromosomes, in which females have two identical "X" chromosomes and males have one "X" and one "Y" chromosome). The genome includes about 20,000 to 30,000 sub-sequences of base-pairs called genes, which contain information that regulates biological processes, most notably the construction of proteins.

The base-pairs across the genome are indexed based on their chromosome and location in the sequence. In most genome locations, the base-pairs are identical across all humans, and hence are uninformative about variability across people. Nonetheless, there are some locations (less than 2 percent) where individuals commonly differ, called *polymorphisms*. There are at least eighty-eight million known genetic polymorphisms in humans; many of them are located outside genes. The most common type of polymorphism, called *single-nucleotide polymorphism* (SNP), occurs where a single base-pair differs across individuals in a genome location. Non-SNP variants include short insertions or deletions of groups of nucleotides (called *indels*) and other structural variants such as *inversions, duplications, and translocations*. In this chapter, we focus on SNP variations that are more commonly measured in large-scale genetic databases.

For most SNPs, only two possible base-pairs are observed in the population. The more frequently observed base-pair variation is called the *major allele*, and the other is called the *minor allele*. Because all humans inherit a copy of every chromosome from each parent, they also inherit two copies of each SNP, and thus have either zero, one, or two minor alleles in every SNP location. This allows to describe each individual's genetic data via the numbers of minor alleles at each SNP location (zero, one, or two). Genetic measurement techniques typically measure variations in selected genome locations (under 1 million SNPs) where humans commonly differ. From there around twenty million other SNPs can be imputed.

2.2. Twin Studies and the Three Laws of Behavioral Genetics

The *heritability* (denoted h^2) of a trait (or a *phenotype*) is the proportion of its variation across individuals that can be ascribed to genetic factors. Heritability can be estimated using twin studies, which are based on the fact that genetically identical twins are on average two times more genetically similar to each other than fraternal twins. Three empirical regularities, often referred to as the "three laws of behavioral genetics" summarize the common findings in twin studies:[5]

(i)   All human behavioral traits are, to some extent, heritable.

This discovery stems from the common observation that identical twins raised apart will be (usually highly) similar in every conceivable measurement, compared to non-identical twins. It has been shown for a wide range of phenotypes, from real-life outcomes such as income and the tendency to divorce, to cognitive and psychological traits such as IQ and risk tolerance.

(ii)   The influence of being raised in the same family is typically smaller than that of genetics.

This discovery stems from the common observation that identical twins raised apart are almost as similar as identical twins raised together, and non-related individuals raised together are almost as different as random strangers.

(iii) The lion's share of behavioral variation across individuals cannot be accounted for by either genetics or family environment.

This discovery stems from the common observation that identical twins (even raised together) are in fact far from completely identical and differ in significant ways.

The three laws are applicable to most behavioral traits, yet there are some exceptions. First, some physiological characteristics such as lactose intolerance, alcohol intolerance, and having freckles are highly heritable. The downstream behavioral consequences of these physiological traits (e.g., buying dairy alternative products), are expected to be more highly heritable than what is observed for other behavioral traits. Second, the variance in traits such as the religion one chooses to practice or her native language are almost fully determined by non-genetic factors (e.g., the language and religion of one's parents). Nonetheless, even such traits can be inferred from one's genome because of non-causal correlations between genetics and geo-location.

The three laws of behavioral genetics demonstrate the promises and potential drawbacks of applications that rely on genetic data for precision retail. While genomes contain information that is (to some degree) predictive of virtually all human traits, genetic data alone is not expected to be sufficiently informative for making accurate individual-level predictions. Nonetheless, genetic data has the unique characteristic of remaining constant across the lifespan. Therefore, one's genome could be predictive of future behavioral tendencies much earlier than other variables (e.g., demographic and behavioral data). For instance, genetic data would clearly not be particularly effective (relative to behavioral data) when predicting the future chocolate intake of a person who has been consuming dark chocolate every day for the past decade. However, such data may be valuable for singling out segments of customers that have the potential of developing the habit of chocolate consumption before they are locked-in to a brand, providing companies (such as Godiva or Lindt) a means to reach segments of customers with high expected lifetime value earlier than their competitors.

2.3. Candidate-Gene Studies

Although twin studies indicate that most human behavioral traits are heritable and allow estimating the heritability of specific traits, they do not inform us on the relationships between specific genetic variants and behavioral disposition across individuals. Estimating such relationships requires access to direct measures of the genome. The first methodological approach for addressing this important question was *candidate-gene studies*. This method crucially relies on the construction of mechanistic hypotheses for the existence of relationships between variation in specific genome locations and behavior and involves directly testing these hypotheses in convenience samples of up to several hundred genotyped individuals. For example, a high-profile publication proposing that intranasal administration of the hormone oxytocin increases trust sparked follow-up candidate-gene studies, which hypothesized that one's behavioral disposition to trust others is associated with SNPs located on the oxytocin receptor gene. Although early studies using the candidate-gene approach for studying the genetic underpinnings of similarly complex behavioral traits have led to high-profile publications, the vast majority of these studies (if not all) could not be replicated in independent samples. In retrospect, these replication failures can be accounted for by methodological issues, including low statistical power, lack of correction for multiple hypotheses testing by researchers, reliance on non-representative samples, and the absence of control for the influence of non-genetic confounding variables.[6] For these reasons, many scientific journals have established editorial policies that preclude publication of candidate-gene studies that do not include well-powered replication in an independent sample.

2.4. Genome-Wide Association Studies (GWAS)

With the maturation of techniques for inexpensively measuring SNPs, the volumes of datasets that include both genetic and behavioral measures have also grown rapidly. This expansion has opened a door for a new approach of studying associations between genomes and behaviors, namely *genome-wide association studies* (GWAS). In contrast to the theory-driven candidate-gene approach, the GWAS method is data-driven and encompasses scanning the entire genome for SNPs associated with any target trait. Because of the vast number of possible associations that are tested in a GWAS, this approach requires adhering to strict methodological standards, which include preregistration and correction for multiple hypothesis testing (the common genome-wide corrected significance threshold is $p<5 \times 10^{-8}$). Because of this stringent threshold, GWAS require very large samples to obtain the required statistical power for reliably detecting small effects.

The first wave of GWAS of behavioral traits consisted of studies with samples of a few thousands of participants and could not identify any SNP whose association with behavioral traits reached genome-wide significance. Continuing development of genotyping techniques together with massive data collection efforts has led to a rapid increase in GWAS samples sizes, which are reaching over one million participants. The increase in statistical power has led to identification of many associations between SNPs and complex behavioral traits, such as 1,271 SNPs associated with educational attainment and 124 SNPs associated with general risk tolerance.

The associations between each SNP and behavioral traits were small (R^2<0.01 percent). These findings indicate that most human behavioral traits are associated with many genetic variants, each of them accounting for a small percentage of the variance across individuals, an empirical regularity commonly referred to as the "fourth law of behavioral genetics."[7]

POLYGENIC RISK SCORES (PRS)

Although each individual SNP explains very little of the variance in most behavioral traits across humans, it is possible to use genetic data to explain a greater part of the behavioral variance using a *polygenic risk score* (PRS). PRSs aggregate the small effects of many genetic variants by calculating a linear combination that weights their contributions based on GWAS results. PRSs become increasingly informative of a target trait as the sample size of the GWAS used to construct them increases thanks to a more accurate estimation of each SNP's effect. This is illustrated in Figure 2.2, representing the share of the (out of sample) variance in height and educational attainment (EA) that can be accounted for using PRSs, based on GWAS results of these traits. For example, back in 2013, a GWAS of EA in a sample of N=126,559 participants identified three genome-wide significant SNPs, and constructed a PRS that explained less than 0.1 percent of the variance in an independent sample. A later EA GWAS in over 1.1 million participants identified 1,271 SNPs and constructed a PRS that explained as much as 13 percent of the variance in an independent sample. While 13 percent might not be sufficiently precise for guiding individual-level actions, this information can be combined with traditional variables such as demographics or behavioral data to increase performance in at least some cases. Moreover, the field of Genomics and related disciplines (biostatistics, social genomics, precision medicine, etc.) are rapidly advancing to develop methods incorporating multimodal data sources: genome, exome, gene expression, microbiome, brain-imaging, physiology, behavioral, environmental, and demographic data. The combination of these modalities within methods considering interactions between variables, together with access to

Figure 2.2. The relationship between GWAS sample size and the variance in a target trait that its PRS explains, for height and educational attainment (EA).[8]

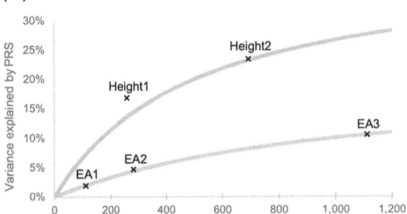

genetic databases of multiple millions of consumers, is expected to increase the prediction accuracy in the future. As a result, this newly achieved predictive performance may allow businesses and institutions to work increasingly at the individual level.

2.5. Genetic Ancestry

The capacity to measure how the genome varies between individuals further enables researchers to study how it varies across population groups. The most prevalent approach for comparing genetic variation across populations relies on dimensional reduction techniques such as principal component analysis (PCA). Such analysis allows identification of a small set (typically 10–40) of high-order variables – the *principal components* (PCs) of a population genome – which explain as much of the genetic variability in the sample as possible. These genetic PCs were shown to be highly informative about the geographic location of one's ancestry, a finding that can be traced back to a study by Li et al.[9] that performed PCA on the genomes of individuals from an ethnically diverse sample from across the world. In this study, the first genetic PC could separate between

Figure 2.3. The two first principal components from a sample of European subjects present similarities to a map of Europe, with the first PC separating Northern from Southern Europeans and the second PC distinguishing Eastern from Western Europeans.[10]

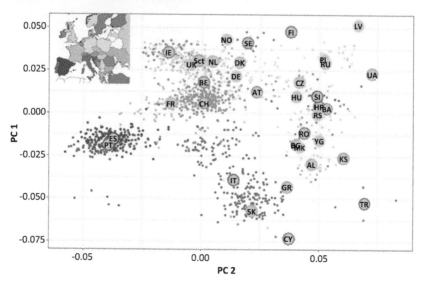

Africans (sub-Saharan) and non-Africans, and the second differentiated individuals from Eastern Eurasia and Western Eurasia. Following Li et al. (2008), many other studies of populations that were less ethnically diverse similarly found relationships between the genetic PCs and people's geographic origin (see Figure 2.3 for illustration).

Because genetic PCs allow researchers to closely track ancestry, they are often used in studies of historical demographic processes such as mass migration. The PCs are also often used as control variables in GWAS and observational studies of other biomarkers in order to reduce concerns about *population stratification* – a problem arising when environmental factors correlate with genetic differences across groups and generate spurious associations between genetic variants and traits. For example, a SNP which is highly predictive of lactase persistence, was found to correlate with many traits, including height and educational attainment. However, these associations are entirely driven by the SNP's higher frequency in

Southeastern (versus Northwestern) parts of Europe, and the relationship vanishes once genetic PCs are controlled for.

3. PRECISION RETAILING APPLICATIONS OF GENETIC DATA

In this section we detail how retailers may be able to use genetic data when developing strategies that aim to deliver the right marketing mix to the right people. Our approach incorporates genetics into the different stages of the well-known Segmentation, Targeting, and Positioning framework.

3.1. Segmentation

Segmentation is the division of a market into subsets of consumers that have similar needs. Traditionally, marketers rely on demographics, psychographics, and behavioral variables as segmentation bases. When genetic variation among customers can be observed and directly tied to differences in product-related needs, reliance on genetic variables for segmentation is straightforward. As noted by the third law of behavioral genetics, the genome only explains a small part of the variance in most behavioral dispositions among humans, and therefore the use of genetic data for segmentation is not always appealing, relative to other variables. However, in some cases – most notably in applications related to nutrition, healthcare, and beauty – genetics is expected to play a more prominent role.

For example, consider a gourmet pizza restaurant chain trying to penetrate a crowded market. The chain offers a large number of pizza toppings, including anchovies, pineapple, sausage, and jalapeños. It also has several lines of unique product offerings, such as gluten-free and lactose-free pizzas. The CMO would like to launch a campaign that sends potential customers personalized coupons in an attempt to lure them into trying the pizza. Ideally, the CMO would know the favorite toppings and dietary restrictions of every customer. However, she does not have access to any historical data. She partners with a DT-GTC company and tries to overcome this limitation by getting insight from genetic data.

In cases such as the above, one would expect to see several direct links between customer needs and their genetic markup. Twin studies show that a non-negligible variance in food preferences across individuals is stable and heritable – an unsurprising finding, as dietary preferences are influenced by genetically regulated biological processes related to metabolism and sensory perception.[11] The CMO could use genetics to segment the market in at least three possible manners. First, she could divide the market based on genetic variants related to people's sensitivity to flavors and odors. For example, liking of salty foods – such as anchovies – is related to one's sensitivity to salty taste, which is linked to SNPs in genes involved in sensory processes. Second, the CMO could segment the market based on genetic variants that are strongly tied to having dietary restrictions, such as lactose and gluten intolerance. Third, she could rely on the genetic PCs for segmenting the market based on genetic ancestry and develop product offerings that appeal to different ancestry groups (e.g., Mediterranean or Mexican pizzas).

Firms may be able to use similar strategies for segmenting the market based on genetic variants in many other domains. For example, a beauty retailer could send coupons for sunscreen to sunburn-prone consumers or advertise products against hair-loss to men who are genetically prone to alopecia. Because one's genome does not change throughout the lifespan, in some cases brand managers may even be able to identify segments of future potential customers long before they show any other indication that they need the product and increase brand awareness among them. For example, a marketer of hair-loss products can identify segments of young men in their twenties who have thick hair but may need the product in their mid-thirties. While this approach might be counterintuitive, it may allow the firm to capture consumers who have not yet locked into a particular brand.

While most prior research has focused on healthcare related variations, research for non-medically relevant causal relations is expected to yield new discoveries that are relevant for marketing strategy across other domains as genetic databases grow, starting with beauty, wellness, and nutrition. Indeed, leading DTC-GT companies already provide non-healthcare related information to their consumers, such as expected food preferences, and are expected to introduce recommendation systems that may be used for advertising.

3.2. Targeting

After dividing the market into segments, marketers must decide which of them to target and with what marketing mix. This decision is typically based on many factors, including the size of each segment, the average lifetime value of its customers, the competition's offering, and – most relevant for this chapter – the capacity to reach consumers. Genetic data can naturally also play a role in this decision and its implementation. The most straightforward application is when genetic variation has been directly used as a base for the segmentation phase. In such cases, the CMO can make a calculated decision based on the attractiveness of each segment, and simply use genetic data for reaching targets.

While the use of single-gene variations that affect consumer needs via known mechanisms can be powerful, it remains limited to few specific applications. However, as discussed in section 2, genome-wide variations – including SNPs located outside of genes – correlate with almost every personal characteristic. Therefore, when genetic data is readily available, marketers can rely on it to infer managerially relevant segmentation variables that otherwise could not have been easily observed at scale. For example, suppose that based on market research, the pizza chain CMO would like to target a segment of consumers who score high on the personality dimension of *openness to experience* (e.g., with offerings of unconventional pizza toppings such as kiwi fruit). Carrying out this strategy requires inferring customers' personality, an approach with limited actionability, as it would require conducting psychological surveys at scale. Instead, the CMO may be able to use genetic data – ideally in combination with other variables that are easy to obtain such as demographics – to construct PRSs that predict high openness. This approach would be feasible for every trait for which a GWAS has ever been performed. Based on the first law of behavioral genetics, such strategies are expected to work for a wide range of outcomes, though their efficiency would vary by trait. Of course, when using this approach, marketers should pay close attention to the utility of genetic data relative to other potential sources. For example, social media data (e.g., Facebook "Likes" is expected to be much more predictive of personality than genetics). If such data is available, it would have greater utility for personality-based targeting strategies.[12]

Given the vast amount of information that genetic data carries (as stated by the first law of behavioral genetics), it can also be used in a large panel of targeting tasks from a retailing perspective, even without an explicit segmentation strategy. It can potentially predict consumer behaviors, such as purchasing a product, clicking on an ad, or carrying word of mouth (though we are not aware of empirical studies of the topic to date). Another approach is to use PRSs and other genetic measures in addition to other variables, which may improve the overall predictive power of the model beyond what could be achieved by using only one or the other.

Finally, genetic data can be used to draw a comprehensive map of family relations between individuals by estimating genetic kinship. Such a map can then be used in a similar manner to social network graphs for targeting.[13] Even without drawing such a map, a simple estimate of genetic relatedness (or inversely genetic distance) between individuals[14] can be leveraged to predict consumer behaviors by identifying clusters of closely related individuals with similar behavioral patterns. A straightforward example would be to target consumers who are within a small genetic distance from existing clusters of high lifetime-value customers. Marketers can use a large panel of methods for this task, such as collaborative filtering, nearest neighbors, or more advanced machine learning algorithms. It has for instance been shown that 51 percent of the general population variance in fluid intelligence could be explained by genetic distance (quantified from SNPs) using only a sample of a few thousand.[15]

3.3. Positioning

Last but not least, genetic data can also play a role in a firm's efforts to shape its image in the consumers' minds via positioning strategies. Over the years, the DNA's double helix has become a "cultural icon" by itself,[16] which opens the door for creative marketing applications where genetics is an integral part of the brands' communication strategy. Consumers may perceive genetic data as a new vehicle to "knowing thyself" as means to discover previously unknown family history, and as a technology for building bridges between people and their heritage. Indeed, such appeal to the fascination of consumers with their DNA has been a fundamental part of the highly successful positioning strategies of two DTC-GT companies, Ancestry and myHeritage. A recent prominent example of this approach comes from a controversial (and viral) video ad, released by the national Mexican air-carrier Aeroméxico in 2018. In the video, the company interviewed Southern Americans who didn't suspect having Mexican ancestry and offered them discounted flights to Mexico, with rates that would be proportional to their percentage of Mexican DNA. To their surprise, most of the customers discovered (after taking a genetic test) that their genomes are, to some degree, "Mexican," and happily received a discount. Although such a DNA discount was never offered to the general public, the ad used the DNA testing to spark the public's interest, in a "know thyself" fashion.

The leading DT-GTC companies have already managed to come up with strategies to translate their customers' allure for genetics into applications that advance their sense of self-knowledge, community, and personalization, most notably via a partnership with other retailers. The previously mentioned collaborations between Spotify and Ancestry and between 23andMe and AirBnB (Figure 2.1) are prominent examples of how genetics can be placed at the center of the positioning strategy. Many products and services in other domains could similarly benefit from the appeal of positioning that connects consumers to their history and heritage. Examples include movies and TV shows that are linked to specific heritage, traditional dining, history books, and museums.

4. ETHICAL CHALLENGES

Genetic data is identifiable, immutable, informative about a very large range of outcomes, and partially shared between family members. These unique properties raise several ethical challenges that must be addressed by regulating the use of genetic data by retailers and marketers.[17]

4.1. Identifiability and Informed Consent

Unless consumers are monozygotic twins, their genetic data can be uniquely attributed to them. Anonymizing genetic data without destroying a significant amount of information is difficult, as research has shown that 60 to 300 randomly chosen SNPs are sufficient to identify most individuals. While some methods try to balance the trade-offs between anonymization and information preservation, the anonymized data is always subject to potential re-identification attacks, threatening confidentiality.[18] It is not always clear that consumers clearly understand the scale of information embedded in their genetic data and the consequent identifiability issues. Even in a strict research setting, the degree of required anonymization and informed consent is subject to debate and varying standards. This makes it difficult to obtain an unambiguous informed consent from consumers on how their or genetic data will be used, posing a threat to their autonomy.[19]

Another serious challenge is that consumers' genetic data are not only informative about themselves, but also about their non-genotyped relatives. Even though relatives of genotyped individuals could potentially be identified, current practices do not require companies holding genetic data to obtain their consent. While these practices might change in the future as the technology gets more widely adopted, it is unclear whether such change could happen without regulatory oversight to enforce it.

4.2. Privacy and Security

The identifiability and informativeness of genetic data also raise important privacy and security issues. First, several companies have been shown to maintain "shadow profiles" of consumers who did not register or consent to the use of their data. A similar approach could be directly applied to the case of genetic data, particularly regarding the mining of information regarding non-genotyped relatives.

A second issue is the rise of data breaches, including prominent cases of reputable companies, where unauthorized third parties obtain data through illegal means. Once such data is leaked, it is unlikely that it will be used following any regulation or ethical norm.

These issues have raised concerns that genetic data could be used against consumers' will or interests. Privacy policies provided by companies are often ambiguous, and even when it is suggested that the data will not be mined for secondary purposes or shared with third parties, companies often reserve the rights to unilaterally modify the policy without notification, or to share the data following a merger, acquisition, or bankruptcy.

A possible solution may result from the emergence of privacy-preserving algorithms, some of which are specifically tailored for genetic data.[20] In such cases the data is kept by the consumer, and mined on the consumer device, without sharing any identifiable information with companies. As the field of privacy-preserving AI advances, a larger panel of algorithms should be accessible to companies, allowing them to use the data for a wide range of applications, without compromising privacy or security.

4.3. Discrimination

Genetic data can directly lead to a broad range of discriminations based on consumers' immutable characteristics. The example of Aeroméxico giving a discount proportional to the percentage of DNA associated with Mexican ancestry is a flagrant case of genetic-based price discrimination. While it is unclear whether the discounts were actually offered, the advertising campaign was quite successful and received positively by the general public and news media outlets.

Another indirect but potentially significant source of discrimination is through the creation of involuntary self-reinforcing loops. Marketers relying on genetic data for prediction and targeting might perpetuate inequalities by reducing the number of options advertised to some consumers whose genetic background does not align with the targeted profile. For example, credit cards providers could offer promotional rates to consumers who are genetically disposed to have a higher income, and doing so, give preferential treatment to consumers who are already socially advantaged.

Unfortunately, current regulations mostly fail to address this issue in the context of retail and marketing. In the US, the 1996 Health Insurance Portability and Accountability Act and the 2008 Genetic Information Nondiscrimination Act (GINA) prohibit employers and insurance companies (only for specific types of policies) from discriminating against people based on genetic information. Some states also have specific provisions to forbid companies from discriminating against consumers based on genetic data (California), or to require the consumer to be notified if genetic information was used to grant or deny insurance, employment, credit (including mortgage and loans), or educational opportunities (Florida).

4.4. Misinformation and Misrepresentation

The lack of consumer understanding regarding genetic data and associated technologies can lead companies to use misleading or misrepresenting claims. Genetic applications are strongly associated with science in the minds of consumers, and this link might be exploited by marketers to oversell the reliability of genetic-based predictions. Until consumers are adequately educated on the highly probabilistic nature of genetics-based predictions, regulation might be needed to prevent abuses.

5. CONCLUSION

This chapter sought to evaluate how the growing availability of genetic data may impact the future of precision retailing. We recognize that the utility of the applications that we discussed critically depends on answers to several key questions, which at the time of writing this chapter have remained open.[21] Most crucially, little research to date assessed the degree to which genetic data is predictive of outcomes that are of direct relevance to retailers, such as consumers' attitudes towards brands, variety seeking behavior, responsiveness to promotions and ads, or word-of-mouth activity. In particular, it is not known to what extent genetic data has predictive power above and beyond other variables that are more readily available to marketers (such as demographics). Last but not least, there is a gap of knowledge concerning how consumers would react to the use of their genetic data for marketing purposes, and whether the unique features of genetic data, discussed in section 4, play a role in consumers' perceptions of such practices. Despite these knowledge gaps, we stress that large-scale genetic databases are already in the possession of private firms and governments, and the use of such data for marketing purposes has already started to take place. The exponential accumulation of genetic data, together with developments of statistical methods for fine-grained genetic-based inference, make it likely that uses and misuses of genetic data in the marketplace will become more prevalent in the near future.

NOTES

1 Harden, K.P., & Koellinger, P.D. (2020). Using genetics for social science. *Nature Human Behaviour, 4*, 567–76. https://doi.org/10.1038/s41562-020-0862-5.
2 Harden & Koellinger (2020).
3 Daviet, R., & Nave, G. (2021). Is genetic data predictive of taste? A genome-wide study of 150,000 individuals (in prep.).
4 Lewis, R. (2016). *Human genetics: The basics.* Garland Science.
5 Turkheimer, E. (2000). Three laws of behavior genetics and what they mean. *Current Directions in Psychological Science, 9*(5), 160–4. https://doi.org/10.1111/1467-8721 .00084.
6 Chabris, C.F., Lee, J.J., Cesarini, D., Benjamin, D.J., & Laibson, D.I. (2015). The fourth law of behavior genetics. *Current Directions in Psychological Science, 24*(4), 304–12. https://doi.org/10.1177/0963721415580430.
7 Chabris et al. (2015).
8 Figure adapted from Harden & Koellinger (2020).
9 Li, J.Z., Absher, D.M., Tang, H., Southwick, A.M., Casto, A.M., Ramachandran, S., Cann, H.M., Barsh, G.S., Feldman, M., Cavalli-Sforza, L.L., & Myers, R.M. (2008). Worldwide human relationships inferred from genome-wide patterns of variation. *Science, 319*(5866), 1100–4. https://doi.org/10.1126/science.1153717.
10 Novembre, J., Johnson, T., Bryc, K., Kutalik, Z., Boyko, A.R., Auton, A., Indap, A., King, K.S., Bergmann, S., Nelson, M.R., Stephens, M., & Bustamante, C.D. (2008). Genes mirror geography within Europe. *Nature, 456*(7218), 98–101. https://doi.org /10.1038/nature07566.
11 Daviet & Nave. (2021).
12 Matz, S.C., Kosinski, M., Nave, G., & Stillwell, D.J. (2017). Psychological targeting as an effective approach to digital mass persuasion. *Proceedings of the National Academy*

of Sciences of the United States of America, 114(48), 12714–19. https://www.pnas.org/doi/pdf/10.1073/pnas.1710966114.

13 Wind, Y. (1994). Marketing and social networks. *Advances in Social Network Analysis: Research in the Social and Behavioral Sciences,171,* 254.

14 Queller, D.C., & Goodnight, K.F. (1989). Estimating relatedness using genetic markers. *Evolution, 43*(2), 258. https://doi.org/10.1111/j.1558-5646.1989.tb04226.x.

15 Davies, G., Tenesa, A., Payton, A., Yang, J., Harris, S.E., Liewald, D., Ke, X., Le Hellard, S., Christoforou, A., Luciano, M., McGhee, K., Lopez, L., Gow, A.J., Corley, J., Redmond, P., Fox, H.C., Haggarty, P., Whalley, L.J., McNeill, G., ... Deary, I.J. (2011). Genome-wide association studies establish that human intelligence is highly heritable and polygenic. *Molecular Psychiatry, 16,* 996–1005. https://doi.org/10.1038/mp.2011.85

16 Nelkin, D., & Susan Lindee, M. (2010). *The DNA mystique: The gene as a cultural icon.* University of Michigan Press.

17 Daviet, R., Nave, G., & Wind, J. (2020). Genetic data: potential uses and misuses in marketing. *Journal of Marketing, 86*(1), 7–26. https://doi.org/10.1177/0022242920980767.

18 Wjst, M. (2010). Caught you: Threats to confidentiality due to the public release of large-scale genetic data sets. *BMC Medical Ethics,11,* 21. https://doi.org/10.1186/1472-6939-11-21.

19 Daviet, Nave, & Wind (2020).

20 Uhler, C., Slavkovic, A.B., & Fienberg, S.E. (2013). Privacy-preserving data sharing for genome-wide association studies. *Journal of Privacy and Confidentiality, 5*(1). https://doi.org/10.29012/jpc.v5i1.629.

21 Daviet, Nave, & Wind (2020).

CHAPTER THREE

Neuroscience Methods, Neuroforecasting, and Digital Media Impact

Gina M. Kemp and Bruce Doré

SUMMARY OF CHAPTER

This chapter provides a framework in which behavioral and neuro-scientific approaches provide complementary insights about the mechanisms that drive message sharing decisions on online media and their impact. Neuroscience tools offer a unique approach to generating insights about what causes digital content to be widely shared, complementing traditional self-report behavioral methods which are widely used in marketing and social sciences.

MANAGERIAL IMPLICATIONS (GENERAL)
- Managers in the precision retail industry are invited to monitor, through their R&D and innovation centers, the new developments in neuroscience methods and tools. More than that, they are invited to be part of this long innovation journey by forging strategic partnerships with neuroscience and behavioral science researchers.
- Managers in many other sectors and industries (including technology companies, venture capitals, start-ups

and entrepreneurs, AI companies, electronic sensors manufacturers, wearable electronics, etc.) might spot new opportunities for products and services development.

MANAGERIAL IMPLICATIONS (ORGANIZATIONAL)

- From the organizational perspective, managers must ensure that their innovation centers are well connected with other departments, especially IT, media, marketing, and sales departments. They need to leverage their internal assets and data to explore ways in which they can collaborate with behavioral and neuroscience researchers.

MANAGERIAL IMPLICATIONS (STRATEGIC, TACTICAL, AND OPERATIONAL)

- From the strategic perspective, it is important to have such multidisciplinary research and development initiatives active as they have strong future potential. What is more important for a retail manager than understanding customers? Openness to input from such initiatives provides managers with much-needed insights to ensure delivering value to their customers. To achieve such insights, managers need to forge the right win-win partnerships. We know that researchers can bring strategic value, so managers need to think how to leverage their online operational data to explore ways to collaborate with researchers on complementing the existing data with new data when technology allows.
- At this stage, there are no immediate tactical and operational implications other than maintaining an adequate budget to support R&D activities.

MANAGERIAL IMPLICATIONS (RISK ASSESSMENT)

- There are ethical but also regulatory and compliance risks involved when it comes to privacy protection.
- The risk of involuntary harm might exist by leakage of protected data.
- Financial risks are very limited, and they are the easiest ones to deal with when compared to personal data risks and associated liabilities.

1. INTRODUCTION

The internet has dramatically expanded opportunities for consumers to connect with and influence each other, transforming the flow of information, opinions, and behaviors through society. Exposure to an online message, as a unit of information, can shape consumer behavior, but the reach and impact of a message depends in large part on whether consumers decide to share it with their peers. Theories in psychology and marketing provide accounts of how psychological processes contribute to message-sharing decisions, but traditional behavioral methods have limitations in predicting behavior and in understanding its underlying mechanisms. We argue that neuroscience methods can generate novel insights about what causes online messages to spread and trigger behavioral changes at population scale. In this pursuit, we first introduce our reader to popular methodologies in cognitive neuroscience followed by a primer on the neuroscience of decision-making. We then introduce *neuroforecasting* as an emerging field which aims to predict population behavior from studying the brains of representative individuals. Furthermore, we showcase the application of neuroforecasting in message-sharing behavior and digital marketing, highlighting implications for managers and policymakers. Finally, we identify next steps for this field towards the development of highly contextualized and individual-specific models that can be applied within the precision retail context. Taken together, this chapter introduces neuroscience as a complementary field to psychology which can yield valuable insights about the mechanisms that drive the impact of digital media and its implications.

2. NEUROIMAGING AS A TOOL TO STUDY BEHAVIOR

Generally, there are two main types of neuroimaging: structural and functional. The first type produces static anatomical representations of the brain while the second allows us to trace the neural activity that accompanies mental and behavioral events in specific parts of the brain. The neural activity is often described as the "neural correlates" of said processes. Such mapping allows us to understand the relationships between mental and behavioral processes and to minimize the bias of the observing researcher and the reporting subject by looking directly at the brain's activities, bypassing the need for speech to access mental processes. Therefore, neuroimaging provides us with objective measurements of the brain activity that is linked to mental processes, allowing us to build mechanistic models that can explain and predict behavior that is closely linked to both brain activities and the related mental processes.

Advances in functional neuroimaging were based on early observations from the second half of the nineteenth century of (1) the electrical nature of brain activity, and (2) the link between the increase in blood flow to specific brain regions in response to an increase in mental activities. These observations gave rise to two types of neuroimaging techniques. The first directly measures the absolute electric activity of the brain (electroencephalography) as well as the resultant electromagnetic fields (magnetoencephalography). These techniques score high in their temporal resolution – that is, the ability to distinguish two consecutive signals on the scale of milliseconds – which allows for real-time detection of fluctuations in brain activities in specific regions. However, these methods are limited because they are susceptible to interfering electric signals and noise from close-by brain areas, which limit access to detecting activity from deeper brain structures. These methods are also susceptible to noise from moving and/or from electric signals in the surrounding environment. These limitations decrease the spatial resolution of the described techniques.

The second type of functional neuroimaging techniques relies on detecting the amount of blood that flows to a specific brain region, as a proxy for brain activation. In this chapter, we focus on the second type of neuroimaging techniques called functional magnetic resonance imaging (fMRI), which measures changes in blood flow as an indirect indicator of brain activity on the scale of single-digit seconds. It is important to point out that the mere detection of an increase in blood flow signal at a particular brain region does not mean that a specific brain region is causing a mental activity or vice versa, just simply that we can visualize a mental activity by measuring the physical activity of a brain. Causality requires combining multiple research approaches that are beyond the scope of this chapter.

Table 3.1. Comparison of popular neuroimaging techniques. Figures created using biorender.com

	Measuring the electric activety of the brain	Measuring blood flow to the brain
Temporal Resolution	Faster	Slower
Spatial Resolution	Low	High
Relative Cost	Low	High

Neuroimaging is a powerful tool that allows us to directly probe the brain activity which underlies mental processes and behaviors. This valuable tool has given rise to numerous applications and fields of research such as "neuro-economics" or the neuroscience of decision-making, which we discuss next.

3. NEUROSCIENCE OF DECISION-MAKING

We make numerous decisions every day, from the food we eat, to clothes we wear, to the information we share. A prevalent framework for choice emphasizes subjective *value* as the input to decision-making.[1]

Value can be defined as "the relative attractiveness of a particular good at the time of choice which is maximized as a result of the decision process."[2] In this process, an individual forms neural representations of the self as well as the environment, including the set of available choice options and their expected outcomes. Individuals then determine the subjective value of each option in a valuation step and selects action based on the outcomes of this step.[3] Moreover, there are different types of valuation: value can be assigned to different possible options (also called *goal valuation*), the expected value for the selected option (*anticipation value*), and the actual value of the outcome (*outcome value*).[4] As for the action selection stage, it is thought to occur when accumulating evidence from the valuation processes reaches a threshold needed to trigger action.[5] Valuation is also sensitive to the timing of the anticipated reward as subjective values depreciate over time in a well-documented phenomenon called *intertemporal discounting*. The *discount rate* (i.e., the speed at which value decreases with time) varies from one individual to another. This phenomenon prompts us to choose immediate rewards over delayed ones. Therefore, valuation does not only depend on options and their outcomes, but also on the anticipated timing of a certain reward.

In terms of the neurobiology of valuation, several studies have demonstrated that valuation is associated with processes in the ventromedial prefrontal cortex (vmPFC) as well as in the ventral striatum.[6] Furthermore, the decrease in monetary rewards with time also corresponds with a decrease in the activity of the vmPFC and the ventral striatum.[7] Moreover, information retention and manipulation in the working memory has been linked to the activity of the dorsolateral prefrontal cortex (dlPFC), which is closely associated with the vmPFC. In addition, computing the net value of different actions is hypothesized to take place in the central prefrontal cortex.[8] The approximate locations of these regions are shown in Table 3.2.

Previous experiences are also integrated in this process of value-based decision-making. Such integration occurs through comparing the actual outcome value to the anticipated value to compute *prediction error*. This allows for the agile adaptation of the assumptions that underlie decision. The biological basis of prediction error was uncovered by the seminal works of Shultz and colleagues.[12] They demonstrated through the meticulous recordings of certain cells in the primate brains that dopamine producing neurons get activated in response to the occurrence of unexpected rewards as well as to the absence of expected rewards. Since then, the prediction error signal has also been detected in the substantia nigra (SN) of humans.[13] Therefore, Shultz and others have revealed a unique property of dopaminergic neurons in reward prediction, which is hypothesized to underlie reinforcement learning from previous experiences.

In addition to learning, attentional processes are integral to the valuation stage as attributing value to various stimuli in the environment requires correctly identifying relevant and irrelevant features and linking them to certain outcomes.[14] This is further supported by the finding that value and *salience* of stimuli, that is, how

Table 3.2. A summary of the brain regions implicated in value-based decision-making. Figures created using biorender.com

Brain Regions	Mental Processes Relevant to Decision-Making	Key References
	– Assigning values – Intertemporal discounting	Delgado (2007); Hare et al. (2009);[9] Kable & Glimcher (2007); Plassmann et al. (2010)
	– Net valuation of multiple options	Hare et al. (2008)
	– Retaining and manipulating information in working memory – Self-control	Hare et al. (2009)
	– Error prediction and reinforcement learning	Zaghloul et al. (2009)[10]
	– Attentional processes	Seeley et al. (2007)[11]

attention grabbing something is, are neuroanatomically dissociable. Cues driving attentional control underlying decision-making can be *endogenous*, where an agent voluntarily chooses to attend to a certain stimulus that is behaviorally relevant, or *exogenous*, where a reorientation of attention occurs, and the agent shifts their task-sets based on the characteristics of a stimulus. In the brain, attentional processes have been attributed to the activity of the salience network, which mainly comprises the anterior insula (AI) and dorsal anterior cingulate cortex (dACC).[15] Therefore, understanding the neurobiology of decision-making involves studying the neural correlates of attention among other mental processes.

4. "NEUROFORECASTING": PREDICTING POPULATION BEHAVIOR BY MEASURING INDIVIDUAL BRAINS

Our goal in this section is to update the reader on the development of the brain-as-a-predictor approach, present examples where it has been used, explore its caveats, and provide an outlook onto its potential and short-term applications. The desire to foresee and predict population-level behaviors that give rise to future events predates modern neuroscience. This can be seen in the archaic practices of fortune-telling and science-fiction writings of powerful future prediction tools with unparalleled accuracy. To empirically actualize this desire, we have depended on the assumption that there are persistent laws and rules that govern and underlie phenomena. Thus, by probing such laws by analyzing past incidents, we may be able to build predicting models of future occurrences.[16] This methodology has been widely applied in the field of meteorology where the term forecasting is abundantly used. Such an approach has also been applied in the consumer behavior domain to varying degrees of success, from difficult-to-predict fashion trends to the robust mathematical modeling of energy consumption.[17]

Traditionally, prediction in the domain of behavior has involved building models from experts' anecdotes and scenarios. Social scientists and psychologists have also been attempting to build predictive models through the gold standard of understanding the causal mechanisms of behavioral phenomena, or the less powerful understanding of the associations between various parameters and behavior that are collected through self-reports and projective ratings of intentions, attitudes, and personality traits.[18] In psychology and marketing, further physiological methods have been used to probe the state of arousal in individuals as they engage with advertising materials by measuring their pupil response, heart rate changes, eye movement, and voice pitch analysis.

Neuroimaging as an emerging tool in behavior prediction provides a compromise between understanding some of the mechanisms underlying behavior and obtaining efficient predictive models that can be potentially operationalized without a complete model of the behavior systems. For example, Knutson and colleagues conducted an experiment with individuals who were presented with items they could purchase while their brain activities were being scanned. A positive correlation was observed between purchase behavior and the activity of the nucleus accumbens (NAcc; part of the ventral striatum) during the price evaluation period as well as between purchase behavior and the activity of the medial prefrontal cortex in the choice period.[19] These two areas are related to value prediction error and valuation respectively, as has been reviewed in another section of this chapter. Brain activity in these areas has further been used to predict individuals' subsequent choice behavior outside the scanner. For example, the level of brain activity in the medial prefrontal cortex and striatum, the latter including the nucleus accumbens, was recorded when an individual was presented with various items. This activity was then used to rank the items and to build a model for individual preferences in a subsequent task. Indeed, items that were previously highly ranked with a high brain activity in the aforementioned areas were preferred in a subsequent out-of-the scanner choice context. Neural correlates were also found to track future purchase behavior within individuals, regardless of their conscious engagement at the time of exposure.[20] This finding was further corroborated in the domain of self-control where the reduced activity in the ventromedial prefrontal cortex correlated with long-term consequences was predictive of the real-world choice of shortsighted behaviors.[21] An important finding to note from Krönke et al.'s (2020) work is that when they combined brain imaging methods with self-reported measures of the self-control personality trait, they found that the two methods are complementary rather than redundant.[22] In other words, brain activity is complementary to classical psychological approaches to predict behavior through surveys in building more predictive models.

Predicting population-level behavior from brain activity patterns of a small sample of individuals, that is, neuroforecasting, has been demonstrated through a number of studies that span the domains of finance,[23] health messaging,[24] news sharing,[25] and retail communications.[26] Overall, these studies suggest the involvement of the nucleus accumbens as well as the medial prefrontal cortex, areas involved in value-based decisions and predictive of individual level behavior.

Table 3.3. Applying neuroforecasting to predict population-level behavior in the real-world

Domains	Applications	References
Brand Advertisements on Television	– The effectiveness of television advertising on sales can be predicted by measuring the activity of the NAcc.	Venkatraman et al. (2015)[27]
Crowdfunding	– Predicting the success of funding appeals in the population through the activity of NAcc of individuals. Choice behavior of the same individuals did not predict population behavior.	Genevsky et al. (2017)
Health Messaging	– The activity in the medial prefrontal cortex (MPFC) when viewing anti-smoking advertisements predicts the population behavior of calling the campaign hotline in the month that follows the airing of the advertisement. Self-reports failed to predict population-level behavior.	Falk et al. (2012); Falk et al. (2016)[28]
Microlending	– Predicting population-level behavior towards loan appeals through measuring the NAcc of individuals.	Genevsky & Knutson (2015)
Music Popularity	– Song downloads on a market-level can be predicted from the brain activity of NAcc of a small group of people.	Berns & Moore (2012)[29]
News Article Sharing	– The combined activity of the vmPFC and the NAcc in individuals who viewed *New York Times* article summaries predicts the sharing behavior of these articles by the population. – The activity in the vmPFC in a subset of the population when viewing *New York Times* article summaries predicts real-world sharing behavior on a population level. Interestingly, the vmPFC signal of individuals showed a stronger correlation with the virality of news summaries in those who read news infrequently.	Doré et al. (2019)
Online Video Popularity	– Video popularity captured by the number of views and the duration of viewing on the internet (youtube.com) were positively correlated by the increase in NAcc and the decrease in the anterior insula.	Tong et al. (2020)[30]
Product Communications	– Sales of chocolate bars correlated positively with the combined and weighted activity of the following brain regions: NAcc, medial orbitofrontal cortex (OFC), amygdala, hippocampus, dorsomedial PFC, and the inferiorfrontal gyrus. On the other hand, the activity in the dorsolateral PFC and insula correlated negatively with market-level behavior.	Kühn et al. (2016)

As for the limitations of neuroforecasting methods, they include the following: i) the high cost associated with fMRI compared to traditional and machine learning methods, ii) sensitivity to the expertise and the design of the test in terms of defining the parameters they are measuring and the control for confounding factors, iii) the relatively low explanatory power at this early stage of this approach considering the current focus of decision-making models to rational valuation and the lack of incorporating the individual's emotions and self as constant yet variable constructs, influenced by real-world contexts outside the laboratory, and iv) the potential ethical considerations in providing direct and undeclared insights into one's mental life and in the intentions to predict and forecast with the intent to introduce change to systems.[31]

5. CASE STUDY: USING NEUROSCIENCE TO HARNESS THE POWER OF DIGITAL MEDIA AND CONSUMER WORD OF MOUTH

As of December 2020, 63 percent of the world population has access to the internet, representing a 1,271 percent increase since the turn of the century.[32] Such a boom in access amplifies the importance of digital media and its role in shaping the behaviors of individuals and societies across our world. A core feature of the modern internet is its profoundly social nature – online environments are saturated with signals reflecting the thoughts, emotions, and behaviors of other people. The impact of these social constructs can take hold in domains such as advertising, public health, politics, and philanthropy. A vivid example of this impact can be found in the 2014 "Ice Bucket Challenge," which engaged over seventeen million individuals and raised over $115 million in eight weeks for Amyotrophic Lateral Sclerosis (ALS) research funds.[33]

Consequently, extensive research in marketing and social science focuses on understanding the origins of content sharing behavior. Within marketing, content sharing, especially when accompanied with new, consumer-generated information, can be understood as a form of consumer word of mouth (WOM) communication, and the more recently developed framework of "viral" marketing (e.g., Berger).[34] Through this theoretical lens, content becomes viral when it is rapidly shared in a short period of time leading to a spreading of the content through a population of consumers. Moreover, it has been found that this type of communication is person-centric, rather than firm-centric, and can impact the behavior of the consumer on the receiving end either positively or negatively. Berger argues that consumers share information on social media that they consider to be self-relevant and valuable, while anticipating how others will respond to the content they share. Thus, the individual plays a central role in this type of social phenomena, and understanding the individual behavior and its mechanisms are of essence.

A desire to engineer this viral spread motivates marketing managers and content creators to design and implement strategies that boost sharing of marketing communications at an accelerated pace with a high return on investment. To date, most research on consumer word of mouth and self-relevance has relied on traditional self-report and behavioral tools drawn from marketing and psychology. However, these traditional methods suffer from limitations such as the introduction of bias by the studied subjects and researchers. Therefore, neuroimaging offers a unique approach to generating insights about what causes digital content to be widely shared through a direct access to brain activity. This type of information can complement and fortify traditional self-report behavioral methods widely used in marketing and social science.

Neuroscience work suggests that decisions to share information are fundamentally value-based and involve *self-* as well as *social-relevance*. Self-relevance refers to experiencing content as relevant to one's own self, while social-relevance is when an individual perceives content as relevant to others. These are two psychological processes that are also important to consider. Theories of message sharing posit that experienced self- and social-relevance are important inputs to subjective value, and that choice options that have higher self- and social-relevance are more likely to be enacted. Indirect evidence from neuroimaging studies suggests that activity in brain regions associated with self- and social-relevance are related to message sharing intentions[35] and virality.[36]

Moreover, neuroimaging research suggests that social information plays into the potential costs and benefits that our brains calculate for sharing, to arrive at a decision about what and when to share. For example, early fMRI research demonstrated that people were willing to forgo money when making the decision to share information about themselves with others, which suggests that sharing information with others is inherently rewarding for the sharer. Other work has suggested that people whose brains show stronger connections between regions involved in valuation, emotion, and self-relevance processing also reported engaging in more self-disclosure on social media.[37]

Neuroforecasting has also been demonstrated in the domain of news article sharing behavior, relevant to WOM behavior and viral messaging.[38] In particular, Doré et al. (2019) provide further insights into the mechanisms driving brain-behavior relationships allowing for prediction of population-level news sharing. Specifically, their study suggests that there are individual differences in terms of how predictive certain individual's neural activity signals are; the neural activity of individuals who consume news less frequently was a better predictor of the popularity of a certain article on a population level.[39] Such insight expands the utility of the brain-as-a-predictor approach beyond a tool into understanding the mechanisms that govern a complex phenomenon such as real-world behavior.

All in all, emerging literature has been investigating the connections between brain activity and the success of online messaging. But while researchers have shown that the spread of online messages relates to activity in particular brain systems, we have only begun to understand the implications of these findings. What drives people to talk about and share content? Why do some things get shared more than others? And how do person-specific motivations and contexts change how people share? By continuing to study brain-behavior relationships in the context of online messaging, the field will learn more about the social and individual underpinnings of word-of-mouth communication and viral marketing, with potential applications to a variety of fields and industries.

6. MANAGERIAL IMPLICATIONS

Though this field is still at its early stages, practitioners can benefit from some insights as well as contribute to our body of knowledge through case studies and field findings. Businesses have more access to rich consumer data than ever before, and many industries are incorporating various approaches to developing and offering personalized product and service experiences that hinge on appraisals of self- and social-relevance. This is enabled through increased computational capacity and the rise in accessibility to technology.

However, forecasting inherently leads to unintended behavioral change, which would require constant forecasting and updating of methods. Thus, we need to adapt our operations to embrace continuous and real-time forecasting that can incorporate multiple scales and domains of information, from personal behavior to environmental factors, for successful integration of any type of forecasting.

There is also a need to invite more multidisciplinary stakeholders to the table and invest more in understanding where and how the ethics, rights, benefits, and risks intersect to maximize outcomes and harvest the advantages. This is an exciting technological era; however, adhering to good practices and upholding the highest standards of practice is key for the sustainability of this technology.

7. FUTURE DIRECTIONS

Currently, online media environments are the context for a large proportion of our daily-life communication. Improving our decisions related to sharing quality materials is important to cope with the ever-increasing volume of online messaging. In this section, we outline future directions for work in this area that we see as critical for continued theoretical advances in the neuroscience of information sharing towards the development of practical applications in marketing and retailing.

7.1. From Region-as-Predictor to Whole-Brain Predictive Modelling

Prior work in the neuroforecasting tradition tends to quantify brain responses by computing *univariate* average activity in isolated brain regions of interest. However, in future work, it will be important to leverage machine learning tools to define *multivariate* whole-brain patterns of neural activity that can serve as signatures of the population-level impact of online messages. This will include using dimension reduction, regularization, and cross-validation to minimize overfitting and thereby enhance the generalizability of the derived brain patterns across different perceivers and message sets.

7.2. Building a Knowledge Base That Is Grounded in Person-Specific Processes

A core premise of precision retailing is that the utility of any marketing action (such as a persuasive online message) will depend on the person responding to it and the context that person is situated in. Because neuroforecasting studies have so far focused on main effects of stimuli or messages, these kinds of message-by-person-by-situation interactions have not yet played a central role in this literature, nor, indeed, in social science models more generally. However, recent trends in functional neuroimaging towards the integration of various methods, such as computational social science and daily-life experience sampling, suggest a path for more complex and realistic studies that assess mechanisms of successful messaging from multiple perspectives within a single research program or even a single study. In our view, the goal to generate highly contextualized and person-specific models of consumer behavior will be greatly facilitated by work that leverages methods affording highly dense measurements of daily-life behavior and that models these measurements through the theoretical lens of person-by-situation interactions. Work of this kind may help to identify when message sharing is driven more by features of content (i.e., the content of the message itself compels people to share on average) versus by particular contexts (i.e., the message is shared because it is relevant to a particular situation or interaction).

8. SUMMARY AND CONCLUSION

We live in an exciting era where brain activity can be directly probed for information to understand and predict our mental processes and behaviors. This chapter provides an overview of neuroscience and its implications in understanding decision-making and predicting behavior on a population level. We first introduced our readers to fMRI as a commonly used neuroimaging methodology in neuroscience to capture brain activity and its correlation with mental processes and behavior. We then provided a primer on choice and value-based decision-making. Furthermore, we introduced the emerging field of neuroforecasting as a relevant application of neuroscience in marketing and retailing. We also included media-sharing behavior as a domain which can benefit from our understanding of the brain and its activity in designing effective marketing campaigns. The chapter was concluded with implications for practitioners and what the future could hold for this area of study and work.

Although the field of neuroforecasting and its implications in media-sharing behavior are still in their early days, rapid advances in machine learning and complexity science are exponentially expanding our understanding of whole-brain activity patterns and of the link between these patterns and behavior. This is exciting as this new avenue of research and practice has the potential to bring us closer to highly individualized person-specific modelling and prediction of consumer behavior in the near future.

NOTES

1 Rangel, A., Camerer, C., & Montague, P.R. (2008). A framework for studying the neurobiology of value-based decision making. *Nature Reviews Neuroscience, 9(7)*, 545–56. https://doi.org/10.1038/nrn2357.

2 Rangel & Montague (2008).

3 Rangel & Montague (2008).

4 Plassmann, H., O'Doherty, J.P., & Rangel, A. (2010). Appetitive and aversive goal values are encoded in the medial orbitofrontal cortex at the time of decision making. *The Journal of Neuroscience: The Official Journal of the Society for Neuroscience, 30*(32), 10799–808. https://doi.org/10.1523/jneurosci.0788-10.2010.

5 Basten, U., Biele, G., Heekeren, H.R., & Fiebach, C.J. (2010). How the brain integrates costs and benefits during decision making. *Proceedings of the National Academy of Sciences, 107*(50), 21767–72. https://doi.org/10.1073/pnas.0908104107.

6 Plassman, O'Doherty, & Rangel (2010); Delgado, M.R. (2007). Reward-related responses in the human striatum. *Annals of the New York Academy of Sciences, 1104*(1), 70–88. https://doi.org/10.1196/annals.1390.002.

7 Kable, J.W., & Glimcher, P.W. (2007). The neural correlates of subjective value during intertemporal choice. *Nature Neuroscience, 10*(12), 1625–33. https://doi.org/10.1038/nn2007.

8 Hare, T.A., O'Doherty, J., Camerer, C.F., Schultz, W., & Rangel, A. (2008). Dissociating the role of the orbitofrontal cortex and the striatum in the computation of goal values and prediction errors. *The Journal of Neuroscience, 28*(22), 5623–30. https://doi.org/10.1523/JNEUROSCI.1309-08.2008.

9 Hare, T.A., Camerer, C.F., & Rangel, A. (2009). Self-control in decision-making involves modulation of the vmPFC valuation system. *Science, 324*(5927), 646–8. https://doi.org/10.1126/science.1168450.

10 Zaghloul, K.A., Blanco, J.A., Weidemann, C.T., McGill, K., Jaggi, J.L., Baltuch, G.H., & Kahana, M.J. (2009). Human substantia nigra neurons encode unexpected financial rewards. *Science, 323*(5920), 1496–9. https://doi.org/10.1126/science.1167342.

11 Seeley, W.W., Menon, V., Schatzberg, A.F., Keller, J., Glover, G.H., Kenna, H., Reiss, A.L., & Greicius, M.D. (2007). Dissociable intrinsic connectivity networks for salience processing and executive control. *The Journal of Neuroscience, 27*(9), 2349–56. https://doi.org/10.1523/jneurosci.5587-06.2007.

12 Shultz, W., Dayan, P., & Montague, P.R. (1997). A neural substrate of prediction and reward. *Science, 275*(5306), 1593–99. https://doi.org/10.1126/science.275.5306.1593.

13 Zaghloul et al. (2009).

14 Vaidya, A.R., & Fellows, L.K. (2016). Necessary contributions of human frontal lobe subregions to reward learning in a dynamic, multidimensional environment. *The Journal of Neuroscience, 36*(38), 9843–58. https://doi.org/10.1523/JNEUROSCI.1337-16.2016.

15 Seeley et al. (2007).

16 Walonick, D.S. (1993). An overview of forecasting methodology. In *Survival Statistics*. StatPac Incorporated.

17 Hare et al. (2009).

18 Hare et al. (2009).

19 Knutson, B., Rick, S., Wimmer, G.E., Prelec, D., & Loewenstein, G. (2007). Neural predictors of purchases. *Neuron, 53*(1), 147–56. https://doi.org/10.1016/j.neuron.2006.11.010.

20 Tusche, A., Bode, S., & Haynes, J.-D. (2010). Neural responses to unattended products predict later consumer choices. *The Journal of Neuroscience, 30*(23), 8024–31. https://doi.org/10.1523/JNEUROSCI.0064-10.2010.

21 Krönke, K.M., Wolff, M., Mohr, H., Kräplin, A., Smolka, M.N., Bühringer, G., & Goschke, T. (2020). Predicting real-life self-control from brain activity encoding the value of anticipated future outcomes. *Psychological Science, 31*(3), 268–79. https://doi.org/10.1177/0956797619896357.

22 Tusche et al. (2010).

23 Genevsky, A., & Knutson, B. (2015). Neural affective mechanisms predict market-level microlending. *Psychological Science, 26*(9), 1411–22. https://doi.org/10.1177/0956797615588467.

24 Falk, E.B., Berkman, E.T., & Lieberman, M.D. (2012). From neural responses to population behavior: Neural focus group predicts population-level media effects. *Psychological Science, 23*(5), 439–45. https://www.jstor.org/stable/41489721.

25 Doré, B.P., Scholz, C., Baek, E.C., Garcia, J.O., O'Donnell, M.B., Bassett, D.S., Vettel, J.M., & Falk, E.B. (2019). Brain activity tracks population information sharing by capturing consensus judgments of value. *Cerebral Cortex, 29*(7), 3102–10. https://doi.org/10.1093/cercor/bhy176.

26 Kühn, S., Strelow, E., & Gallinat, J. (2016). Multiple "buy buttons" in the brain: Forecasting chocolate sales at point-of-sale based on functional brain activation using fMRI. *Neuroimage, 136*, 122–8. https://doi.org/10.1016/j.neuroimage.2016.05.021.

27 Venkatraman, V., Dimoka, A., Pavlou, P.A., Vo, K., Hampton, W., Bollinger, B., Hershfield, H.E., Ishihara, M., & Winer, R.S. (2015). Predicting advertising success beyond traditional measures: New insights from neurophysiological methods and market response modeling. *Journal of Marketing Research, 52*(4), 436–52. https://dx.doi.org/10.2139/ssrn.2498095.

28 Falk, E.B., O'Donnell, M.B., Tompson, S., Gonzalez, R., Dal Cin, S., Strecher, V., Cummings, K.M., & An, L. (2016). Functional brain imaging predicts public health campaign success. *Social Cognitive and Affective Neuroscience, 11*(2), 204–14. https://doi.org/10.1093/scan/nsv108.

29 Berns, G.S., & Moore, S.E. (2012). A neural predictor of cultural popularity. *Journal of Consumer Psychology, 22*(1), 154–60. https://doi.org/10.1016/j.jcps.2011.05.001.

30 Tong, L.C., Acikalin, M.Y., Genevsky, A., Shiv, B., & Knutson, B. (2020). Brain activity forecasts video engagement in an internet attention market. *Proceedings of the National Academy of Sciences, 117*(12), 6936–41. https://doi.org/10.1073/pnas.1905178117.

31 Hare et al. (2009).

32 Internet World Stats. (2020). Internet usage statistics: The internet big picture. https://internetworldstats.com/stats.htm

33 Oppenheim, M. (2017, November 30). Man who inspired ice bucket challenge dies aged 46. *The Independent.* https://www.independent.co.uk/news/world/americas/man-inspired-ice-bucket-challenge-facebook-dies-death-anthony-senerchia-jnr-a8084621.html.

34 Berger, J. (2016). *Contagious: Why things catch on.* Simon and Schuster.

35 Baek, E.C., Scholz, C., O'Donnell, M.B., & Falk, E.B. (2017). The value of sharing information: A neural account of information transmission. *Psychological Science, 28*(7), 851–61. https://doi.org/10.1177/0956797617695073.

36 Falk et al. (2012).

37 Meshi, D., Tamir, D.I., & Heekeren, H.R. (2015). The emerging neuroscience of social media. *Trends in Cognitive Sciences, 19*(12), 771–82. https://psycnet.apa.org/doi/10.1016/j.tics.2015.09.004.

38 Falk et al. (2012).

39 Doré et al. (2019).

CHAPTER FOUR

Unlocking Unconscious Truths: Adapting Linguistics, Semiotics, and Evidence-Based Behavioral Modeling to Inform Corporate Strategy and Brand

Joanna Castellano, Matthew E.C. Bourkas, and Chris McCarthy

SUMMARY OF CHAPTER

The chapter provides an approach to deriving behavioral insights from traditional and non-traditional market research techniques with many real case studies. The first section focuses on the organization's emphasis on uncovering and characterizing the "true meaning" of a consumer's words. The authors explain how these techniques decode people's unconscious needs and expectations of brands and product solutions. The second section delves into the development of mindset and need-state segments when analyzing consumers. Effectively assigning mindsets with powerful AI-driven tools allows a more precise targeting of the right solutions and communications campaigns.

MANAGERIAL IMPLICATIONS (GENERAL)

- The understanding of consumer linguistic cues and relevant sensory modalities is very important. Of critical value is the capturing and storing of textual data, words, and contexts as major assets for further mining.

- The combination of different techniques coming from linguistics, semiotics, and behavioral sciences is highlighted in this chapter as different teams typically deal with these different aspects separately.

MANAGERIAL IMPLICATIONS (ORGANIZATIONAL)

- A chief data officer role is important to get the benefits from textual data mining using the advanced techniques proposed in this chapter.
- It is recommended to create multidisciplinary teams that combine at least linguists, behavioral scientists, AI scientists, and marketing & communication experts among others.

MANAGERIAL IMPLICATIONS (STRATEGIC, TACTICAL, AND OPERATIONAL)

- The strategic planning exercise must consider the advanced techniques described in this chapter. At least, it is recommended to include a proof of concept in the road map.
- From a tactical perspective, managers need to start climbing the maturity level to be able to implement such advanced models and provision the adequate resources (human & technical) to get there. Iterative business value cases need to be developed where investments are justified by business value outcomes.
- From the operational perspective, consider every piece of data (from contact center, chatbots, portal, mobile, etc.) exchanged with customers as an asset that needs to be captured with high quality in the context of an operational governance model that preserves security and compliance.

MANAGERIAL IMPLICATIONS (RISK ASSESSMENT)

- There are risks associated with security, privacy, and compliance considerations that are not limited to the data level but extend to the level of the discovered models and insights.

- There are financial risks associated, but they are limited and calculated if managers adopt an iterative business value cases where investments are justified by business value outcomes.
- There could be brand risks if the models are not tuned or developed correctly, or if they contain any biases.

1. INTRODUCTION AND OVERVIEW

Most leading corporations that sell directly to consumers have well-structured and disciplined approaches to sustaining market growth and identifying new white space opportunities, and yet 80–95 percent of new product launches underperform.[1] In addition, new market entrants with breakthrough innovations in customer and brand engagement, technologies, products, channels, and services can blindside even the best of companies and put them at risk, as Amazon and Netflix, for instance, achieved against their respective competitors. The COVID-19 pandemic has intensified this risk to entrenched market leaders by introducing challenges not accounted for in their risk management rosters of serious threats to organizational resilience. Although many have struggled to evolve (e.g., with supply chain adaptations), other companies have thrived in this new environment. For example, Home Depot has significantly increased its emphasis on e-commerce distribution channels, helping it flourish. To succeed in the new environment, leading corporations will need to move beyond traditional characterizations of the consumer by understanding their rational, emotional, and aspirational relationships to products and brand.

The emergence of COVID-19 has accelerated the reliance on and acceptance of technological innovations that many consumers would have likely resisted or ignored pre-pandemic. It has disrupted virtually every industry by forcing consumers to change habitual behaviors: for example, how they shop, work, interact with healthcare, and perceive social constructs, all of which force consumers to suddenly make numerous and significant adaptations.[2] The forced adaptations that elevate the consumer experience in some manner, either through the addition of positives or elimination of barriers, are those that are likely to continue even after the pandemic subsides.[3] Moving forward, it will be critical to better understand and influence which adaptations consumers adopt as long-term behaviors and which they abandon.

COVID, spiraling inflation, supply chain issues, and other factors have introduced consumers to a wide range of novel experiences, such as how they shop, find entertainment sources, source food, etc. It appears these external forces have accelerated slow-moving consumer trends and pushed them into the mainstream. Conversely, these factors have also introduced significant challenges to most, and there may be a strong urge to revert to the status quo with individuals who have lost a sense of control and comfort. We hypothesize this era of change will escalate consumers' assertiveness and power to demand what products and services corporations deliver as well as when, where, and how they are delivered. Consumers are increasingly turning to products, services, and brands to fulfill the lifestyle or societal aspirations that governments have failed to help them with, such as those relating to climate change or social responsibility. This era of change has kick-started a new era of consumer empowerment.

Consequently, there is a greater urgency for corporations and brands to leverage the expansive paradigm of precision retailing and tailor their value offers to specific segments of consumer mindsets. As discussed in the other chapters of this book, precision retailing provides a framework to tap into the new ecosystem of advanced analytics, AI, technology, and human biology to better understand what drives and actualizes behavior. In this chapter, we will discuss why it is critical to pursue deeper interdisciplinary approaches to understand why and how consumers react to this era of change.

The approach we will outline integrates concepts from multiple disciplines, including psycholinguistics, behavioral economics, Jungian psychoanalysis, and natural language processing. Psycholinguistics is the study of psychological processes as they relate to the use, production, and comprehension of language. It can help interpret the language of consumers to develop a deeper understanding of what is driving their choice of wording, for example, by learning what emotional states associate with what words. Jungian psychoanalysis has proven valuable in establishing a methodology for interviewing individuals and grouping behaviors using universal and cultural archetypes.[4] Behavioral economics has had a significant role in determining how precision retailers can frame and interpret choices as well as the biases influencing them. And natural language processing is a type of AI that can process large volumes of text to complement the analysis of in-depth interviews.

This unique approach has been tested quantitatively with numerous clients across a broad range of sectors and geographies, and it has been scaled using machine learning and advanced analytics. For over thirty years, this approach has proven its value in a practical setting by helping clients discover new market opportunities and innovations, consistently expanding their market shares. Successful precision retailing requires strong advocacy of the consumer as an individual, and practitioners must be mindful of the role they play as custodians of behavioral insights with the power to influence how major corporations shape society and connect to consumers. By collaboratively working with clients to respectfully build choice architectures in the consumer's best interest,[5] organizations using this approach continue to experience a growing positive sentiment of their brands.

We will discuss a framework for deriving behavioral insights from traditional and non-traditional market research techniques throughout this chapter. The first section will focus on uncovering and characterizing the "true meaning" of a consumer's words, and the power of maintaining a psychoanalytic approach to smaller scale, in-depth interviews when initially segmenting consumer behavior. Psychoanalysis attributes weight to the unconscious mind of an individual, including thoughts, feelings, and desires that lie outside of conscious awareness. We will outline techniques to decode people's unconscious needs and expectations of brands and product solutions. Case examples will be provided to show how understanding the impact of linguistic cues can be translated into market success.

The second section will delve into the development of mindset and need-state segments when analyzing consumers. It will outline the sequential, three-part process that precision retailers can conduct: the **discovery and investigation phase**, which models mindsets and

behaviors; the quantitative **validation phase**, which refines and prior-
itizes the prior phase's hypothesized behavioral cohorts; and finally,
the **scaling and typing** phase, which scales, matches, and types validated mindsets to an organization's existing consumer databases. By
effectively assigning mindsets with powerful AI-driven tools, this
final phase can be reliably scaled to analyze the larger sets of consumer
data often built by major multinational corporations. This allows precision retailers to better target the right solutions and communications
campaigns, and we will demonstrate this process through a practical
case study involving financial institution (FI) clients.

2. UNDERSTANDING THE "WHY" AND "HOW" OF CONSUMERS THROUGH LINGUISTICS ANALYSIS

*A language is not just words. It's a culture, a tradition, a unification of a community, a
whole history that creates what a community is. It's all embodied in a language.*

Noam Chomsky

Discussed in this section are the underlying principles that can be
applied to build a behavioral framework that incorporates a deeper,
more holistic approach to understanding consumers' purchasing
behaviors. By understanding the cognitive, emotional, linguistic,
behavioral, neurological, and cultural aspects to a person's decision-
making process in specific contexts, organizations are able to better predict human behavior in a large swathe of diverse industries,
including financial services, food and beverage, healthcare, and consumer packaged goods.

A critical foundation common to all such behavioral frameworks
is the exploration and investigation of the unconscious drivers that
influence spoken language. This helps bridge the gap between "what
people say" and "what people do." Over a decade of practical experience applying and validating this paradigm suggests that a consumer's unconscious beliefs, motivations, and linguistic cues are just as
important, if not more so, than the literal content of their words. Profiling the emotional and cognitive underpinnings of an individual's
behavior can inform the decoding of their linguistic patterns and associated meanings, providing a lens to see what other approaches often

miss while at the same time avoiding false positives, when a consumer confidently expresses a behavior they will fail to follow through with.

Language has many layers of meaning and subtext to it, and we go through a continual process of discovery and reinterpretation as we grow and develop as individuals.

There is typically a large amount of cultural, interpersonal, and emotional "baggage" embedded within a language.[6] Even fluent, non-native speakers often struggle to capture the figurative connotations that specific words carry when translating into their native tongue, and this is why even common idiomatic expressions can be so hard to translate intuitively. This phenomenon is perhaps best evinced by the host of competing translations that exist for many major literary works, even within the same language, as each version attempts to better capture the subtext of the original prose or poetry.

Every culture has its own "DNA" of language that begins imprinting from birth,[7] and it is often lost in translation by non-native speakers, who have no frame of reference for the language's nuanced meanings. The unique circumstances with which a person learns and uses language leaves a "blueprint of language," which can be decoded to provide deeper insight into the interrelated rational and emotional beliefs, attitudes, and actions of an individual. For example, by decoding linguistic cues, this holistic approach can better understand which sensory cues have the greatest impact on a consumer's decision-making process when purchasing certain products. These revelations help brands and corporations provide innovative solutions to the unmet, and often unconscious, needs of consumers.

3. UNCOVERING HIDDEN MOTIVATIONS IN CONSUMER BEHAVIOR: CASE STUDIES IN BEVERAGES, FOOD, AND PHARMA

Case Study 1: Beverages

People who exhibit similar behavior under certain contexts often share common linguistic cues and patterns, which can be used to segment consumers and create predictive models of behavior.

Three examples follow that depict how the initial framing of language sharpens precision retailing and how an understanding of the physical, neurological aspects to a decision-making process, such as when an individual is most responsive to sensory cues, can further strengthen these models. More specifically, we will provide snapshots of projects at the qualitative phase, which will be later outlined in greater detail as the first "discovery and investigation" phase.

The first case revolves around the beverage industry. One of the largest beverage companies in the world wanted to better position its products with consumers. The client felt consumer tastes were evolving, and they feared their products did not fit the palette of prevailing trends. Despite hundreds of millions of dollars spent in consumer research globally, the client did not understand the deep-rooted "why" and "how" of these hypothesized trends in consumer tastes. The project identified new insights around sensory cues that better framed the brand and product in numerous consumption contexts. It was also able to decode the deeper affective states associated with early brand memories that the company had not identified.

To achieve this, consumers were asked to recount their experiences from childhood to present day in various contexts. They were also asked to individually write a fable and select Jungian imagery from a set of seventy-eight visual cards that best expressed their feelings around the moral of the fable. In analyzing the linguistic cues across qualitative data as well as the consumer relationships with certain imagery and Jungian archetypes, we discovered that early brand experiences imprinted on older generations provided strong nostalgic memories of people, foods, and shared experiences – most of which were absent in younger demographics.

This meant that the immediate product experience was the main determinant in securing loyalty for younger consumers, and it signaled a generational gap in messaging that the client had to address. This allowed the client to further tailor their messaging across demographic cohorts, and they found great success in retooling their youth-focused product lines' presentation, including glassware, accompanying food, and general context, such as the food's surrounding environment when displayed.

In discovering the role of emotional associations and carefully assessing the influence of specific sensory cues, particularly visual, auditory, and tactile cues for advertising, the client developed a framework for optimizing "the perfect product experience" by demographics. In addition to age, geography and local culture had particularly important roles in determining the importance of food pairing when messaging to consumers. These insights also disproved the client's hypothesis that shifting palettes were mainly to blame for declining volume, avoiding a false positive and leading the client to overhaul the visuals and accompanying instructions in their foodservice manuals.

Case Study 2: Food

This second case study went beyond the usual cognitive, affective, and behavioral analyses performed in the discovery and investigation phase to incorporate additional physical metrics during customer segmentation: for example, accounting for morphometric measurements like BMI throughout and nutritional genetic markers during a subset of the study. Further, interview discussion guides were adapted to elucidate specifically how the developing consumer segments reflected the neuroscience field's current views on hedonic eating: that is, eating for reward rather than metabolic need.

The project was a syndicated study funded by several multinational food and beverage corporations that were seeking to better position their brands in an increasingly health-conscious world. These companies wanted to understand why their push towards healthier food and beverage portfolios were often met with tepid demand, particularly considering the tremendous societal and political movements towards healthier living. In addition to brand and marketing concerns, these insights carried relevance for product innovation strategies: for example, in understanding which sensory modalities allowed the strongest response when experiencing an advertisement versus consuming a given product. To better understand the gap between a consumer's needs and wants, which is particularly discrepant when investigating eating behaviors, we turned to peer-reviewed medical literature to help frame our initial studies.

One of the earlier models explaining the population variability in obesity relates to the dopamine deficiency hypothesis, which posits that individuals with lowered dopamine signaling are less able to experience reward when eating – in turn, leading to a positive feedback loop of continued reward seeking via hedonic eating.[8] However, the concept was increasingly challenged with conflicting genetic studies around the time of this project, and dopamine's proposed role during consumption is now better understood to relate to impulsivity, adherence to diet, and the ability to correct inflated expectations of reward.[9] The initial discovery phase of research was informed by this understanding of the unique product experience that obese consumers are predisposed to undergo during consumption.

However, dopamine's complex role in mediating eating behaviors is context specific, and this is well illustrated in the distinct role dopamine plays in the brain's striatum. Excess dopaminergic (dopamine-releasing), striatal activity in response to food cues *before consumption* associates strongly with obesity.[10,11] It is notable that this region of the brain mediates Pavlovian conditioning and reward systems.[12,13] And in addition to associating the inherent reward of high caloric intake with certain gustatory sensations, individuals with excessive dopaminergic activity in their striatum are predisposed to further condition these gustatory cues with additional sensory cues that the less obese are less likely to develop. Consequently, it is important to understand the context-specific relationship that different consumer segments have with food cues and the vital role that a selected advertising medium will play in establishing saliency and creating desirable choice architectures.

Contextualized with the dopamine deficiency research, this paints a nuanced model where obese consumers are more likely to struggle with impulsivity and food cues during the "want" phase of eating, due to overactive dopamine, while simultaneously contending with a blunted reward or "like" during consumption, due to underactive dopamine.[14,15,16]

Understanding the neurological basis of eating behaviors and the distinct phases that a person undergoes (e.g., goal-directed food seeking versus hedonic consumption) all contributed to the framework developed to interpret the first phase's in-depth interviews. This allowed us to categorize consumers via literature defined measurements of obesity, to develop mindsets around these different weight categories, and finally, to inform the characterization and development of these cohorts with scientifically relevant processes.

For example, the development of mindsets within BMI-defined cohorts exhibited consistent trends with respect to vulnerability to food cues and sensitivity to specific sensory modalities. As a result, the mindsets that emerged were more nuanced and extensive, informing our sponsors' product pipeline-fills to better innovate, position, and communicate their future health and wellness offerings, so as to increase the odds of success for those mindset cohorts struggling with weight.

Case Study 3: Pharma

The third case study is a project related to smoking cessation and provides another strong example of the lasting benefits afforded by the successful decoding of consumer language cues. A major pharmaceutical company sought to increase the market share of two of its over-the-counter smoking cessation products, and like the previous beverage case, the insights provided by this approach continue to be embedded in the client's brand tenets more than twenty years later. The work was first conducted during a period when smoking bans were becoming increasingly prevalent across many states. The pharmaceutical company believed that more smokers would seek aids to stop smoking as these new laws became the norm.

The company wanted to ensure that they had a better understanding of their existing and potential customer base, so they could "do right by them." During this time, smokers were starting to feel more like outcasts as opposed to being a part of the "fun, cool crowd."

They felt tremendous pressure to change their smoking behaviors and were often experiencing alienation and disgust with themselves over their ongoing failures to quit smoking.

Many smokers require multiple attempts to successfully quit their smoking habit, even with the help of smoking cessation products. However, a segment of smokers was identified that would consistently give up by their second or third trial with cessation aids, blame the products, and then spread negative word of mouth to other consumers. For this group, it was pivotal to integrate the client's intervention programs as part of the brand solution and to indicate clearly how to use both. It was of mutual interest for both the pharmaceutical company and the smokers to experience success after fewer product trials. From the company's perspective, it enhanced their brand image and ensured their brand experience was not being defamed, and from the consumer's perspective, it allowed earlier success, improved self-confidence, and motivation to "stay on track."

During the interview process, respondents were asked to mentally return to experiences they'd had when they attempted to quit smoking with varying degrees of success. This was executed by having each respondent take a few minutes to relax and mentally transport themselves to these memories, describing their environment, actions, thoughts, and most importantly, feelings during the process. Once attuned to their emotional and mental state while reliving these events, consumers were then able to better imagine themselves acting in future experiences, communicating how they would feel and think during these events, as though they were real.

This process borrows from an evidence-informed psychological intervention used by CBT (cognitive behavioral therapy) practitioners, termed interoceptive exposure, in which an individual can desensitize themselves to difficult stimuli by imagining themselves in relevant contexts and *feeling* what the event would be like.[17] Although its usage in behavioral insights is not to desensitize, it still leverages the ability of individuals to effectively relive, physically feel, and even learn from their mental experiences. Additionally, consumers were asked to empathize by placing themselves in the position of those affected by their smoking, allowing us to further characterize the importance consumers placed on their loved ones' experiences during cessation.

This technique led to the development of a new strategy that better framed the consumer's choice of product solutions within the client's brand umbrella. The product solutions were presented to reflect the emotional and functional criteria of the smoker's frame of mind around quitting, employing visuals that presented the consumer in situations they associated with success, such as happy family interactions or physical activities. The product materials, which included these visuals in packaging, inserts, and advertising, were also conveyed in a very structured and step-by-step manner. This encouraged a routinized procedure, which evidence showed improved the smoker's confidence and probability of success significantly. During validation, this approach was contrasted to alternative framings that presented information as itemized benefits with less personally relevant visual stimuli. This communication format resulted in stressing consumers and curbing purchases as they felt less capable of following a routine during cessation. In addition, smokers were particularly drawn to material that promoted the multi-therapeutic modality of the company's portfolio by including materials for the brand's intervention program. This encouraged purchases and provided smokers with a structured and methodical approach they could follow to better adopt nonsmoking behaviors into their long-term routines.

The strategic implementation of these behavioral insights also revealed the fine line between providing a structured routine and appearing paternalistic, as the advertising proofs were initially found to carry a voice and tone perceived as condescending and fearmongering by consumers. Fine-tuning the activation of the insights gained during discovery and validation revealed a sweet spot between benevolence and paternalism that made the product and the brand more appealing. The more compassionate yet authoritative voice that was iteratively developed helped consumers feel they had agency to quit smoking, without being left alone to figure out their own routines.

4. MOVING FROM LINGUISTIC ANALYSIS TO MINDSETS AND BEHAVIORAL TYPING: A THREE-PHASED APPROACH

Traditional consumer segmentation hinging on geographic, demographic, and psychographic data is useful and helps an organization understand its place in the market, who their consumers are, and what their consumers need and buy. This type of data is useful, but precision retailing can be sharpened by supplementing it with a deeper investigation into the nuances of consumer decision-making, with a specific focus on *context-specific* behavior. In doing so, precision retailers can avoid generalizing consumer behavior that may be context specific. Understanding the deeper cognitive and affective processes that are in play when a consumer makes decisions is vital to helping shape their customer journey as well as the information and choices presented to them. Although examples of validation and implementation have been covered, the prior section was focused on qualitative discovery and investigation. This section will provide a more detailed overview of the three-stage holistic approach recommended to identify and activate behavioral insights, particularly the second stage of validation and refinement.

In the stage 1 discovery and investigation phase, a multidisciplinary approach reveals how people relate to their external or objective world, their internal or perceived world, and how they construct and evaluate trade-offs, such as in risk versus reward. One of the outcomes of this unique behavioral approach is a *mindset framework* that captures the fluidity of consumer decision-making by examining the shifting mindsets that consumers adopt across varied contexts as well as their default predispositions. It reveals distinct cohorts of people in which consumers share similar beliefs, motivations, behaviors, and linguistic cues, all of which provide markers for unconscious behavioral patterns and internal dialogues around decision-making. For stage 2, we recommend replacing classic segmentation inputs (attitude and behavior inputs) with more holistic inputs. Stage 1 outcomes become stage 2 inputs, and the mindsets and aspirations of consumers are translated into different jobs to be done (JTBD)[18] associated with each mindset segment. These JTBD are future-leaning as they are aspirational in nature and less about describing who a person is but instead, who they might aspire to be and how a given product can help them achieve this.

It is critical that the mindset language of the consumer, discovered and decoded during the qualitative phase, be emulated and carried forward into the second stage survey and validated through quantitative analysis. Large market-representative samples should include a mix of both existing consumers and aspirational consumers, who are not current consumers but desirable future ones. Attitudinal and belief statements given by individuals during the qualitative stage are grouped into segments that are then validated and prioritized based on quantitative surveying. The wording of these statements not only captures an attitude and belief but mirrors the linguistic cues most aligned with the customer prospects holding each attitude and belief.

Responses are cluster analyzed to reveal differentiated mindsets. Next, respondents review a large variety of possible JTBD, what a product or service might do for them, and respondents prioritize them via a trade-off type survey process. Individual respondent prioritizations are cluster analyzed to uncover distinct and differentiated jobs that the market wishes to be done. The final step asks consumers to indicate how well the current market delivers each JTBD. Broadly valued JTBD which underperform in the market represent white space potential. These JTBD segments are integrated with the mindset segments to reveal a targeting and product strategy. The mindsets describe the WHO and WHY, while the JTBD segments reveal the WHAT and HOW, that is, what to build for consumers and how, allowing for a "whole person" market strategy.

The final, third stage is a scaling and typing phase in which we apply an algorithm to type the client's customer databases, enabling precision targeting and messaging at scale. Predictive accuracy of such typing tools varies, with a mean of approximately 70 percent, at times achieving predictive rates as high 85 percent depending on the project in question. This allows our clients to target the "right" offers and communications and match them to the "right" mindsets, increasing consumer engagement (Figure 4.1) through optimized precision retailing.

It is our experience that a consumer discovery and innovation approach is more likely to arrive at leading-edge business results if it is rooted in the rigor of scientific research, a deep understanding of people's unconscious motivations, and real-world business practices. Traditional attitudinal segmentations are insight-rich, but they are often backward looking or lacking in the ability to inspire winning strategies. This three-phased approach marries whole-consumer

Figure 4.1. Research Phases

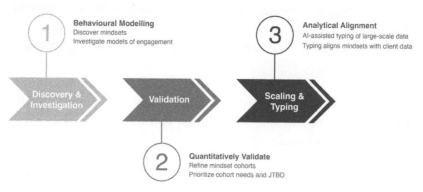

Source: Q:Quest Inc.

insights with client data findability to better engage consumers, even in larger scale marketing efforts.

Understanding the Retail Investor's Relationship with Risk by Developing and Validating Mindsets: A Financial Institution (FI) Case Study

A major North American FI sought to understand risk in the context of wealth accumulation and investment management among multimillionaires. The client wanted to derive a risk-profile algorithm that typed each investor with an accurate and reliable risk tolerance score. Using the unique linguistic and behavioral processes described in this chapter, we uncovered the underlying motivations around the wealth-management consumer's investment decision-making that enabled investment counselors to more appropriately group their clients, gauge their financial, emotional, and aspirational goals, and build stronger relationships.[19]

Before developing and validating a predictive big-data, risk-profile algorithm, it was imperative to understand the conscious and subconscious relationship between investors and risk. Whom did they bring into this relationship and how did this impact their interactions with risk and expected rewards? The first phase, the qualitative discovery and investigation phase, used several different in-depth psychoanalytic, CBT, and Jungian archetype interviewing techniques and analysis to decode the language, emotions, and decision-making trade-offs associated with risk realities. This identified cultural imprints relating to money and risk, which constituted memories retained from childhood. These cultural imprints were representative of the culture that individual investors came from, and they contributed significantly to investors' assessed trade-offs.

As we delved deeper into each individual's personal history with risk and reward, different mindset classifications emerged around the trade-offs between risk and returns: (i) survival (fearful), (ii) security (skeptical), (iii) enhancement seeking (pragmatic), (iv) adventure seeking (confident), and (v) high risk-seekers (gamblers). These behaviors were found to exist in a non-hierarchical and dynamic model, and mindsets were influential to differing degrees depending on the person, their circumstances, and their preferences. The model is depicted in Figure 4.2.

A holistic risk-profile questionnaire that addressed an investor's preferred returns, risk tolerances, and psychological state was developed. It is important to note that our interpretation of risk tolerance differs from the industry standard, which typically focuses purely on the financial consequences of an investment decision. The risk-profile questionnaire constituted an evaluation of investor characteristics: (i) circumstances (e.g., financial situation, age, employment, and assets); (ii) realties and capacity for risk (e.g., short- and long-term investment goals, and the mental calculus around various owned investible and non-investible assets); (iii) preferences and desire to outperform indexed assets (e.g., presenting what-if scenarios where investors are asked to decide and react on various investment situations framed as opportunities for gains or losses); (iv) attributes relating to beliefs, attitudes, and behaviors that reflect cognitive biases and cultural imprints around money, investing, and legacy (e.g., cultural beliefs on gender roles and family hierarchy).

Figure 4.2. Dynamic Risk Model

Circumstances and preferences will determine which risk mindsets have influence on behaviours.

Source: Q:Quest Inc.

The intent of the risk-profile questionnaire was to empower both the investment manager and the investor. By helping both parties develop a more accurate and authentic assessment of the investor's cognitive and emotional biases, managers were better able to identify a best-fit asset mix and investment portfolio for clients. The resulting portfolio structure provided an anchor for the client and set the stage for effective future discussions about portfolio adjustments that focused on strategy rather than recent market events. Further, it enabled the investment counselor to have a more personalized and authentic conversation about a client's relationship to risk, further strengthening their working relationship and facilitating compliance with best practices that aligned with the client's mindsets and desired outcomes.

The mindsets were validated and refined using a large representative sample of the FI's investor pool, and a risk-profile algorithm was created and scaled to type all of the investment management subsidiary's pool of wealthy investors. The success of the risk-profile research led the parent FI to adapt and launch the proven risk-profile algorithm to all their retail investors. Additionally, the qualitative findings on investor mindsets were valuable in further refining and developing the asset allocation portfolios designed for different types of investors.

The discovery and investigation phase identified significant and varied emotional utility associated with each asset class, which added a dimension to the analysis of retail investors' mental accounting bias. Behavioral economics stresses the value of recognizing the cognitive biases involved when individuals code, group, and evaluate economic outcomes. And delving into the context-specific affective states that each investor experiences when making decisions can further complement this approach. For example, although investors tend to bias towards selling strong-performing assets, in the hopes of realizing gains, and holding poor-performing assets, due to a fear of realizing losses, we found that the powerful emotional attachments to certain assets overrode these general trends. Cottages represent one of the strongest examples as consumers often associate powerful family memories with these assets and struggle to sell them, independent of economic performance or the rationale predicted by traditional behavioral economics. Consequently, advisers must employ delicate and tailored communication if they wish to recommend the liquidation of cottages, a non-revenue-generating asset, to contribute towards a retirement investment portfolio.

The qualitative discovery and investigation phase also revealed important insights relating to the relationship between retail investors and their counselors. Even investors that expressed a desire for greater agency and collaboration with their counselors were found to have a marked desire for a clearly defined, hierarchal relationship with a strong element of deference. In addition, investors held an entrenched belief that their advisors should treat their profession like researchers, remaining on the cutting edge of capital markets both in terms of financial news and investment theory. We were initially working with wealthy investors who held investible assets in excess of $5 million and had high expectations for their advisors, and it was quickly discovered that these expectations extended beyond knowledge. Clients wanted to feel that their counselors were not only logical in their decision making, but also empathetic and capable of conveying the appropriate emotions during difficult discussions.

The risk research insights defined how to interact with investors when discussing their investment portfolios, and how to better position monetary and non-monetary rewards so they aligned with each mindset's acceptable risk tolerance. This included customizing how the data and visuals were presented, as well as how rewards and expected outcomes were framed relative to a client's capacity for risk. Investment counselors were trained to utilize the investment management tools empathetically during initial client assessments, so they could form a strong working relationship early in the process. This personalized focus and behaviorally informed choice architecture facilitated the investor's ability to accurately assess information, experience stronger self-agency, and deeply engage with the investment counselor's recommendations. And the approach helped the FI shift to a more proactive and personalized engagement that resulted in investors adopting more beneficial and sustainable behaviors towards their management of risk and returns.

6. FINAL THOUGHTS AND DISCUSSION

Central to this precision retailing approach is an interdisciplinary framework for investigating consumer behavior and developing strategic recommendations. Also common is a deeper and more intimate approach to deriving behavioral insights. The discovery and investigation phase relies on effective qualitative research that depends heavily on psychoanalytic techniques and a cognitive behavioral approach when conducting and analyzing in-depth interviews. By quantitatively validating these qualitative insights before scaling our behavioral models, we challenge our initial findings and mitigate the biases inherent to any open-ended interview process.

Irrespective of industry or client type, we have repeatedly found that psycholinguistics and semiotics, oftentimes in relation to specific Jungian archetypes, provide valuable tools to uncover the unconscious meanings behind a consumer's words. This allows precision retailers to develop predictive behavioral models that fit the contemporary body of relevant peer-reviewed literature, including psychology, semiotics, neuroscience, and behavioral economics. Perhaps most importantly, precision retailers can better uncover the underlying drivers of behavior by delving deeper into the individual and contextualizing consumer profiles with their cultural, societal, and interpersonal roles. This rigorous, in-depth approach more effectively aligns the brand with its consumers' needs, helping build stronger brand loyalty. In the greater context of this textbook, we have outlined an approach that closely follows the core concepts of precision retailing, moving beyond traditional definitions and characterizations of the consumer.

NOTES

1 According to Harvard Business School's Clayton Christensen, each year more than thirty-thousand new consumer products are launched and 95 percent of them fail. According to University of Toronto professor Inez Blackburn, the failure rate of new grocery store products is 70 to 80 percent. The Nielsen static is more than 85 percent of new consumer packaged goods.

2 Charm, T., Gillis, H., Grimmelt, A., Hua, G., Robinson, K., & Sanchez Cabellero, R. (2021, May 13). *Consumer sentiment in the US during the coronavirus crisis.* McKinsey. https://www.mckinsey.com/business-functions/marketing-and-sales/our-insights/survey-usconsumer-sentiment-during-the-coronavirus-crisis#.

3 Wilson, M. (2021, March 15). *Harris Poll: Pandemic shopping habits will remain as life returns to "normal."* Chain Store Age. https://chainstoreage.com/harris-poll-pandemicshopping-habits-will-remain-life-returns-normal.

4 Jung, C.G. (1991). *The archetypes and the collective unconscious* (R.F.C. Hull, Trans; 2nd ed.). *Collected works of C.G. Jung.* Routledge.

5 Thaler, Richard H, & Sunstein, Cass R. (2009). *Nudge, Improving decisions about health, wealth, and happiness.* Penguin Books.

6 Fishman, Joshua A. (2019). "The Sociology of language: An interdisciplinary social science approach to language in society." In J.A. Fishman (Ed.), *Volume 1 Basic concepts, theories and problems: alternative approaches* (pp. 217–404). De Gruyter Mouton. https://doi.org/10.1515/9783111417509-005.

7 University College London. (2009, January 19). *Language driven by culture, not biology, study shows.* ScienceDaily. https://www.sciencedaily.com/releases/2009/01/090119210614.htm.

8   Wang, G.-J., Volkow, N.D., Logan, J., Pappas, N.R., Wong, C.T., Zhu, W., Netusll, N., & Fowler, J.S. (2001). Brain dopamine and obesity. *The Lancet, 357*(9253), 354–7. https://doi.org/10.1016/S0140-6736(00)03643-6.

9   Benton, D., & Young, H.A. (2016). A meta-analysis of the relationship between brain dopamine receptors and obesity: A matter of changes in behaviour rather than food addiction? *International Journal of Obesity, 40*(S1), S12–S21. https://doi.org/10.1038/ijo.2016.9.

10 Demos, K.E., Heatherton, T.F., & Kelley, W.M. (2012). Individual differences in nucleus accumbens activity to food and sexual images predict weight gain and sexual behavior. *J. Neurosci., 32*(16), 5549–52. https://psycnet.apa.org/doi/10.1523/JNEUROSCI.5958-11.2012.

11 Yokum, S, Gearhardt, A.N., Harris, J.L., Brownell, K.D., & Stice, E. (2014). Individual differences in striatum activity to food commercials predict weight gain in adolescents. *Obesity, 22*(12), 2544–51. https://dx.doi.org/10.1002/oby.20882.

12 O'Doherty J., Dayan P., Schultz J., Deichmann R., Friston K., & Dolan R.J. (2004). Dissociable roles of ventral and dorsal striatum in instrumental conditioning. *Science, 304*(5669), 452–4. https://doi.org/10.1126/science.1094285.

13 Salgado, S., & Kaplitt, M.G. (2015). The nucleus accumbens: A comprehensive review. *Stereotactic and Functional Neurosurgery, 93*(2), 75–93. https://doi.org/10.1159/000368279.

14 Green, E., Jacobson, A., Haase, L., & Murphy, C. (2011). Reduced nucleus accumbens and caudate nucleus activation to a pleasant taste is associated with obesity in older adults. *Brain Research, 1386*, 109–17. https://doi.org/10.1016/j.brainres.2011.02.071.

15 Stice, E., Spoor, S., Bohon, C., & Small, D.M. (2008). Relation between obesity and blunted striatal response to food is moderated by TaqIA1 gene. *Science, 322*(5900), 449–52. https://doi.org/10.1126/science.1161550.

16 Stice, E., Spoor, S., Bohon, C., Veldhuizen, M.G., & Small, D.M. (2008). Relation of reward from food intake and anticipated food intake to obesity: A functional magnetic resonance imaging study. *Journal of Abnormal Psychology, 117*(4), 924–35. https://doi.org/10.1037/a0013600.

17 Boettcher, H., Brake, C.A., & Barlow, D.H. (2015). Origins and outlook of interoceptive exposure. *Journal of Behaviour Therapy and Experimental Psychiatry, 53*, 41–51. https://doi.org/10.1016/j.jbtep.2015.10.009.

18 Christensen, C.M., Hall, T., Dillon, K., & Duncan, D.S. (2016, September 1). Know your customers' "jobs to be done." *Harvard Business Review.* https://hbr.org/2016/09/knowyour-customers-jobs-to-be-done.

19 Castellano, J., Horton, W.R., & Stewart, J.K. (2021). *Adapting to COVID 19: A behavioural lens on financial institution resilience.* Global Risk Institute. https://globalriskinstitute.org/download/adapting-to-covid-19-a-behavioural-lens-on-financial-institution-resilience/.

CHAPTER FIVE

Rethinking Human-Centered Design in the Age of AI and Humans as Data

Felipe Almeida and Chloe Benaroya

SUMMARY OF CHAPTER

The paper discusses the limits and potential evolution of human-centered design (HCD), a design approach that puts human needs at the center of the innovation process.

The authors explore some of the current changes seen in the field of HCD and user experience design (UXD) to infer a potential future where designers and innovation teams increasingly rely on AI systems to learn about human experience and its relationship with the larger system in which it is embedded.

MANAGERIAL IMPLICATIONS (GENERAL)

The paper:

- Allows businesses to rethink how the design process has been undertaken at organizations. This process is widely used to optimize interfaces and perform usability testings, yet it is much less consistently used for the initial and highly relevant stages of discovery and problem definition.
- Enables businesses and individual designers to think about the roles and skills that might enhance the collaboration

between human designers and intelligent systems, instead of reinforcing the idea of competition between humans and machines.
- Reinforces the role of the design team and designers within the company by describing how design can create added value not only to products but also to the company's strategic plan.

MANAGERIAL IMPLICATIONS (ORGANIZATIONAL)
- Design is put at the center of the organizational chart to become the interface between different departments, driving transdisciplinary collaborations that integrate teams such as sales, marketing, engineering, data science, maintenance, and support.
- An organizational change is to be considered to address this tightened collaboration between the design team and other analytical teams.
- The paper highlights the need to broaden the HCD perspective and embrace a systems-thinking view in order to properly tackle the increasingly complex problems faced by organizations around the world.

MANAGERIAL IMPLICATIONS (STRATEGIC, TACTICAL, AND OPERATIONAL)
- The design-centric model of organization is a strategic consideration that becomes even more important as AI systems are deployed, enabling the processing of large data sets but also requiring a deeper critical thinking about how the data affects the customer experience.
- From a tactical perspective, HR recruitment and training practices should reflect this model of the organization, and this should be translated into the hiring and promotion decisions. This can also lead to new job roles mixing qualitative design, qualitative analysis, and ethical and philosophical analysis skills. These would foster the collaboration between AI systems and human staff and focus on the end-to-end experience and company-to-society impact.

- Developing the skills of critical and systems thinking within the design team is a continuous tactical objective that can add value to the organization by enhancing the collaboration between AI systems and human designers.

MANAGERIAL IMPLICATIONS (RISK ASSESSMENT)
- The context collaboration between AI systems and human designers is still quite recent and not widely present. This might be risky for current companies willing to make the transition to an innovative organizational approach in the short term. A long-term plan might be much more beneficial, and it needs to address technical, experiential, and ethical aspects of its development.
- An organization that adopts this style of working could witness the "first mover advantage," with a new style of organizational culture being created. As the context changes in both tech and socio-environmental aspects, this model will gain in maturity and will be widely pursued by organizations. First movers will likely have an advantage over both other individual professionals and organizations.

1. INTRODUCTION

With the emergence of AI, there is a growing belief that we will increasingly rely on machines to finally decipher the complexity of human behavior and decision-making. Given not only the pressure for fast and continuous progress but also the ingrained cultural aspects such as myths of oracles and omniscient superior entities, machines embedded with artificial intelligence (i.e., that perceive the environment, take actions, and learn how to optimize their decisions to reach specific goals) can easily become the ideal solution in the eyes of corporations and institutions alike. Within the realm of design research, AI promises a faster and more reliable way to analyze the complex and non-linear experience of customers, and, therefore, a supposedly more reliable way to inform design and innovation teams. But outside research and data analysis, AI's popularity has also skyrocketed due to new generative models. Altogether, this increasing adoption of AI models has triggered a new wave of discussions in the field of design, many of these being in their core about the possibility of intelligent machines challenging the narrative of superior human intelligence and creativity.

But independent of a lack of consensus on the true potential of AI, artificially intelligent systems are already having an impact on traditional design approaches such as human-centered design (HCD), and we believe that discussing not only short-term, but also long-term implications is highly important to both academics and practitioners. Thus, we looked at HCD's main characteristics of human centrism, collaborative work, problem definition, and problem-solving to generate the initial questions that motivated us to write this chapter:

- What does the complexity of advanced analytics tell us about the limits of HCD?
- What happens to design practices when people become numbers that have to be abstracted with little to no direct contact with these groups and their daily lives?
- Is there a new design paradigm about to emerge and how will this paradigm work?
- What will be the role of human designers in this new design paradigm?

We believe these questions are crucial for product designers, innovation teams, and academics alike to help forge a way to collaborate in a future where they increasingly rely on AI systems to learn about human cognition, emotion, and behavior. We attempt to explore and discuss these questions as well as some of the current changes we see in the field of HCD and user experience design (UXD). Finally, we conclude our chapter with a speculative design section focused on discussing a few possible scenarios in which solutions for human problems are strongly influenced or even generated by black box processing of big data. We are fully aware of the challenge in writing about such a large topic, and we also know that the abundance of cross-references in this chapter may have led us to write a dense chapter, but we hope that by integrating multiple dimensions we can communicate the relevance and complexity of the above questions, while also igniting a larger discussion about the topic.

2. IS HCD DISRUPTED?

Human-centered design is definitely not perfect, but as an approach it should be carefully criticized with the understanding of the circumstances that led to its creation and the context that might lead it to become outdated. HCD provided a place where many specialists (including data scientists, marketers, designers, engineers, and risk and compliance specialists) could dialog because it created an anchor around a large common topic: the human experience. By doing so, HCD enabled a diverse number of professionals to build solutions through convergent and divergent cycles of communal activities. However, in the age of AI, the HCD approach may reassert that data is the footprints that humans leave behind, and the value of such data is related to the value humans give to their own actions. The solution proposed, the product or service offered, is also a singular arrangement, defined by choices and interpretation, influenced by individual or corporate values. But if maximization of profits is kept at the core of our system, until when will the solutions be generated by humans for humans? Can the human-centered approach be the main approach in an increasingly connected and largely complex world? And given the complexity of our problems, should the measure be indeed centered on humans alone?

2.1. The Teachings of Complexity and Nonlinearity

The debate over the design process is still one of the most central aspects of the design discourse, with the term "design thinking" being adopted by organizations of all kinds and all over the world. The term, first used in 1987 by Peter Rowe in his book *Design Thinking*,[1] comprised an attempt to provide a versatile but systematic approach to the process of designing in both architecture and urban planning. By the early 2000s, design thinking gained vast popularity among other fields outside design and was consolidated as a modern and creative problem-solving process mostly due to the design company IDEO and the Hasso Plattner Institute of Design at Stanford (a.k.a. the "d.school"), as well as by the famous Double Diamond of Design created by the British Design Council.

Design thinking became the template process that supported the human-centered view of design, in which good design was basically a design that embraced, first and foremost, the needs and emotions of humans. The lucrative innovations that emerged under the claim of HCD and design thinking incited many organizations to implement the approach and, as consequence, to demand for clear definitions and a toolkit of easily applicable methods.

However, as the design process gained popularity, the continuous attempts to describe and map the design process started to expose the problem of complexity and nonlinearity in human creativity and decision-making, leading practitioners and academics to question the benefits of attempting to map a nonlinear process and teach the process as such. The problem of nonlinearity, although frustrating to many, takes into consideration the fact that designers usually deal with complex systems (e.g., social groups), and therefore with uncertainty, emerging behaviors, and ill-defined problems.

Cross (1982)[2] further reflects on the nonlinear aspect of the design process by suggesting that nonlinearity in design is probably due to the nature of the design task, the time required to create solutions, and the nature of the problems usually tackled in design. Cross (2001)[3] also suggests that a linear method is not practical in design because the tasks tackled in design require solutions that are unique and are often not reproducible. Despite the comparison the author makes between design and science, the relevance of nonlinearity has also been long discussed by many scientists who understand its relevance when it comes to increasing the applicability of scientific findings to the real world.

Dorst (2011)[4] states that the confusion about the application and nature of the design process has led to a situation in which eminent design researchers have even suggested to completely avoid the term "design thinking." Such a suggestion is based on the fact that in design the basic reasoning pattern shifts from both inductive and deductive to abduction-1 (i.e., a form of "closed" problem-solving where the "how" and the value to be created are known, but the "what" is unknown) and abduction-2 (i.e., a form of "open" problem-solving where both the "what" or the "how" are unknown). Thus, abduction-2 type of problems demand the parallel exploration of two missing variables of the equation, making the reasoning process much more complex than those in traditional problem-solving. Moreover, abduction-2 problems require the definition of the viewpoint with which the problem can be perceived (i.e., frame) so that the designer can apply a certain working principle associated with the viewpoint (i.e., "how") to then create the desired perception of value.

On the practical level, a design problem such as "how might we provide a digital solution to answer the most frequent questions from users to alleviate demand on call centers?" can be reduced to different sets of proposed hypotheses (e.g., a list of frequent Q&A, a digital chatbot, or video tutorials) even if its frame is relatively narrow. However, by using causal-effect techniques such as the "five whys," designers are able to reframe the scope of the problem to tackle the central problem (e.g., how can we efficiently answer users' questions using multiple communication channels?) with more creative ways (e.g., by integrating chatbots, videos, online forums/ social media groups, and call centers in distributive and adaptive systems of communication).

The reader may correctly identify that the problem above is still highly descriptive, already directing the type of solution ("digital"), but it is often the case that designers have to constrain their creativity accordingly to business focus and strategy. The point here is to try to demonstrate that abductive reasoning, in higher or lower complexity, represents nonlinearity in the design process because, at least at the human level, it requires an iterative process in which information is constantly retrieved and updated until a solution is generated and seen as satisfying by any type of strategic metric. This type of creative solution generation is still a big challenge for AI systems, given that these systems haven't yet reached a similar level of generalization that humans have. But it is exactly the effort to make AI systems learn how to generalize that is teaching us designers about another main limitation in HCD, human centrism in itself.

Unsupervised AI systems (i.e., systems that learn without human supervision) such as the now highly popular clustering algorithms (e.g., used in Netflix and Amazon platforms for shows and product display), have increased their performance and efficiency, and have surprised humans with their outputs. Although still limited, these models are also focused on acquiring knowledge about the user context and actions that they perceive as relevant to perform their task (i.e., optimize their accuracy). Within the design practice, this perspective becomes an important mirror to expose human biases but also our limited capacity of understanding multiple contexts that can comprise a single design problem, especially when these contexts appear contradictory or paradoxical to designers. Moreover, as these new models evolve and are applied to larger technological and realistic societal contexts, they end up not only teaching us about the intricate relationship of multiple agents in complex systems, but they also push for new paradigms that seem to require a view that surpasses the narrowed traditional human-centered approach.

The debate about the limits of HCD is much deeper than what we can address here, but thinking about it and creating efforts to visualize a new paradigm also means rethinking the role of human designers even before machines become intelligent enough to provide us with a solution or set of solutions for problems that we thought only humans could solve. Is the designer's task really just the proposal of solutions without deep concern about cause and effect, which Lawson argues against (1979)?[5] What is the true nature of design? Is it the blind proposal of utilitarian and aesthetically pleasing solutions that fit a problem? And what if it is not the nature of design that keeps on pushing for a superficial thinking aimed at palliative types of solutions? What if it is our current context, as proposed by Victor Papanek (1970/2019),[6] that is constraining design by creating a very limited view of it?

3. HOW HCD EVOLVES WITH THE USE OF ANALYTICS AND AI

While the HCD process might fall short in addressing some of the complexity of designing in today's world, many designers do their best to be actively involved in product development and business strategy, gathering preexisting assumptions, identifying key learnings from past experiences, performing competitive analyses, producing generative research, and providing methods to validate design assumptions. Yet, step-by-step models of the design process, which should be used as pedagogical reference for discussion, are used by practitioners as a recipe to face the increasing pressure to reduce research time, accommodate financial-related metrics (e.g., ROIs), and deliver value fast.

Such a pressure reduces even more the scope of HCD and design thinking activities by usually putting aside important tasks such as problem identification and definition, contextual analysis, and reframing perspectives. Often, HCD teams fall into the trap of utilitarian solution-driven perspectives that seem to have an almost total lack of interest in the *qualia* of the experience, reducing most or all exploration of customer needs into quick conversations about their product or feature preferences, and thus failing to properly understand the relationship between the problem, the individual customer, and context in which they are embedded. In doing so, they may fail to properly understand the relationships between the problem, the individual, and the social-environmental context that surrounds them.

Comparatively, further stages of product design, such as development and testing, with their various metrics and empirical paradigms, seem to only grow in popularity. Big data from social media and digital market analytics are seen by many product teams as a way to capture vast amounts of knowledge on current and potential new consumer segments. But quantitative data-driven perspectives in design may be gaining influence with teams not because the data is necessarily relevant or sufficient, but because this type of data may be the teams' only method to learn about their users given the disincentive towards in-depth time-consuming research methods such as ethnographic exploration.

With digital interfaces being entrenched in their lives, the customer as a person appears further away, isolated on the other side of the screen and reduced to a number in a normal curve, or worse, to an average. Paradoxically, this context is progressively incentivizing designers to get out of their comfort zone and get training on multiple disciplines in order not only to understand digital metrics but also to come up with more advanced mixed methods to investigate the customer experience.

Design research teams used to rely on various tools, such as simple log analysis tools to collect basic funnel metrics such as hits, page views, visits, unique visitors, etc. Nowadays, as users interact with interfaces, more powerful tools with large-scale web analysis and even biometric capabilities allow companies to also track and visualize granular event-based data to help improve all product goals, from awareness to conversion (e.g., measuring campaign or conversion funnels effectiveness) and retention (e.g., creating heat maps and graphs to reflect the user's point of interests and conflict during the experience journey).

In leveraging big data, new technologies have also allowed teams to automate, at least to a certain extent, some of the tasks designers often performed as they fine-tuned their solutions: running A/B or multivariate tests on layout and content variations within an interface, reporting how these variations are efficient to targeted segments of the audience for a designated micro-goal or event, and generating various types of content (e.g., through products based on natural language processing models, such as Midjourney, DALL•E, ChatGPT, etc.)

These new tools may enable new ways of thinking about the experiential journey that are adaptable by using machine learning models to explore the variation and formation of new patterns in real time for relatively simple website funnel navigation or registration page flow. And while the AI uses the information to adapt this flow and UI elements to the goals and profiles of various audiences, it is up to the design team to think about the broader experience (e.g., adaptable elements and types of adaptation) and how it can be optimized for a positive response and engagement with the platform in ethical ways to avoid harm such as impulsive buying, addiction, and prejudice.

The increasing ability to perform large-scale collection of data on low-level user interactions is a growing trend. Digital micro-behaviors such as bird's nest or multi-click, which are micro-movements of the user's mouse on a computer screen or the user's finger on a tactile interface, are compounded in single key indicators proposed as measurable values of "engagement" or "frustration." As these blended metrics and new key performance indicators surge – many under "black box" processing of deep learning models – designers are pushed not only to gain more technical knowledge but are also adding to the push for more ethical discussions and systemic thinking.

One of the highly discussed topics is the one pertaining to natural user interfaces using bio signals (body and brain activity), which also require new techniques, metrics, and knowledge to capture and interpret adequately, in real time or not, the user's response. The growing interest of both private and university labs in the exploration of the neurophysiology of user experience is directly related to the possibility of inferring about various users' states (e.g., engagement, frustration, cognitive overload, visual attention, etc.) without the need to break the flow of the experience or rely solely on the participants ability to accurately describe their experiences.

In this context, relying only on quantitative KPIs to measure the user experience may appear attractive to many stakeholders as they supposedly provide clear metrics for decision-making and may not be as time-consuming as in-depth qualitative studies. Moreover, many third-party companies are now providing user-friendly biometric technologies that do not require highly technical knowledge by the team to use them. However, many of these companies use their own proprietary algorithms to make inferences about the same metrics (e.g., engagement), or they use biased assumptions in both the training data set and theoretical aspects behind it (e.g., in identification of biomarkers of emotional categories), making it very hard to actually understand what is truly being measured and in which context the measure might actually be valuable.

Thus, it is relevant to question how able these algorithms and AI based systems actually are to propose a fair narrative of the user's pain points and delights. Moreover, can open-loop systems (i.e., algorithms that do not take feedback from the environment to adjust their behavior, thus ignoring users' subjective response in adjusting output) be truly successful to measure human experience? There is definitely an open debate that still divides researchers and practitioners, but some leading researchers are concerned that we might be placing too much attention into what we wish these machines could do and forgetting to properly critique or understand their limitations. The constant and almost overwhelming interactions with machines along with the innate human capacity to mimic behavior, may lead us to try to mimic AI behavior, similarly to what happened in the mechanistic Cartesian views that highly influenced us and made us lose sight of the wholeness of our experience.

Yet, we wonder if soon we will still need interpretations and narratives around the users and their contexts, or if we will recommend the next best actions or outputs purely based on correlations and other metrics. While the notion of user centricity has become increasingly popular, there may be fewer humans bending over the cradle of customer experience. Are we leaving empathy behind?

4. CAN HCD ADDRESS THE CHALLENGES OF AUTOMATING USER INSIGHTS?

As mentioned in the previous section, automated user insights and their algorithms have their flaws, too. First, automating the assessment of the user experience with digital analytics might only have some relevance in a stable and mature digital platform, where key variables of the user experience are clearly defined, validated, and benchmarked. As soon as the system evolves – for example, if a development team practices a continuous improvement delivery model that generates constant variations in the system – the evaluation of the user experience through pure metrics becomes challenged.

For example, in gaming, the blend of KPIs such as performance score, level of difficulty, and gameplay time can be used to create a simple algorithm for an adaptive interface that may initially increase engagement but in the long term may lead to negative user feedback. In such a scenario, a short-term increase in engagement levels might be achieved by adjusting the game's level of difficulty using the correlation between performance and gameplay time, which could be a proxy for fatigue levels.

However, without taking into consideration the user's subjective response in a sort of closed-loop system (e.g., highlighting the adaptations and enabling the user to edit some game parameters), the company may actually create various negative situations such as false sense of improved skills and reinforcement of addictive behavior. Similarly, if the audience of a system is significantly different than that used to create the model (training set), for instance, due to a change in the marketing acquisition channels leading to a slightly different playstyle, the outputs of the system may not reflect the reality of the actual user.

Second, insights are often delivered in silos. Data is usually collected by different tools and systems, at different stages of the user life cycle, and by different teams, and it rarely reflects an immediately real-time and consistent view of the end-to-end journey of the customer. In addition to tracking a customer's navigation, large-scale quantitative surveys are also used to capture their overall perception and attitude through tools such as System Usability Scale (SUS), Net Promoter Score (NPS) or Customer Satisfaction Score (CSAT). In these situations, machine learning algorithms can help by finding hidden correlations and clusters that provide additional information when trying to decipher users' comments and feedback, but these algorithms do not signal or understand the limits of the data provided to them. Simply put, the idea that more data is always better is highly dependent on the quality of the data and how it is relevant to the question being explored.

In fact, automating data insights becomes an even greater challenge as the data collected becomes more complex and abstract, such as in the case of emotional perception, where inferences about emotional categories are highly impacted by contextual and cultural constructs, and neuroimaging data, in which a cause and effect relationship is often and wrongfully derived from correlations and in which a single data set can be interpreted in different ways by different teams due to variations in analytical approach.[7]

The quality of the insights from these studies can, in principle, be improved by integrating them all. However, none of these activities are easily synthesized, and that might be impossible to do without a transdisciplinary team. Moreover, the increasing complexity in user data is also turning the spotlight back on critical thinking, an ability that is typically encountered in the convergence between science, design, and philosophy. Thus, the increasing importance of design as a distinctive business value goes side-by-side with the growing importance of metrics and data.[8]

But even when corporations do use a mixed method approach to capture various types of subjective and objective data about the users and their contexts, they still have to face the challenge of how to create a full and integrated view of the customers' experience. According to a 2019 HBR Analytical Services report,[9] only 15 per cent of the CEOs surveyed rate their organization as very effective at integrating small data with big data to create a holistic view of the customer.

That means that for the time being, it's still up to HCD practitioners to take on the challenge of connecting the dots and providing a critical perspective for each stream of data input and output. But giving such a responsibility to designers also means moving beyond the aesthetic and utilitarian view of design. It's also often up to designers to solve ill-defined problems, where judgments and decisions have to be made using incomplete information and by breaking formal or technical constraints. But while HCD methods have helped designers to learn about the innovation process, they may also be applied to at least facilitate the creation of a new design approach that may fit better with our current context.

Thus, if HCD is honestly applied to generate its next iteration, it will first and foremost try to identify its limitations based on the current needs and context in our society, and that means not only rethinking the role of human designers in the age of AI but also understanding that our biggest problems are now systemic issues that go way beyond the realm of human society. So, what may be ahead of us?

5. THE FUTURE AHEAD

This chapter is challenging because it must make many assumptions, and although assumptions about the future are rarely accurate, they can spur a valid and important debate for the benefit of the whole community. This was our intent: to generate a debate. In this final section, we thus take a speculative design perspective to first infer about the emergence of a new design paradigm and its characteristics, following up with our final thoughts about how it might be connected to different human-machine relationship scenarios. We conclude by distilling those scenarios down to two: complementary collaboration and human-machine symbiosis.

5.1. The Call for Transdisciplinarity, Temporal Adaptation, and Critical Thinking

So far, we have discussed the limits of HCD given the current technological context and the increased complexity in the problems we are facing. We believe these aspects are also leading to the emergence of a new design paradigm, one that fits the current context better than the original HCD. We believe that this new context requires designers to continually broaden their perspectives and skills, and it will continuously push mainstream design perspectives to look at systemic interactions between the knowledge required to innovate and the consequences of innovation. That is, we believe a new paradigm will reinforce a transdisciplinary view of design, making it, for example, not only very comfortable with but also highly interested in philosophy and science (and vice-versa). We also believe this new paradigm will reward strong systemic thinking for product innovation, enabling designers to jump into a blend of technical and philosophical discussions about data collection and available data sets, the knowledge they bring, their biases and limitations, and the additional information needed to make the outputs more accurate and generalizable in different contexts.

Moreover, the development of a new design paradigm that truly integrates complexity and nonlinearity also requires a stronger focus on the tracking of temporal changes of the user experience, which has always been a challenging HCD activity. As a purely human-related task, detailed temporal tracking seems impossible, and its complexity only increases with time. This, however, might be a great opportunity to explore and maybe deploy AI based systems that can highlight novel information to optimize human-machine collaboration (e.g., warning systems that inform about changes in the accuracy of the autopilot model enabling the user to know when to trust the model or not). These systems can also act in real time to enhance the experience according to the context (e.g., self-driving cars automatically taking action to reduce speed, sending a second warning layer to the passengers or alerting them through different sensorial channels such as tactile ones in case accuracy thresholds are very low and no human action is detected). But while machines may take the more specialized roles of quickly processing multiple data points and generating the changes in the experience, human designers might take a much more strategic role, one that is focused on truly thinking about the end-to-end experience and its impact on society.

The temporal and learning aspect may not be the biggest challenges for intelligent design systems, but defining the scope of these variables and an ethical way to optimize the quality of predictions and inferences is a challenge that machines alone cannot currently tackle. As sources of information grow exponentially – for example, storing and leveraging health and personal information in the health industries with the Internet of Things (IoTs) and Internet of Bodies (IoBs)[10] – critical thinking about the knowledge and ethics on which a product or service development strategy is built is a key part of the strategy itself, especially in the absence of clear regulations.

As with other services and human activities, HCD will be largely impacted by AI, requiring a recalibration of human activity to find its added value. With more and more insights and metrics about customers, HCD practice needs to evolve to host a robust dialogue between the different sets of expertise and allow for a more holistic and integrative view. Moreover, the human side of design will possibly transition from the solution-driven mode to focus on the critical thinking and developmental view, thus shifting from reacting to problems to preventing problems. We believe that these are undeniable skills in today's world already but will only grow in importance as we become aware of the systemic social-environmental problems we face. These skills are the basis for the identification of the true value of human designers, possibly enabling humans to work with intelligent machines, instead of being fully replaced by AI systems.

5.2. Human-Machine Cooperative Design: Collaborative or Symbiotic?

Of all the major problems with AI-based systems, the limited common sense and understanding of causality are possibly on the top of the list when it comes to artificial and human intelligence – efficiency is also a big one, given how energy hungry some of these recent models are. On various other tasks, including comprehension of large data sets, AI either outperforms humans or has a strong potential to do so in the near future. However, complexity is part of human society, and it involves a level of uncertainty that is improbable to predict. Social complexity is composed of different agents within different contexts and no central control, thus creating dynamic and heterogeneous needs and forms of interactions.

Since human-centered design has the human as the central part of the process, it is also understandable that in a good design practice one needs to consider social complexity also as a consequence of highly dispersed data and the presence of implicit and tacit knowledge – information that people are unable to communicate.[11] But how much of our experience can actually be understood by intelligent machines via a reductionistic process even if the data includes the description of phenomenological experience? Using

Nagel's philosophical frame[12] two fundamental questions about the role of AI in the future of design seem to emerge: Can data only allow machines to understand what it is like to be a human? And is there any value for a machine in understanding what is like *for a human* to be a human? These questions are fundamental to the development of a new design paradigm because it might be the ultimate test to the idea that human empathy is necessary to generate strong innovation. For human-centered designers, perspective-taking is an ability that enables the understanding and embodiment, at least to a certain extent, of what the users or group of users feel and need. It ultimately enables the generation of solutions that are aimed at solving the users' needs given the context in which they live. Thus, if empathy and embodied experience turn out to be complementary to artificial intelligence, then there is a solid case for human designers even in the age of intelligent machines.

Taking this as our assumption, we believe that there is a good possibility of cooperation instead of competition between machines and humans – although this also depends on overcoming dangerous narratives such as profit over people and the planet – opening the doors to a new paradigm that we will call "human-machine cooperative design." This new paradigm is already emerging, although not yet prevailing, and among many things is enabling humans to slowly grasp that we are just a part of a much larger system and, therefore, to truly innovate we will have to understand how our needs are linked to other systemic variables and how they can be fulfilled given such a complex network of relationships.

Although it is impossible to predict what paradigm will emerge and when, it doesn't seem so eccentric to suggest an increasing depth in the collaboration between humans and machines in the next few decades. We also understand that this collaboration can happen in various ways: (a) the complementary collaboration scenario, where human designers provide directions and perform some sort of selection of the solutions proposed by the machines, and (b) the symbiosis between AI and humans.

The first scenario is consistent with the difficulty that AI may have with generalizations and common sense (e.g., outputs of conversational models such as ChatGPT can highly differ depending on small variations in the prompt related to one's awareness of implicit bias and common-sense expectations in communication), enabling it to find interesting solutions and patterns but only under the premise of a critical human perspective. This scenario might represent the chance to truly shift towards the core aspects of HCD, meaning, to free design from the chains of utilitarianism and mercantilism so it can increasingly help us to contemplate, question, and freely explore the richness of human complexity and emotions.

Of course, the relationship between human designers and machines might also change not only according to the progress of AI but also according to the context of each company. The ability that some intelligent systems have in finding correlations in a large data set can be enough for some companies or departments that are satisfied with statistical proxies. Anderson,[13] for example, mentions how Google supposedly uses this idea to optimize their services such as translation of texts without any knowledge of aspects such as culture. This might be very efficient as long as corrections and refinements can be done by a human, which is why even with recent progress in automatic translation, people can still often infer when a text was automatically translated or not. Thus, as AI improves, its direct outputs might be sufficient for certain offerings, but for companies in niche markets and those competing for strong value-added positioning, proxies may not necessarily lead to a successful future.

Within this scenario, provided that two companies have similar access to data and technology, the key differentiator might be the goals assigned to the AI systems, based on the underlying values defined through the HCD exploration. Moreover, when we acknowledge that there is no perfect product for all groups and all contexts, we see again the strategic relevance of human designers and their capacity to question with empathy and pose the "whys."

Design experience might then start to be more commonly desired in executive roles and for those willing to have seats on boards of directors. Solid inter- and transdisciplinary training with enhanced critical thinking and perspective taking skills will probably facilitate the translation of human experiences and contexts to machines while also constantly analyzing the company's direction given its vision and mission. So, while machines might take the problem-solving part of the design process, they might not be responsible for the direction of the development and the selection of the problems to be solved. And this is important because, to a good extent, it is the "why" that makes the difference between random correlation and the identification of relevant findings.

We are trying to say that machines may never have the same sort of understanding of our experiences as we do, yet they might offer us a different point of view that could lead to new perspectives in human experiences, as long as we try to understand the whys. But for that to happen, we will need humans that are skilled enough in providing and assessing directions about ethics, contextualized human needs, and experiences to the machines.

This leads us to the second and most speculative scenario discussed here: symbiosis between humans and AI. Although considered far-fetched by many, this might be a real possibility at some point in the future given the advancements in the field of brain-computer interfaces (BCI) and brain-machine interfaces (BMI), a blend of AI, neuroscience, and engineering. Neuralink™, a company funded by Elon Musk, is currently the most popular example in this scenario, attempting to have digital data translated into electrical impulses to ultimately augment human perception and physical abilities, while the user's biological activity is collected by the machine to be further and continuously optimized.

Currently, various other applications can emerge according to the development of BMIs and BCIs, which have been mostly used in the medical domain with their primary motivation being the monitoring of biometrics and restoration of impaired sensory and motor functions.[14] However, there is also a wide range of parallel applications for BMIs that go from web browsing to the control of avatars and robots, gaming, and VR.

Designing for experiences that use BMI with just the above initial applications is already a sign that points to the evolution of HCD, since it demands a highly interdisciplinary team that is able to deal with deep questions in technology, psychology, biology, and ethics, all in a given context or set of contexts. As these technologies reach a massive audience, it is more than reasonable to imagine the further development of these systems towards the idea of human perceptual augmentation. This could mean several variations in human perception, from learning and feeling digital data to being able to experience one or multiple points of view of different people and even different species.

If, or maybe when, symbiosis is achieved, machines might then be able to perform very accurate inferences about human experience by making sense of systemic processes and relationships within individual and social levels. Then, human experience will be, at least partially, a machine experience and vice-versa, opening the way to new concepts through "an objective phenomenology not dependent on empathy or the imagination."[15] Finally, symbiosis may also allow us to experience an even deeper sense of empathy for one or many individuals, of the same or different species, by using machines to "download" memories and feelings of others and "upload" them into ours – yet the ethical and potentially harmful consequences of such an experiment are not to be taken lightly.[16]

It's obvious that the future is open to big changes and to so-called "black swans," and our speculations may be completely wrong. Yet, we have been gaining awareness of the complexity around us, which, with or without AI, is already revealing the need to create a design paradigm that is systems-centric, and we hope that AI will support us in achieving such a goal. It might be that just like the development of photography helped painting to move away from realism and opened a whole new world of explorations in abstraction, AI might force us to finally adopt a view where "we" means a lot more than just humans.

NOTES

1 Rowe, P.G. (1987). *Design thinking*. MIT Press.
2 Cross, N. (1982). Designerly ways of knowing. *Design Studies*, 3(4), 221–7. https://doi.org/10.1016/0142-694X(82)90040-0.
3 Cross, N. (2001). Designerly ways of knowing: Design discipline versus design science. *Design Issues*, 17(3), 49–55. https://www.jstor.org/stable/1511801
4 Dorst, K. (2011). The core of "design thinking" and its application. *Design Studies*, 32(6), 521–32. https://doi.org/10.1016/j.destud.2011.07.006.
5 Lawson, B.R. (1979). Cognitive strategies in architectural design. *Ergonomics*, 22(1), 59–68. https://doi.org/10.1080/00140137908924589.

6 Papanek, V. (2019). *Design for the real world* (3rd ed.). Thames & Hudson. (Original work published 1970)

7 Barret, L.F. (2017). *How emotions are made: The secret life of the brain.* Houghton Mifflin Harcourt.

8 McKinsey Design. (2018). *The business value of design.* McKinsey. https://www .mckinsey.com/~/media/McKinsey/Business%20Functions/McKinsey%20Design /Our%20insights/The%20business%20value%20of%20design/The-business-value -of-design-full-report.pdf?shouldIndex=false.

9 Harvard Business Review Analytic Services. (2019). *Beyond big data: Why small data integration is the bey to CXM success.* Harvard Business Review. https://hbr.org /resources/pdfs/comm/focusvision/Beyondbigdata.pdf.

10 World Economic Forum. (2020). *The internet of bodies is here: Tackling new challenges of technology governance.* https://www.weforum.org/reports/the-internet-of-bodies-is -here-tackling-new-challenges-of-technology-governance.

11 Hayek, F. (2017). The theory of complex phenomena. In M. Bunge (Ed.), *Critical approaches to science & philosophy* (pp. 332–49). Routledge. (Original work published 1964).

12 Nagel, T. (1974). What is it like to be a bat? *The Philosophical Review, 83*(4), 435–50. https://doi.org/10.2307/2183914.

13 Anderson, C. (2008). The end of theory: The data deluge makes the scientific method obsolete. *Wired.* https://www.wired.com/2008/06/pb-theory/.

14 Rao, R.P. (2013). *Brain-computer interfacing: An introduction.* Cambridge University Press.

15 Nagel, T. (1974).

16 Orth, M. (2020). 10 TechnoSupremacy and the final frontier: Other minds. In I. Pedersen & A. Illiadis (Eds.), *Embodied computing: Wearables, implantables, embeddables, ingestibles* (pp. 211–35). MIT Press.

PART TWO

Weaving Behavioral and Precision Consumer Research into Marketing and Retail Strategy

CHAPTER SIX

Personalized Retailing: A State-of-Theory & State-of-Practice Review

Murali K. Mantrala and Arun Shastri

SUMMARY OF CHAPTER

The chapter covers the latest academic and managerial perspectives on retailing strategy and offers insights and directions for the traditional retailer's journey towards personalization at scale.

MANAGERIAL IMPLICATIONS (GENERAL)

- Managers in the retail industry will find extremely valuable "lessons learned" as well as "best practices" when it comes to personalizing their customer experience and their customer engagements. This chapter could be one of the main inputs of design thinking sessions for the elaboration of a strategy road map for a retailer.

MANAGERIAL IMPLICATIONS (ORGANIZATIONAL)

- Organizational changes must go hand in hand with a strategy road map for the retailer as participants in many different departments (IT, marketing, media, sales, inventory, finance, procurement, supply chain) at the retailer must cooperate very closely to implement strategic initiatives.

- One way to achieve this end is through establishing an excellence center for data, analytics, and AI, engaging and coordinating closely with each of the departments.

MANAGERIAL IMPLICATIONS (STRATEGIC, TACTICAL, AND OPERATIONAL)

- The chapter provides very rich ideas that help retailers understand the state of the art in theory and practice and enable them to craft their strategy or reassess it if it is already developed.
- From the tactical perspective, it gives great guidelines on how to procure multiple types of resources to be able to execute the initiatives of the strategy road map.

MANAGERIAL IMPLICATIONS (RISK ASSESSMENT)

- Interestingly, this chapter goes beyond the hype of solution providers and offers real lessons learned from real experiences. By doing so, it helps managers mitigate their risks when it comes to embarking on very costly but far from efficient solutions.

1. INTRODUCTION

Tailoring firms' offerings to the changing needs of customers has always been a fundamental tenet of marketing since the articulation of the *marketing concept*. However, it was only about the early '90s, at the dawn of the electronic interactive marketing age, that the possibility and power of truly executing the marketing concept at the individual level via low-cost electronic data-based "addressability marketing" began to be articulated. Industry observers pointed to a number of ways retailers and retail service providers could create and take advantage of databases of addressable customer-level transactions, behaviors, and characteristics to mail tailored, that is, "personalized" advertising, promotions, and offerings to individual customers. Following the marketing concept, the general theory was that the provision of offerings closely matching your customers' needs would lead to a stronger and more rewarding customer relationship for both the retailer and the customer.

In the following decades, "intelligent technologies" for knowledge discovery in databases (KDD),[1] which include capturing, storing, analyzing, and deriving insights from huge volumes of "big data" on customers, have rapidly evolved. These have opened the door for many powerful applications, especially in online retailing and e-commerce. In particular, in the domain of personalization, pioneering work by Amazon researchers established how smart item-based collaborative filtering techniques could be used to provide effective personalized product recommendations to online shoppers. Early applications included recommending books and gifts. Since then, Amazon's recommendation algorithm has tremendously improved, and new developments offering even more sophisticated, model-based collaborative filtering recommendation systems using data mining and machine learning algorithms continue to emerge. As a result, as early as 2013, it was reported that nearly 35 percent of the company's sales revenues came from such personalized recommendations.

In other online retailing settings, digital goods companies like Netflix and Spotify have especially profited from personalized recommendations by leveraging machine learning technologies. Netflix, the streaming entertainment content company, today has over 180 million subscribers and is available all over the world.[2] A huge part of its success, its "secret sauce," is undoubtedly its recommendation system's personalized offerings to its users. Netflix employs an army of designers, data scientists, and product specialists to create an engine that analyzes precisely how subscribers click, watch, search, play, and pause. These data are used to identify over two thousand "taste communities," namely, clusters of people who have the same content preferences. Combining these taste clusters with individual behavioral data, Netflix executes "predictive personalization" with algorithms for "content ranking," surfacing only the content with a high probability of being of interest to the subscriber, along with "evidence selection": endorsement of the product with the most effective cue, message, tag, or label. Netflix even personalizes how elements are presented on screen (e.g., the rows, the titles in those rows, the order of those titles within the rows, and the artwork in thumbnails). As a result of such extreme personalization, the company has reported that its recommendation engine influences users' choices in over 80 percent of streaming cases.

Similarly, music streaming giant Spotify today has nearly 300 million active users, 50 million tracks, and over 4 billion playlists. A big reason for Spotify's success is its "Discover Weekly" playlist. Every Monday, Spotify gives its millions of users thirty new song recommendations generated by an artificial intelligence (AI) system called "Bandits for Recommendations as Treatments" (BaRT), based on "exploit" and "explore" concepts. Exploit makes use of the user's listening history, songs skipped, playlists the user has created, social media activity on platforms, and even their location to recommend music. With "explore," similar to Netflix's taste communities, Spotify studies the rest of the world: it searches for playlists and artists similar to a user's listening taste and recommends popular artists in that area that the user has apparently not yet heard.

There have been advances in offline retail personalization technologies as well, especially in the domain of shopper-facing interactive technologies. For example, mobile apps allow retailers to advertise directly to shoppers, provide online in-store navigation, and enhance customers' shopping experiences. In-store proximity marketing combines smartphone technology and loyalty card data and allows retailers to reach shoppers with personalized offers in real time by tracking their position in the store through their smartphones. Other technologies include digital display walls, interactive fitting rooms, smart and social mirrors that utilize RFID, cameras for facial recognition, or body-scanning to offer context-specific personalized product recommendations.[3] Commentators in both academia and practice have argued that utilizing such and similar technologies will be the way physical retailers, often written off as history, will survive and even thrive in an increasingly omnichannel world where shoppers easily transition between online and physical channels over their customer journeys.

However, despite technological advances, even at the time of writing, the understanding and record of personalized retailing strategy and management by physical retailers are spotty, and the adoption of the latest technologies is slow relative to the need, especially in the post-COVID environment. Although the general proposition that personalized recommendations and offers can be appealing and will keep customers is intuitively plausible, knowledge about the drivers and barriers to consumer acceptance of technology-enabled personalization (TEP), especially in physical retail stores, is still evolving.[4] This knowledge gap is one of the reasons there remains a high degree of uncertainty among retailers about personalized retailing strategies' benefits versus costs, which to pursue in their contexts, and how to execute them well. Indeed, despite all the hype from technology consultants, a recent report by Gartner predicts 80 percent of marketers are set to abandon personalization efforts by 2025 because of the lack of ROI and the difficulty of setting up a clear personalization strategy to collect, integrate, and protect customer data.[5]

Such continuing skepticism and confusion among marketers in general and retailers in particular are understandable. Many are still struggling to understand, design, and implement successful personalization strategies for their targeted customer segments. This is despite the fact that technologies and algorithms for doing so are exploding in sophistication and possibilities. Even though there is still no universally accepted definition of "personalization" in retailing, its next-generation version known as "hyper-personalization" (personalization 2.0 or predictive personalization as used by Netflix and Spotify) is being touted by technology and analytics firms. Moreover, the findings about the efficacy of this strategy for "precision retailing" in the academic literature remain quite mixed, indicating the need for careful formulation of retail personalization strategy as much as greater understanding and the use of facilitating technologies.

Therefore, the objective of this chapter is to review and document the "state of the art" of personalization in retailing – especially from the viewpoint of bricks-and-mortar retailers, where the payoffs of this strategy seem to be considerable, but the related understanding and experience are quite limited. In this review, we aim to concisely summarize the latest academic and managerial perspectives of this retailing strategy – the "state of theory" and "state of practice" – and offer an agenda for practice and further research in this domain.

More specifically, after reviewing definitions and underlying economic and consumer psychology theory of why and how personalization can be beneficial in retailing, we summarize how well it works in practice, what is known about drivers and barriers to consumer acceptance of personalization in physical and omnichannel retailing contexts, and how current and emerging AI and machine learning (ML) methods and algorithms promise to improve the picture. We then focus on the current state of retailers' understanding and adoption of these latest personalization technologies, specifically in relation to the findings and takeaways from a recent survey that we conducted. We close with recommendations for the traditional retailer's journey towards personalization at scale.

2. DEFINITIONS

Although there is no universally accepted definition of personalization, the following definitions are quite consistent regarding what is entailed:

> "Personalization is when the firm decides, usually based on previously collected customer data, what marketing mix is suitable for the individual."[6]
>
> "The process offering the right content in the right format to the right person at the right time."[7]

Thus, these definitions converge on the idea that *personalization is a targeted, individual-level data-driven marketing strategy, relevant to the customer's context, in which the customer is passive.* That is, all personalization efforts, such as Amazon's Recommender System, are initiated by the company. In this crucial aspect, personalization is distinct from the one-to-one marketing strategy of "customization," in which the customer proactively specifies one or more elements of their marketing mix. An example of the latter would be Dell Technologies allowing customers to customize the computer they order.

In this chapter we exclusively focus on the strategy of *personalization in retailing*.

Of course, the concept of personalization itself is not new, and in fact this has been the hallmark of "personal selling" in retailing since time immemorial. But traditionally retail salespeople collected data on consumers by asking questions in a conversation and then adapting their message to provide content that was particularly suited to the customer. Today, vastly greater amounts of customer data can be collected and automatically processed to provide a personalized advertising message, product recommendation, price, or promotional offer to a customer. The customer may not even be present in-store, but rather shopping online or simply passing by a physical branch. Moreover, traditional personalization tactics are giving way to much more sophisticated "hyper-personalization" strategies with the help of AI and ML, using data collected about individual consumers as well as the sequence of actions they have gone through before each touchpoint in their purchase journey. But before proceeding to the latest technologies and developments, it is worth dwelling on the underlying theory and what academic research has revealed about the efficacy, challenges, and opportunities in precision retailing via personalization.

3. HOW AND WHY PERSONALIZATION WORKS: THEORY AND UNDERLYING MECHANISMS

A quick scan of contemporary retailing literature, academic as well as practitioner-oriented, will reveal that the dominant themes of retailing strategy today are *customer experience* and *customer engagement*. In a nutshell, the prevailing paradigm is that if a retailer can provide a superior customer experience (known by the popular initialism "CX") at all stages of the *customer's buying journey* (i.e., "pre-purchase," "purchase," "post-purchase"), then that would, in turn, enhance customer engagement and firm performance. More specifically, according to Verhoef et al. (2009),[8] CX (a) involves the customer's cognitive, affective, emotional, social, and physical responses to a retailer, created by elements that the retailer controls (e.g., service interface, retail atmosphere, assortment, price), and others the retailer does not control (e.g., influence of others, purpose of shopping); and (b) CX encompasses all stages of the consumer's purchase journey and all channels utilized during this journey. Previous research has suggested that a customer's assessment of a CX is likely to influence outcomes like customer satisfaction, customer loyalty, and customer lifetime value (CLV).[9]

In contrast, customer engagement (CE) focuses on the extent to which the customer reaches out to and initiates contact with the firm, whether attitudinally or behaviorally. In effect, CE can be viewed as specific interactional touchpoints a customer has with a retailer. Positive CX should lead to more CE. According to Pansari and Kumar's framework,[10] a positive CX should engender positive emotion and customer satisfaction and in turn lead to greater CE that could include greater repeat purchases (loyalty) as well as customer referrals. From this perspective, personalization then is a process that improves the CX and solidifies the relationship, especially emotional bonding, between the retailer and the customer leading to greater engagement. To reiterate, personalization concepts once limited mainly to targeted offers now extend to the entire customer experience over the multiple touchpoints with the retailer over the customer purchase journey.

Several attitudinal and behavioral mechanisms underlying the above-theorized effects have been posited and subjected to some study in the literature. For example, in the context of web personalization, Ho and Bodoff (2014)[11] propose and experimentally test a combination of cognitive information process theory from psychology and normative economic consumer search theory as the mechanisms underlying consumer attitude formation and behaviors in relation to a personalization *agent*. Among their results, they find that with increasing quality (relevance) of personalization, the consumer's attitude towards the personalization agent improves and they are more likely to select a recommended option. In short, personalization can contribute to improved customer experience and thereby greater CE and increased customer equity or lifetime value. Intuitively, the company heightens its relevance to customers by offering content or products of interest as solutions to their needs.

Relevance implicitly incorporates *context specificity*, which is essential for effective personalization.

The above discussion raises the question: Does personalization in practice always work as theorized? In the next section, we consider the empirical evidence about personalization's effects and their boundary conditions.

4. DOES PERSONALIZATION WORK? EMPIRICAL EVIDENCE FROM PRACTICE AND RESEARCH

In general, the consensus in both practice and academia is that personalization's main effects on CE and firm performance are positive in both digital and non-digital environments.

Evidence from Practice

The news from practice is generally good. For example, according to a report by McKinsey & Co. (2020),[12] personalization at scale (i.e., when companies have personal interactions with most of their customers) "often delivers a 1 to 2 percent lift in total sales for grocery companies and an even higher lift for other retailers, by driving up loyalty and share-of-wallet and reducing marketing and sales costs by around 10 to 20 percent." This McKinsey study reported over 80 percent of customers saying they want their shopping experience to be personalized in some way, and that effective personalization "can increase store revenues by 20 to 30 percent." Similarly, an Accenture study[13] found 91 percent of consumers are more likely to shop with brands which recognize, remember, and provide relevant offers and recommendations, and 44 percent of these customers will become repeat buyers after a satisfying personalized shopping experience. Moreover, the latter customers are more likely to purchase a product that they did not initially intend to buy, as well as buy something more expensive than originally planned, according to a Pure360 survey.[14]

Another recent survey (May 2019) of two hundred marketing leaders by Forbes Insights and Arm Treasure Data[15] reveals that where personalization is being applied in a robust way, enterprises are seeing positive results. In the survey, 40 percent of respondents said that their customer personalization efforts have had a direct impact on maximizing sales, basket size, and profits in direct-to-consumer channels, such as e-commerce, while 37 percent cited increased sales and CLV through product or content recommendations. More than one-third of respondents have seen increases in their transaction frequency as a result of personalization strategies.

Some of the notable success stories are multichannel retailers that utilize both online and offline stores. For example, Sephora, the beauty products retailer, has for the third year in a row topped the fourth Annual Retail Personalization Index (ARPI 2021) rankings put out by Sailthru and Livekicker, the former a marketing automation firm that helps clients engage their customers with personalized experiences across email, mobile, and web channels, and the latter a global provider of real-time email personalization solutions.[16] Sephora's performance in recent times has been the envy of the field, and much of its success is attributed to offering a seamless personalized shopping experience to its customers across both its physical and digital channels, where staff have been merged and incentive-aligned since 2019. Beauty products are personal by nature and Sephora quickly learns about shoppers' skin, habits, and lifestyles to recommend the most relevant products. Other retailers ranked among the top twenty-five in the 2021 ARPI report include Best Buy, Bloomingdale's, Nordstrom, Macy's, Bed Bath & Beyond, Office Depot & Office Max, Walmart, and Target. Notably, the presence in this list of several bricks-and-mortar chains that have recently been in the news for being in trouble and closing large numbers of their store outlets (e.g., Macy's and Bed Bath & Beyond) indicates the importance of personalized retailing in their recovery strategies.

More generally, in the latest ARPI Index report, Sailthru notes that the goal of personalization should be to engage customers where they are rather than where you would ideally like them to be. The report claims that their long-term data indicates that customer targets of retailer communications are more likely to convert if content is personalized using predictive analytics, while repeat purchases and CLV are increased if customers are nurtured using personalization.

Furthermore, fewer customers will opt out when personalization is effectively integrated. Interestingly, this fourth ARPI report notes that despite Amazon's cutting-edge and pioneering product recommendation systems that accounted for over a third of its sales – about $125 billion in the last quarter of 2020 – the company actually slipped down the ARPI rankings significantly. This is because, in response to competition from Amazon, many specialty multichannel retailers and even department stores have been greatly improving their personalization efforts to hold on to their customers.

Evidence from Academics

The academic literature contains numerous studies of retail personalization's effects on various outcomes across the customer journey (see, e.g., Mehmood et al.).[17] As already mentioned, the findings in this literature are mixed: many studies report positive customer outcomes while others report negative ones. The outcomes of interest are manifold, from, for example, usage to behavioral intentions to loyalty. The effects of personalization on these outcomes can be mediated by CX and CE as already mentioned, as well as by *customer trust*. Moderators can include the *type of personalization (personalization strategy)* and *type of personalized offering*, among other factors. The academic literature has shown that it matters whether the firm uses a personalization strategy that is *product-based* (i.e., focused on recommending products based on information on past purchases as well as the current context that is not explicitly mentioned) or *interaction-based* (based on explicitly mentioned personally identifiable information, e.g., personalized greetings). Findings are that consumers tend to respond positively to personalization that is product-based and respond negatively when the personalization is interaction-based. Similarly, *the type of offerings* makes a difference. For example, personalized recommendations work better for *experience products* than for *search products*, and when they are perceived to be useful, that is, reducing the consumers' evaluation costs.

A comprehensive review of the voluminous academic literature on personalization's effects on various consumer response outcomes is beyond the scope of this chapter. Suffice it to say that the overall research findings indicate that personalization is a double-edged sword, eliciting both favorable and unfavorable consumer outcomes. That is, whether personalization has positive or negative effects on consumers (and ultimately, the retailer's performance) and the strengths of these effects depend on a host of contextual, technology-related, firm-related, and consumer-related factors. In particular, a contextual factor of considerable importance is whether consumer interactions with the retailer are occurring online or in physical stores. Much of the early developments occurred in the online retailing and e-commerce contexts where digitalized consumer-level data for personalized recommendations and offerings were immediately and abundantly available. However, advancing technologies are elevating the quantity and richness of digitalized consumer data available to bricks-and-mortar retailers as well. The latter are beginning to exploit these in conjunction with their natural advantages to provide richer consumer experiences to consumers than those available online. As stated at the outset, these developments are of considerable interest at this time, and shedding light on the state of the art on personalization in these retailing arenas is an important goal of this paper. Therefore, in the next section, we focus on reviewing what is currently known about the drivers of and barriers to consumer acceptance of retail personalization in these environments.

5. DRIVERS AND BARRIERS TO CONSUMER ACCEPTANCE OF IN-STORE PERSONALIZATION

In their recent article, Riegger et al.[18] offer a typology of drivers and barriers to consumer acceptance of technology-enabled personalization (TEP) in physical stores. First, Riegger et al. define TEP as a process that essentially relies on information technology and specifically draws on databases of customers' past behavior for personalization approaches, with the help of smart retail technologies (e.g., interactive fitting rooms, digital touch screens, etc.). TEP integrates physical and digital personalization dimensions at the point of sale to provide individual customers with relevant, context-specific information, based on a combination of historic and real-time data. Thereby, TEP introduces the amenities of online retailing, such as data-driven personalization, into physical interactions.

Second, based on twenty-five in-depth consumer interviews, Riegger et al. identify five types of drivers of TEP acceptance by consumers: *utilitarian, hedonic, control, interaction,* and *integration;* and four barriers: *exploitation, interaction misfit, privacy,* and *lack of confidence.* Putting these drivers and barriers together then reveals five *paradoxes* with respect to consumer acceptance of TEP (*exploration-limitation, staff presence-absence, humanization-dehumanization, personalization-privacy, personal-retailer devices*). These paradoxes are summarized below.

Personalization-privacy paradox: This paradox is probably the most prominent and has received the most attention in both research and practice. It refers to the well-known phenomenon that consumers want personalization but are wary of businesses harvesting the data needed to achieve it. From a customer viewpoint, there exists a fine line between "personalized" and "invasive" or "intrusive" interactions with the retailer. Accenture[19] reports that 41 percent of consumers find it creepy when they receive a text from a brand or retailer as they walk past a physical store, and 35 percent find it creepy when they receive ads on social sites for items they had browsed on a website. Not surprisingly, HubSpot[20] reports that 79 percent of consumers say they had blocked ads for this reason but, interestingly, 77 percent of consumers prefer to filter ads rather than block them, as they do pay greater attention to personalized ads if they are aligned with their interests. More specifically, older consumers tend to feel more violated by personalized digital targeting, whereas younger groups appreciate seeing ads that are relevant to them. Consumers also experience particular discomfort if other customers take notice of their personalized information, and if identity disclosures based on personal information occur in unfamiliar environments. It is evident that minimizing privacy concerns relative to personal data collection and use needs more understanding and delicate handling.

More specifically, given the personalization-privacy paradox retailers need to be very circumspect in their use of available customer data as well as its collection. For example, consider recent research in the context of online retailing by Aiello et al. (2020).[21] This research finds that compared to the pre-purchase phase of the customer journey, asking for personal information at the end of the online customer purchase journey leads to a higher perception of *warmth* (i.e., perceptions that the other party has good intentions) and lower privacy concerns, thereby increasing consumers' disclosure of personal data. Put simply, warmth judgments increase perceived sincerity, kindness, and friendliness, generate positive emotional reactions and behaviors, and reassure consumers about the intentions of the company. Warmth perceptions increase once the relationship is already established (post-purchase phase of the customer journey) because the focus is on the customer more than getting a sale at that time.

Exploration-limitation paradox: According to Riegger et al.,[22] this paradox refers to when consumers appreciate getting highly tailored suggestions from some TEP technology ("machine") but at the same time feel restricted in their choices and have a fear of missing out ("FOMO") on other new options they have not tried before and have no human agent available to discuss the matter.

Staff presence-absence paradox: This paradox emerges as a result of consumers' contradictory feelings towards humans versus TEP personalization in physical retail settings. Consumers often want to shop independently or with the help of technology without human interactions, but they also seek human interaction when they are confused about the value of the offering recommended by a chatbot, etc.

Humanization-dehumanization paradox: This paradox arises when consumers perceive interactions with too humanlike machines as strange but at the same time want the technology to have human traits, such as being more empathic.

Personal-retailer devices paradox: This refers to the ambivalent feelings that consumers have regarding which medium or device should transmit personalized content. They recognize the functionality of receiving personalized content on their own device, but they also perceive personalized messages on their smartphones as invasive or identity-revealing.

In short, aside from the well-known personalization-privacy paradox, consumers experience other tensions that can create pitfalls in

TEP provision by retailers. Not surprisingly, this has led to mixed findings with respect to the effectiveness of adopting a personalization strategy. For example, negative outcomes have been reported due to consumers' increased feelings of intrusiveness, privacy concerns, and perceived loss of choice.[23] In turn, such personalization misfires have aroused skepticism and slowed the adoption of personalization by many retailers. We now probe whether the latest technologies and data science methods can mitigate some of these hurdles in the way of TEP.

6. OVERVIEW OF AI AND ML TECHNOLOGIES FOR PERSONALIZATION

In general, AI in marketing is currently gaining importance due to increasing computing power, lower computing costs, the availability of big data, and the advance of ML algorithms and models. Whereas AI combines different technologies to enable machines to sense, comprehend, act, and learn with humanlike levels of intelligence, ML refers to the process by which a system learns patterns from data and improves through experience. The two technologies clearly are related and have a similar purpose, namely, to harness data to the fullest extent possible.

Indeed, several scholars have declared that AI will change the future of marketing substantially. Shankar (2018)[24] has noted two main ways in which AI can impact retailing: (i) *demand-side applications* (e.g., personalization/recommendation systems, customer relationship management, in-store customer experience management, payment management), and (ii) *supply-side applications* (e.g., inventory optimization, logistics, store payout optimization).

Customer-facing retailing AI applications include ML prediction for mobile marketing personalization, in-store technology (e.g., robots, smart displays, or augmented reality) for convenience or social presence, and AI for personalized CE. In their various writings, Ming-hui Huang and Roland Rust conceptualize AI as the use of computational machinery to emulate capabilities inherent in humans, such as *doing physical or mechanical tasks, thinking, and feeling.*[25,26] Huang and Rust posit that *mechanical AI* is best for standardization, *thinking AI* is good for personalization, and *feeling AI* is ideal for relationalization (i.e., personalizing relationships), due to its capability to recognize and respond to emotions.

In particular, thinking AI provides personalization benefits due to its ability to recognize patterns from data (e.g., text mining, speech recognition, facial recognition). Given this data, Huang and Rust[27] note that marketing analytics can predict market trends for product designs that cater more precisely to target customers' preferences, big data analytics can be used to inform product development to quickly adapt to consumer trends and changing preferences, adaptive systems can be used to personalize service to each consumer's preference, and deep learning can be used to personalize point-of-interest recommendations.

Thinking AI-based personalization, for example, can facilitate in-store shopping for individual customers. Once again, Amazon has taken the lead in this domain. Its experimental Amazon Go grocery store uses facial recognition technology to identify and remember each customer. Similarly, Alibaba's Fashion AI system uses smart mirrors on the sales floor and changing rooms to display items that each customer selects and suggests complementary items. Another smart technology is Macy's query-based response AI system, On Call, a mobile app and shopping personal aid that provides in-store information to help customers locate items they are looking for. Such AI-based responses via mobile apps can tremendously impact customers as they shop, whether physically or online. They can gather information about where products are physically located within a store, answer questions about the product attributes and uses, and suggest what other products might work well in combination with the purchased item. Further, using historical customer data and predictive analytics, the responses to customer's queries can be personalized to recommend relevant information or products, thereby enhancing customer experience and engagement.

As a final example of the "power of the personal"[28] in offline retailing, consider Starbucks's relentless efforts to offer a personalized "Starbucks Experience" to its consumers. Specifically, Starbucks has been using reinforcement learning technology – a type of ML – to provide a more personalized experience for customers who use the Starbucks mobile app. Within the app, 16 million active Starbucks Rewards members receive tailor-made, thoughtful recommendations, generated via a reinforcement learning platform, built by Microsoft Azure in collaboration with Starbucks data scientists, for food and drinks based on local store inventory, popular selections, weather, time of day, community preferences, and previous orders. Thus, customers are more likely to get suggestions for items they will enjoy. For example, if a customer consistently orders dairy-free beverages, the platform can infer a non-dairy preference, not recommend items containing dairy, and suggest dairy-free food and drinks. In essence, reinforcement learning allows Starbucks to better understand the customer with the ultimate goal of personalized interactions and recommendations.

This effort is aptly summarized in the following quotes:

> "Starbucks is an experience, and it's centered around that customer connection in the store, the human connection, one person, one cup, one neighborhood at a time. I think that mission is so critical to how technology has to show up for us." Gerri Martin-Flickinger, Starbucks executive vice president and chief technology officer[29]
>
> "Just like their relationship with a barista, customers receive the same care and personalized recommendations when it comes from our digital platforms." Jon Francis, senior vice president, Starbucks analytics and market research[30]

Notwithstanding the above examples, however, as discussed in the next sections, retailers vary considerably in terms of their *personalization maturity*.

7. PERSONALIZATION USAGE IN PRACTICE: A SURVEY

In late fall 2020, we conducted a survey of multichannel marketers and retailers in order to better understand the adoption, perceived opportunities, challenges in the way of adoption, and application of AI and ML in their personalization strategies. A total of 437 corporate executives received the survey, with nearly half (48.7 percent) working in B2C marketing or marketing analytics. Over 40 percent of the respondents were at the level of vice president or higher.

Out of the survey sample, 138 respondents responded to the item "select all focus areas from below where you spend significant time in your current role (e.g., at least 30–40 percent of time)." The top three focus areas were general marketing (57.2 percent), digital marketing (54.3 percent), and customer experience management (50 percent). Over 38 percent of these respondents worked in retail while 21 percent worked in e-commerce. On average, about 59 percent of sales of these respondents' organizations came through direct channels (digital/company website or app) while 41 percent of sales came through indirect channels (e.g., through resellers, selling partners, third party websites, retailers, wholesalers, etc.)

Over 90 percent of the above respondents felt that personalization was somewhat, very, or extremely important for their companies (29 percent answered it was extremely important). While 63 percent said they were currently offering segmented marketing (customer offers at the segment level), 45.3 percent said they were currently engaged in web content personalization to their customers and 45.8 percent were currently offering curated experiences to select, high-value customers. However, in the future, over 58 percent of respondents were planning to offer web content personalization and curated experiences while only 43 percent were planning to offer segmented marketing.

Interestingly, 93 percent of the respondents were currently delivering personalization through email to their customers while only 41 percent were using mobile apps for this purpose, and just 31 percent were delivering personalization in-store. Further, 64 percent of respondents ranked email as the top channel for personalization. Far lower proportions, 44 percent and 32 percent respectively, ranked in-store and mobile app as the top channel for delivering personalization to customers.

The enthusiasm for individualized personalization, however, seems high. About 89 percent of the respondents indicated they planned to use individualized personalization tactics in their one-to-one marketing efforts in the next twelve to twenty-four months.

Over 60 percent were planning to deploy an AI solution to drive one-to-one product recommendations with customers, while 57 percent were planning to deploy limited-scope handcrafted experiences for select audiences.

However, there are clearly perceived hurdles in the way. Specifically, 58.1 percent of 128 respondents pointed to "lack of integrated tools" (e.g., integration across customer relationship management and mobile app systems) as the biggest challenge/obstacle to making personalization a bigger opportunity in their organizations. The biggest obstacle picked by the second largest proportion of respondents (47 percent) was "lack of trained staff" (e.g., data scientists) to execute a strategy, while about 43 percent of the respondents picked lack of data/low quality data as the biggest obstacle to personalization becoming a bigger opportunity.

Interestingly, when asked, "What steps is your organization planning to take to mitigate some of these challenges discussed above?" 57 percent of 128 respondents indicated "Hire different types of talent (e.g., data scientists, more experienced marketers, etc.)" as the next step, while 46 percent picked "Employ newer AI tools/technology adoption" and 40 percent picked "Obtain better data (data integration with 3rd party vendors)."

When asked, "How important is AI in your approach to personalization?" 45 percent of the respondents answered, "very important" or "extremely important." Strikingly, however, 31 percent of 129 respondents answered, "Not leveraged as of today" when asked to "describe the current status of how your organization is leveraging AI for personalization." Another 30 percent answered, "Recently begun our journey – currently evaluating." Only 16 percent of respondents answered, "Advanced – deployed AI for 1+ years."

Encouragingly, however, in response to the question "Compared to last year, how will your personalization budget/spending change this year?" 66 percent of 129 respondents answered either "somewhat increase (up to 15 percent increase)" or "significant increase (>25 percent increase)." Another 26 percent expected the budget to "stay the same."

Next, focusing on tools and metrics, when asked, "What tools are you currently using for personalization? (Select all that apply from a list)," 33 percent of 129 respondents said "None," 25 percent picked Salesforce Marketing Cloud (SFMC)/Einstein and 24 percent picked Adobe Marketing. As regards metrics, in response to the question "What metrics do you use to measure the impact personalization has had in your organization? (Please select all that apply)," 65 percent of 129 respondents picked "Topline (sales) increase," 59 percent picked "Customer engagement/satisfaction improvement," and 53 percent picked "Increase in customer retention."

Finally, in response to the question "What is the impact you have observed from personalization efforts in your organization (in incremental revenue/customer growth)?" 44 percent of 116 respondents indicated "greater than 15 percent," which seems promising.

Summary of Takeaways from Survey

There are several noteworthy takeaways from the above survey results. Below, we summarize them along with managerial implications.

Perceptions and use of personalization strategy: Despite all the hype by consultants and technology providers, less than 50 percent of respondents currently employ truly personalized strategies towards their customers even though over 90 percent feel such an approach is somewhat important or extremely important for their organizations. This suggests some clear gaps in understanding and/or agreement within the organization on what precisely personalization is or how much of a priority it should be for the company. Hopefully, getting a balanced view of both theory and practice of this strategy will alleviate some of the confusion and misgivings. Clearly, however, the sense that personalization should be a greater priority than it is currently is growing as over 58 percent of respondents were planning to offer web content personalization and curated experiences in the future, 89 percent of the respondents indicated they planned to use individualized personalization tactics in their one-to-one marketing efforts in the next twelve to twenty-four months, and over 66 percent respondents were planning to increase their budget for personalization by over 15 percent in the coming year. However, even with budget increases, some major hurdles in the way of implementation of personalization strategies evidently exist.

First, the level of understanding or experience with the range of personalization opportunities still seems fairly rudimentary and unsophisticated compared to the advances in retail personalization technologies we discussed in earlier sections of this chapter. For example, it is interesting to see that email is still the dominant channel for delivering personalization in fall 2020, just as has been observed in earlier surveys. Drawing on one such survey, a Forbes blog post[31] offers three key reasons for this: (i) email is central to the mobile experience, that is, email is mobile users' preferred type of notification (cited by 46 percent of respondents); it is strongly preferred over push notifications (15 percent) and in-app messaging (20 percent); and it integrates well with other channels (e.g., text, social media in the consumers' native mobile experience). (ii) Email benefits from the shift to real-time opening of messages on smartphones and messages sent by marketers and can be richly informative as well as more personal, delivering relevant information in time-sensitive contexts. A retailer equipped with a customer-aware Wi-Fi network, for example, can send a tailored offer and a personalized note that shows awareness of the consumer's purchases and preferences. (iii) Email can be a powerful engine of CE for personalization and relationship-building. For instance, it is well-known that simply adding the recipient's name to an email's subject line hugely increases open rates. Yet many retailers still have yet to achieve or go beyond even such a modest degree of personalization.

The fact is, despite the merits of email personalization, it too can be enhanced in sophistication, and it is surprising to find the relatively lower proportions of respondents who rank in-store and mobile app as the top channel for delivering personalization to customers. Much of this may have to do with the survey's findings that lack of integration across systems (e.g., CRM, mobile app), lack of trained staff and data scientists to execute a strategy, and lack of high-quality data are the three big challenges to implementation of personalization strategies. Undoubtedly, these are pervasive shortfalls along three key dimensions that many multichannel retailers suffer from that lead to their failure to meet today's personalization expectations, putting them at a significant competitive disadvantage relative to agile and well-endowed omnichannel retailers like

Amazon and Alibaba. Indeed, this confluence of very common and persistent shortfalls that we see in our very recent survey even has a name in the trade – the "retail personalization gap"[32] – meaning that while 90 percent of retailers recognize the importance of personalization, the majority of these retailers lack the advanced technologies they need to improve their personalization capabilities, exactly as we found in our own survey summarized above.

More specifically, a majority of bricks-and-mortar retailers are low on the "personalization maturity vs. revenue" curve relative to leaders such as Amazon, Spotify, and Starbucks (see Figure 6.1). They are delivering what can be called *commodity content personalization*, relying on single channel messages, rules-based content, and messages based on events, triggers, and business rules. In contrast, as already described, the leaders such as Amazon, Netflix, Starbucks, and Spotify are well into *predictive content personalization* or more popularly, *hyper-personalization*. The key differences between the two are as follows:

In rules-based personalization, the content is generated and targeted based on a number of manually predefined rules. The content is modified and displayed to different visitors based on information such as demographics, location, and past visits to the site, but this method is not dynamic – each version of the landing page has to be manually designed. Then, each rule works consistently, displaying the same result until someone changes it. In contrast, predictive personalization involves real-time segmentation of users and employs machine learning methods to automatically match each person to a group of like-minded users. Then, the recommendations are based on the actual actions (like purchases) of the people in the segment, making them extremely accurate. Predictive personalization also analyzes visitor behavior on different pages (channels) and predicts possible purchase intent before a single dollar is spent, shortening the path to conversion.

Both approaches have their uses in different settings. Specifically, rules-based personalization is better suited to smaller sites that do not necessarily have vast amounts of user data at hand. It can be used to display personalized callouts (using each user's name, for instance) or pop-up messages to new customers. For example, a mobile-phone store can display mobile-phone banners only to

Figure 6.1. Personalization Maturity vs. Revenue Curve

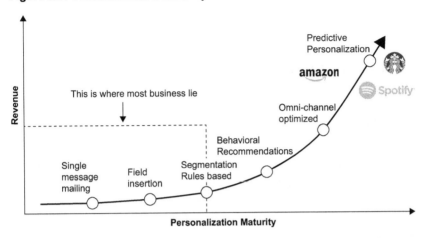

known visitors who have expressed interest in a specific brand and, say, offer them applicable discounts and promotions. In this way, first-time, return, and high-value visitors can be addressed differently. On the other hand, predictive personalization is more complex as it can offer visitors specific products ("often bought together," "you may also like …" "people like you also bought …" etc.) based on their demonstrated behavior. Because it uses machine learning algorithms, no manual work is required to put these rules into place. This is most suitable when big data generated by huge numbers of customer visits to the site or store is available.

To overcome this retail personalization gap, bricks-and-mortar retailers need the right combination of data science talent, the right data collection, classification, and management tools, and the right combination of technologies (e.g., CRM suites, e-commerce platforms, email engines, loyalty programs, recommendation engines, live chatbots, and social media capabilities). Further, these must be orchestrated across several departments, including marketing, IT, e-commerce, and store operations. Hiring the right talent is a good place to start. Additionally, however, significant technology investments and help from specialized, experienced consultants is needed to overcome the retail personalization gap and accelerate the adoption of more effective personalization strategies by offline retailers.

8. THE ROAD TO PERSONALIZATION AT SCALE

In the previous sections we discussed what personalization is: how it works, the drivers and barriers to its acceptance, and the contributions of AI and ML technologies. Based on the survey we conducted, we also discussed what organizations are currently doing with regards to personalization and highlighted the retail personalization gap that exists among the majority of retailers. In this section we will discuss key considerations of the journey of retail organizations as they consider their customer needs and how to enable personalization success.

Personalization creates business value in many ways: (i) driving sales by increasing the size of the basket and choice of products in direct-to-consumer channels; (ii) increasing the number of transactions and further directing the customer to specific products by tailoring content and recommendations at a customer level; and (iii) driving affinity to the brand by enriching the experience and elevating service levels. Realizing all this requires strategy, technology, data, and insight. For most retailers this is a journey.

We view the retailer journey towards personalization as transiting through four stages: "Basic," "Foundational," "Advanced," and "Transformational" (see Figure 6.2 below).

While many retailers strive to offer a *transformational personalized customer experience,* few have achieved that level of sophistication yet. As indicated by the retail personalization gap revealed by our survey and others, most retailers have not advanced beyond the Basic or Foundational level in their personalization efforts. At the Basic level, digital tactics are used but they are not integrated, content is created by each promotional channel such as email, all customers receive all tactics and content, and deployments follow a campaign calendar that is periodic and set at the start of the planning cycle. At the Foundational level, an organization is beginning its digital journey. Digital is understood as a priority, long-term

Figure 6.2. The Retailer Personalization Journey

Sophistication of capabilities

commitments on budgets and resourcing exist, and elements of a sophisticated approach begin to appear. Market research provides insights which are then leveraged to drive content and experiences by customer segment.

At the Advanced level the focus is on scaling digital experiences. Organizations are learning, iterating, and refining their approaches, and decision engines are increasingly sophisticated in delivering the right content to the right customer at the right time and through the right channel. A truly transformational organization behaves as a digitally native organization would. AI/ML informs every interaction with the customer, and everything happens dynamically. To realize this potential, organizations need an increased sophistication in capabilities accompanied by a shift in mindset and alignment with business priorities. There are different ways to embark on this journey but there are some common foundational capabilities namely *digital, content,* and *the decision engine.*

As capabilities get to be more sophisticated, organizations transition from Basic to Foundational stages where *digitalization* is an increasingly important driver. The impact of digital capabilities is enormous. Intermittent decision-making is now of a more continuous nature, planning which could potentially be independent is now linked, and organizations need to have an "always ready never done" mindset. Finally, there must be increased coordination across business units. In more elementary stages of maturity, digital is simply a channel for tactics. From there, the next step is for leadership to understand that digital is more than simply a channel, and for its full potential to be realized, it must be a priority for the organization. To achieve these priorities, the organization needs a plan to get there.

Content is also a critical element in personalization. In early stages of maturity, content is created by channel and all customers receive all tactics and content. Market research produces insights and campaign stories can be created based on these insights. However, as organizations get more sophisticated, ML algorithms can drive segments and determine needs so content can be tailored in real time. Finally, to ensure that the right content is delivered to the right customer at the right moment in their journey, *a decision engine* must piece together modular content to hyper-personalize and dynamically deploy tactics tailored to preferences. Due to the lack of a sophisticated decision engine, *trigger or rules-based approaches* are predominantly used in practice. Figure 6.3 depicts steps and stages along an illustrative Road to Personalization at Scale.

Personalization at scale takes time. Even for an organization that is deeply committed to the cause, this is likely a multi-year process. Here are a few insights and observations. The North Star must be defined and well understood, and senior management has to constantly focus the organization on it to achieve it. Acquiring and building out technology is almost always never the first step. In fact, it can be a detriment. An agile approach, with short sprints as opposed to long planning and execution cycles, keeps the engagement consistent. Sacrifice accuracy (complexity) for transparency if the situation merits.

Many personalization solutions exist in the market and can be helpful to an organization on its journey, but each presents its specific set of challenges that need to be understood and tackled. CRM providers and platform providers have standard solutions with generic ML algorithms, but some effort is required to craft these to suit the unique needs of a retail organization and its circumstance.

Figure 6.3. Road to Personalization at Scale

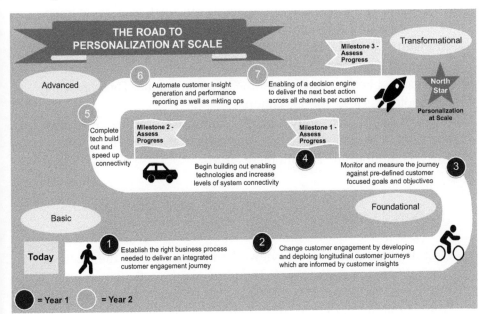

Many niche players address narrow use cases which look attractive but create challenges when attempts are made to link these more broadly with other technology and business. Solutions focus on generating insights and others on guiding actions, but few provide the combination of recommendations and targeting. And as is the case with any technology solutions, effort is required to ensure that these are deployed well and adopted across the organization to drive the impact they promise.

What exactly is the nature of the technology and analytics that is required to support the solution? It depends on how personalization as a capability is delivered. If the approach is rather rudimentary with content chosen based on rules, and messages are based on events, triggers, and business rules, then ease-of-integration and business process automation are the primary considerations. If the goal is to leverage AI-curated experiences that deliver relevant content and preference-based recommendations, a cohesive marketing platform is essential. Standardization is the key decision driver. The trade-off in these circumstances is often between deployment complexity and agile marketing. And finally, if the aim is to drive transformation, the entire marketing design process, the communication strategy, and the customer-centric messaging have to be re-engineered before focusing on the decision engine. The remaining technology is to enable execution.

In order to successfully navigate this journey, organizations must be willing to make the commitment, take the steps necessary to drive adoption, and sustain these efforts.

9. CONCLUSION

In this chapter, we have reviewed and documented the "state of the art" of personalization in retailing – with particular emphasis on bricks-and-mortar retailers. In this review, we have endeavored to concisely cover and summarize the latest academic as well as managerial perspectives and insights into personalization as a core retailing strategy: the "state of theory" and "state of practice." We have discussed personalization's role in enhancing customer experience and engagement along the customer purchase journey and what is known about drivers and barriers to consumer acceptance of personalization. Clearly, there is much scope and there are many opportunities for more research into these questions, but two general truths can be stated about the need for further research: (i) Personalization in retail can be a double-edged sword: it can be highly beneficial but can also backfire if it is not sensitive to its nuanced acceptance or the "paradoxes" of consumers; and (ii) effective personalization strategy requires extensive and holistic digitalization or digital transformation of traditional retailers that is not inexpensive, simple, or straightforward. Considering these truths, we have offered several insights and directions for the traditional retailer's journey and progress towards personalization at scale. In conclusion, we hope this chapter stimulates greater research and effective practice in retail personalization.

NOTES

1 Ravi, V., Raman, K., & Mantrala, M.K. (2006). Applications of intelligent technologies in retail marketing. In M. Krafft & M.K. Mantrala (Eds.), *Retailing in the 21st Century* (pp. 127–41). Springer.

2 Kay, M. (2020, July 15). *Netflix: A marketing and business powerhouse*. Digital Marketing Institute. https://digitalmarketinginstitute.com/blog/netflix-a-marketing-and -business-powerhouse.

3 Riegger, A.S., Klein, J.F., Merfeld, K., & Henkel, S. (2021). Technology-enabled personalization in retail stores: Understanding drivers and barriers. *Journal of Business Research, 123*, 140–55. https://doi.org/10.1016/j.jbusres.2020.09.039.

4 Riegger et al. (2021).

5 Gartner Newsroom. (2019 December). *Gartner Predicts 80% of Marketers Will Abandon Personalization by 2025*. https://www.gartner.com/en/newsroom/press -releases/2019-12-02-gartner-predicts-80--of-marketers-will-abandon-person.

6 Murthi, B.P.S., & Sarkar, S. (2003). The role of the management sciences in research on personalization. *Management Science, 49*(10), 1344–62. https://www.jstor.org /stable/4134010.

7 Aguirre, E., Mahr, D., Grewal, D., De Ruyter, K., & Wetzels, M. (2015). Unraveling the personalization paradox: The effect of information collection and trust-building strategies on online advertisement effectiveness. *Journal of Retailing, 91*(1), 34–49. https://doi.org/10.1016/j.jretai.2014.09.005.

8 Verhoef, P.C., Lemon, K.N., Parasuraman, A., Roggeveen, A., Tsiros, M., & Schlesinger, L.A. (2009). Customer experience creation: Determinants, dynamics and management strategies. *Journal of Retailing, 85*(1), 31–41. https://psycnet.apa.org /doi/10.1016/j.jretai.2008.11.001.

9 Pansari, A., & Kumar, V. (2017). Customer engagement: The construct, antecedents, and consequences. *Journal of the Academy of Marketing Science, 45*(3), 294–311. https:// psycnet.apa.org/doi/10.1007/s11747-016-0485-6.

10 Pansari & Kumar (2017).

11 Ho, S.Y., & Bodoff, D. (2014). The effects of web personalization on user attitude and behavior. *MIS Quarterly, 38*(2), 497–510. https://doi.org/10.25300/MISQ/2014 /38.2.08

12 Lindecrantz, E., Gi, M.T.P., & Zerbi, S. (2020, April 28). *Personalizing the customer experience: Driving differentiation in retail*. McKinsey & Company. https://www .mckinsey.com/industries/retail/our-insights/personalizing-the-customer -experience-driving-differentiation-in-retail.

13 Accenture Interactive. (2018). *Personalizationpulse check*. Accenture. https://www .accenture.com/_acnmedia/pdf-83/accenture-making-personal.pdf.

14 Spotler. (2018, April 24). *Are your personalisation tactics intelligent enough to meet consumer demand?* https://spotler.co.uk/blog/consumers-want-intelligent -personalisation.

15 Insights Team. (2021, August 10). *Forbes insights: The path to personalization*. Forbes. https://www.forbes.com/sites/insights-treasuredata/2019/05/01/the-path-to -personalization/?sh=2e4c8e437a76.

16 Bloomberg. (2021, March 3). *Sailthru's fourth annual retail personalization index highlights thriving retail brands*. https://www.bloomberg.com/press-releases /2021-03-03/sailthru-s-fourth-annual-retail-personalization-index-highlights -thriving-retail-brands

17 Mehmood, K., Verleye, K., & De Keyser, A. (2020). *Making personalization work: A review of 45 years of personalization research and its customer outcomes*. La Londe Conference 2020. La Londe les Maures, France.

18 Riegger et al. (2021).
19 Accenture Interactive (2018).
20 Powles, M. (2019). *Personalization versus privacy: Making sense of the privacy Paradox.* Hubspot. https://blog.hubspot.com/marketing/personalization-versus-privacy
21 Aiello, G., Donvito, R., Acuti, D., Grazzini, L., Mazzoli, V., Vannucci, V., & Viglia, G. (2020). Customers' willingness to disclose personal information throughout the customer purchase journey in retailing: The role of perceived warmth. *Journal of Retailing, 96*(4), 490–506. https://doi.org/10.1016/j.jretai.2020.07.001.
22 Riegger et al. (2021).
23 Boerman, S.C., Kruikemeier, S., & Zuiderveen Borgesius, F.J. (2017). Online behavioral advertising: A literature review and research agenda. *Journal of Advertising, 46*(3), 363–76. https://doi.org/10.1080/00913367.2017.1339368.
24 Shankar, V. (2018). How artificial intelligence (AI) is reshaping retailing. *Journal of Retailing, 94*(4), vi–xi. http://dx.doi.org/10.1016/S0022-4359(18)30076-9.
25 Huang, M.H., & Rust, R.T. (2021). A strategic framework for artificial intelligence in marketing. *Journal of the Academy of Marketing Science, 49*, 30–50. https://doi.org/10.1007/s11747-020-00749-9.
26 Rust, R.T., & Huang, M.H. (2021). *The feeling economy: How artificial intelligence is creating the era of empathy.* Springer Nature.
27 Huang & Rust (2021).
28 Sokolowsky, J. (2019, May 6). *Starbucks turns to technology to brew up a more personal connection with its customers.* Microsoft. https://news.microsoft.com/transform/starbucks-turns-to-technology-to-brew-up-a-more-personal-connection-with-its-customers/
29 Sokolowsky (2019).
30 Sokolowsky (2019).
31 Kyurkchiev, M. (2019, September 24). *Council post: Email is not dead – Here's why.* Forbes. https://www.forbes.com/sites/forbestechcouncil/2019/09/24/email-is-not-dead-heres-why/?sh=5b7e88322211.
32 Shapiro, S. (n.d.). *Mind the gap: The real store of personalization in retail.* Bluecore. https://www.bluecore.com/blog/retail-personalization-gap/.

CHAPTER SEVEN

How Resource Scarcity Shapes Consumer Behavior: Implications from the COVID-19 Pandemic

Caroline Roux, Christopher Cannon, and Kelly Goldsmith

SUMMARY OF CHAPTER

The chapter uses the *Self-Regulatory Model of Resource Scarcity* framework to explain how resource scarcity shaped consumer behavior during the COVID-19 pandemic and how consumers generally respond to experiencing a lack of resources.

MANAGERIAL IMPLICATIONS (GENERAL)

- The chapter provides an important conceptual framework for managers to understand the behavioral patterns of their customers during times of scarcity.
- Managers need to be ready to react to future scarcity-related events caused by different types of crises.
- Managers in the private and public sectors alike need to design and develop plans based on a set of well-identified crisis scenarios that can be deployed easily in times of scarcity.

MANAGERIAL IMPLICATIONS (ORGANIZATIONAL)

- Include an analytic, forward-looking function in the marketing department that would provide continuous monitoring through market watch, news trend, and social media analytics to detect any potential regional or global disruptions likely to increase various forms of scarcity.
- Develop policies and procedures for all departments (marketing, sales, procurement, logistics, etc.) to deal with unexpected scarcity-related events or with longer crises.

MANAGERIAL IMPLICATIONS (STRATEGIC, TACTICAL, AND OPERATIONAL)

- From the strategic perspective, managers need to assess the different scarcity-related risk or crisis situations they might face in the future and reflect on their plan to stay in business and continue serving their customers in times of scarcity.
- From the tactical perspective, managers need to review at least the two following systems that they already have in place:
  - Demand forecasting: The demand forecasting system must be reviewed to address scarcity-related situations by considering the framework of this chapter.
  - Recommender systems: An additional profiling of customers is necessary to cope with scarcity-related situations as their behavioral patterns will be different, and classical recommendations may no longer be relevant.
- From the tactical perspective, managers need to review the structure of all their partnerships, from suppliers to logistics, to be better prepared to face potential supply disruptions and/ or sharp demand increases.
- Managers need to design and develop new operational models to deal with scarcity-related situations.

1. INTRODUCTION

COVID-19 started spreading globally in late 2019. By early 2020, numerous countries across the world had experienced the first wave of the pandemic. Notably, the pandemic affected not only the health and lives of consumers around the world but also their purchasing habits and consumption preferences. For instance, consumers from several countries began hoarding toilet paper. It was so prevalent that it has been recognized by many as the hallmark of the "panic buying" trend during the first wave of the pandemic.[1] Beyond toilet paper, retailers were faced with increased demand for numerous other products. Many of these highly sought-after products were directly related to preventing the spread of the virus (e.g., hand sanitizer, face masks, cleaning products). However, other highly in-demand products had little to do with promoting one's physical health (e.g., beauty products, ready-made cookie dough, hair dye). What caused consumers to go from panic buying health-related products such as disinfecting wipes to purchasing unrelated products such as ready-made cookie dough?

To answer this question, we need to consider the key characteristics of the COVID-19 pandemic. Although it was a complex societal phenomenon, one aspect that was central to people's experiences of the pandemic was the *experience of resource scarcity*. We define a *resource* as any quantifiable entity that offers value to an individual and has the potential to be depleted or consumed. We define resource scarcity as *"sensing or observing a discrepancy between one's current level of resources and a higher, more desirable reference point."*[2] For instance, during the pandemic, many people were furloughed or laid off from their jobs and thus faced financial constraints, consumers were hoarding products leaving a scarcity of goods on the shelves at major retailers, and frontline workers often dealt with an insufficient supply of personal protective equipment relative to their needs. While consumers regularly deal with limited financial resources, time constraints, and the occasional stockout under normal circumstances, the pandemic amplified consumers' experiences of resource scarcity in intensity, duration, and variety (i.e., types of scarcity).

In this chapter, we draw from our conceptual review[3] to offer a framework that helps explain how resource scarcity shaped consumer behavior during the COVID-19 pandemic. We start by further explaining what we mean by "resource scarcity," as well as other important concepts related to our framework. Next, we present the different ways consumers tend to cope with resource scarcity – direct, indirect, and dual resolution – that are derived from our framework. Finally, we conclude with managerially relevant implications of our framework to help retailers better understand consumer behavior during and following the COVID-19 pandemic.

Having a clearer understanding of how the COVID-19 pandemic changed consumers' purchasing habits and consumption preferences is especially important as scientists predict that events that exacerbate resource scarcity, such as pandemics and natural disasters, will become increasingly frequent. Therefore, our insights apply not only to the most recent COVID-19 pandemic but also to other economic crises and scarcity-related events (e.g., water, food, or oil shortages). Our framework allows marketers to be better equipped to deal with such events in the future. For example, our framework can help marketers understand and predict how market disruptions may impact consumers' needs and behaviors when resources are scarce, and thus it provides retailers with an important strategic tool for better serving customers during trying times.

2. RESOURCE SCARCITY AND RELATED CONCEPTS

In response to the 2008 financial crisis, there was a notable increase in academic research on the psychology of resource scarcity. Over the following decade, researchers across various disciplines, such as behavioral economics, marketing, and psychology, contributed to our understanding of how resource scarcity can impact consumer decision-making.[4,5,6] One reason why so much attention has been devoted to understanding the impact of resource scarcity is that, as a phenomenon, it can take many forms.[7,8] For example, resource scarcity can take the form of monetary scarcity, which can further manifest as financial constraints, poverty, or the long-term effect of one's socioeconomic status during childhood.[9] Consumers can also experience a scarcity of many other types of resources, such as time, food, products, jobs, and potential romantic partners.[10,11] In addition, consumers can be exposed to information that simply reminds them of current or future resource scarcity, such as news articles about an economic recession, marketing appeals such as limited-quantity or limited-time promotions, comparisons to better-off peers (e.g., through social media), and many more.[12,13,14] As these examples illustrate, resource scarcity can be experienced both objectively (e.g., poverty) and subjectively (e.g., feeling financially constrained after comparing oneself to a wealthier friend). Despite these many differences, our conceptual review identified one critical feature that the most commonly studied types of resource scarcity share: an unfavorable discrepancy in resources. This is why we defined resource scarcity as believing that one's current level of resources is below a desired reference point.[15]

As noted above, we also defined a *resource* as any quantifiable entity that offers value to an individual and can be depleted or consumed.[16] Although some types of resources are more universal (e.g., money, time, food), what constitutes a resource depends on what the consumer personally values. For instance, consumers who did not ever use hand sanitizer before the pandemic might not have considered it a resource during the pandemic. This is because they would not have considered it to be a valuable product and would thus not have been impacted by a shortage of hand sanitizer. However, for most consumers, the COVID-19 pandemic did, in fact, significantly shift the perceived value of hand sanitizer, as it helped protect them from the coronavirus. This prompted consumers to invest effort to acquire and consume such products, leaving many impacted by its shortage. Some consumers were even willing to pay exorbitant prices to acquire it during times of peak demand, which illustrates the scarcity principle[17] (i.e., the fact that resources become increasingly valuable as they become scarcer).

Our conceptual review[18] integrates empirical research on resource scarcity into a unifying framework – the *Self-Regulatory*

Figure 7.1. How resource scarcity shapes consumer behavior, according to the *Self-Regulatory Model of Resource Scarcity*

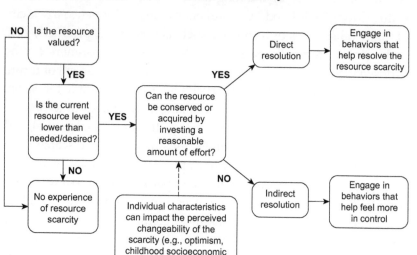

Model of Resource Scarcity – which identified two strategies consumers generally use to deal with their experiences of resource scarcity. The strategy used depends on the extent to which a consumer perceives the situation to be *changeable*. When a consumer believes that investing a reasonable amount of effort (e.g., money, time, energy, cognitive capacities) can help reduce the discrepancy between their current and desired level of resources, they believe that change is possible. As a result, the consumer attempts to resolve their experience of resource scarcity *directly* by acquiring the scarce resource (e.g., working a second job when money is tight) or preserving their scarce resources (e.g., cutting nonessential expenses when money is tight). Conversely, when a consumer believes that change is not possible (i.e., investing a reasonable amount of effort cannot increase their resource levels), they cannot attenuate their scarcity directly. As a result, the consumer attempts to resolve their experience of resource scarcity *indirectly* by findings various ways to feel more in control over their life,

Figure 7.2. How the *Self-Regulatory Model of Resource Scarcity* maps onto examples from the COVID-19 pandemic: hand sanitizer (*top*) and monetary resources (*bottom*)

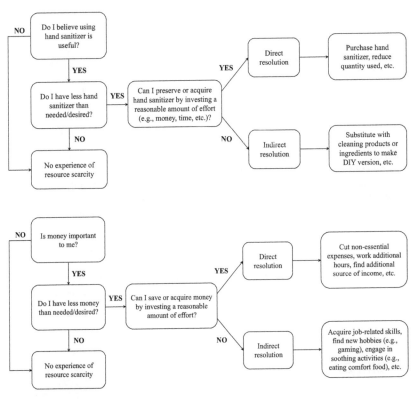

even if these means do not actually solve their scarcity-related problems (e.g., purchasing a suit to feel successful).

The second flow chart uses the example of monetary resources. If a consumer experiences monetary scarcity but can save or acquire money through reasonable efforts, the direct resolution might be to cut nonessential expenses, work additional hours, find additional sources of income, etc. If the consumer cannot save or acquire money through reasonable efforts, the indirect resolution might be acquiring job-related skills, finding new hobbies (e.g., gaming), engaging in soothing activities (e.g., eating comfort food), etc.

Table 7.1. Implications of the *Self-Regulatory Model of Resource Scarcity*

	Impact for Consumers	Implications for Retailers
Direct Resolution (When the situation seems relatively easy to change)	• Scarce resource is valued more • Budgeting, planning, and/or prioritization of scarce resource • Greater focus on trade-offs and/or opportunity costs	• Greater willingness to spend effort (e.g., money, time) to acquire scarce resource • Shifts the share of different types of expenses (e.g., essentials vs. nonessentials) • Increases the importance of attributes related to acquiring or saving the scarce resource (e.g., price of product vs. time spent shopping)
Indirect Resolution (When the situation seems hard to change)	• Increased need for personal control • Substitutions • Competition and aggression • Compensatory consumption	• Increases the importance of attributes related to personal control (e.g., agency, safety, familiarity) • Changes the set of alternatives, which can impact loyalty • Increases aggressive behaviors, both direct (for acquiring the scarce resource) and indirect (redirected aggression) • Increases the desire for products offering compensatory benefits (e.g., comfort, status, self-improvement)

3. DIRECT RESOLUTION

When a consumer believes that investing a reasonable amount of effort can help reduce the present or anticipated discrepancy between their current and desired level of resources (i.e., when they believe that change is possible), they attempt to resolve their experience of resource scarcity *directly*.[19] The most direct way of resolving one's resource scarcity is by acquiring the scarce resource. Most instances of panic buying observed during the COVID-19 pandemic were the result of consumers attempting to reduce their current or anticipated resource scarcity. For example, most public health organizations around the world (e.g., the Center for Disease Control in the United States) recommended that consumers purchase various products to help reduce the spread of the coronavirus, such as hand sanitizer, cleaning products, and face masks. As a result, retailers faced widespread stockouts of many of these items due to heightened demand. The stockouts created scarcity, which further increased the desirability of these products. Similarly, lockdown and stay-at-home orders – as well as the uncertainty surrounding their duration and impact on access to businesses – prompted many consumers to stock up on various products (e.g., non-perishable food, toilet paper), partly due to the fear of not having enough to sustain an increased in-home consumption. In addition, although only a minority of consumers engaged in more extreme forms of panic buying,[20] seeing the news and social media flooded with images of empty store shelves and consumer stockpiling prompted more consumers to follow suit. This ironically exacerbated product shortages and, consequently, perpetuated panic buying.

Consumers can also directly resolve their resource scarcity through budgeting, planning, and prioritizing the scarce resource.[21] For instance, many consumers shifted their spending during the pandemic to include only essential purchases while cutting back on discretionary spending due to ongoing financial constraints and anticipated shortfalls. Consumers' motivation to maintain financial wealth during times of economic uncertainty can even overpower the desire to stick to a moral compass.[22] For instance, as previously discussed, hand sanitizer became increasingly scarce, and thus valued, after the pandemic began.[23] Some "entrepreneurial" consumers, whose financial situation had been negatively impacted by the pandemic, attempted to improve their financial standing by hoarding this highly sought-after product and attempting to resell it at inflated prices.[24] This sparked public outcry as consumers were selfishly prioritizing their own needs during a pandemic that affected everyone.

It is worthwhile to note that scarcity only elicits the motivation for direct resolution when consumers believe they are able to acquire the scarce resource by investing a reasonable amount of effort.[25] Relevant to the recent pandemic, as many consumers' financial resources diminished during the initial stages of COVID-19, most did what they could to maintain their financial standing by trying to increase their wealth (e.g., take on a second job) or stretch their current wealth (e.g., budget, clip coupons). These are examples of direct resolution because a singular type of resource is scarce (i.e., money), and direct efforts for increasing one's amount of money are possible.

However, consumers will not be motivated to directly resolve their resource scarcity if any of the following three conditions[26] are met: (1) If consumers believe they are unable to allocate additional effort towards acquiring or preserving the scarce resource. For instance, an individual would feel unable to save money when it seems there is nothing left to cut out of their budget, or they would feel unable to acquire money when they believe they have no time available for working longer hours or taking on a second job. (2) If consumers do not value the scarce resource. For example, a consumer would not be motivated to acquire hand sanitizer if they doubt the effectiveness of the product. (3) If consumers do not value having more of the scarce resource. For instance, consumers concerned about food waste would not want to acquire more perishable food than needed, even if it may be scarce. Marketers thus need to understand their customer base well enough to know if any of their target customer segments will be more (or less) likely to pursue direct resolution.

4. INDIRECT RESOLUTION

When the COVID-19 pandemic hit, hoarding hand sanitizer and other cleaning products, as well as tracking one's spending and staying within budget, were reasonable strategies for consumers. These were relatively straightforward actions that helped directly resolve their experienced or anticipated resource scarcity. However, as the pandemic continued, and consumers' resource levels became more uncertain, such direct strategies were insufficient for many of them. For instance, as bills began piling up and income was dwindling, no matter how much budgeting was prioritized, spending began to seem unmanageable. In such cases, consumers engaged in a different type of consumption behavior. When a consumer believes that increasing their resource levels is unlikely, they attempt to resolve their experience of resource scarcity *indirectly*. Indirect resolution involves engaging in behaviors that help the consumer feel more in control over their life (e.g., adopting a new exercise routine), even if those behaviors do not directly solve the scarcity-related problem – as consumers want to feel safe and secure in times of instability and uncertainty.[27]

For instance, many employees were faced with potential or actual salary cuts, furloughs, or job losses during the pandemic, which often strained their financial situations. Given the unprecedented unemployment rates observed during the pandemic and increased constraints put on people's time (e.g., due to homeschooling), directly resolving their resource scarcity by finding additional employment was not an option for many. Some employees turned to acquiring job-related skills (e.g., software skills, online certifications, and professional degrees) to increase their competitiveness in an increasingly tight job market as an indirect strategy for maintaining or improving their financial situation. Many consumers started taking on new hobbies that helped them feel more in control over their life – such as baking, gardening, or exercising – or even hobbies that gave them control over an alternative reality, such as playing video games (e.g., Animal Crossing: New Horizons, which was released March 20, 2020). People also increasingly engaged in soothing behaviors, such as eating comfort foods and watching nostalgic television shows. Consumers took on these activities not because they could directly resolve their experienced resource scarcity but because they helped them feel more in control over other aspects of their lives and provided them with a sense of comfort and relief. In support of this, even when product stockouts were at their peak during the pandemic, brands and products that did not allow for a sense of control (e.g., through safety, familiarity, or comfort) tended to be left on the shelves. For instance, green cleaning products tended to be shunned due to their perceived lower effectiveness and thus fears that they would not protect against the coronavirus as well.[28] Additionally, foods that did not satisfy a need for comfort or nostalgia experienced lower demand, and consumers spurned unfamiliar products, such as chocolate hummus, during the pandemic.

Importantly, there are many other ways through which consumers can satisfy their need for control. For instance, being unable to acquire or consume a scarce resource can prompt consumers to make substitutions,[29] which can help maintain their sense of control by providing them with alternative means to reach their goals. A consumer unable to purchase hand sanitizer during a pandemic, due to product stockouts and price gouging, may instead purchase cleaning products or ingredients to make homemade hand sanitizer to feel safe and protected. Many substitution behaviors have been observed during the pandemic, including both the type of product consumed (e.g., purchasing gluten-free bread when not gluten intolerant) and trying do-it-yourself activities (e.g., baking bread at home). As another example, experiencing resource scarcity can activate competitiveness and aggression.[30,31] Aggressive behaviors have been shown to help consumers feel more in control. These motivations and tendencies help explain why some consumers were aggressively fighting in stores over toilet paper at the start of the pandemic, as competitive hoarding provides a way for consumers to feel secure and in control.[32]

The *lipstick effect*, or a rise in sales of "affordable luxuries" such as lipstick during times of economic crises – which has been identified by both practitioners[33] and academics[34] – is another example of indirect resolution. Indeed, purchasing affordable luxuries allows consumers to treat themselves when their finances are limited, while also offering some sense of control or security through compensatory benefits, namely social status. This type of consumer behavior was also observed during the pandemic but took a different form than the purchase of lipstick. For instance, a mascara (or eye make-up) effect was observed because most people had to wear a face mask, moving focus from the now-covered lips to the eyes.[35] Regardless of the type of cosmetic purchased, the underlying motive remained the same: consumers desired to restore their sense of control and thus indirectly address their resource scarcity.

This shift from attempting to directly resolve one's resource scarcity to wanting to feel more in control in other areas of one's life can occur for several reasons. Consumers will attempt to indirectly resolve their resource scarcity when they cannot attribute their scarcity to a specific quantifiable resource.[36] For instance, much of the COVID-19 pandemic coverage emphasized how a variety of resources, from consumer packaged goods and personal protective equipment to time and money, were scarce. Consumers will also attempt to indirectly resolve their resource scarcity when they are aware of a specific resource that is scarce, or will be scarce in the future, but which they are unable to acquire by investing a reasonable amount of effort (e.g., hand sanitizer due to product stockouts or price gouging).[37] In each situation, consumers need to resolve this tension by increasing their sense of control through alternative ways (e.g., comfort, safety, status, self-improvement). For instance, during the pandemic, many consumers interpreted not having enough hand sanitizer as a threat to one's health. Consumers unable to acquire the product had to find alternative ways to alleviate its scarcity, such as substituting disinfecting wipes for hand sanitizer, wearing gloves, or exercising to improve their immune system.

However, consumers will not be motivated to indirectly resolve their resource scarcity if either of the following two conditions are met: (1) As with direct resolution, consumers will not be affected by resource scarcity if they do not value the resource that is scarce (e.g., when one doubts the effectiveness of hand sanitizer). (2) If consumers are not threatened by the resource scarcity.[38] For instance, an upper-class consumer may have still felt relatively well-off even if their income was reduced during the pandemic. Marketers thus again need to understand their customer base well enough to know which, if any, of their target segments will be likely to pursue indirect resolution.

5. DUAL RESOLUTION AND THE MULTIPURPOSE OF RESOURCES

Having discussed two strategies consumers often use to deal with their experiences of resource scarcity, it is important to note that their pursuit is not always clear-cut. This is because certain resources are *multipurpose*, such that the same resource can address multiple goals. Specifically, certain resources can address both the direct and indirect ways of resolving one's resource scarcity, thus resulting in *dual resolution*.[39] For example, hoarding toilet paper during a pandemic allows consumers to buffer against future resource scarcity (i.e., direct resolution), especially when the product is out of stock.

However, toilet paper also allows consumers to feel safe and in control (i.e., indirect resolution), as it is a long-lasting good that ensures some sense of normalcy in one's home during uncertain times.[40] Likewise, many other products, such as non-perishable food, baking ingredients, and cleaning products, can offer these dual benefits of directly reducing resource scarcity and indirectly improving one's sense of control.

Furthermore, how a consumer responds to resource scarcity can create a feedback loop that influences subsequent decision-making. For instance, a consumer that has been temporarily laid off due to the pandemic may reduce their expenses in order to stretch their financial resources[41,42] (i.e., direct resolution) and may also shift to indulging in highly caloric food as the pandemic drags on and the situation feels increasingly harder to change (i.e., indirect resolution).[43,44] Similarly, consumers can also oscillate between the two routes as their beliefs change over time about whether investing a reasonable amount of effort will help address their scarcity-related situation. For instance, the above consumer could attempt to find another job to address their financial constraints while they are temporarily laid off (i.e., direct resolution), but they could also respond by trying to restore their sense of control through exercising or baking (i.e., indirect resolution). Recent research has shown that consumers can even attempt to pursue both strategies simultaneously by concurrently planning to save a substantial portion of their money (i.e., direct resolution) and spending more money on nonessential items (i.e., indirect resolution). For example, consumers may attempt to balance where they allocate their income, from saving money and consuming basic goods to enjoying more indulgent, premium purchases.[45]

In addition, when consumers are unsure how to address their scarcity-related situation, they tend to rely on individual characteristics and prior experiences to determine how to respond.[46] For instance, individuals naturally vary in how optimistic they are.[47,48] People who are optimistic have positive outcome expectancies and believe that if they invest effort, good things will come to them. Conversely, people who are pessimistic have negative outcome expectancies and believe that if they invest effort, it is unlikely that good things will come to them. As a result, consumers who have more positive outcome expectancies are more likely to attempt to resolve their resource scarcity through direct resolution, as they believe investing a reasonable amount of effort will help resolve their situation (e.g., they believe they will manage to find some hand sanitizer if they search more stores). In contrast, consumers who have more negative outcomes expectancies are more likely to attempt to resolve their resource scarcity through indirect resolution, as they believe investing a reasonable amount of effort will *not* help improve their situation (e.g., they believe no amount of searching will turn up sanitizer, so they had better make it from scratch).

As another example, consumers who grew up in relatively poor environments (i.e., lower socioeconomic status during childhood) tend to have less rosy expectations about their future.[49] Conversely, consumers who grew up in relatively wealthy environments (i.e., higher socioeconomic status during childhood) tend to think that good things will often come to them. These differences are a result of the predictability, certainty, and availability of opportunities (or lack thereof) experienced during a person's major stages of life development.[50,51] As a result, life experiences during childhood shape how consumers deal with resource scarcity well into adulthood, such that adults from poorer childhoods tend to opt for indirect resolution (e.g., purchasing products that help them feel more in control), whereas adults from wealthier childhoods tend to opt for direct resolution (e.g., budgeting and saving money).[52] Outcome expectancies and childhood socioeconomic status are only two of the many individual characteristics that can shape how consumers respond to resource scarcity.

6. IMPLICATIONS FOR RETAILERS AND MARKETERS

In sum, our *Self-Regulatory Model of Resource Scarcity* offers a novel perspective on how resource scarcity shaped consumer behavior during the COVID-19 pandemic. Having discussed our model, it is important to note that it rests on the assumption that it would still be possible for consumers to acquire the scarce resource and to thus change their scarcity-related situation, even if they believe that they may be unable to do so given the amount of effort required. Therefore, we caution against the application of our model in situations in which the resource scarcity is unchangeable (e.g., water drought) or especially difficult to change (e.g., extreme poverty, homelessness). Under such situations of resource unavailability, rather than finding direct or indirect ways to resolve their resource scarcity, consumers might instead respond with behaviors such as dissociation (e.g., by devaluing the scarce resource) or escapism (e.g., binge eating or drinking).[53]

The insights generated by our model can be applied to a variety of scarcity-related contexts. Retailers and marketers can use our model to generate deeper insights from their customer data by better understanding the motives underlying their behavior. For instance, consumer stockpiling, such as hoarding toilet paper, may suggest a direct resolution, as consumers were mainly motivated to acquire current or anticipated scarce resources. However, being able to acquire and hoard resources requires a certain level of *resource slack*, or a surplus of resources. Stocking up on toilet paper, for instance, requires a surplus of money and storage space that many consumers did not have before[54] or were not willing or able to forgo after the pandemic hit. Although consumer stockpiling and hoarding were widely covered by the news and on social media during the pandemic, this helps explain why "accidental stockpiling" was actually much more common.[55] Indeed, adding a few extra products (e.g., purchasing an additional box of dry pasta) each time a consumer visited a store helped address resource scarcity both directly, by allowing consumers to acquire scarce resources while being mindful of their budget, and indirectly, by restoring their sense of control by having a consistent supply of comforting products. Retailers could thus employ data about consumers' resource slack (e.g., income level), habitual purchase quantities, and sudden deviations from these quantities to try to determine whether their customers are engaging in direct resolution (e.g., hoarding in-demand products), indirect resolution (e.g., shifts in the types of products purchased), or dual resolution (e.g., accidental stockpiling).

Better understanding the pull that resource scarcity can have on consumers can also help retailers and marketers develop more responsible policies to address consumers' responses when faced with product stockouts and shortages. For instance, when faced with exceptional demand for certain types of products (e.g., hand sanitizer) during the pandemic, many retailers attempted to dissuade consumer stockpiling and hoarding through various retail policies. One approach was to impose a steep price premium on additional items purchased after the first one (e.g., $4 for the first bottle of hand sanitizer purchased and $95 for each additional bottle).[56] While this pricing strategy may help deter consumers from overbuying scarce products, it disadvantages poorer and more vulnerable consumers, especially when wealthier consumers are willing to pay the higher price. Such pricing policies reduced the availability of certain products to consumers who needed them the most, such as poorer essential workers who needed hand sanitizer more than wealthier individuals working from home during the pandemic. Another approach used by retailers to curb consumer stockpiling and hoarding during the pandemic was to introduce purchase quantity restrictions (e.g., two bottles per customer), which was a fairer and more effective response to product stockouts and shortages, as it allowed wider access to the products while helping curb consumers' increased desire to acquire the scarce resource. Retailers should thus be mindful of the broader impact that in-store, pricing, and purchase policies may have, especially during times of widespread resource scarcity. Relatedly, knowing that some consumers are willing to employ immoral or dishonest means to acquire resources highlights the need for retailers to be more proactive in terms of policies that can help curb such behavior. For instance, one of the most effective solutions to "entrepreneurial" consumers hoarding and price gouging essential products (e.g., hand sanitizer, disinfecting wipes, N95 masks) during the pandemic was when online retailers, such as Amazon, blocked them from reselling these products on their platform.[57] Both examples illustrate how retailers may have to find counterintuitive ways to temper consumers' desire to directly resolve their resource scarcity when demand for certain products is very high. This is especially important during a pandemic, or other types of crises, when retailers or brands need to be the most socially responsible.

Furthermore, knowing that many consumers were trying to secure a scarce resource (e.g., hand sanitizer) in order to protect themselves and their loved ones from the pandemic can also help retailers and marketers design more effective communication strategies. Although altruistic messaging (e.g., protect vulnerable elderly adults) can be effective in increasing preventive behaviors such as social distancing, curbing undesirable resource-related behaviors (e.g., consumer stockpiling) may require an appeal to consumers' more self-focused motivations of control or security.[58] For instance, it may have helped curb consumer stockpiling to emphasize that hoarding preventive health products, such as hand sanitizer, was actually against their own self-interest, as the greater the overall number of infected consumers, the greater the chance they themselves would become personally infected. Several other health-related behaviors (e.g., hand washing, mask wearing, social distancing) could have been similarly encouraged by also highlighting how they helped enhance one's sense of control (e.g., faster return to normal) or security (e.g., reduced likelihood of getting sick), rather than by focusing mostly on their benefits to others' well-being.

Finally, retailers and marketers should track the long-term impact of the COVID-19 pandemic on consumer behavior as it may have enduring effects on how consumers respond to resource scarcity in the future. Indeed, as discussed previously, experiencing resource scarcity during crucial developmental times, such as during one's childhood,[59] has lasting effects later in life. In addition, repeated exposure to certain scarcity-related cues, such as time-limited promotions, can weaken their effectiveness over time.[60] It will therefore be interesting to track whether consumers respond more negatively to scarcity-related approaches used in marketing in the future, such as limited product availability, given the unprecedented product stockouts and shortages that consumers experienced during the pandemic.

7. CONCLUSION

The COVID-19 pandemic set the stage for a unique time to explore consumer behavior. Although the pandemic may have been a novel experience for many, what we know about the psychology of resource scarcity is well-established. Our *Self-Regulatory Model of Resource Scarcity* can be readily applied to this unprecedented situation to unpack how consumers approached scarcity brought on by the pandemic, either through direct, indirect, or dual resolution. Some behaviors like budgeting allowed consumers to directly improve their financial situation, whereas other behaviors, such as at-home baking, allowed them to develop skills to feel a greater sense of control in their life. Other behaviors like hoarding toilet paper were even able to simultaneously accomplish direct and indirect resolution by both acquiring a highly valued scarce resource and offering a sense of security. Understanding that consumers have these two overarching goals are important for retailers and marketers hoping to meet the needs of consumers during crucial times of resource scarcity.

Further, marketers need to design and develop plans based on a set of well-identified crisis scenarios that can be easily deployed to deal with unexpected events (e.g., natural disasters) or longer periods of shocks (e.g., the COVID-19 pandemic). Our *Self-Regulatory Model of Resource Scarcity* offers a framework that helps better understand consumers' new or changing behavioral patterns during such crises. This allows marketers to more appropriately continue serving them, for instance, by better forecasting demand for various types of goods or offering more relevant recommendations. However, consumer profiling based on our framework should be done in an ethical and socially responsible manner, as many consumers experiencing resource scarcity also tend to be more vulnerable, especially during crises. Finally, the insights gained for our framework need to be supported by all marketing functions, such as an analytic, forward-looking function that can detect potential regional (e.g., hurricane) or global (e.g., pandemic) disruptions leading to crisis situations, as well as updated operational models and supply chain logistics that can more efficiently adapt to market disruptions.

NOTES

1 Zagorsky, Jay L. (2020, March 11). *There's plenty of toilet paper – so why are people hoarding it?* The Conversation. https://theconversation.com/theres-plenty-of-toilet-paper-so-why-are-people-hoarding-it-133300.

2 Cannon, C., Goldsmith, K., & Roux, C. (2019). A self-regulatory model of resource scarcity. *Journal of Consumer Psychology, 29*(1), 104–27. https://doi.org/10.1002/jcpy.1035.
3 Cannon et al. (2019).
4 Cannon et al. (2019).
5 Hamilton, R., Mittal, C., Shah, A., Thompson, D., & Griskevicius, V. (2019). How financial constraints influence consumer behavior: An integrative framework. *Journal of Consumer Psychology, 29*(2), 285–305. https://psycnet.apa.org/doi/10.1002/jcpy.1074.
6 Hamilton, R., Thompson, D., Bone, S., Chaplin, L.N., Griskevicius, V., Goldsmith, K., Hill, R., Roedder John, D., Mittal, C., O'Guinn, T., Piff, P., Roux, C., Shah, A., & Zhu, M. (2019). The effects of scarcity on consumer decision journeys. *Journal of the Academy of Marketing Science, 47*(3), 532–50. https://doi.org/10.1007/s11747-018-0604-7.
7 Cannon et al. (2019).
8 Hamilton, Thompson, et al. (2019).
9 Hamilton, Mittal, et al. (2019).
10 Cannon et al. (2019).
11 Hamilton, Thompson, et al. (2019).
12 Cannon et al. (2019).
13 Hamilton, Mittal, et al. (2019).
14 Hamilton, Thompson, et al. (2019).
15 Cannon et al. (2019).
16 Cannon et al. (2019).
17 Hamilton, Thompson, et al. (2019).
18 Cannon et al. (2019).
19 Cannon et al. (2019).
20 Hammett, E. (2020, March 24). *"Accidental" stockpilers driving shelf shortages.* MarketingWeek. https://www.marketingweek.com/accidental-stockpilers-supermarkets-coronavirus/.
21 Fernbach, P.M., Kan, C., & Lynch, J.G. Jr. (2015). Squeezed: Coping with constraint through efficiency and prioritization. *Journal of Consumer Research, 41*(5), 1204–27. https://doi.org/10.1086/679118.
22 Cannon et al. (2019).
23 Froelich, P. (2020, March 21). *Danish store instills pricing trick to stop hand sanitizer hoarders.* New York Post. https://nypost.com/2020/03/21/danish-store-instills-pricing-trick-to-stop-hand-sanitizer-hoarders/.
24 Nicas, J. (2020, March 15). *He has 17,700 bottles of hand sanitizer and nowhere to sell them.* The New York Times. https://www.nytimes.com/2020/03/14/technology/coronavirus-purell-wipes-amazon-sellers.html.
25 Cannon et al. (2019).
26 Cannon et al. (2019).
27 Cannon et al. (2019).
28 Terlep, S. (2020, April 23). *Shoppers go green to clean because there is nothing else left.* The Wall Street Journal. https://www.wsj.com/articles/shoppers-go-green-to-clean-because-there-is-nothing-else-left-11587645952.
29 Hamilton, Thompson, et al. (2019).
30 Cannon et al. (2019).
31 Hamilton, Thompson, et al. (2019).
32 Zagorsky (2020).
33 Biron, B. (2020, August 11). *Masks may be causing a blow to lipstick sales, but eye makeup sales are booming as Americans find creative ways to use cosmetics.* Business Insider.

https://www.businessinsider.com/eye-makeup-sales-rise-lipstick-dips-due-to-mask
-wearing-2020-8.

34 Netchaeva, E., & Rees, M. (2016). Strategically stunning: The professional motivations
behind the lipstick effect. *Psychological Science, 27*(8), 1157–68. https://doi.org/10.1177
/0956797616654677.

35 Biron (2020).

36 Cannon et al. (2019).

37 Cannon et al. (2019).

38 Cannon et al. (2019).

39 Cannon et al. (2019).

40 Zagorsky. (2020).

41 Hamilton, Mittal, et al. (2019).

42 Fernbach. (2015).

43 Cannon et al. (2019).

44 Hamilton, Thompson, et al. (2019).

45 Pomerance, J., Light, N., & Williams, L.E. (2022). In these uncertain times: Fake
news amplifies the desires to save and spend in response to COVID-19. *Journal of the
Association for Consumer Research, 7*(1), 45–53. https://doi.org/10.1086/711836.

46 Cannon et al. (2019).

47 Cannon et al. (2019).

48 Mittal, C., Laran, J., & Griskevicius, V. (2021). How early-life resource scarcity influences
self-confidence and task completion judgments. *Journal of the Association for Consumer
Research, 5*(4), 404–14. https://doi.org/10.1086/709884.

49 Mittal (2021).

50 Hamilton, Mittal, et al. (2019).

51 Mittal (2021).

52 Hamilton, Mittal, et al. (2019).

53 Cannon et al. (2019).

54 Orhun, A.Y., & Palazzolo, M. (2019). Frugality is hard to afford. *Journal of Marketing
Research, 56*(1), 1–17. https://doi.org/10.1177/0022243718821660.

55 Hammett (2020).

56 Froelich (2020).

57 Nicas (2020).

58 Cannon et al. (2019).

59 Hamilton, Mittal, et al. (2019).

60 Hmurovic, J., Lamberton, C., & Goldsmith, K. (2022). Examining the efficacy of time
scarcity marketing promotions in online retail. *Journal of Marketing Research, 60*(2),
299–328. https://doi.org/10.1177/00222437221118856

CHAPTER EIGHT

Interface Design for Evolving Consumers and Retail Contexts

Tim Derksen and Kyle B. Murray

SUMMARY OF CHAPTER

The chapter provides a novel model for understanding retail success based on ease-of-use and repeated shopping experience as they elevate or attenuate consumer satisfaction. The chapter concludes with a discussion of what the future may hold for the retail-consumer interface and thoughts on how full-service retailers can compete in an increasingly self-service world.

MANAGERIAL IMPLICATIONS (GENERAL)

This chapter:

- Makes managers in retail business think about the attributes of their customer interface and the importance of creating an adequate balance between these attributes.
- Provides a thorough summary of the accumulated experiences in interface designs in retail business and highlights the accelerated innovations.

MANAGERIAL IMPLICATIONS (ORGANIZATIONAL)

- From an organizational perspective, managers must ensure that teams working on the interface design of technological systems are multidisciplinary. By multidisciplinary, we mean much more than technology experts and marketing and sales businesspeople.
- These teams must include experts in behavioral science who understand the complex behavior of customers and their experience.

MANAGERIAL IMPLICATIONS (STRATEGIC, TACTICAL, AND OPERATIONAL)

- Managers in retail must elaborate a strategy and a road map for their interface design as this is one of the most important strategic components for their business.
- From a tactical perspective, it is important to assess the value of any investment in technological innovations. Managers ought to ask themselves critical questions: What is the optimal investment in interface technologies (as a resource) compared to other investments? How should I have a balanced set of investments to enhance my business?
- From the operational perspective, managers need to understand how their customers perceive the current interface in light of the criteria elaborated in this chapter then proceed to immediate corrections, if any.

MANAGERIAL IMPLICATIONS (RISK ASSESSMENT)

- Early adoption of some interfaces could be risky as the technology readiness of the customers is not there yet.

1. INTRODUCTION: PIGGLY WIGGLY AND THE ADVENT OF SELF-SERVICE RETAIL

In 1916, a grocery store named Piggly Wiggly upended the traditional practice of retailing.[1] It was the first *self-service* grocery store in North America and likely the world. It was a pioneer in allowing consumers to browse aisles of goods and pick items for themselves. Consumers no longer had to present their lists or give their orders to a store representative. Prices were visible on individual goods, and those prices were reduced as the self-service model generated savings with lower labor costs. Checkout stands were installed so that customers could now bring their goods to clerks, and goods were sold "cash-and-carry" with payment required at the time of purchase.

Aware that consumers needed to be convinced about this new format, Clarence Saunders, the founder of Piggly Wiggly, went all out. He hired a brass band to play in the lobby, handed out flowers and balloons to children, and had a "beauty contest" in which fake judges handed out gold coins to women entering the store when it opened.[2] While the self-service aspect of the store was front and center, Saunders was a sophisticated retailer who introduced other advances in more subtle ways. Foreshadowing the future of retail, his new interface carefully considered consumer self-efficacy,[3] satisfaction, time, and convenience. As a result, the retail-consumer interface was forever changed.

In this chapter, we review the evolution of the retail-consumer interface from Piggly Wiggly to Amazon's prototype Go stores. We explain why consumers tend to choose self-service shopping and how they can become locked into interfaces that they have more experience using. We propose a novel model for understanding retail success based on ease-of-use and repeated shopping experience – both of which have the potential to elevate or attenuate consumer satisfaction. The chapter concludes with a discussion of what the future may hold for the retail-consumer interface and our thoughts on how full-service retailers can compete in an increasingly self-service world.

The Evolving Retail-Consumer Interface. For many years, retailers refined and enhanced the model that Piggly Wiggly pioneered. The next major step forward came as technology advanced and firms developed self-service interfaces that further automated the customer experience. One early example comes from the banking industry with the Automated Teller Machine (ATM). For basic banking services, ATMs allowed customers to forgo interpersonal interactions altogether. Such machines were leaders in introducing consumers to the potential of self-service technology (SST).

Self-checkout stands were another early SST with which many consumers are now familiar. Today, SST interfaces have become commonplace among grocery, hardware, and other retailers who wish to offer consumers the option of avoiding the traditional checkout process. More recently, SST has advanced to include shopping carts that can automatically scan items and automate grocery fulfillment.

In the 1990s, retail took its first steps towards the revolutionary retail-consumer interfaces made possible with the advent of e-commerce. Online shopping interfaces may give shoppers the impression of physical stores, but they offer substantially enhanced convenience via their ubiquitous accessibility and enormous selection of products.

Amazon.com, for example, started with books because the potential product selection vastly exceeded the space available in a bricks-and-mortar store, and even within a very large physical store searching for a particular title was difficult and inconvenient. Today, many retailers provide a hybrid interface to customers that offers both in-store selections and an "endless aisle" that allows consumers to browse products beyond the physical store and then make purchases for home delivery. Amazon was a leader in the early days of e-commerce interface design, and it continues to build on that innovative spirit in the design of physical stores that have no checkout stands at all. The company's Go stores offer "Just Walk Out Shopping" – an SST interface that tracks consumers as they grab goods from store shelves and then allows them to simply walk away from the store. Consumers are later charged through their Amazon accounts.

2. THE INTERFACES OF INTERMEDIARIES

E-commerce has wrought a great deal of disruption in the world of retail, but even SST is now being disrupted as new entrants move from product sales to service-based options. This includes companies such as Uber Eats, DoorDash, and InstaCart. These businesses work with existing product sellers, bringing them into a new channel for online distribution and providing the complex logistical support required to quickly deliver goods to consumers. They are changing the retail interface from one built on a direct interaction between a consumer and a company into one that is mediated by a third party. While Amazon Go allows consumers to walk into a store and walk out with their goods without any service interaction, InstaCart allows anyone to purchase goods online from a partner retailer and then delivers those goods to the consumer's door. The only interpersonal interaction (if there is one at all) is between Insta-Cart's temporary "gig" worker and the consumer.

While the retail interface initially changed slowly after Piggy Wiggly, taking more than sixty years to introduce automated and technology-driven self-service options, today innovations are being introduced much more rapidly. Technology has been a disruptive force in retailing, opening doors to new and exciting opportunities while simultaneously closing other doors forever, which has been met with resistance for a variety of reasons.

The fundamental challenge for retailers, however, has not changed. At the core, success is driven by meeting the needs and desires of the customers the business wishes to serve. For example, it will continue to be important for retailers to offer the right mix of a comfortable shopping environment, product selection, and customer engagement. Although it will not be easy for retailers to anticipate the capabilities of future SSTs or predict the limitations of the next generation of consumer interfaces, a clear trend in the ongoing stream of innovations is a push to enhance ease-of-use.

3. BALANCING USEFULNESS AND EASE-OF-USE

There has always been a segment of "do it yourself" (DIY) consumers who like to jump in and take control. An enduring characteristic of this segment is their self-efficacy – that is, their "beliefs about their capabilities to exercise control over their own level of function and over events that affect their lives."[4] Essentially, greater self-efficacy increases the probability of SST adoption.

4. SELF-EFFICACY AND SELF-SERVICE TECHNOLOGY

In the context of SST interfaces, greater ability, role clarity, and motivation all tend to increase the probability that a consumer will try a self-service technology.[5] This increased preference for trial of SSTs is related to self-efficacy. This is likely an iterative process where consumers are learning and increasing their abilities and, as a result, improving on their past performance. Role clarity should also increase with practice, as knowing what to do to exercise control of the environment is a component of elevated self-efficacy. Higher levels of self-efficacy have also been shown to reduce anxiety related to using an SST.[6] Given the importance of self-efficacy in the adoption of SST, consideration should be given to how interface design affects consumer self-efficacy.

Starting from the basics, the technology acceptance model explains that usefulness and perceived ease-of-use are at the heart of the consumer's adoption decision process.[7] Both of these factors are also likely to impact consumer self-efficacy[8] – that is, both usefulness and perceived ease-of-use will have a positive effect on consumers' perceptions of their own ability and control over their environment. For example, as an interface is more useful, it should provide the consumer with greater control over the shopping experience. Similarly, as it is easier to use, it should have a positive effect on the consumer's perceptions of their own ability to accomplish their shopping goals. When discussing technology, an early example of capitalizing on perceived ease-of-use in interface design is the computer "desktop," which was designed to be analogous to an actual desktop. In doing so, Apple created an intuitive, useful, and easy-to-use graphical user interface, which led to its successful adoption on a wide scale and, ultimately, the birth of home computing.

5. LOCK-IN AND FEATURE FATIGUE

Ease-of-use has also been shown to increase customer loyalty. Specifically, practice makes shopping with a particular interface easier, and that makes it more difficult to switch to a store that the consumer knows less well or is completely unfamiliar with.[9] This creates *lock-in*, where consumers choose not to use, or even consider using, other interfaces.[10] As a result, new interfaces that are easy to learn and easy to use can lock customers in and create powerful barriers to entry that drive competitive advantage.

In addition to ease-of-use, the technology acceptance model relies upon the usefulness of the interface.[11] Increased interface usefulness is likely to result in greater self-efficacy as consumers have increased control over their environment. For example, imagine comparing a home phone of the 1980s to a modern smartphone. While the home phone could accomplish many things – from connecting with friends to checking the weather to shopping for groceries – it was not nearly as useful as a modern smartphone. A consumer equipped with a smartphone will have far greater control over their environment, and they are likely to feel greater self-efficacy because they are more capable with this technology in hand. The more features that are added to the smartphone the more it can do and the more potentially useful it is.

However, adding additional features can also make it much more difficult to use. A traditional home phone could do less but was very easy to master compared to a modern smartphone. Thus, although consumers will want interfaces that provide as many capabilities as possible, there is likely a point where more usefulness starts to interfere with ease-of-use. Thompson et al.[12] called this "feature fatigue" and suggested that it can be difficult to balance an optimal number of features, and the corresponding increase in capabilities, with the right level of ease-of-use. As the retail-consumer interface evolves, this balance will continue to be critical to success.

Recommendations and Double Agents. One way to simplify an SST with many features is to include artificial intelligence that personalizes the experience for consumers. For example, a recommendation agent that suggests products to consumers may simplify the shopping process at an online store, making the SST both easier to use and more useful. There is also the potential for the retailer to influence consumers' preferences through the recommendation process. For example, Häubl and Murray[13] found that by focusing on particular features during the recommendation process, consumers came to see those as the key features of the product, and ultimately those features determined the choices that they made. This preference for particular features persisted for consumers into future purchase occasions. Today's voice-activated assistants – such as Apple's Siri, Amazon's Alexa, Samsung's Bixby, and Google's Assistant – are likely to be even more effective as shopping interfaces that are not only easy to use and useful but also capable of influencing consumer decision-making. In the future, such assistants are likely to become even more useful and easier to use, thus making them an increasingly powerful part of the retail-consumer interface.

However, research has also demonstrated that while consumers enjoy using and can benefit from recommendation agents, they are not comfortable with shopping interfaces that appear to have a built-in bias. If the recommendation agent seems to be focused primarily on creating value for the retailer rather than truly assisting the consumer, it runs the risk of being perceived as a "double agent" – that is, an artificial intelligence that pretends to be on the side of the consumer when it really is working to generate sales for the business. This is a fine line to walk, as research has clearly shown that consumers are more likely to buy what is recommended by an assistive agent.[14] However, if the agent loses credibility as an assistant and is instead seen as a salesperson, the consumer is unlikely to trust its advice and may stop shopping with the retailer altogether.[15] Therefore, it is essential that the evolution of the retail-consumer interface be one that continues to build consumer trust and credibility, alongside ease-of-use and usefulness.

6. THE DILEMMA OF ADOPTION VERSUS SATISFACTION

Convenience, defined as perceived time and effort or ease-of-use, plays a special role in adoption decisions when it comes to the retail-consumer interface because it can be an antecedent of other important factors, such as usefulness, trustworthiness, and satisfaction.[16] Put another way, when an interface is easy to use, it is likely to make people feel more in control and capable of using it – thus increasing self-efficacy. Similarly, when an interface feels intuitive and simple, it is also likely to be more useful and easier to use because it "just seems to work."[17] This will tend to enhance consumer satisfaction with an interface and increase consumers' usage intentions.[18]

Repetition is highly correlated with enhanced ease-of-use, such that people improve their performance over time and through practice with a particular interface.[19] This, in turn, tends to elevate self-efficacy, improving usefulness and the perceived trustworthiness of the interface. Further, when people do something repetitively, the gains made through usage continue to grow, which makes the benefit of early adoption more prevalent. With repeated use, habits tend to develop, which then further increase usage of the particular retail interface.[20] When we break down the factors of ease-of-use and repetition into a two-by-two matrix, both are necessary for widespread market adoption (Table 8.1: Adoption Matrix). Without both repeated experience and high perceived ease-of-use, a retail interface will – at best – be able to achieve adoption within niche segments.

Looking at Table 8.1, it is clear that retailers will tend to avoid interfaces characterized by low repetition and low ease-of-use. With low ease-of-use, there is a greater likelihood of increasing technology anxiety,[21] and without repetitive use, perceived usefulness is likely to decrease.[22] The high repetition, low ease-of-use quadrant is better but likely to lead to only segmented adoption. With high repetition, users will tend to increase their ability with the interface and even develop habits of use.[23] This is likely to increase self-efficacy and, to the extent that habits develop, drive continued use of the SST.[24] However, because initial ease-of-use is low, the SST will struggle to attract users and, therefore, adoption will be limited to segments of DIY consumers or other niches willing to put in the time to learn to use the interface.

If the interface is initially perceived as easy to use, then consumers will be more likely to adopt it.[25] Initial ease-of-use will increase convenience and control, reducing the time necessary for achieving the consumers' goals. For some of the early adopters, ease-of-use will be enough to convince them to try a technology, and it should contribute to higher technology readiness, even among skeptics.[26] However, ease-of-use without experience with the interface will also

Table 8.1. Adoption Matrix

	Low Repetition	High Repetition
High Ease-of-Use	Segmented Adoption (e.g., Sears catalog, Fuller Brush men, Tupperware parties)	Market Adoption (e.g., ATMs, Google Search, Mobile payments)
Low Ease-of-Use	Limited Adoption and/or Market Failure (e.g., Voice-assisted purchasing, Segway, Oculus VR)	Segmented Adoption (e.g., Computer programming, cryptocurrencies)

Source: Author

tend to lead to segmented adoption because repetition is the key to creating a loyal base of locked-in consumers. This larger market of consumers is interested in the convenience of an easy-to-use interface, but they also value familiarity and the efficiency that can be gained through experience. As mentioned above, repetitive use leads to greater self-efficacy, which further increases preference for the interface.[27] Together, ease-of-use combined with repetition will tend to drive market-wide adoption of a retail interface.

7. INTERFACE CHOICE AND CUSTOMER SATISFACTION

Prior research has demonstrated that satisfaction becomes critically important to the consumer after the initial trial and evaluation of an SST.[28] So, while adoption is the first stage of interface design, it is necessary to deliver on consumer satisfaction over the longer term. Satisfaction with the interface will depend on the technology readiness of the consumers,[29] which again relates to the ease-of-use and the repetition matrix outlined above. When the interface is easy to use, and the consumer has repeated experience with it, they are more likely to be highly satisfied.

The perceived quality of an SST is influenced by ease-of-use, performance, control, efficiency, and convenience.[30] Delivering each of those attributes is a challenge because when control or performance increases, ease-of-use and efficiency may decrease, which in turn can have a negative effect on consumer satisfaction. Consider that as number of features increases, consumers are more likely to adopt an interface because it is perceived to be more useful and capable, but they may end up being less satisfied with the interface because it is less easy to use.[31] Alternatively, an interface that is adopted because it is easy to use may end up dissatisfying consumers because it is less capable than those of competitors. Put another way, the aspects of the SST retail-consumer interface that initially led to adoption may ultimately lead to dissatisfaction.

Consumers also want the ability to choose when they use an SST and when they receive a higher level of personal service. Interpersonal service interactions have been shown to be integral to increasing future purchase intentions.[32] Offering only one option and thereby restricting consumers' choice leads to a negative response, known as psychological reactance.[33] Without the freedom to choose a preferred level of service, consumers may feel that they are being treated poorly and even see the offered interface as less useful, being less satisfied if forced to adopt an SST when they do not have the option of a higher level of service.

Further, if the technology is complex, it will demand more time from the consumer for skill acquisition. Skill acquisition can also be especially hard if consumers are anxious due to others waiting or a lack of available staff.[34] The increased cost of time, combined with time pressure, will lead to abandonment of the technology or the firm.[35] This may lead consumers to pay for time-saving services, and using an SST or having to learn the SST could decrease satisfaction.

In designing the retail interface, it is important to consider perceived ease-of-use and the consumer's level of experience or familiarity with the interface while at the same time understanding the corresponding disadvantages. It is important for retailers to keep in mind that the design features of the SST interface that initially lead to adoption may ultimately lead to dissatisfaction. For example, consumers may adopt a self-service retail interface, but then become unhappy – and discontinue use – when they experience a transaction with little or no service. This dilemma is not simple to resolve, but addressing it is essential to the successful design of retail interfaces that consumers will be both likely to adopt and repeatedly use.

8. IMPLICATIONS OF EMERGING TECHNOLOGIES FOR PRECISION RETAILING

We fully expect that the retail-consumer interface will continue to evolve with technology – including emerging SST options, such as self-checkout shopping carts or Amazon Go-type stores. Amazon, for example, has begun to sell its technology to other retailers, which will increase the repetitive interactions consumers have with the Go interface. In the future, there are opportunities that Go-style stores have yet to capitalize on. Consider, for example, what Clarence Saunders had envisioned as the future of grocery retailing: a fully robotic store that eliminated human labor costs.[36] That vision was well ahead of the technological capabilities of his time, but today it is ever closer to being a reality. Ultimately, these advances have the potential to make retail-consumer interfaces easier to use than ever before.

At the same time, without the option of human interaction and without competing visions of the future of the consumer-retail interface, psychological reactance or similar negative responses might limit adoption of Amazon's SST.[37] One possible negative response is a backlash to cashless technology. It should be noted that some consumers may be "unbanked" and only have the option to pay with cash. A simple fix is to offer in-store personal assistance to those who want it but make the automated SST the default mode of operations – in contrast to the traditional model that makes personal assistance the default and SST an option. Ensuring a competitive market for future retail SST interfaces may take time but is likely inevitable as consumer demand draws new players into the marketplace. As an analogous example, consider the effect of Tesla's success on more traditional auto manufacturers, moving the industry rapidly towards full lines of electric vehicles. Start-ups have already begun to enter the SST interface space and are developing their own models to compete with Amazon.

Other possible developments in adaptive retail interfaces include the addition of augmented (AR) or virtual realities (VR). AR in particular could enhance the endless aisle, allowing stores to keep few or no products on the physical shelves, employing automated fulfillment technologies in the back of the store while consumers add to their virtual carts in the front of the store. Using VR would go further and eliminate the physical aisle entirely. Along the same lines, wearables such as smart watches may open new avenues through which retailers can interface with consumers. Initially this may include location-based services and GPS-targeted promotions, but ultimately there is potential to use data collected by such devices to better understand customers and provide more personal, yet still automated, services, such as emotional analysis through smart speaker interactions to customize playlists and suggestions. Similar technology could create a retail-consumer interface that adapts to consumers' moods. Of course, this further highlights potential concerns around privacy and the use of data in the ongoing quest to improve the retail interface.

Although there is almost unlimited potential for the future of adaptive retail interfaces, even the emerging technologies discussed so far will need to be introduced slowly. As has been mentioned, the ease of using familiar interfaces can prevent consumers from upgrading to more useful alternatives as they begin to get locked-in. One strategy is the gradual introduction of new features to allow consumers time to develop their abilities and habitual behaviors. As self-efficacy increases, consumers are more likely to adopt new and innovative retail interfaces.

There are, of course, still opportunities for existing retail interfaces to evolve alongside emerging SST technologies. As discussed above, purchase intentions can be higher with greater interpersonal interaction, which can be enhanced with the use of SST. This will become a necessary tool in adapting to a changed retail world. These interactions will need to focus on providing consumer solutions that are credible and trustworthy. The representatives will need to demonstrate expertise and provide opportunities for experiential shopping to the consumer. This will demand elevated emotional connections and excellent communication between the representative and consumer. It will also likely require a high-touch in-store experience that is complemented by a more automated SST alternative. Many higher price-point retailers, from lululemon to Hugo Boss to Tiffany, have already adopted this strategy. In addition, it may be possible to connect SST consumer information to a consumer's social media interactions with a firm. Representatives could have an entire customer history available when a customer enters the store to make that customer feel as though they have a personal shopper.

The retail interface has come a long way since Piggly Wiggly. Some form of SST is nearly ubiquitous in today's retail-consumer interfaces. Consumers will continue to demand interfaces that are useful, easy to learn, and easy to use. Retailers will continue to innovate and compete to attract customers who become increasingly locked-in to incumbent interfaces. Finally, retailers will need to maintain their focus on consumer satisfaction. There is a risk that consumers reach a tipping point in the near future, whereby self-service simplicity makes many traditional retailers seem extraneous. This may have already happened to some as the continued growth of e-commerce upends traditional store models. We recommend that retailers with higher-service levels compete by driving superior service in-store while also offering consumers an SST alternative. In general, as consumers and retail contexts evolve, we expect interface designs will increasingly adopt a hybrid approach that combines highly automated, technology-driven interactions with an option for high-touch and human-mediated service.

NOTES

1 Eschner, K. (2017, September 6). The bizarre story of Piggly Wiggly, the first self-service grocery store. *Smithsonian Mag.* https://www.smithsonianmag.com/smart-news/bizarre-story-piggly-wiggly-first-self-service-grocery-store-180964708/.
2 Eschner (2017).
3 Defined as "the belief in one's capabilities to organize and execute the courses of action required to manage prospective situations." Bandura, A. (1991). Social cognitive theory of self-regulation. *Organizational Behavior and Human Decision Processes, 50*(2), 248–87. https://psycnet.apa.org/doi/10.1016/0749-5978(91)90022-L.
4 Bandura (1991, p. 257).
5 Meuter, M.L., Bitner, M., Ostrom, A.L., & Brown, S.W. (2005). Choosing among alternative delivery service modes: An investigation of customer trial of self-service technologies. *Journal of Marketing, 69*(2), 61–83. https://psycnet.apa.org/doi/10.1509/jmkg.69.2.61.60759
6 Gelbrich, K., & Sattler, B. (2014). Anxiety, crowding, and time pressure in public self-service technology acceptance. *Journal of Services Marketing, 28*(1), 82–94. https://doi.org/10.1108/JSM-02-2012-0051.

7   Davis, F.D., Bagozzi, R.P., & Warshaw, P.R. (1989). User acceptance of computer technology: A comparison of two theoretical models. *Management Science, 35*(8), 903–1028. https://doi.org/10.1287/mnsc.35.8.982.

8   Gelbrich & Sattler (2014).

9   Murray, K., & Häubl, G. (2007). Explaining cognitive lock-in: The role of skill-based habits of use in consumer choice. *Journal of Consumer Research, 34*(1), 77–88. https://ssrn.com/abstract=964189.

10 Murray & Häubl (2007).

11 Davis et al. (1989).

12 Thompson, D.V., Hamilton, R.W., & Rust, R.T. (2005). Feature fatigue: When product capabilities become too much of a good thing. *Journal of Marketing Research, 42*(4), 431–42. https://psycnet.apa.org/doi/10.1509/jmkr.2005.42.4.431.

13 Häubl, G., & Murray, K.B. (2003). Preference construction and persistence in digital marketplaces: The role of electronic recommendation agents. *Journal of Consumer Psychology, 13*(1–2), 75–91. https://doi.org/10.1207/S15327663JCP13-1&2_07.

14 Senecal, S., & Nantel, J. (2004). The influence of online product recommendations on consumers' online choices. *Journal of Retailing, 80*(2), 159–69. https://doi.org/10.1016/j.jretai.2004.04.001.

15 Fogg, B. (2002) *Persuasive technology: Using computers to change what we think and do.* Morgan Kaufmann Publishers.

16 Collier, J.E., & Sherrell, D.L. (2010). Examining the influence of control and convenience in a consumer self-service setting. *Journal of the Academy of Marketing Science, 38*(4), 490–509. https://psycnet.apa.org/doi/10.1007/s11747-009-0179-4.

17 Davis et al. (1989).

18 Wang, C., Harris, J., & Patterson, P. (2013). The roles of habit, self-efficacy, and satisfaction in driving continued use of self-service technologies: A longitudinal study. *Journal of Service Research, 16*(3), 400–14. https://doi.org/10.1177/1094670512473200.

19 Murray & Häubl (2007).

20 Wang et al. (2013).

21 Gelbrich & Sattler (2014).

22 Davis et al. (1989).

23 Murray & Häubl (2007).

24 Wang et al. (2013).

25 Davis et al. (1989); Collier & Sherrell (2010).

26 Wang et al. (2013).

27 Murray & Häubl (2007).

28 Wang et al. (2013).

29 Wang et al. (2013).

30 HsiuJu, R.Y. (2005). An attribute-based model of quality satisfaction for internet self-service technology. *The Services Industries Journal, 25*(5), 641–59. https://doi.org/10.1080/02642060500100833.

31 Thompson et al. (2005).

32 Lee, H.-J. (2015). Consumer-to-store employee and consumer-to-self-service technology (SST) interactions in a retail setting. *International Journal of Retail and Distribution Management, 43*(8), 676–92. https://doi.org/10.1108/IJRDM-04-2014-0049.

33 Liu, S. (2012). The impact of forced use on consumer adoption of self-service technologies. *Computers in Human Behavior, 28*(4), 1194–201. https://doi.org/10.1016/j.chb.2012.02.002.

34 Gelbrich & Sattler (2014).

35 Gelbrich & Sattler (2014).

36 Eschner (2017).

37 Liu (2012).

CHAPTER NINE

Real-Time Retail Analytics

Harpreet Singh, Olivier Rubel, and Prasad A. Naik

SUMMARY OF CHAPTER

The paper provides a practical overview of an analytics journey in retail and identifies best practices for practitioners to create a decision-oriented analytics mindset. This journey is illustrated by a case study (Planters).

MANAGERIAL IMPLICATIONS (GENERAL)
- This chapter provides a road map for an analytics journey in retail, with a set of best practices in retail analytics that retailers should consider independently of the maturity level their business has reached.
- It also provides retail managers with a set of analytical tools that can be deployed depending on the problem at stake. Retail managers must be able to revisit their road map in analytics and explore additional use cases or additional venues to be developed. They must also be able to reconsider the priorities in their road map.

MANAGERIAL IMPLICATIONS (ORGANIZATIONAL)
- Retail analytics will have a profound impact on retailers' organizational structures and workflows. Many departments that used to work independently can now collaborate thanks to blended data.

MANAGERIAL IMPLICATIONS (STRATEGIC, TACTICAL, AND OPERATIONAL)
- All levels of decisions are addressed by analytical models: Strategic, Tactical, and Operational, as shown in Table 9.4: Tools and Their Applications.
- Prescriptive analytics and optimization models address marketing decisions with a dynamic perspective.

MANAGERIAL IMPLICATIONS (RISK ASSESSMENT)
- Still, a retail manager has to assess the risks associated with investing in such analytical tools against the risk of doing nothing.

1. INTRODUCTION

On June 16, 2020, the US technology firm Google and the French retailer Carrefour announced a strategic partnership aimed at creating synergistic growth opportunities in the retail sector.[1] This partnership reveals the new Zeitgeist of the retail industry, where technology firms and retailers use analytics to create and deliver value.[2,3] For this value to materialize, retail firms must embrace transformative analytics journeys to identify new strategic orientations and gain operational efficiencies. Technological advances such as machine learning and artificial intelligence allow these businesses to monitor brand health and sales dynamics and to make decisions in real time.[4] Therefore, the role of analytics for retail firms is crucial, but it relies on their abilities to implement rapid measurement systems within their organizations. With these systems, firms can learn how marketing actions (e.g., search advertising, online display advertising, advertising on social media platforms, social media activities, TV spots, Out-Of-Home billboards) impact key performance indicators (e.g., brand awareness, consumer sentiments, market-share, sales).

Rapid measurement systems create value for retailers when analytics are used to build data-driven marketing campaigns that can be dynamically adjusted based on real-time algorithmic attribution. Big data and technology thus empower retailers to replace postmortem analyses of marketing campaigns with live campaign analyses and dynamic marketing strategies. In order to do so, retailers can use a plethora of data sources generated by different sides of the business, especially data regarding (1) sales and transactions, (2) store operations, (3) firm-controlled demand shifters, (4) supply-chain data, and (5) other exogenous environmental factors likely to influence sales.

More precisely, *sales data and transactions data* come from the different retail channels used by firms to sell to customers, such as bricks-and-mortar stores, online (web) presence, mobile channels, affiliate networks, and so on. Such data informs on what is sold, to whom, and at what time, and provide crucial information to understand customers and to identify emerging sales patterns. Retailers also combine sales and transactions data with information regarding *store operations*, in other words, "what is going on at the store level." This data will differ depending on the nature of the store: bricks-and-mortar store information includes, for example, information about product inventory, out-of-stock information, product movement and waste (in the case of perishables), rotation and tenure of retail associates, and so on. In the case of digital storefronts, store operations data include the cost of running the website, storage and sourcing information regarding distribution centers, the efficiency of fulfillment and return processes, as well as information about how shoppers interact with websites, mobile apps, and other sources of commerce (e.g., WhatsApp, WeChat, Line, etc.). *Demand shifters data* include information at the product level, as well as information about all actions the brand or the company undertakes to manage sales, such as pricing, promotional activities, online and offline marketing campaigns, and so on. *Supply-chain data* is generated from the day-to-day execution of various components in the supply chain, such as warehouses, distribution centers, and stores. Finally, retail dynamics is also related to *exogenous factors* that impact sales, such as weather patterns, structured and unstructured information about competitive activities, changes in legal environments, emerging consumer trends, exogenous shocks affecting demand (such as a pandemic), and so on.

To make the most of the data that retailers collect, managers need to ask the right questions and choose the appropriate tools to address them. The main goal of the chapter is to embed questions and answers in a retail analytics journey and to provide a practitioner's view of best practices to create a decision-oriented analytics mindset.

2.   CASE STUDY: PLANTERS

In order to best illustrate the value of data and analytics for retailers, we have created a case study based on the fictitious company Planters, modeled after real-world fast food chains.

2.1. *Sales Growth: A Tale of Two Worlds*

Historically, Planters has been offering a wide range of burger menu options targeted towards the lunch and dinner needs of its consumers. While Planters has shown significant growth in its sales and transactions over the past five years, some worrying trends are emerging, as shown in Table 9.1. More specifically, while overall sales have been growing, a deeper look at the data shows that this growth masks two opposite trends: on the one hand, there has been an increase in the average order value (AOV), but at the same time, there has been a decline in the overall number of transactions. From Planters' perspective, the question is then whether the company is experiencing a change in consumption trends, and if so, how to address it.

Table 9.1. Planter's Performance

Year	Transactions	Sales	AOV	Transaction Growth	Sales Growth	AOV Growth
2010	2,000,000	$24,514,600	$12.26			
2011	2,109,544	$25,610,926	$12.14	5.5%	4.5%	−1.0%
2012	2,258,711	$27,013,694	$11.96	7.1%	5.5%	−1.5%
2013	2,447,689	$28,722,190	$11.73	8.4%	6.3%	−1.9%
2014	2,679,897	$30,753,156	$11.48	9.5%	7.1%	−2.2%
2015	2,887,481	$33,135,285	$11.48	7.7%	7.7%	0.0%
2016	3,091,657	$35,907,582	$11.61	7.1%	8.4%	1.2%
2017	3,287,190	$39,119,254	$11.90	6.3%	8.9%	2.5%
2018	3,434,198	$42,830,432	$12.47	4.5%	9.5%	4.8%
2019	3,325,599	$47,113,475	$14.17	−3.2%	10.0%	13.6%
2020	2,993,039	$52,054,778	$17.39	−10.0%	10.5%	22.8%

2.2. A Multichannel Firm

Like many players in this industry,[5,6] Planters started as a dine-in business only, focusing on selling its products to retail customers only through its restaurants. However, around 2017 when platforms[7] like DoorDash started to drive home-delivery of food items, including burgers, they quickly established and scaled up their own delivery practice. The company thus became a multichannel retailer.[8] As a result, while in 2010, 90 per cent of their sales were realized on-premises (Planters' physical stores, i.e., restaurants), in 2020, the share of this channel in Planters's overall sales dropped to 45 per cent. In contrast, while in 2010, Planters did not generate any sales from delivery channels, the combined shares of Uber Eats, DoorDash, and Planters' own delivery channel accounted for 34 per cent of their sales, as shown in Table 9.2.

Further analysis also revealed a link between increased sales at Uber Eats and DoorDash with higher AOVs: while the AOV was on average $17.39 in 2020 across channels, AOVs for Uber Eats and DoorDash were at $21.72 and $20.81, respectively.

Because of this correlation, executives at Planters believed that they were witnessing longer-term consumer trends around AOVs and the volume of transactions. In particular, Planters's management

Table 9.2. Multichannel Sales

Year	Uber Eats	Doordash	Own Delivery	Takeaway	Dine-In
2010	0%	0%	0%	10%	90%
2011	0%	0%	0%	12%	88%
2012	0%	0%	0%	14%	86%
2013	0%	0%	0%	14%	86%
2014	0%	0%	0%	15%	85%
2015	0%	0%	0%	16%	84%
2016	0%	0%	0%	17%	83%
2017	0%	1%	5%	18%	76%
2018	0%	3%	30%	20%	47%
2019	5%	4%	25%	21%	45%
2020	8%	6%	20%	22%	45%

Table 9.3. AOV across Channels in 2020

	Uber Eats	Doordash	Own Delivery	Takeaway	Dine-In
AOV	$21.72	$20.81	$12.10	$18.15	$21.02

worried about the decline in transactions, since negative transaction growth has usually been a leading indicator of future sale declines overall. Therefore, while sales growth is a positive indicator, Planters' leadership also believed that they were witnessing a shrinkage in their consumer base, which required a deeper analysis. The analysis needed by Planters was very similar to the type of analysis needed by other retailers trying to understand sales dynamics. Next, we present a simple but effective framework to understand how to use data to provide insights to address the challenges faced by Planters.

3. RETAIL ANALYTICS JOURNEY

This framework is guided by three questions regarding data, or more precisely, around how to use data to improve retail decision-making. First, what is interesting in my data? Where do I pay attention?

Such questions can be answered with *exploratory data analytics*. They are crucial as they will determine further analyses. Second, what are the significant relationships? What are the key variables? The strategic importance of such questions comes from the fact that the ultimate value of data is to help managers make better decisions. Thus, having a clear view of the causal relationships that drive business outcomes is important to decide which marketing levers (e.g., advertising vs. promo) to activate. Such questions usually require the use of *advanced data analytics* (i.e., causal inference) to identify relationships between variables. The goal of such analytics is to learn, for example, what the incremental sales lift would be if the marketing budget were increased.

Finally, based on the insights learned from the first two stages, one should ask what the desirable course of action should be moving forward, which corresponds to the simple question of "what should I do?" In the case of advertising, for example, what should be the "optimal" advertising budget, and how should I allocate it across different media? Such questions are best addressed with *prescriptive analytics*[9,10,11]

These three questions – (i) What is interesting in my data? (ii) What are the relationships between my actions and my key performance indicators? and (iii) How do I make better decisions? – define the backbone of the analytics journey that retail firms should put in place. It is important to recognize that each of these questions can be addressed with different tools, as illustrated in the table below.

3.1. Analyzing Planters's Problem

The first step in analyzing Planters's problem is to have a representation of sales. Sales can be decomposed into three primary drivers: number of consumers (i.e., N), purchase frequency (i.e., F) , and order size (AOV),[12] such that:

Sales = Number of Customers × Purchase Frequency × AOV,

or written in a more compact form:

Sales = N × F × AOV.

Table 9.4. Tools and Their Applications

Techniques	Retail Applications
Exploratory Data Analytics: What is interesting in my data? Where do I pay attention?	
Clustering (e.g., k-mean)	How to group – customers, stores, products (Customer Segmentation, Market Basket, Product Affinities)
Fourier Transforms | Wavelet Transforms	Temporal-frequency analysis (seasonality analysis, extraction of sales patterns, frequency-based clustering, denoising of sales patterns, evaluate day of the week effects)
Data Distribution: Gaussian Mixture Models (GMM), Negative Binomial Distributions, Beta Distributions	GMM – Modality in data NBD – Across store behavior of the same SKUs, Beta Distributions (customer-SKU segmentation, sales forecasting across stores)
Advanced Data Analytics: What are the significant relationships?	
Random Forests (Decision Trees)	Black-box estimation: understanding variable influence of a larger set of variables (evaluating multimedia advertising campaigns)
Kalman Filtering	Estimating dynamic sales processes with hidden states (marketing attribution, measurement of brand equity)
Prescriptive Analytics: What should be the decisions?	
Static Optimization	Optimizing store location, self-space allocation, price promotion
Dynamic Optimization	Setting advertising budget, media allocation, mark-down pricing

This representation is a good start as it helps identify important drivers of sales growth. This representation, however, is missing the fact that sales are likely to come from different customer segments, that is, customers are likely to be different, with different purchase frequencies and different order sizes. Hence, to understand sales dynamics, one needs to account for the existence of these segments, and to do so, we rewrite the first equation as

$$Sales = \underbrace{N_1 \times F_1 \times AOV_1}_{Sales\ from\ Segment\ 1} + \underbrace{N_2 \times F_2 \times AOV_2}_{Sales\ from\ Segment\ 2} + \cdots + \underbrace{N_K \times F_K \times AOV_K}_{Sales\ from\ Segment\ K},$$

or written in a more compact way

$$Sales = \sum_{i=1}^{K} N_i \times F_i \times AOV_i,$$

where $i = \{1, 2, \ldots, K\}$ is used to designate segment 1 to K.

The next step in analyzing Planters's problem is to understand how sales are generated by different customer groups, or segments, that have different behaviors and propensities to buy Planters's products.

3.2. Segmentation Part 1

The data required to conduct segment-level analysis is typically a form of longitudinal customer data: a single row of data per customer that can provide all of their purchase behavior history. This data can come from multiple sources, not only within the firm (e.g., CRM data, transactions data, online clickstream data, store operations data) but also from third-party data sources (for instance, regarding exogenous demand shifters like competitors' actions). For example, there are many panel data providers like Visa that can provide purchase history data. Such data sets typically contain fields such as Customer ID that can be used to link a particular customer's transactions, Transaction ID that identifies a specific transaction associated with a purchase event, and Transaction Header, which represents aggregated information for a transaction. Typically, this includes date-time of order, order value, discounts or coupons, and sales taxes applied to the order. Finally, Transaction Detail, which represents line-item level information for a given order, includes the details of each item purchased, the item selling price, and item quantity.

This data is not directly useful for understanding customer segments but can be transformed into variables reflective of a customer's purchase behavior. While purchase behavior for a customer is specific to a given retail sector, there are some common variables that can be extracted from transaction data irrespective of the industry. These include, for example, purchase frequency, days between orders, and average order values.

3.2.1. FREQUENCY OF PURCHASE

Frequency of purchase metrics provide insight into the average frequency associated with a particular customer's product purchase. This frequency may range from 1–2 times per week (e.g., grocery) to 45–60 days (e.g., restaurants). In some industries, such as the automotive industry, frequency of purchase may be low (once every few years). Compared to durable goods, retail environments move at a faster pace and have a higher frequency of purchase. Typically, frequency of purchase is defined as the number of purchase events by a customer in a year/fifty-two weeks. By doing so, we can better generalize a customer's purchase behavior. In the case of Planters, as in other firms, the choice of the appropriate window for analysis is not uniform, and different time frames will reveal different patterns.

The figures above suggest, for example, that most customers typically purchase products from Planters once or twice in a given two-week period. However, when this timeframe is extended to 30 days, an average consumer would consume about 2.6 times in a 30-day period, i.e., once every 11 days. These trends tend to flatten out when considering a 365-day frequency. At 365 days, there is a much flatter distribution of people across consumption events. This example shows the distribution of the number of purchases for a two-week, 30-day and 365-day timeframe. However, an analyst can experiment with different windows to establish the most appropriate window that provides the best differentiation among different types of customer purchase behavior. A good heuristic to use is to capture at least two to three purchase cycles.

3.2.2. DAYS BETWEEN ORDERS AND AGE

Days between orders is another metric that represents the average duration between a customer's orders. Another related metric is the average customer tenure with the brand. These metrics should be contrasted with average frequency to understand the proximity of a customer's ordering behavior.

For Planters, the average number of days between transactions is 25 days, which is quite close to the number derived from the average

Figure 9.1. Purchase Frequencies at Planters

Average Frequency: 1.4

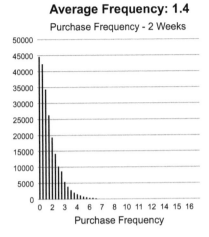

Average Frequency: 2.6

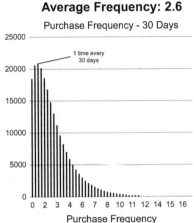

Average Frequency: 13.7

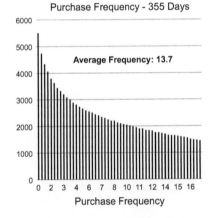

365-day frequency of 13.7 times/year (26 days between orders). However, there is a wide distribution of days between transactions around the mean value. Being able to segment customers based on the days between orders allows for better discrimination between different types of customers and hence better development of more targeted marketing campaigns.[13] Similarly, the average customer age is about ten months. However, the average tenure follows a multi-modal distribution with a mode of one month and thirteen months, respectively. Again, these insights point to the need to segment customers to craft appropriate strategies for each segment.

Figure 9.2. Days between Transaction and Customer Age

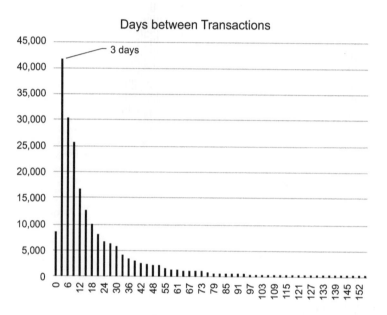

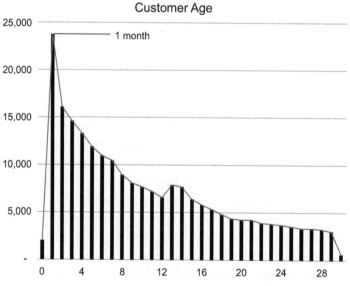

Figure 9.3. Average Order Value for Different Windows

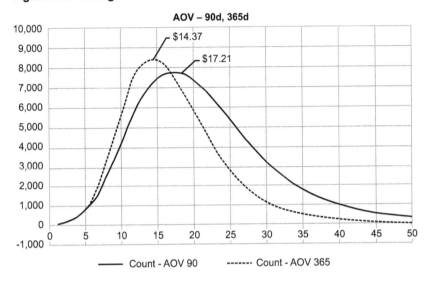

3.2.3. *AVERAGE ORDER VALUE*

Finally, data regarding AOVs provide insights regarding the typical order size for a given customer segment. This helps the retailer determine customers' values and hence the investments that the retailer needs to make in acquiring or retaining customers. For Planters, the AOV for the past 365 days has been $17.40. However, the AOV for the past 90 days has increased significantly compared to a 365-day average. This represents a *significant* shift towards high-value transactions.

While an increase in high-value transactions is positive, it is important to recognize that a retailer needs to acquire both high-value and low-value customers since low-value customers tend to be very high in number and thus contribute significantly to overall revenue.

3.3. *Building Segments*

Once the consumer's purchase behavior features have been generated, consumers can be segmented (or grouped) into distinct clusters. There are multiple clustering algorithms that can be used for segmentation, including K-Means, Gaussian Mixture Models, Agglomerative Clustering, and many other methods. While each algorithm has its own nuances, practical segmentation of the customer does not really depend significantly on the type of mathematics used in such clustering schemes.

The features to be used for segmentation are based on the objectives of segmentation. In its simplest form, segmentation can be done organically by segmenting on all available features. However, this comes with the challenges inherent with the dimensionality of data, as well as with the inability to really understand how the algorithm segmented the way it did. A better way to segment, from a practical perspective, would be to establish an objective and corresponding features that are directly relevant to the segmentation objective. In our case study, the segmentation objective is to cluster consumers on their purchase behaviors with the goal of increasing both the overall volume of transactions, as well as their frequencies. Hence the segmentation approach should be focused on using the least possible number of features required to establish transaction characteristics.

For Planters, the following steps were followed to identify the appropriate features for segmentation.

1. Partition data on consumers based on their 30-day purchase frequency. Based on these partitions, consumers are then classified into multiple classes.
2. Use a variable influence algorithm to identify the purchase behavior variables that best predict a consumer's frequency classification established in step 1. This provides an initial list of variables that can be used for segmentation.
   - For Planters, we used a random forest algorithm to establish variable influence. This algorithm is an ensemble of decision trees, which works well with relatively uncorrelated variables. This algorithm is computationally efficient and reliable for establishing variable influence. We did not use consumer demographic data, including age, household income, gender, location, etc., for segmentation. These variables help cluster consumers, but the resulting

segments do not reflect enough differentiation in purchase behavior.
3. Establish consumer clusters based on the features identified in step 2.

Once the clusters were obtained, these segments were then profiled based on their key characteristics – Sales, Transactions, AOV, Frequency, and Recency. These characteristics can also include additional attributes like age, gender, household income, education, trade area, etc. A segment can be defined further by comparing segment-level attributes with overall customer population attributes.

For Planters this analysis was conducted on purchase behavior characteristics, typical promotions used by such consumers, and the marketing channels associated with converting these consumers. The following table provides a summary of the segments identified as of January 1, 2021.

The next step was to label these segments based on their purchase behavior characteristics and help establish relevant targeting strategies for each of the segments. By creating these relatively exclusive groups, the retailer can reason about these segments independently, as illustrated in the visualization of segments provided in Figure 9.4.

In this figure, "Fill Leaky Bucket" segments contribute the most to transactions. These segments correspond to an annual frequency of about "twelve": in other words, consumers in these segments would consume about once a month at Planters. These consumers tend to be new consumers and help manage customer churn. Hence, we named them "Fill Leaky Bucket." "Maintain" segments contribute significantly to the total volume of transactions but tend to have lower AOV. Planters simply needs to maintain these segments as this is a source of new consumers that can be developed into loyal consumers in the future. Finally, "Build a Relationship" segments correspond to customers that have been cultivated by Planters through customer loyalty programs and through brand-building efforts. These customers are high frequency customers who order two to four times a month and have a long-term relationship with the brand. In dynamic markets, it is also important to recognize that

Table 9.5. Segments at Planters

Segment Name	Orders	Sales	AOV	Freq**	Customers (#)	DBO*	Recency
Value Seekers	814,488	11,533,474	$14.16	12.3	66,057	25	12
New, High AOV	737,240	14,783,151	$20.05	10.6	69,508	29	11
New, Low AOV	422,864	3,808,755	$9.01	12.1	34,833	25	21
Family/Group Buys	186,968	6,057,997	$32.40	10.0	18,635	31	25
Need Attention	159,601	2,518,875	$15.78	26.3	6,076	11	17
Promising	155,406	2,823,456	$18.17	20.2	7,692	16	20
Potential Loyalists	152,891	3,092,420	$20.23	27.3	5,596	12	18
Slipping	130,964	2,637,134	$20.14	25.4	5,156	12	18
Loyalists	123,876	2,657,122	$21.45	42.1	2,939	7	16
Champions	108,741	2,142,393	$19.70	55.0	1,978	5	16
All	**2,993,039**	**52,054,777**	**$17.40**	**13.7**	**218,470**	**25**	**15**

*DBO means days between orders
**Freq implies a 365-day frequency

Figure 9.4. Segments at Planters

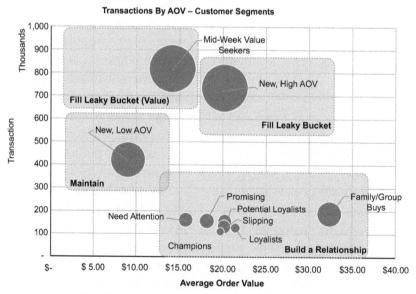

Size of bubbles represents the # of customers in the segment

Figure 9.5. Customers Change over Time

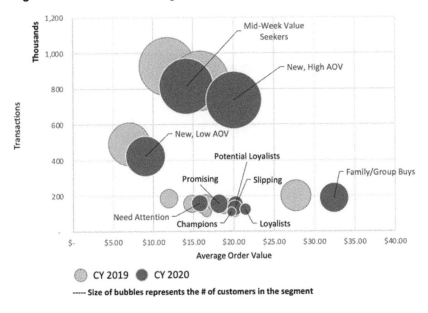

CY 2019 CY 2020

----- Size of bubbles represents the # of customers in the segment

customers change over time and as a result, segmentation cannot be a static exercise, as illustrated in Figure 9.5 below.

Additional analysis about the evolution of customer segments, provided in Table 9.6, shows more precisely which consumer segments contribute to the overall decline in transaction volume. More specifically, the "Mid-Week Value Seekers," "New Customers/High AOV," and "New Customers/Low AOV" segments have all seen significant transaction declines in 2020 as compared to 2019. Most segments with higher AOVs and higher frequency of transactions have maintained transactions year over year.

Given the importance of the top three clusters, we dived deeper into weekly trends for these clusters. As a result, we obtained the following insights, which are summarized in Figure 9.6. First, we learned that the AOV metrics for all three main segments seems to follow an increasing trend through the year. However, at the same time, weekly transactions for all three segments follow declining trends, which is even more pronounced for the New, High AOV segment in comparison to other segments.

Table 9.6. Evolution of Segments between 2019 and 2020

Segment Name	Sales	Δ	Orders	Δ	AOV	Δ	Freq**	Δ	Customers	Δ
Mid-Week Value Seekers	11,533,474	6%	814,488	-12%	$14.16	21%	12.3	-7%	66,057	-5%
New, High AOV	14,783,151	10%	737,240	-13%	$20.05	26%	10.6	-8%	69,508	-5%
New, Low AOV	3,808,755	10%	422,864	-14%	$9.01	28%	12.1	-6%	34,833	-8%
Family/Group Buys	6,057,997	10%	186,968	-6%	$32.40	17%	10.0	-1%	18,635	-5%
Need Attention	2,518,875	14%	159,601	-14%	$15.78	32%	26.3	0%	6,076	-14%
Promising	2,823,456	13%	155,406	2%	$18.17	11%	20.2	0%	7,692	2%
Potential Loyalists	3,092,420	14%	152,891	5%	$20.23	8%	27.3	0%	5,596	5%
Slipping	2,637,134	14%	130,964	-16%	$20.14	36%	25.4	0%	5,156	-16%
Loyalists	2,657,122	16%	123,876	8%	$21.45	7%	42.1	0%	2,939	8%
Champions	2,142,393	18%	108,741	-1%	$19.70	19%	55.0	0%	1,978	-1%
All	**52,054,777**	**10%**	**2,993,039**	**-10%**	**$17.40**	**23%**	**13.7**	**-5%**	**218,470**	**-5%**

Figure 9.6. Metrics Evolve over Time

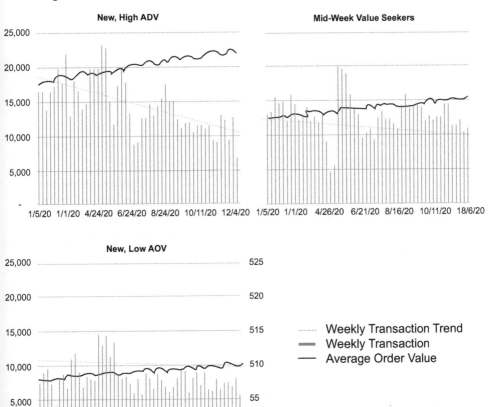

Based on these insights, the most pressing issue is to gain a better understanding of the role of marketing in driving sales growth.

3.4. *Marketing Dynamics*

Several time-series models are available to conduct such analyses. In order to build such a time-series model to evaluate the temporal trends of customer segments, we need to have some hypotheses regarding sales dynamics. For instance, it is reasonable to assume, based on past academic research and past experience, that marketing and promotional actions have both short-term and long-term effects on sales, that is, TV advertising in a given week will impact sales not only today but also in subsequent weeks.[14] Moreover, it is likely that marketing and promotional actions have time-varying effects, that is, the effect of today's search advertising expenditures on today's sales can be different from the effect of tomorrow's search advertising expenditures on tomorrow's sales.[15] Finally, demand is seasonal, which means that ignoring seasonal demand shifters can lead to erroneous evaluations of marketing campaigns.

Given these assumptions and the dynamic nature of sales, we use a state-space modeling approach known as Kalman filtering to establish the relationship between the volume of transactions for a given segment and the retailer's marketing and promotional activities.[16] The Kalman filter, which was originally designed to land the first astronauts on the moon, is a powerful algorithm that takes into account the "recursive" nature of the data generating process,[17] that is, today's sales are not only a function of today's marketing activities, but also of yesterday's sales, as described in the equation below:

$$Sales_t = \beta_t \times Marketing\ Actions_t + \lambda_t \times Sales_{t-1} + Errors,$$

where the subscript t corresponds to the temporal unit of analysis (e.g., a week in our case), β_t corresponds to the time-varying effectiveness of marketing actions taken in week t, while λ_t captures the carry-over effect in week t of sales realized in the previous week $(t - 1)$. Finally, errors capture all the other random factors affecting sales. As a result, one can rewrite the sales dynamics as a combination of "baseline sales", that is, $\lambda_t \times Sales_{t-1}$, and the incremental effect of marketing activities in a given week, that is, $\beta_t \times Marketing\ Actions_t$.

For Planters, this analysis was conducted for each of the segments that needed to be studied. The Planters team had a hypothesis that TV helped them generate brand awareness, and Paid Search helped drives conversions. Hence a significant portion of their total marketing budget is spent on TV. In addition to paid media (e.g., online display advertising, online video advertising, advertising on social media platforms), Planters spends a significant amount of budget on running CRM promotions, as illustrated in Table 9.7 below.

Table 9.7. Marketing Expenditures for Planters in 2020

	Impressions/Clicks	Spend	Average CPM/CPC	# of Weeks
Paid Search	51,717	$172,238	$3.33	50
Online Display	12,964,320	$21,574	$1.66	24
OLV	22,170,160	$167,198	$7.54	47
Social	17,149,144	$42,970	$2.51	32
TV	105,192,854	$1,198,345	$11.39	20
CRM Promotions	2,916,340	$5,913,848	$5.03	48
TOTAL		**$7,516,173**		

Based on this data, we analyzed the dynamics of transactions for the Mid-Week Value Seekers customer segment, based on the assumption that the volume of transactions in this segment in a given week is a function of past transactions as well as current marketing actions, such that

– *Transactions ~ function (Transactions Lag, Paid Search Clicks, OLA Impressions, OLV Impressions, Social Impressions, CRM Promotions, TV Impressions, Aggregator Index),*

where the aggregator index is an index variable of all aggregator driven transactions, which provides a signal of aggregator activity. We note that "aggregators ... [offer] access to multiple restaurants through a single online portal"[18] (e.g., Uber Eats), and the aggregator index captures the relative importance of the food aggregators to the Planters business over time. The results of the statistical analysis allow us to then quantify the contribution of each marketing instrument to the overall transaction volume above and beyond the baseline sales levels as shown in Table 9.8 below.

The following insights emerge from this table. First, marketing activities contribute to 39 per cent of overall sales, compared to 13 per cent for aggregators and 48 per cent for the baseline. Thus, marketing matters. However, the second insight that we obtain is that Planters is not getting a good return on investment from either TV or CRM promotions, compared to other instruments. They are over-leveraged on the use of promotions especially given that CRM promotions spend is effectively almost half of their overall sales from

Table 9.8. Marketing Attribution in a Retail Setting

	% Sales	Sales	ROAS	Spend
Baseline	48%	$5,497,660		
Aggregators	13%	$1,514,822		
CRM Promotions	3%	$3,780,893	$0.6	$5,913,848
TV	5%	$570,468	$0.5	$1,198,345
Paid Search	7%	$798,584	$4.6	$ 172,238
Online Display	4%	$470,672	$21.8	$21,574
OLV	10%	$1,117,816	$6.7	$167,198
Social	10%	$1,114,327	$25.9	$42,970

this customer segment. The third insight then pertains to how Planters should reallocate resources. In particular, to drive transaction growth for this segment, Planters should be reducing the level of promotions they are providing to customers, and they should focus on increasing the use of paid social and online display channels in order to improve their ROIs on these instruments, but most importantly to increase transactions for this specific segment.

4. CONCLUSION

The value of analytics for retailers comes from their ability to learn useful insights from data. We argue that to do so, managers need to ask three questions: (1) What is in my data? (2) What are the interesting relationships? (3) How do I make marketing decisions that drive profitable growth? To illustrate these three questions, we used a case study. We first performed some exploratory data analysis to identify emerging trends – while sales are increasing overall, the volume of transactions has been decreasing. We learned, after segmenting the data, that this decrease in transactions is driven by specific segments. Next, using a dynamic sales response model, we evaluated the effect of marketing on transactions for a given segment. As a result, we learned that to increase sales and obtain better ROIs for its marketing investments, Planters should reallocate part of its marketing budget towards paid social advertising and online display advertising. These results comport with the increasing importance of online delivery channels for Planters.

We want to close this chapter by providing a few words of caution with respect to the risk of cascading decision errors, confirmation bias in model building, and "p-hacking." First, as described in this chapter, the retail analytics process requires synergies between different levels of analyses that build on each other. For instance, in our case, the estimation of the dynamic sales response function hinges on how we derived segments, which were themselves built on our exploratory data analysis.

As a result, a risk of *cascading errors* can emerge. For example, erroneous or biased identification of sales patterns will lead to incorrect estimation of causal effects and therefore poor managerial decisions. Second, there is a *risk of confirmation bias* when conducting model building. Managers or analysts probably tend to overlook emerging patterns that contradict their current assumptions or "views" of the world and instead favor results that confirm what they initially believe. Therefore, it is important to be aware of such biases in order to maximize the value of analytics in retail environments. Finally, there also exists an *agency risk* between those conducting analyses, those implementing the recommendations, and those who will have to justify performance to stakeholders. This issue is heightened not only by time constraints in senior leadership to carefully digest results from analytics, but also by the fact that senior managers might have an understanding of analytics limited to the concepts such as p-values and R^2. In conclusion, while we firmly believe that analytics will deliver new growth opportunities to retailers, we also believe that it is important to be knowledgeable about the possible risks that come with big data.

NOTES

1 Vidalon, D. (2020, June 16). Carrefour, Google to launch voice grocery shopping service in France. Reuters. https://www.reuters.com/article/us-carrefour -google/carrefour-google-to-launch-voice-grocery-shopping-service-in-france -idUSKBN23N1RC.
2 Padmanabhan, V.P., & Lecossois D. (2018, March 15). *Where Amazon is headed with Whole Foods*. INSEAD Blog. https://knowledge.insead.edu/blog/insead-blog /where-amazon-is-headed-with- whole-foods-8601.

3 Padmanabhan, V.P. (2019, March 4). *Three cornerstones of global retail innovation.* INSEAD Blog. https://knowledge.insead.edu/marketing/three-cornerstones -global-retail-innovation

4 Guha, A., Grewal, D., Kopalle, P.K., Haenlein, M., Scheinder, M.J., Jung, H., Moustafa, R., Hedge, D.R., & Hawkins, G. (2021). How artificial intelligence will affect the future of retailing. *Journal of Retailing, 97*(1), 28–41. https://doi.org /10.1016/j.jretai.2021.01.005.

5 Bhargava, H.K., Rubel, O., Altman, E.J., Arora, R., Boehnke, J., Daniels, K., Derdenger, T., Kirschner, B., LaFramboise, D., Loupos, P., Parker, G., & Pattabhiramaiah, A. (2020). Platform data strategy. *Marketing Letters, 31,* 323–34. https://doi.org/10.1007/s11002 -020-09539-3.

6 Neslin, S.A., & Shankar, V. (2009). Key issues in multichannel customer management: Current knowledge and future directions. *Journal of Interactive Marketing, 23,* 70–81. https://ssrn.com/abstract=2061792.

7 Bhargava et. al. (2020).

8 Neslin & Shankar (2009).

9 Shankar, V. (2008). Strategic allocation of marketing resources: Methods and managerial insights. In R. Kerin and R. O'Regan (Eds.), *Marketing Mix Decisions: New Perspectives and Practices.* American Marketing Association.

10 Cohen, M.C., Leung, N.H.Z., Panchamgam, K., Perakis, G., & Smith, A. (2017). The impact of linear optimization on promotion planning. *Operations Research, 65*(2), 446–68. https://doi.org/10.1287/opre.2016.1573.

11 Mantrala, M., & Kanuri, V.K. (2018). Marketing optimization methods. In N. Mizik & D.M. Hansens (Eds.), *Handbook of Marketing Analytics* (pp. 324–70). Edward Elgar Publishing.

12 Store count is an important variable that has a bearing on sales. However, given the significant role of ecommerce, we are considering number of consumers as a proxy of offline store and online commerce reach.

13 Pan, X., Ratchford, B.T., & Shankar, V. (2001). Why aren't the prices of the same item the same at me.com and you.com?: Drivers of price dispersion among e-tailers. University of Maryland Department of Marketing. https://dx.doi.org/10.2139 /ssrn.328820.

14 Rubel, O., Naik, P.A., & Srinivasan, S. (2011). Optimal advertising when envisioning a product-harm crisis. *Marketing Science, 30*(6), 1048–65. https://www.jstor.org /stable/41408417.

15 Kolsarici, C., & Vakratsas, D. (2015). Correcting for misspecification in parameter dynamics to improve forecast accuracy with adaptively estimated models. *Management Science, 61*(10), 2495–513. https://doi.org/10.1287/mnsc.2014.2027.

16 Naik, P. (2015). Marketing dynamics: A primer on estimation and control. *Foundations and Trends in Marketing, 9*(3), 175–266. http://dx.doi.org/10.1561/1700000031.

17 Rubel, O., & Naik, P. (2017). Robust dynamic estimation. *Marketing Science, 36*(3), 453–67. https://doi.org/10.1287/mksc.2016.1010.

18 Hirschberg, C., Rajko, A., Schumacher, T., & Wrulich, M. (2016, November 9). *The charging market for food delivery.* McKinsey. https://www.mckinsey.com/industries /technology-media-and-telecommunications/our-insights/the-changing-market -for-food-delivery#.

PART THREE

Data Analytics and Machine Learning for Retail Design and Strategy

CHAPTER TEN

The Promotion Planning Optimization Problem with Bounded Memory Demand Models

Tamar Cohen-Hillel and Georgia Perakis

SUMMARY OF CHAPTER

This chapter reviews the most recent advances in tools and methodologies to tackle the problem of promotion planning optimization with bounded memory demand models.

MANAGERIAL IMPLICATIONS (GENERAL)

- This chapter provides retail managers with a highly valuable solution for optimizing the planning of promotion of the items they are selling. The solution takes into consideration the negative indirect effect of promotions on future sales but also many business rules that retailers consider as constraints when they apply promotions on items.
- All marketing managers in the retail industry are confronted with this problem and need a solution. The proposed computational models are extremely beneficial when augmenting the experience and intuition of marketing people. They might run multiple simulations and iterations of the optimization model with different sets of business rules and constraints to reach a final solution that meets their expectations.

MANAGERIAL IMPLICATIONS (ORGANIZATIONAL)

- The implementation and operationalization of a promotion planning optimization process requires cooperation between different departments inside the retail company: marketing, sales, finance, procurement, and logistics, including inventory, transportation, and IT.
- This also requires the integration of the various IT systems supporting different stakeholders in the retail company.
- The inter-department cooperation could be implemented in the form of a multidisciplinary center of excellence inside the retail company, grouping representatives of the main stakeholders, with the responsibility of designing, developing, deploying, and monitoring such types of advanced analytics and optimization models.

MANAGERIAL IMPLICATIONS (STRATEGIC, TACTICAL, AND OPERATIONAL)

- From a strategic perspective, the promotion planning optimization project must be mapped to other projects in the context of the strategic plan. The road map of projects must take into consideration the dependency between projects, the availability of data, and the complexity of integration with the different IT systems in place.
- From a tactical perspective the implementation of such a project requires the provisioning of a data and advanced analytics platform as well as sourcing the required skills. Luckily, these platforms are becoming affordable with all major cloud providers.
- The operationalization of this optimization will differ if the supermarket is a bricks-and-mortar store or an e-commerce business. For bricks-and-mortar businesses, the physical location (heat map of the store) of the item in promotion is an essential complementary action. For e-commerce, the integration rules with the existing recommender system are critical.
- From the operational point of view, it might be interesting to have different optimization criteria based on sales-rate, revenue, or margin.

> **MANAGERIAL IMPLICATIONS (RISK ASSESSMENT)**
> - Implementing promotion planning optimization problems can be described as a limited risk project. The only risk is that the benefits are in the low end while the cost to implement and operationalize the solution are high for a low margin retail business. To mitigate the risk, managers could proceed with a proof-of-concept project or a proof-of-value project before proceeding with a larger implementation.
> - Other risks arise from the fact that noise signals (other factors that drive demand like weather, social media trends, events, competition, economics, and pandemics, etc.) are so high that they might hide the benefits associated with the optimized solution.
> - The assumptions used might not reflect the complexity of the operation of a retail business.

1. INTRODUCTION

Sales promotions is a marketing strategy where products are promoted using short-term price reductions to stimulate demand and increase sales. Sales promotions are extremely common in the retail industry. This practice of temporary price reduction to boost sales is one of the most commonly used promotion tactics. In this chapter, we focus on the planning process for these temporary price reductions.

When undertaking a sales promotion, retailers must consider both the direct and indirect effects of price promotions on consumers, and consequently on demand. The direct effect of a price promotion includes the increase in sales due to the price decrease. Nonetheless, price promotions can have indirect effects due to consumers' behavior. One such effect is anchoring on past prices.

When consumers are anchoring on past prices, they are either consciously or subconsciously comparing the current price of an item to its previous prices. When the current price is lower than past prices, consumers are much more likely to purchase the item. However, while having a positive impact on current sales, price promotions may have a negative effect on future sales. This negative effect is referred to as the post-promotion dip or the post-promotion slow-down. The set of past prices that impact the demand is referred to as the anchoring set, and it is crucial for retailers to be able to identify it. In this chapter, we focus on some of the most commonly used sets of anchoring prices, referred to as bounded memory anchoring models, and we consider the impact of this indirect effect on the promotion planning process.

There are several steps that retailers must take when planning pricing policies, from negotiating vendor contracts, which can set price restrictions for the retailer, to promotion scheduling, promotion vehicle planning, and inventory and replenishment planning. In this chapter, we focus on the second step, the promotion planning process. Due to the complexity of the promotion planning problem, many retailers opt to use manual processes based on intuition and experience. However, with the growing availability of data and computing power there is more potential for retailers to increase profit using state-of-the-art algorithms and analysis. In this chapter, we describe some of these methodologies and demonstrate that by adopting the proposed approaches, retailers can increase their profit by 3–15.6 percent.

The promotion planning process gives rise to several challenges. The first challenge involves retailers being able to understand how price promotions affect current and future demand. The academic literature provides several models to describe this relationship. Nonetheless, to identify the model that best fits their data, retailers need to have access to large data sets, statistical analysis tools, and computational power. Choosing the wrong model can have a significant impact on the resulting promotion policy. The second major challenge is the impact of prices on the demand for other items due to the cross-item effect, such as substitution or complementary effects. Retailers must be able to characterize this effect and incorporate this dependency in their decision process when planning a promotion policy. In today's economy, retailers sell thousands of items simultaneously, and accounting for all the cross-item effects can result in an intractable problem.

Another challenge retailers face when planning a promotion is the additional complexity due to business constraints. In many cases, due to store norms, physical restrictions, and vendor funds-related constraints, retailers impose a set of business rules that any promotion policy must follow.

The result of the above-mentioned challenges is a large and complex optimization problem that requires more computational power than most retailers have available as well as long processing time. For retailers who must plan promotions frequently, this becomes a major challenge.

In this chapter, we review the most recent advances in tools and methodologies to tackle the above-mentioned challenges. The main contributions of the work that we review here can be summarized as follows: (1) formulation of the promotion planning optimization problem; (2) formulation of and motivation for the two recently introduced bounded memory demand models; (3) presentation of several variations of the problem and review of the state-of-the-art solution approaches; and (4) discussion of the impact of the proposed approaches on retailers in practice.

This chapter is organized as follows. In section 2, we review some of the related literature. In section 3, we present the notation and assumptions, as well as the problem statement and mathematical formulation. In section 4, we discuss the state-of-the-art solution approaches to the promotion planning optimization problem with bounded memory demand models. Finally, in section 5, we discuss the potential impact and implications of the proposed approaches on retailers in practice.

2. LITERATURE REVIEW

The question of promotion planning optimization and dynamic pricing is well-studied in the literature. Our problem is related to several streams of literature, including dynamic pricing, promotions in marketing, and retail operations. The post-promotion slowdown is studied in the marketing community. The main driver of post-promotion slowdown is anchoring behavior, where consumers' evaluation of item value changes if they observe a different set of past prices. Another factor that contributes to post-promotion slowdown is *stockpiling* or the *pull-forward* effect. In this case, when consumers see that an item they regularly purchase is on promotion, they tend to buy a significantly larger volume than they normally would. Consumers stock up on the item and therefore do not buy it in the following periods. Anchoring demand models account for both drivers of the post-promotion slowdown (see Macé and Neslin [2004][1] for a detailed review of the post-promotion slowdown literature).

2.1. Dynamic Pricing with Post-Promotion Slowdown

There is a significant amount of research on post-promotion slowdown and anchoring behavior. In the traditional literature, strategic consumers are associated with a utility function that captures the consumers' preferences with respect to the current price of an item and a set of *reference prices* (an internal reference price that is determined based on past prices, and an external reference price that is determined by, among other factors, the prices of other items). Consumers will buy the item if their utility function is non-negative. When considering retailers who operate in bricks-and-mortar stores, retailers are usually unable to implement such dynamic pricing policies, nor can they estimate the parameters of the utility function. Therefore, the majority of the promotion planning literature is focused on the settings in which the demand is aggregated. In this chapter, we focus on problems with aggregated anchoring demand models.

Perhaps the most common anchoring demand model is the Reference Price with Exponential Smoothing (RPES) model, in which the demand is a function of the current price and a reference price. The reference price in the RPES model is assumed to be an exponential smoothing of all past prices. Popescu and Wu (2007)[2] have studied the problem of dynamic pricing with RPES. In the case of an unconstrained promotion planning problem using the RPES model, the authors showed that the optimal promotion policy converges to a constant study-state price; otherwise, the optimal policy cycles. Cohen et al. (2020)[3] studied a similar problem and were able to identify two special cases in which the optimal promotion policy can be computed in a tractable time. For the general case, they suggested a heuristic and demonstrated that the proposed approach can compute a near-optimal solution when tested on real data. A review of the literature on dynamic pricing with RPES can be found Hu (2015).[4]

A different approach to anchoring demand models was presented in Nasiry and Popescu (2011),[5] where the authors studied an anchoring set that is referred to as *Peak-End*. In this model, the set of prices that are affecting the anchoring behavior includes the minimum price over all previous periods (referred to as *Peak price*) and the last seen price (referred to as *End price*). This approach is based on the behavioral study in Kahneman et al. (1993).[6] Nasiry and Popescu (2011) showed that in light of such a demand model, the optimal price converges to a fixed promotion price.

In contrast to the Peak-End and RPES models, in which prices from a long time in the past can impact the anchoring behavior (and thus, can impact current demand), in models with bounded memory the consumers are anchoring on a finite set of past prices within a fixed memory. In this chapter, we focus on the promotion planning optimization problem with these bounded memory demand models. There are two main types of bounded memory demand models in the literature, the Bounded Memory and the Bounded Memory Peak-End models.

In the case of the Bounded Memory demand model, the set of prices that are affecting the anchoring behavior include all prices within the past M periods, where M is the length of the memory window.[7,8]

In Cohen-Hillel et al. (2022)[9] and Cohen-Hillel et al. (2023),[10] the authors considered a bounded memory version of the Peak-End demand model. In this case, the set of prices that are affecting the anchoring behavior include the End price (last seen price), similar to the Peak-End demand model. However, unlike the Peak-End demand model, the Peak price in the Bounded Memory Peak-End demand model is equal to the minimum price within the last M periods. Here, similar to the Bounded Memory demand model, M is the length of the memory window. There are many ways in which past prices can impact current sales. For example, Baardman et al. (2020),[11] illustrated that through social interactions, for trendy items such as fashion, selling an item at a low price to an influential consumer can have a positive effect on future sales. Nonetheless, in this chapter, we focus on the post-promotion slowdown that is caused by temporary price reduction in supermarkets.

2.2. Dynamic Pricing with Business Constraints

In addition to the type of demand model, another way to distinguish between the papers above is by the set of business constraints imposed by the dynamic pricing problem formulation. Kristofferson et al. (2017)[12] suggested that repeated and too frequent promotions can lead to negative implications for consumer behavior. Indeed, too frequent promotions may change consumers' price sensitivity. As a result of the negative response to frequent promotions, retailers often consider a variation of the dynamic pricing problem in which the retailer is restricted in terms of the number of periods in which they can use a discounted price. Such a constraint eliminates the fixed price policies that were suggested in the previous literature.

The question of limiting the number of promotions is part of a long-lasting debate on whether retailers should use dynamic pricing or stick with the Every-Day Low Price (EDLP). Adida and Ozer (2019)[13] studied the question of dynamic pricing compared to the EDLP approach. The authors showed that dynamic pricing can lead to higher profits, even in the presence of competition, compared to EDLP, which can lead to significant losses. This result is supported by Cohen-Hillel et al. (2022) among others.

2.3. Dynamic Pricing for Multiple Items

While the literature on the single-item dynamic pricing problem with anchoring demand functions is substantial, the research on the more general multiple-item dynamic pricing problem with anchoring demand functions is limited. One main reason for this is the repeated evidence of brand loyalty in the supermarket industry. This evidence has been found in field experiments that show that for many types of products, consumers remain loyal to their favorite brand. Examples of such research can be found in Dickson and Sawyer (1990).[14]

Nevertheless, when planning a promotion, retailers may choose to promote some items while keeping the prices of the other items of the same brand high. In such cases, one must consider the impact of an external reference price. This captures the dependency of the demand on the prices of comparable items. Kopalle et al. (1996)[15] studied the question of the dynamic pricing of multiple items using the RPES model and no limit on the number of promotions. The authors showed that the optimal policy in this case admits a cyclic structure. Cohen et al. (2021) studied the problem of dynamic pricing with a Bounded Memory demand model and business constraints. The authors proposed an efficient algorithm to find a near-optimal pricing policy. Finally, Cohen-Hillel et al. (2022) studied a similar problem with the Bounded Memory Peak-End demand model and proposed a Polynomial Time Approximation Scheme (PTAS). The proposed PTAS allowed retailers to balance between the running time and the optimality guarantee.

3. PROBLEM STATEMENT

In this section, we formulate the promotion planning optimization problem (PPOP). First, we introduce some notations, assumptions, and business rules that are important for the PPOP. We then provide a mathematical formulation for the PPOP.

The PPOP considers a single retailer selling N non-perishable items over a season (time horizon) of T periods. In the problem, the retailer decides at each time period and for each item the selling price of the item.

We denote by $p_{t,i}$ the promotion price of item i at time t and by $d_{t,i}(p)$ the corresponding demand function. To capture the cross-item effect, we consider for each item i the corresponding set C_i, which includes all "comparable" items such that the demand for item i at time t is impacted by the price $p_{t,j}$ for all items $j \in C_i$. In section 3.4, we discuss the structure of the demand as a function of the pricing policy.

For a demand function $d(p)$, the PPOP objective is to maximize profit throughout the season. The profit at period t for item i is the product of the offering price and the corresponding demand. Formally, the retailer will maximize the following objective function.

$$\max_{\vec{p},\vec{\gamma}} \sum_{i=1}^{N} \sum_{t=1}^{T} p_{t,i} d_{t,i}(\vec{p}) \tag{1}$$

3.1. Assumptions

In this variation of the PPOP, the retailer decides all price promotions at the beginning of the season. Retailers need to commit up front for the entire selling season for several reasons, including vendor funds constraints.

We assume that the retailer has a sufficient amount of inventory to account for the expected demand associated with any pricing policy. Due to the nature of the supermarket industry, in which retailers make frequent replenishment decisions, pricing decisions are made ahead of time, but retailers can make replenishment decisions in reaction to excess demand. This observation was also documented in recent reports in the literature (see for example, Griswold [2011],[16] Cohen et al. [2017], and Cohen-Hillel et al. [2022]).

Following the analysis in Cohen-Hillel et al. (2023), here we consider bounded memory demand models. In bounded memory demand models, the demand for item i at time t depends explicitly on self-current price $(p_{t,i})$, past M_i prices $(p_{t-M_i,i},...,p_{t-1,i})$, and crosscurrent prices (i.e., prices $p_{t,j}$ for all items $j \in C_i$, where C_i is the set of all items that are comparable to item i.). In section 3.4, we discuss the structure of the demand model in more detail.

The negative impact of current price promotion on future sales implies that the objective function in (1) does not account for all post-promotion slowdown. In particular, a promotion for item i at time $t > T - M_i$ will have a negative impact due to the anchoring effect on merely $T - t < M_i$ periods. To amend this bias, we consider the following objective function which includes for each item i M_i periods after the end of the time horizon. During these periods, we do not allow for a promotion.

$$\max_{\bar{p},\bar{\gamma}} \sum_{i=1}^{N} \sum_{t=1}^{T+M_i} p_{t,i} d_{t,i}(\vec{p})$$

3.2. Business Rules

When planning a promotion policy, retailers impose a set of restrictions called business rules. In what follows, we discuss some of the most common business rules used by retailers in the grocery industry.

The first business rule is the *Discrete Price Ladder*. This business rule restricts the retailer to use at each time period t and for each item i a price $p_{t,i}$ that is chosen from a discrete set of potential prices. This set of potential prices is also referred to as a price ladder and is denoted as $Q_i = q_{0,i},\ldots,q_{K_i,i}$, where K_i is the length of the price ladder associated with item i, and $q_{0,i} > q_{1,i} > \ldots > q_{K_i,i}$. The full price, $q_{0,i}$, is also referred to as the *regular price* or the *base price*. More formally, this constraint can be formulated as follows.

$$p_{t,i} = \sum_{k=0}^{K_i} \gamma_{t,i}^k \cdot q_{k,i}, \qquad \forall 1 \le t \le T, 1 \le i \le N$$

$$p_{t,i} = q_{0,i}, \qquad \forall T+1 \le t \le T+M_i, 1 \le i \le N$$

$$\sum_{k=0}^{K_i} \gamma_{t,i}^k = 1, \qquad \forall 1 \le t \le T, 1 \le i \le N$$

$$\gamma_{t,i}^k \in \{0,1\} \qquad \forall 1 \le t \le T, 0 \le K_i, 1 \le i \le N$$

In this set of constraints, the parameter $\gamma_{t,i}^k$ reflects a binary decision. $\gamma_{t,i}^k$ is equal to 1 if at time t item i was priced with price $q_{k,i}$.

The size of the price ladder can have significant implications in terms of the tractability of the resulting problem. In Cohen-Hillel et al. (2022), the authors studied the question of the size and structure of the optimal price ladder. The authors showed that under mild conditions, which are being satisfied by the data, an optimal solution uses at most two prices for each item, the regular price and one promotion price. This type of promotion policy is referred to as a *High-Low policy*. The conditions that are required to determine whether the optimal solution is indeed a High-Low policy are referred to as the *High-Low conditions*.

In the case of a High-Low policy, the constraint above can be reformulated as follows.

$$p_{t,i} = \gamma_{t,i} \cdot q_{\kappa,i} + (1 - \gamma_{t,i}) \cdot q_{0,i}, \qquad \forall T \leq t \leq T, 1 \leq i \leq N$$
$$p_{t,i} = q_{0,i}, \qquad \forall T + 1 \leq t \leq T + M_i, 1 \leq i \leq N$$
$$\gamma_{t,i}^k \in \{0,1\} \qquad \forall 1 \leq t \leq T, 1 \leq i \leq N$$

The second business rule is the *Limit on the Number of Promotions*. Retailers often require limiting the number of periods during which each item is under a price promotion. The main driver for this limit is the attempt to avoid low-quality perceptions. If a product is often being discounted, it may be perceived in the eye of the consumer as a product of lower quality. To avoid this lower quality perception, manufacturers usually predetermine the full price and limit the percentage of the time during which the price is discounted. These requirements are usually reflected in the vendor fund agreements.

$$\sum_{t=1}^{T} \sum_{k=1}^{K_i} \gamma_{t,i}^k \leq L_i \qquad \forall 1 \leq i \leq N$$

The final business rule we consider is the *Separation Constraint*. The Separation Constraint is designed to mitigate the post-promotion dip. This business rule requires that for each item *i* every two consecutive promotions must be separated by at least S_i periods. This business rule can be achieved by including the following constraint.

$$\sum_{t=\tau}^{\tau+S_i} \sum_{k=1}^{K_i} \gamma_{t,i}^k \leq 1 \qquad \forall 1 \leq \tau \leq T, 1 \leq i \leq N.$$

3.3. Problem Formulation

In what follows, we present the promotion optimization problem that captures the assumptions and the business rules.

$$\max_{\vec{p},\vec{\gamma}} \sum_{i=1}^{N} \sum_{t=1}^{T+M_i} p_{t,i} d_{t,i}(\vec{p}) \tag{2a}$$

$$\text{s.t. } p_{t,i} = \sum_{k=0}^{K_i} \gamma_{t,i}^k \cdot q_{k,i}, \qquad \forall 1 \le t \le T, 1 \le i \le N \tag{2b}$$

$$p_{t,i} = q_{0,i}, \qquad \forall T+1 \le t \le T+M_i, 1 \le i \le N \tag{2c}$$

$$\sum_{k=0}^{K_i} \gamma_{t,i}^k = 1 \qquad \forall 1 \le t \le T, 1 \le i \le N \tag{2d}$$

$$\sum_{t=1}^{T} \sum_{k=1}^{K_i} \gamma_{t,i}^k \le L_i \qquad \forall 1 \le i \le N \tag{2e}$$

$$\sum_{t=\tau}^{\tau+S_i} \sum_{k=1}^{K_i} \gamma_{t,i}^k \le 1 \qquad \forall 1 \le \tau \le T, 1 \le i \le N \tag{2f}$$

$$\gamma_{t,i}^k \in \{0,1\} \qquad \forall 1 \le t \le T, 0 \le k \le K_i, 1 \le i \le N \tag{2g}$$

In this problem, the objective is to maximize the total profit from all N items during the selling season. In the above formulation, we have included all business rules.

In section 4, we discuss several solution approaches to the problem in (2) for different settings. First, we consider the problem in (2) when assuming different bounded memory demand models. The structure of the demand model can have significant implications regarding the interactions between the different decision variables and therefore, it may require different solution approaches. In addition, we consider the special case of the Single-Item PPOP. This case can be relevant, for example, when the demand for different items is independent of the prices of all other items in the store.

3.4. Anchoring Demand Models

In this chapter, we focus on the PPOP with bounded memory demand models. There are two main types of bounded memory demand models, the Bounded Memory and Bounded Memory Peak-End demand models.

In all cases, we assume that the demand for item i at time t is a function of the current price, the anchoring set (let it be the Bounded Memory or the Bounded Memory Peak-End), the current prices of all the items in the set C_i, and a set of exogenous parameters, such as seasonality, store location, brand quality, etc. We denote the set of exogenous parameters for item i at time t with $\sim x_{i,t}$.

The demand function is also characterized by the structure of the demand as a function of the parameters (current price, anchoring set, prices of other items, and the exogenous parameters). Many demand functions have been studied in the literature. The most common functions are linear, where the demand is a linear combination of the parameters, and the log-log, where the log of the demand is a linear combination of the log of the parameters as well as several non-parametric functions, such as those arising from a random forest, a Gaussian Process, and a Neural Network.

Cohen-Hillel et al. (2023) conducted an empirical study to evaluate the fit of each demand model to a data set from large supermarket retailers. The authors found that among all anchoring sets that were tested, the Bounded Memory Peak-End with log-log demand functions fit the data best, with the Bounded Memory coming a close second.

Formally, the Bounded Memory Peak-End and the Bounded Memory demand models with linear and log-log functions are as follows.

$$d_{t,i}(\vec{p}) = \alpha_0 - \alpha_1 p_{t,i} + \alpha_2 p_{t-1,i} + \alpha_3 \left(\min_{t-m \le \tau < t} p_{\tau,i} \right) + \alpha_4 \left(\sum_{j \in C_i} p_{t,j} \right) \qquad \text{(BMPE-Linear)}$$

$$\log(d_{t,i}(\vec{p})) = \beta_0 - \beta_1 \log(p_{t,i}) + \beta_2 \log(p_{t-1,i}) \beta_3 \log \left(\min_{t-m \le \tau < t} p_{\tau,i} \right) \beta_4 \left(\sum_{j \in C_i} p_{t,j} \right) \qquad \text{(BMPE-Log-log)}$$

$$d_{t,i}(\vec{p}) - = \alpha_0 - \alpha_1 p_{t,i} + \sum_{m=1}^{M} \alpha_2^{(m)} p_{t-m,i} + \alpha_3 \left(\sum_{j \in C_i} p_{t,j} \right) \qquad \text{(BM-Linear)}$$

$$\log(d_{t,i}(\vec{p})) = \beta_0 - \beta_1 \log(p_{t,i}) + \sum_{m=1}^{M} \beta_2^{(m)} \log(p_{t-m,i}) + \beta_3 \left(\sum_{j \in C_i} \log(p_{t,j}) \right) \qquad \text{(BM-Log-log)}$$

4. SOLUTION APPROACHES

In the retail environment, where decisions are made by local managers, the tractability of solution approaches for the PPOP is vital. Retailers must be able to solve the PPOP quickly and often.

Including past prices in the demand function leads to a non-linear objective function. Unfortunately, this implies that the problem in (2) is a complex problem to solve. Cohen-Hillel et al. (2022) showed that the PPOP with bounded memory demand models is NP-hard, even with a High-Low price ladder. These results suggest that finding an optimal solution for the PPOP requires long computations, longer than is acceptable by retailers in practice. Therefore, retailers have opted for suboptimal heuristics and approximation algorithms.

In what follows, we review some of the most recent approximation algorithms that were suggested for the PPOP with bounded memory demand models, and different variations of the problem.

4.1. Solution Approaches for the Promotion Planning Optimization Problem with Bounded Memory Peak-End Demand Model

First, we discuss solution approaches for the PPOP with the Bounded Memory Peak-End demand model. We begin with a special case of the Single-Item PPOP, where the demand is stationary. We then discuss a solution approach for the more general Single-Item PPOP. Finally, we discuss the Multiple-Item PPOP with the Bounded Memory Peak-End demand model.

4.1.1. SINGLE-ITEM AND STATIONARY DEMAND SETTING

First, we present an efficient solution for the Single-Item PPOP with stationary Bounded Memory Peak-End demand model and High-Low price ladder. A stationary Bounded Memory Peak-End demand model is a demand model that reacts merely to price changes and includes no exogenous parameters.

The lack of exogenous parameters allowed Cohen-Hillel et al. (2023) to identify the structure of an optimal promotion policy. The authors characterized the promotions in an optimal promotion policy based on the time that has passed since the previous promotion. Due to the nature of the Bounded Memory Peak-End demand model, the authors showed that there are at most three types of promotions in an optimal policy.

This analysis allowed Cohen-Hillel et al. (2023) to find the optimal separation between consecutive promotions without imposing the restrictive separation constraint. The optimal separation can help retailers to avoid the reduction in sales during promotion periods due to the post-promotion dip.

Finally, the authors used a process of elimination to identify the optimal solutions for the Single-Item PPOP with stationary Bounded Memory Peak-End demand model and High-Low price ladder in a constant computation time ($O(1)$).

To evaluate the practical impact of the proposed approach in terms of the profit that could be gained over the retailer's existing practice, the authors showed a significant improvement of 4–6 percent.

4.1.2. SINGLE-ITEM AND NON-STATIONARY DEMAND SETTING

The more general Single-Item PPOP with Bounded Memory Peak-End demand model presents several challenges that make this problem less tractable than the special case discussed above. Therefore, more sophisticated algorithms are required for this optimization problem.

In Cohen et al. (2020), the authors studied the Single-Item PPOP with general bounded memory demand models. The authors proposed a Dynamic Programming (DP) formulation that is exponential in the memory parameter M. Unfortunately, with the memory window spreading up to seven weeks for some items, this formulation is not tractable enough to be used by retailers in practice.

Cohen-Hillel et al. (2022) utilized the structure of the Bounded Memory Peak-End demand model and the low number of demand parameters to propose a more tractable DP formulation. The authors refer to this DP formulation as High-Low Dynamic Programming (HLDP). This DP formulation is exponential only in the number of prices in the price ladder.

The complexity of the DP that was proposed in Cohen-Hillel et al. (2022) suggests that for the case of the Single-Item PPOP with Bounded Memory Peak-End demand model and High-Low price ladder, the DP can find the optimal promotion policy in polynomial time. In fact, the authors demonstrated that in practice this algorithm can find the optimal promotion policy in seconds.

For the more general problem of the Single-Item PPOP with Bounded Memory Peak-End demand model and general price ladder, the authors proposed using the HLDP as an approximation algorithm. The authors provide both theoretical and empirical evidence to show that the HLDP can find a near-optimal solution, even if the High-Low conditions are not met. Therefore, the optimal solution is not necessarily a High-Low policy.

Finally, the authors tested the approach on real data to illustrate a potential increase in profit of 8.5% –15.6% compared to the retailer's current practice.

4.1.3. MULTIPLE-ITEM SETTING

The new HLDP formulation allowed Cohen-Hillel et al. (2022) to also address the more complex problem of Multiple-Item PPOP with Bounded Memory Peak-End demand model. Cohen-Hillel et al. (2022) extended the HLDP to the multiple-item setting and proposed using the DP formulation as a subroutine in an algorithm that allows the retailer to balance between the algorithm running time and the optimality gap of the resulting policy.

First, Cohen-Hillel et al. (2022) showed a natural extension of the HLDP to the Multiple-Item PPOP with Bounded Memory Peak-End demand model. While the resulting DP, referred to as the N-HLDP (where N represents the number of items), can find the optimal solution, the computation time required for this algorithm is exponential in N, the number of items. Therefore, the proposed algorithm is not tractable enough to be used by retailers in practice.

To address the tractability challenge, Cohen-Hillel et al. (2022) proposed splitting the set of items into smaller subsets. For each subset, the authors proposed to solve the Multiple-Item PPOP while considering only the items within the subset and assuming the worst-case prices for all items outside of the set. The authors referred to this algorithm as the Subset-Approximation algorithm.

Using this approach, the authors showed that the worst-case gap between the profit from an optimal promotion policy and the profit from the policy found by the Subset-Approximation algorithm is empirically low and theoretically linear in the number of subsets. The algorithm runs in time that is exponential only in the size of the largest subset (compared to an exponential in the total number of items for the optimal DP formulation).

The authors quantified this trade-off between the running time and the worst-case optimality gap by proposing a PTAS. A PTAS is an algorithm that, given a number (ε), can find a policy with a profit that is lower by at most ε of the optimal solution yet runs in a time that is exponential only in $\frac{1}{\varepsilon}$. In essence, given a value of ε, the proposed PTAS can help retailers find the right way to split items into subsets to be used in the Subset-Approximation algorithm. The resulting policy will yield profit that is at most ε of the optimal solution and can be found in time that is exponential only in $\frac{1}{\varepsilon}$.

Table 10.1 illustrates this trade-off between the running time and the optimality of the resulting policy for different values of ε. For each value of ε, we calculate the optimal number of subsets and find both the theoretical and empirical running time, and the ratio between the profit from the resulting policy and the profit that was achieved by the policy that was implemented in practice by the retailer. Table 10.1 illustrates that the retailer could have improved the profit by 4.7 percent with a computation time of merely 18 seconds.

4.2. Solution Approaches for the Promotion Planning Optimization Problem with Bounded Memory Demand Model

In this section, we discuss the PPOP with the Bounded Memory demand model. We discuss solution approaches for both the single-item setting and the multiple-item setting. In both cases, due to the complexity of the problem, we present approximation algorithms. Finally, we discuss a recent approach for an approximation

Table 10.1. Revenue and running time of PTAS formulation for different values of ε

	Revenue (%)	Running Time (s)
8 subsets, $\varepsilon = 0.91$	0.5%	3.56
4 subsets, $\varepsilon = 0.45$	4.7%	17.54
2 subsets, $\varepsilon = 0.22$	5.1%	416.65

algorithm for the PPOP with the Bounded Memory demand model, which includes a solution using demand approximation.

4.2.1. SINGLE-ITEM SETTING

First, we discuss the special case of the Single-Item PPOP with Bounded Memory demand model. While the Single-Item PPOP with Bounded Memory demand model is less complex than the Multiple-Item PPOP with Bounded Memory demand model, the non-linearity that is the result of including the past price in the demand function remains, and therefore, it is unlikely to find an optimal solution in a tractable manner.

In Cohen et al. (2017), the authors found that the source of the complexity lies in the non-linearity of the objective function. They therefore proposed to approximate the objective function using a linear function.

In particular, Cohen et al. (2017) proposed approximating the objective function by the sum of the marginal contributions of having a single promotion at a time. To calculate the marginal contribution of a single promotion at time t, the algorithm assumes a solution where the price was set to the regular price at any period other than period t ($\tau \neq t$), while maintaining the promotion at time period t. The algorithm then calculates the marginal contribution of this virtual policy by subtracting the profit from a policy with no promotions at all. The resulting marginal profit is an approximation of the true marginal profit from the promotion at time t. The authors referred to this algorithm as $App(1)$.

Using real-world data, Cohen et al. (2017) demonstrated that the proposed approach can find a near-optimal solution in seconds, with an increase of 3–5 percent compared to the promotion policy that was implemented by the retailer.

4.2.2. MULTIPLE-ITEM SETTING

Extending the $App(1)$ algorithm, Cohen and Perakis (2021) proposed adopting a similar approach of approximating the marginal contributions for the general case of Multiple-Item PPOP with Bounded Memory demand model.

In the case of the Multiple-Item PPOP with Bounded Memory demand model, the algorithm must linearize not only the cross-time effect but also the cross-item effect. Therefore, Cohen and Perakis (2021) proposed the $App(\kappa)$ algorithm. The main idea behind the $App(\kappa)$ algorithm is to balance the problem complexity and the approximation gap achieved by the marginals. The parameter κ reflects the number of items we consider when calculating the marginal profit. More precisely, $App(\kappa)$ includes the marginal contributions, the pairwise contributions, and the three-way, four-way, and up to k-way contributions.

On one extreme, for $\kappa = 1$, the algorithm will find a promotion policy while ignoring all the cross-item effects. For $\kappa = 2$, the algorithm approximates the objective function of (2a) by the sum of unilateral deviations (i.e., having a single promotion at a time) and the pairwise contributions. On the other extreme, for $\kappa = N$, the algorithm successfully captures all cross-item effects.

While $App(\kappa)$ is designed to find the optimal policy, even in the case where $\kappa=N$, Cohen and Perakis (2021) demonstrated that when tested on real data, the approximation yields a solution that is optimal or very close to optimal. The authors also provided an analytical bound on the worst-case approximation gap.

Note that Cohen and Perakis (2021) considered, in addition to the business rules in (2), additional cross-item constraints, such as that the retailer cannot promote more than L_t items in each time period t.

4.2.3. USING BOUNDED MEMORY PEAK-END FOR DEMAND APPROXIMATION

A different approach for the PPOP with the Bounded Memory demand model was proposed in Cohen-Hillel et al. (2023), which approximated the Bounded Memory demand model with a Bounded Memory Peak-End demand model. The authors then proposed using one of the algorithms discussed in section 4 to solve the PPOP with the Bounded Memory Peak-End demand model.

To achieve this approximation algorithm, the authors first showed how to find a Bounded Memory Peak-End demand model such that the worst-case demand approximation error is minimized. In other words, the authors solved the following problem:

$$
\min_{\tilde{\alpha}} \max_{\vec{p}} \left\| \left(\tilde{\alpha}_0 - \tilde{\alpha}_1 p_{t,i} + \tilde{\alpha}_2 p_{t-1,i} + \tilde{\alpha}_3 \left(\min_{t-m \le \tau < t} p_{\tau,i} \right) + \tilde{\alpha}_4 \left(\sum_{j \in C_i} p_{t,j} \right) \right) \right.
$$
$$
\left. - \left(\alpha_0 - \alpha_1 p_{t,i} + \sum_{m=1}^{M} \alpha_2^{(m)} p_{t-m,i} + \alpha_3 \left(\sum_{j \in C_i} p_{t,j} \right) \right) \right\|
$$

where α is the coefficient of the true Bounded Memory demand model, and $\tilde{\alpha}$ denotes the coefficients for the approximating Bounded Memory Peak-End demand model. The problem minimizes the absolute worst-case demand approximation error across all possible pricing policies.

To solve the problem in (3), the authors use principles from duality theory to bound the worst-case demand approximation error. The authors found that if using the proposed approach, the worst-case demand approximation error can be bounded by

$$
0.5 \cdot (q_{0,i} - q_{K,i}) \left(\sum_{m=2}^{M_i} \alpha_2^{(m)} \right) \tag{3}
$$

Finally, Cohen-Hillel et al. (2023) showed how the worst-case demand approximation error affects the optimality of the promotion planning policy that was found by approximating the demand and solving the PPOP with the Bounded Memory Peak-End demand model.

When tested on real data, the authors showed that in using the proposed approach the retailer can improve profit by 5–6 percent compared to their current practice, and by 1 percent above the *App*(1) approach.

4.3. Solution Approaches for the Promotion Planning Optimization Problem with Demand Misspecification

Both in section 4.1 and in section 4.2, we assume that the retailer can fully identify the correct structure of the demand model. In section 4.1, we make the assumption that the demand follows a Bounded Memory Peak-End demand model, and we propose solution approaches. In section 4.2, we make the assumption that the demand follows a Bounded Memory demand model.

Hu (2015) compared the prediction accuracy of different demand models when fitted on real data. While this study allowed the authors to identify which demand models are more likely to fit the data well, it also revealed concerning results. In many cases, multiple demand models can fit the data with similar accuracy. This result was later validated in Cohen-Hillel et al. (2023), in which the authors compared the fit of the Bounded Memory Peak-End, the Bounded Memory, the RPES, and the Peak-End to real-world data. The authors found that while in general the Bounded Memory Peak-End fit the data best, the prediction accuracy achieved by the Bounded Memory demand model came a close second. In fact, in many cases, the prediction accuracy achieved by the Bounded Memory demand model was higher than that of the Bounded Memory Peak-End model.

The prediction accuracy results raise a valid concern, namely the impact of choosing the wrong demand model. Is there a demand model that yields a promotion policy that is more robust in the face of demand misspecification?

Cohen-Hillel et al. (2023) addressed this question. First, by using an empirical study the authors showed that among all anchoring demand models, the Bounded Memory Peak-End is the most robust

Table 10.2. Robustness of the Different Demand Models.[17]

Regression Model	Model Used to Generate the Data			
	Peak-End	RPES	Bounded Memory	Bounded Memory Peak-End
Peak-End	8.96	11.07	9.13	15.95
RPES	13.08	8.89	8.6	11.84
Bounded Memory	10.02	9.46	8.55	11.14
Bounded Memory Peak-End	10.55	9.93	9.28	8.58

to demand misspecification. To show this, the authors generated four synthetic data sets. In each data set, the authors assumed that the demand follows a different demand model. Then, for each of the four data sets, the authors used four linear regressions to find the best fit for the data for each of the four demand models. The results of this experiment can be found in Table 10.2.

Second, Cohen-Hillel et al. (2023) looked into a theoretical bound on this demand misspecification error. Using a statistical analysis, the authors showed that if the retailer has a data set that comes from a Bounded Memory demand model, yet the retailer misspecified the demand and tried to fit a Bounded Memory Peak-End; the equation below is the order of the estimation error.

$$
(q_{0,i} - q_{K,i}) \left(\sum_{m=2}^{M_i} \alpha_2^{(m)} \right).
$$

Finally, as the Peak-End is a simple case of the Bounded Memory Peak-End and the RPES is a simple case of the Bounded Memory demand model, all the results above also apply for the case in which the retailer has a data set that comes from Peak-End or RPES demand models. Combining the theoretical and the empirical results, Cohen-Hillel et al. (2023) conclude that the case where the retailer is unable to determine with a high level of accuracy the nature of the demand model, using a Bounded Memory Peak-End demand model to estimate the demand function and then to find the optimal promotion policy is an optimal approach that minimizes the risk of profit loss.

5. INSIGHTS AND PRACTICAL IMPACT

In this chapter, we reviewed solution approaches for different variations of the PPOP with various bounded memory demand models. In what follows, we summarize some of the main takeaways for practitioners and insights into the promotion planning process.

5.1. The Importance of Understanding the Demand Model

When consumers are making decisions, they are impacted by various sources of information, from the current price sticker to the prices of comparable or complementary items, the prices that they have observed in the past, and more. Understanding the sources of information that impact consumers' purchasing decisions can have significant implications for the retailers' profit.

In many cases, retailers are unable to access all relevant information to be able to perfectly predict demand response to price changes. Nonetheless, for Fast-Moving Consumer Goods products, such as ground coffee and soft drinks, Cohen-Hillel et al. (2023) and Cohen et al. (2017) showed that by using the bounded memory demand models (BMPE-Linear, BMPE-Log-log, BM-Linear, and BM-Log-log), retailers can predict demand with relatively high accuracy of 8.27 percent.[18]

Note that on average, the Bounded Memory Peak-End demand model fits the data with higher accuracy. However, when analyzing the prediction accuracy for each item at each outlet separately, in 25–46 percent of the cases the Bounded Memory fit the data with better accuracy. In addition, the memory parameter M, which represents the number of periods that impact the anchoring effect, also changes from brand to brand and from store to store. Cohen-Hillel et al. (2022) analyzed the length of the memory parameter for different brands of ground coffee. They found that more luxurious items result in a longer anchoring effect. The distribution level of the brand (store brand, national, or international) also plays a role in determining how luxurious a brand is in the eyes of the customer, as the international brand yields a longer memory window compared to the national brand and the store brand.

These results imply that when looking for a demand model that best fits the data, avoiding generalization of the results may improve prediction accuracy. As illustrated in Cohen-Hillel et al. (2023), the impact of demand misspecification (using an incorrect demand mode) can lead to loss of prediction accuracy and consequently loss of profit.

Finally, if the retailer is unable to determine with high accuracy the correct demand model, using more robust demand models, such as the Bounded Memory Peak-End, may help avoid profit loss due to demand misspecification.

5.2. The Impact of Business Rules on the Retailer's Revenue

To this day, many retailers opt to use manual processes to determine their promotion policies. These processes are based on intuition and experience. Some of the business rules that we discuss in this chapter are motivated by retailers' intuition, are based on experience, and do not necessarily reflect physical, financial, or legal requirements.

One of these business rules is the separation between consecutive promotions. Retailers often include the separation between consecutive promotions to avoid the negative effect of the post-promotion dip on promotion sales. Nonetheless, when using a demand model that accounts for the anchoring effect, retailers can avoid the negative effect of the post-promotion dip on promotion sales without imposing additional constraints. In fact, as illustrated in Cohen-Hillel et al. (2023), in many cases the optimal promotion policy may include more frequent promotions, which can help reduce the loss of sales due to the post-promotion dip.

When attempting to solve the problem in (2), retailers tend to assume that a larger price ladder may lead to higher profit. While in general this is not inaccurate, including a large price ladder may increase the complexity of the problem and thus make it intractable. Cohen-Hillel et al. (2022) showed that, due to the optimality of High-Low policies, using more than one promotion price may lead to loss of profit. Therefore, considering a smaller price ladder can improve the tractability of the problem without any negative effect of profit. Interestingly enough, when examining the different prices that were used by retailers in practice, it may appear that retailers chose a very large price ladder. However, while analyzing historical data Cohen-Hillel et al. (2022) noticed that in many cases it seems that retailers are attempting to implement a High-Low promotion policy. The multiple promotion prices come from the search for the correct promotion price to be used.

5.3. Accounting for the Cross-Item Effect

One of the main sources of the complexity of the PPOP is the large number of items that need to be priced. Accounting for all cross-item effects requires the retailers to solve the PPOP for thousands of items at a time, as illustrated in Cohen-Hillel et al. (2022). This task is intractable and may take a long time to solve.

Nonetheless, as illustrated by both approaches described in sections 4.1.3 and 4.2.2, by considering only part of the cross-item effects retailers can find a near-optimal solution in seconds. In both cases, the proposed algorithms account for a partial cross-item effect, either by splitting the items into smaller subsets or by approximating the cross-item effect using marginal profit.

5.4. The Added Value in Sensitivity Analysis

In section 4, we reviewed fast and effective solution approaches for different settings of the PPOP. Another added value to fast solutions is the ability to perform a sensitivity analysis that can help retailers better understand the impact of different factors on their profit.

One such example is a sensitivity analysis on the impact of the limit on the number of promotions. In many cases, this business rule comes from the manufacturer in the form of vendor fund agreements. Using a sensitivity analysis of the impact of these restrictions, the retailer can quantify the monetary impact of such agreements and make educated decisions when negotiating with the manufacturer.

In Cohen-Hillel et al. (2023), the authors have used the proposed approach to show how, due to the anchoring effect, even in the absence of the business rule that limits the number of promotions, in many cases retailers should use less frequent promotions to avoid the negative effect on future sales. Accounting for this anchoring effect, retailers may choose to space out the promotions by at least M periods (where M is the length of the anchoring effect).

6. CONCLUSION

Sales promotion is an important tool for retailers to induce sales. Hence, understanding the impact of promotions on current and future sales is crucial for retailers. Choosing the right items to promote at the right time can help increase profits by an order of 3–15.6 percent.

In this chapter, we considered a retailer who is planning the promotions for multiple items to consumers with bounded memory anchoring behavior, where the demand at a given time depends not only on the current price but also on a limited number of past prices. We formulated the problem, including several important business rules. We then discussed the challenges that arise from the formulation and two of the most common bounded memory demand functions – the Bounded Memory and the Bounded Memory Peak-End demand functions. For each demand function, we discussed recent solution approaches that allow retailers to find an optimal or near-optimal promotion policy that helps retailers to maximize profit.

For both the Bounded Memory and Bounded Memory Peak-End cases, we show that the PPOP can be solved quickly and can help the retailers to improve profit by 3–15.6 percent. Finally, we show how retailers can use the promotion planning algorithms to perform sensitivity analysis and learn more about the structure of the demand, the impact of the business rules on the profit, and the cross-item effect.

NOTES

1 Macé, S., & Neslin, S.A. (2004). The determinants of pre- and postpromotion dips in sales of frequently purchased goods. *Journal of Marketing Research, 41*(3), 339–50. https://doi.org/10.1509/jmkr.41.3.339.35992.
2 Popescu, I., & Wu, Y. (2007). Dynamic pricing strategies with reference effects. *Operations Research, 55*(3), 413–29. https://doi.org/10.1287/opre.1070.0393.

3 Cohen, M.C., Gupta, S., Kalas, J.J., & Perakis, G. (2020). An efficient algorithm for dynamic pricing using a graphical representation. *Production and Operations Management, 29*(10), 2326–49. https://dx.doi.org/10.2139/ssrn.2772231.

4 Hu, Z. (2015). *Dynamic pricing with reference price effects* [Doctoral dissertation]. University of Illinois at Urbana-Champaign.

5 Nasiry, J., & Popescu, I. (2011). Dynamic pricing with loss-averse consumers and peak-end anchoring. *Operations Research, 59*(6), 1361–68. https://doi.org/10.1287/opre.1110.0952.

6 Kahneman, D., Fredrickson, B.L., Schreiber, C.A., & Redelmeier, D.A. (1993). When more pain is preferred to less: Adding a better end. *Psychological Science, 4*(6), 401–5. https://www.jstor.org/stable/40062570.

7 Cohen, M.C., Leung, N.-H.Z., Panchamgam, K., Perakis, G., & Smith, A. (2017). The impact of linear optimization on promotion planning. *Operations Research, 65*(2), 446–68. https://doi.org/10.1287/opre.2016.1573.

8 Cohen, M.C., Kalas, J.J., & Perakis, G. (2021). Promotion optimization for multiple items in supermarkets. *Management Science, 67*(4), 2340–64. https://doi.org/10.1287/mnsc.2020.3641.

9 Cohen-Hillel, T., Panchamgam, K., & Perakis, G. (2022). High-low promotion policies for peak-end demand models. *Management Science, 69*(4), 2016–50. https://doi.org/10.1287/mnsc.2022.4477.

10 Cohen-Hillel, T., Panchamgam, K., & Perakis, G. (2023). Bounded memory peak end models can be surprisingly good. https://ssrn.com/abstract=3360643.

11 Baardman, L., Boroujeni, S.B., Cohen-Hillel, T., Panchamgam, K., & Perakis, G. (2020). Detecting customer trends for optimal promotion targeting. *Manufacturing & Service Operations Management, 25*(2), 448–67. https://doi.org/10.1287/msom.2020.0893.

12 Kristofferson, K., McFerran, B., Morales, A.C., & Dahl, D.W. (2017). The dark side of scarcity promotions: How exposure to limited-quantity promotions can induce aggression. *Journal of Consumer Research, 43*(5), 683–706. https://www.jstor.org/stable/26570336.

13 Adida, E., & Özer, Ö. (2019). Why markdown as a pricing modality? *Management Science, 65*(5), 2161–78. https://doi.org/10.1287/mnsc.2018.3046.

14 Dickson, P.R., & Sawyer, A.G. (1990). The price knowledge and search of supermarket shoppers. *Journal of Marketing, 54*(3), 42–53. https://doi.org/10.2307/1251815.

15 Kopalle, P.K., Rao, A.G., & Assuncao, J.L. (1996). Asymmetric reference price effects and dynamic pricing policies. *Marketing Science, 15*(1), 60–85. https://doi.org/10.1287/mksc.15.1.60.

16 Griswold, M. (2011). *Improving on-shelf availability for retail supply chains requires the balance of process and technology.* Gartner. https://www.gartner.com/en/documents/1701615.

17 The values in this table represent the Weighted Mean Absolute Percentage Error when using the different models.

18 Prediction accuracy is measured in Weighted Mean Absolute Percentage Error (WMAPE). WMAPE gives a weighted measure of the relative prediction error.

CHAPTER ELEVEN

Retail Markdown Optimization under Demand Parameter Uncertainty

Andrew Vakhutinsky

SUMMARY OF CHAPTER

The theoretical model presented within the paper allows retail establishments to fix the *optimal price for various items*, taking into consideration their inventory, in order to maximize the total sales profit. The model allows retail establishments to determine the levels of price markdown they should apply at different points in time, based on the remaining quantity on hand and the expected demand.

MANAGERIAL IMPLICATIONS (GENERAL)

This paper contributes to various aspects of everyday operations of several types of retail establishments.

- The target audience of the paper is any retail establishment, e-commerce establishments, management of fulfillment centers, inventory control supervisors, and retail revenue management specialists – be it a small business or a large e-commerce giant such as Amazon, Shopify, or eBay.
- Retail commodities best suited for testing this model are perishable products of any type, ranging from everyday groceries to medicines, and from fashion to electronics.

- The model enables managers to set an optimal price for any product, considering shipping and handling costs. The optimal price is set based on varied customer groups, thereby allowing managers to maximize revenue for a said product.
- The model also accounts for various real-time business decisions and needs that affect the retail industry – demand fluctuations, distribution networks, and markdowns for retail items.

MANAGERIAL IMPLICATIONS (ORGANIZATIONAL)

- In many retail establishments, there is little communication between the inventory managers and revenue analysts. This model allows for cross-communication, therefore enabling establishments to set dynamic pricing for products based on the available inventory on hand.
- The framework of the paper might result in reorganization or restructuring within retail organizations. The restructuring could, on the one hand, result in value creation by merging functions, but on the other, it could lead to a potential reduction in staff count.

MANAGERIAL IMPLICATIONS (STRATEGIC, TACTICAL, AND OPERATIONAL):

- From a strategic perspective, the implementation of this model should encourage retail establishments to reconsider the locations of their respective fulfillment centers to optimize shipping and handling costs. This potentially reduces the overall shipping costs to their customers and might even subsequently change the customer groups.
- From a tactical perspective, when implementing this model, it is important to optimize the assortment of products to be put on the e-commerce portal, especially when it comes to "conflicting" products because it is a substation product. Another tactical implication is the reallocation of products between different fulfillment centers.

- From an operational perspective, implementing this model must take into consideration other systems that are used internally, typically an internal recommender system that can push sales as it understands who might want certain products. Combining this model with a recommender system contributes to increasing sales as well as profits.

1. INTRODUCTION

A typical e-commerce retailer fulfills orders from multiple warehouses or fulfillment centers (FC) that are generally geographically dispersed, and thus the cost of shipping an order to a customer can differ significantly depending on the FC. At the same time, when an item approaches its end of life, its inventory levels frequently vary greatly among the FCs. Therefore, maximizing total profit should involve both assigning FCs to customers in order to balance the load among the FCs as well as pricing the item based on each customer's price elasticity and cost of service.

On the other hand, more traditional bricks-and-mortar retailers also supply their stores from multiple warehouses. As the stores are usually clustered into so-called price zones, it allows the retailer to execute a flexible pricing policy offering different prices in the price zones with different price sensitivity. In both cases, we have multiple supply centers and customer groups with a variety of demand parameters and service costs.

In this chapter we consider items with a limited life cycle, such as fashion merchandise or electronics. These items lose nearly all their value after a certain amount of time as they must be replaced by the new version of the product. When such an item approaches its end of life, its inventory is usually not replenished. If the inventory level at the beginning of the period is high enough that it cannot be sold by the exit date at its current price, a markdown is applied. Some recent research papers focus on omnichannel retail[1] and markdown with an assortment-dependent demand model.[2,3] In Lei et al. (2018),[4] the authors propose an approach to solving the problem of joint pricing and fulfillment of multiple customers from multiple FCs.

In most of these and other papers, the demand parameters are considered fixed, and the demand uncertainty is modeled as fluctuations in demand realization. The case of mispricing due to the error in estimating the model parameters is explained by an example in Gallego and Van Ryzen (1997).[5] In Mai and Jaillet (2019)[6] the authors solve the problem of price optimization under parameter uncertainty using a robust optimization approach. In this chapter, we consider a stochastic programming formulation of the problem as a way to optimize the expected performance measured either as revenue or profit. This problem is also related to the well-known newsboy problem if we consider the demand distribution as dependent on price. Based on the experience with the practical implementation of the markdown problem for various retailers, they often impose multiple rules essentially aimed at safeguarding against mispricing. For example, a retailer would limit the percentage of the single markdown or set a limit on the earliest markdown and/or minimal time between the two consecutive markdowns. The goal of the latter two restrictions is to improve estimation of the demand and price sensitivity before taking further action. More recently, retailers and, in particular, those with online channels, started using price randomization to arrive at a better estimate of customer demand parameters. Nevertheless, there is always uncertainty in the demand parameters, especially price elasticity, which is usually the most difficult to estimate.

Solving the markdown optimization problem requires a comprehensive predictive model to account for various exogenous and endogenous effects typically confronting the retailer, such as holiday-driven change in customer demand, presence of similar items resulting in demand transference, a.k.a. demand cannibalization, and pricing and promotion effects. Some existing studies in the area of revenue management describe similar models incorporating such effects: Caro and Gallien (2012)[7] for the case of a fast-fashion retailer and Ito and Fujimaki (2017)[8] for a grocery retailer. In more recent papers by Vakhutinsky et al. (2019)[9] and Cohen et al. (2022),[10] the authors proposed methods to estimate the demand model parameters of individual product items by incorporating the sales of other like items with similar demand characteristics such as price elasticity and promotion lift. Our approach extends this idea to estimate the parameter distribution as a posterior to the Bayesian prior using Markov Chain Monte Carlo (MCMC) simulation similar to the approach laid out in Cho et al. (2022).[11]

We formulate the markdown optimization model in section 2. First, in section 2.1, the problem is formulated as a basic markdown problem for a single customer group served from the same FC; then, in section 2.2 we provide a formulation for the model with multiple FCs supplying multiple customer groups at specific service costs and describe a min-cost network flow approach to solving the joint inventory allocation and markdown optimization problem. In both cases we provide a closed-form solution and a gradient descent algorithm for a log-linear demand model and uniform distribution of the price elasticity parameter that allows for a straightforward practical implementation. The predictive modeling approaches are described in section 3.

2. JOINT INVENTORY ALLOCATION AND MARKDOWN OPTIMIZATION PROBLEM

In this section we consider a markdown problem with multiple warehouses or FC that supply goods to different groups of customers. The customers can be individual customers such as online shoppers or customer groups sharing the same demand parameters or, more generally, they could be stores or even groups of stores. We assume that demand model parameters are not known exactly but are measured within certain limits. More precisely, we assume that each customer has their demand modeled as a function of the product price with parameters that follow a known joint distribution. The problem that we would like to solve is to find the best price to maximize the expected profit derived from selling the given amount of product inventory located at multiple FCs accounting for the costs of handling and shipping the product to the customer groups. We also assume that the sales period is bounded by a certain exit date, after which the product is salvaged at near-zero price. In addition, we assume that there is no replenishment of the product in the sales period at the FC level, but the product is replenished at the customer group level when the demand arises. Thus, when a customer group represents a bricks-and-mortar store, our model would ignore the situation when the on-hand inventory at the store is shipped but not sold, thus incurring the shipping costs without revenue.

Regarding the expected demand as a function of price $\bar{d}(p)$ and expected revenue $\bar{R}(p) = p\bar{d}(p)$, we make the following two assumptions:

1. $\bar{d}(p) > 0$ for all $p > 0$ and monotonically decreasing function of price p.
2. $\bar{R}(p) \to 0$ as $p \to 0$ or $p \to +\infty$.

The first assumption does not allow modeling the demand as piece-wise linear function and the second assumption excludes the constant elasticity power law demand model (e.g., in the form $d(p) = \alpha p^{-\beta}, \beta = const > 0$).

The time and price parameters as well as demand output are considered as continuous variables, which does not limit the practical applicability of the model as the integration in the model can be straightforwardly replaced with summation. In the discussion that follows, $p = p(t)$ is assumed to be the function of time.

2.1. Basic Markdown Optimization Problem: A Single Customer Group Served from a Single FC

In order to demonstrate the concept of markdown optimization under parameter uncertainty, we consider a basic markdown optimization problem of a single customer, or a homogeneous customer population served from the same FC.

Suppose there are S units of inventory that must be sold within time horizon T. There is no replenishment during this time period, and all inventory unsold by exit time T is salvaged at a negligibly small near-zero price. We formulate the problem as finding the optimal pricing policy, that is, the price of an item as non-increasing. Other examples of the constraints are limited price drops during markdown events and limited intervals between the drops. We denote the set of the allowed price policies as P. We assume there is a demand function $d(t,p;\theta)$ of pricing policy $p \in P$ at the time t that also depends on parameter vector θ. Since in practice it is impossible to measure the exact parameter values, we assume that θ is a realization of a random variable Θ, which follows a distribution given by p.d.f. $f(\theta)$ defined on domain $dom(f)$. θ may include such components as price elasticity of demand, promotion lift, and sensitivity to the reference price.

In general, the demand as a function of time depends on prior pricing decisions. For example, it could be prior promotions changing the customer reference price point or customer perception of the fair price affecting the future demand through the "pantry-loading" effect (see, e.g., Cohen and Perakis [2018]).[12]

Another example is the inventory depletion effect, when prior sales diminish the current inventory amount, which may negatively affect the current demand (see Vakhutinsky et al. [2012] and Smith and Achabal [1998]).

Since inventory is limited, we can define the sell-off time T_0 for the given pricing policy as the time of the inventory exhaustion under the current pricing policy. It is determined as the solution to the following equation:

$$\int_0^{T_0} d(t,p;\theta)\,dt = S$$

Note that for some combinations of the demand models and pricing policies the sales may last infinitely long. In this case, $T_0 = \infty$. Define the end-of-sale time $T_1 = \min(T,T_0)$, that is, the time when the vendor runs out of inventory or out of time, whichever happens earlier.

The total revenue under pricing policy p can be expressed as

$$R(p,\theta) = \int_0^{T_1} p(t)d(t,p;\theta)\,dt \tag{1}$$

Then the expected revenue can be expressed as

$$\bar{R}(p) = \int_{dom(f)} R(p,\theta)f(\theta)\,d\theta \tag{2}$$

and the markdown optimization problem is to find the optimal pricing policy p^* that would maximize the expected revenue:

$$p^* = \arg\max_{p \in P} \bar{R}(p) \tag{3}$$

While in general, the solution to the above problem may not be computationally tractable when the dimension of the parameter vector θ is relatively high, it can be applied to practical cases when only one or two components of the demand function parameters are estimated with uncertainty. In many practical cases, it is the price sensitivity or price elasticity parameter that is the most difficult to estimate for several reasons. For example, if there are no observed price changes in a product, the only estimation of the price elasticity can be obtained from observing similar products. Another example is when discounts occur during the seasonal decline in demand for the product. In this case, due to the so-called endogeneity effect, when the lower prices correlate with the lower demand for the product, the price sensitivity coefficient can be estimated at a much lower absolute value or even with the opposite sign. The usual practice in this case is also to consider the estimation of the broader product set or apply the range of endogeneity-mitigating instruments. In both examples, the estimation of the price elasticity will be within a certain range. In section 3 we propose a technique to obtain the empirical distribution function of the coefficient estimates. In what follows in this section we demonstrate how this technique can be applied to a widely used special case of log-linear demand model.

2.1.1. SPECIAL CASE OF LOG-LINEAR DEMAND MODEL AND UNIFORM DISTRIBUTION OF THE PRICE COEFFICIENT

In this section we consider one of the simplest demand models, the log-linear demand model, which is formulated as follows:

$$d(p,t) = s(t)\alpha e^{-\beta p} \tag{4}$$

where $s(t)$ is a seasonality factor independent of price. Without loss of generality, we can assume that $\int_0^T s(t)dt = 1$. Then it can be easily shown that the optimal price policy for model (4) with exactly known parameters consists of a single optimal price $p^* = \max\left(p_{opt}, p_{icp}\right) = \max\left(\dfrac{1}{\beta}, \dfrac{1}{\beta}\log\dfrac{\alpha T}{S}\right)$ by finding the revenue-maximizing value p_{opt} from the first-order optimality condition $\dfrac{\partial\left(pd(p,t)\right)}{\partial p} = 0$ and the inventory-clearing price (ICP) value p_{icp} from the total demand over period T, $\int_0^T d(p,t)dt = S$. Therefore, when considering the basic log-linear demand model, instead of function p(t), we will use single variable p omitting its functional dependency on t.

Note that the first-order optimality condition for the revenue-maximizing price is equivalent to the price elasticity of demand being equal to one: $-\dfrac{\partial d(p,t)}{\partial p}\dfrac{p}{d(p,t)} = 1$. The price is set to maximize the revenue when the inventory is high enough relative to the base demand α and the length of the sales period, or $\log\dfrac{S}{\alpha T} > -1$. In this case, some of the inventory is left unsold.

The above is summarized in the following equation:

$$p_{det}^* = \begin{cases} \dfrac{1}{\beta}\log\dfrac{\alpha T}{S} & \text{if}\log\dfrac{\alpha T}{S} > 1; \\[2ex] \dfrac{1}{\beta} & \text{otherwise.} \end{cases} \tag{5}$$

Note that in the optimal solution to the deterministic markdown optimization problem with any demand function, the optimal pricing policy is such that the inventory is never completely sold out before the end of the sales period. Otherwise, the price can be raised, and the same amount of the inventory can yield higher revenue.

When the price coefficient β is not known exactly, it is easy to see that underpricing the item and running out of inventory before the end of the season when the value of β is overestimated results in greater revenue loss than overpricing the product when the value of β is underestimated by the same amount. We will illustrate by considering the following case of a specific distribution.

Assume that the price coefficient β is a realization of the random variable with uniform distribution $\beta \sim U(\beta_1, \beta_2)$. For a fixed price p denote by β_0 the value of the parameter β at which the inventory is cleared within the sales period T:

$$\beta_0 = \frac{1}{p} \log \frac{\alpha T}{S} \tag{6}$$

For values of β in the $[\beta_1, \beta_0]$ interval, the inventory is sold out yielding the revenue pS. For β in the $[\beta_1, \beta_2]$ interval, since the inventory is not depleted, the sales per unit of time are $\alpha T e^{-\beta p}$. If $\beta_0 < \beta_1$, the inventory is never depleted; if $\beta_0 > \beta_2$, the inventory is always sold out. Combining the above, the revenue defined in (1) can be expressed as:

$$R(p, \beta) = p \cdot \begin{cases} S & \text{if } \beta \in [\beta_1, \beta_0]; \\ \alpha T e^{-\beta p} & \text{if } \beta \in [\beta_0, \beta_2]. \end{cases} \tag{7}$$

By substituting the expression for the revenue from (7) and p.d.f. for the uniform distribution $U(\beta_1, \beta_2)$, $f(\beta) = \begin{cases} \dfrac{1}{\beta_2 - \beta_1} & \text{if } \beta \in [\beta_1, \beta_2]; \\ 0 & \text{otherwise} \end{cases}$, into the general expression (2) for the expected revenue, we obtain

$$\bar{R}(p) = \begin{cases} pS & \text{if } p < p_1; \\ \dfrac{1}{\Delta\beta} \left(S\log\dfrac{\alpha T}{S} + S(1 - \beta_1 p) - \alpha T e^{-\beta_2 p} \right) & \text{if } p \in [p_1, p_2]; \\ \dfrac{\alpha T}{\Delta\beta} \left(e^{-\beta_1 p} - e^{-\beta_2 p} \right) & \text{if } p > p_2. \end{cases} \tag{8}$$

where we use notation $\Delta\beta = \beta_2 - \beta_1$, $p_1 = \dfrac{1}{\beta_2} \log \dfrac{\alpha T}{S}$ and $p_2 = \dfrac{1}{\beta_1} \log \dfrac{\alpha T}{S}$.

Notice that when the value of β is known exactly, that is, $\beta_1 = \beta_2 = \beta$, the last line in the equation (8) can be computed as

$$\lim_{\Delta\beta \to 0} \frac{\alpha T\left(e^{-\beta_1 p} - e^{-\beta_2 p}\right)}{\Delta\beta} = -\alpha T \frac{\partial e^{-\beta p}}{\partial \beta} = \alpha T p e^{-\beta p},$$

which coincides with the expression for the revenue for the revenue-maximizing price as stated earlier.

In order to find the revenue-maximizing price $p^* = \arg\max_p \overline{R}(p)$, we differentiate the function for $\overline{R}(p)$ from equation (8) over p and obtain:

$$\overline{R}'^{(p)} = \frac{\partial \overline{R}(p)}{\partial p} = \begin{cases} S & \text{if } p < p_1; \\ \dfrac{1}{\Delta\beta}\left(\beta_2 \alpha T e^{-\beta_2 p} - \beta_1 S\right) & \text{if } p \in [p_1, p_2]; \\ \dfrac{\alpha T}{\Delta\beta}\left(\beta_2 e^{-\beta_2 p} - \beta_1 e^{-\beta_1 p}\right) & \text{if } p > p_2. \end{cases}$$

In order to find the revenue-maximizing price $p^* = \arg\max_p \overline{R}(p)$, we differentiate the function for $\overline{R}(p)$ from equation (8) over p and obtain:

$$\overline{R}'^{(p)} = \frac{\partial \overline{R}(p)}{\partial p} = \begin{cases} S & \text{if } p < p_1; \\ \dfrac{1}{\Delta\beta}\left(\beta_2 \alpha T e^{-\beta_2 p} - \beta_1 S\right) & \text{if } p \in [p_1, p_2]; \\ \dfrac{\alpha T}{\Delta\beta}\left(\beta_2 e^{-\beta_2 p} - \beta_1 e^{-\beta_1 p}\right) & \text{if } p > p_2. \end{cases} \tag{9}$$

It is easy to see that $\overline{R}'^{(p_1)} = \dfrac{1}{\Delta\beta}(\beta_2 - \beta_1)S > 0$, and $\overline{R}''^{(p_1)} = -\dfrac{1}{\Delta\beta}$ $\beta_2^2 \alpha T e^{-\beta_2 p} < 0$. Therefore, the first-order condition $\overline{R}'^{(p)} = 0$ delivers an optimal solution

$$p^* = \frac{1}{\beta_2}\log\frac{\beta_2}{\beta_1}\frac{\alpha T}{S} \qquad (10)$$

When $p^* < p_2$, which is

$$\log\frac{\alpha T}{S} > \beta_1\frac{\log\beta_2 - \log\beta_1}{\beta_2 - \beta_1}. \qquad (11)$$

The price defined in (10) can be thought of as the modified ICP defined in the first line of (5). Interestingly, when the price coefficient is uncertain, the modified ICP is greater than the ICP in the deterministic case for any $\beta \in [\beta_1, \beta_2)$.

It is also interesting to compare conditions (11) and those used to apply ICP in (5). First, the right-hand side of (11) converges to one as $\Delta\beta \to 0$; second, it can be seen that $\beta_1\frac{\log\beta_2 - \log\beta_1}{\beta_2 - \beta_1} < 1$ when $\beta_2 > \beta_1$, which can be interpreted as that a higher level of inventory is required to apply ICP when the price coefficient is not known exactly.

When condition (11) is not satisfied, $\overline{R}'^{(p_2)} > 0$ and the optimal revenue-maximizing price is found in the interval $[p_2, \infty)$ as the solution to the first-order condition:

$$p^* = \frac{\log\frac{\beta_2}{\beta_1}}{\beta_2 - \beta_1}. \qquad (12)$$

Similarly to the revenue-maximizing optimal price in the second line of (5), the optimal price defined in (12) does not depend on the inventory. That is, in this case the optimal markdown solution will have some unsold inventory at the exit date. Also, $\lim_{\beta_1 \to \beta_2} \frac{\log\frac{\beta_2}{\beta_1}}{\beta_2 - \beta_1} = \frac{1}{\beta_2}$ coincides with the optimal price defined in (5).

Interestingly, in the case of an uncertain price coefficient, the optimal revenue-maximizing price is higher than the price that can be "naively" set to the reciprocal of the price coefficient mean value. In our case of the uniform distribution, it can be proved by comparing p^* to $\dfrac{2}{\beta_1 + \beta_2}$ using its Taylor expansions. Indeed, after setting $x = \dfrac{\beta_2}{\beta_1} - 1$ it can be seen that

$$\frac{\log(x+1)}{x} > \frac{1}{1 + \dfrac{x}{2}}.$$

Finally, we summarize the solution to the optimal markdown pricing when the price coefficient is uniformly distributed in the $[\beta_1, \beta_2]$ interval, as follows:

$$p^* = \begin{cases} \dfrac{1}{\beta_2} \log \dfrac{\beta_2}{\beta_1} \dfrac{\alpha T}{S} & \text{if } \log \dfrac{\alpha T}{S} > \beta_1 \dfrac{\log \dfrac{\beta_2}{\beta_1}}{\beta_2 - \beta_1}; \\[2em] \dfrac{\log \dfrac{\beta_2}{\beta_1}}{\beta_2 - \beta_1} & \text{otherwise.} \end{cases}$$

2.2. Joint Inventory Allocation and Markdown Optimization Problem for Multiple Customer Groups Served from Multiple FCs

It is a common practice that the demand for a limited life span item has to be fulfilled from several FCs. The demand is usually coming from several distinct groups with varying demand parameters. For example, the groups may be determined by the geographic locations with different socioeconomic characteristics that affect their price elasticity. In this section we consider the problem of optimal markdown pricing of an item when its inventory is spread over several FCs. We assume that inventory at all FCs has the same exit date, after which it is salvaged at near-zero price. In addition, the cost associated with selling from each FC to each customer group may be distinct. In the example of the geographically dispersed customer groups, the difference could be due to the delivery cost from an FC to a geographic location.

2.2.1. GENERAL CASE OF MULTIPLE CUSTOMER GROUPS SERVED FROM MULTIPLE FCs

Suppose there are M FCs serving L customer groups that may be defined either by their locations or other parameters. At each FC m, there is initial product inventory S_m. The product has its remaining lifetime T. Given the product demand function $d_\ell(p)$ at customer group ℓ and unit delivery cost to the customer group ℓ from FC m as $c_{m\ell}$, the optimization problem is to find the group-specific prices p_ℓ and amount of inventory $x_{m\ell}$ delivered from m to ℓ that maximizes profit, subject to FC inventory constraints.

Denote the total amount of inventory allocated to customer group ℓ as $S_\ell = \sum_{m \in M} x_{m\ell}$. Then the revenue-maximizing markdown price $p_\ell^*(S_\ell)$ for that group can be found by applying equation (3), which now explicitly depends on the allocated inventory. The optimal expected revenue for that location becomes $\bar{R}_\ell^*(S_\ell) = \bar{R}(p_\ell^*, S_\ell)$. The total profit-optimization problem now can be formulated as follows:

$$\max \sum_{\ell \in L} \left(\bar{R}_\ell^*(S_\ell) - \sum_{m \in M} c_{m\ell} x_{m\ell} \right) \tag{14}$$

subject to:

$$\sum_{\ell \in L} x_{m\ell} \le B_m \tag{15}$$

$$\sum_{\ell \in L} x_{m\ell} \le B_m \tag{15}$$

$$S_\ell = \sum_{m \in M} x_{m\ell} \tag{16}$$

$$x_{m\ell} \geq 0 \tag{17}$$

where B_m i s the amount of inventory at FC m. That is, the constraint (15) determines the upper bound of the inventory delivered from FC m.

In practically all cases allocating a greater amount of the inventory to be sold to the customers cannot reduce the revenue as extra inventory can always be left unsold. On the other hand, in order to derive more revenue by selling more inventory within a given time period, the sales price should be lowered, which results in diminishing marginal return of inventory allocation. Mathematically speaking, the second derivative of the optimally-priced revenue as a function of allocated inventory is negative, implying that the function is concave. Therefore, after the sign of the objective function (14) is changed, the optimization problem (14–17) becomes equivalent to a well-studied min-cost network flow problem with convex costs.

We propose another algorithm described below as Algorithm 1 that iteratively solves the Optimal Inventory Allocation problem. The algorithm takes a hyper-parameter δ_0 to determine its initial step length.

At each iteration of the Algorithm 1, we solve the min-cost network flow problem, MCNF(δ), described next. We start by defining the critical product allocation amount σ as a solution to the following equation:

$$\frac{\partial \bar{R}_\ell^*(S_\ell)}{\partial S_\ell}\Big|_{\sigma_\ell} = \min_m c_{m\ell} \tag{18}$$

That is, σ_ℓ can be thought of as the maximal possible allocation of the inventory that can still improve the profit generated by the customer group ℓ. We will use σ_ℓ to scale the amount of inventory to be allocated to the customer group. Next, we design the network consisting of three layers of nodes as shown in the example in Figure 11.1 for two FCs and two customer groups.

Algorithm 1 Optimal Inventory Allocation

Construct an initial feasible solution $x_{m\ell}$ satisfying constraint (15)

$\quad n \leftarrow 1$

while $n < N$ and termination criteria not satisfied

$\quad \delta \leftarrow \delta_0 / n$

obtain $f_{m\ell}$ as the optimal solution to MCNF(δ)

$\quad x_{m\ell} \leftarrow f_{m\ell}$

$\quad S_\ell \leftarrow \sum_{m \in M} x_{m\ell}$

$\quad b_m \leftarrow B_m - \sum_{\ell \in L} x_{m\ell}$

end while
return $x_{m\ell}$

The nodes in the top layer correspond to the FCs; the nodes in the bottom layer correspond to the customer groups as well as nodes in the intermediate layer which serve to "consolidate" the allocations from the FCs to the customer groups. There are arcs connecting each FC to each customer group node that is reachable from the FC as not all FCs may serve all customer groups. The cost of each arc in this layer is the delivery or service cost of the unit of the product from the FC to the customer group. The network flow problem starts with the current feasible solution x_m units of flow in the top arc layer. Consequently, the amount of flow sent from the consolidator nodes to the customer group nodes is $S_\ell = \sum_{m \in M} x_{m\ell}$. The cost of the arc from the "consolidator" node to the customer group node is $-\dfrac{\partial \bar{R}_\ell^*(S_\ell)}{\partial S_\ell}$. Note that the negative sign is used to form the minimization problem. The top-layer nodes serve as flow sources with capacity B_m (framed in red in the diagram). The bottom-layer nodes serve as what is called "sinks" in network flow terminology. The capacity of each sink is set to the interval $\left[(S_\ell - \sigma_\ell \delta_n)^+, S_\ell + \sigma_\ell \delta_n\right]$. That is, the flow is feasible but there are constraints to limit the change of the

Figure 11.1. Illustration of the network flow graph

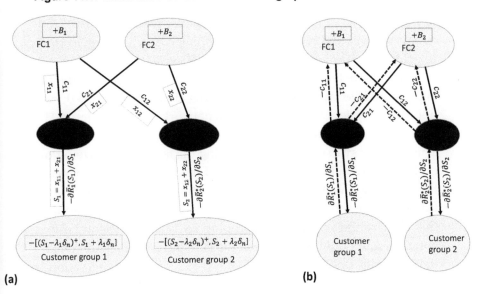

(a)

(b)

total allocated product for each customer group within progressively tighter boundaries. At each call to the MCNF algorithm, it returns the new network flow f_m that decreases the total cost of the flow in the network thus increasing the total profit. The Optimal Inventory Allocation algorithm terminates when it fails to improve the objective function above a certain threshold, or the maximal number of iterations is reached. There are several well-studied fast polynomial-time algorithms to solve the min-cost network flow problem.

Below, we make certain observations regarding the solution to the problem.

We define the cost of an undirected cycle in the directed flow network as the sum of all arc costs with the costs of the arcs traversed in the reversed direction taken with the negative sign. Borrowing the terminology from the network simplex method, we call a network degenerate if it has a zero-cost cycle. The network degeneracy may occur in practice, for example, when the retailer has flat shipping rates that are the same for all origin-destination pairs. It is easy to see that when all shipping costs are the same, then in the optimal solution the marginal revenue $\dfrac{\partial \overline{R}_\ell^*(S_\ell)}{\partial S_\ell}$ is the same for each cus-

tomer group S_ℓ. It exceeds the shipping cost when there is no left-over inventory and is equal to the shipping cost when there is some unsold inventory left at the end of the life cycle.

When the network is non-degenerate, the links between the top and the middle layers with nonzero flow, that is, with $x_{m\ell} > 0$, can-not form a cycle. For example, in the network shown in Figure 11.1 at most three of the four links in the top layer can carry positive flow. This fact is easy to prove by considering the fact that a nonzero flow cycle will have a positive cost in one of the directions, which means that reducing the flow along this cycle improves the objective func-tion implying the suboptimality of the solution. One implication of this observation is that if the shipping costs are sufficiently differ-ent, the number of links between the FCs and intermediate consoli-dating nodes does not exceed $|M| + |L| - 1$. Another observation is that each customer group is supplied from at least one FC. Since by assumption the demand function stays positive for any price, then for any delivery cost values, there is always a positive (although very low) inventory allocation that can make this allocation profit-able. In other words, if there is zero allocation of inventory, a suf-ficiently small reallocation from another customer group will carry overall positive marginal profit. One implication of this observation is that the number of customer groups supplied from two or more FCs is, at most, one less than the number of FCs. These properties of the optimal solution may provide the following two managerial insights: (1) Since in many supply chain cases the number of FCs is significantly lower than the number of customer groups, additional constraints may need to be imposed on planning supply to increase its robustness. One such measure could be imposing hard or soft constraints on link capacities. (2) Most min-cost flow algorithms also compute so-called node potentials or dual costs for the nodes with binding supply constraints. One interpretation of the dual cost is the improvement of the objective function per unit of extra supply at the node. This information may be useful when there is an additional opportunity to transport inventory between the nodes. Usually, it involves a significant fixed cost, and the problem becomes what is known as the network design problem. Its solution may serve as an additional decision tool for planning load balancing between the FCs.

2.2.2. MULTIPLE CUSTOMER GROUPS SERVED FROM MULTIPLE FCs WITH THE PRICE COEFFICIENT UNIFORMLY DISTRIBUTED

In this section we derive a closed-form expression for the marginal revenue to be used in Algorithm 1 in the special case of uniformly distributed price coefficient described in section 2.1.1.

In order to find the derivative of the revenue-maximizing function of the allocated inventory $\dfrac{\partial \bar{R}^*_\ell (S_\ell)}{\partial S_\ell}$, we substitute the expression for the optimal price p^* from (13) to the expression (8) for the expected revenue $\bar{R}$ to get the optimal revenue as a function of the allocated inventory S, $\bar{R}^* (S)$, and take its derivative:

$$\frac{\partial \bar{R}^* (S)}{\partial S} = \begin{cases} \dfrac{1}{\beta_2} \log \dfrac{\alpha T}{S} - \dfrac{\beta_1}{\beta_2} \dfrac{\log \frac{\beta_2}{\beta_1}}{\beta_2 - \beta_1} & \text{if} \log \dfrac{\alpha T}{S} > \beta_1 \dfrac{\log \frac{\beta_2}{\beta_1}}{\beta_2 - \beta_1} ; \\ 0 & \text{otherwise.} \end{cases} \qquad (19)$$

Note that when the inventory exceeds the critical threshold $\alpha T \exp \left(-\beta_1 \dfrac{\log \frac{\beta_2}{\beta_1}}{\beta_2 - \beta_1} \right)$, adding more inventory does not affect the optimal markdown revenue.

3. THE HIERARCHICAL DEMAND MODELS

In this section we consider several approaches to estimating the demand model parameters. Although demand modeling can be considered as a general predictive analytics problem, the model must exhibit certain properties, which narrow the choice of models. The main limitation comes from the fact that demand is a monotonically decreasing function of the product price, which makes the most used machine learning approaches like ensemble methods (e.g., Random Forest, Gradient Boosting) or deep learning neural networks inapplicable. Therefore, we limit our scope to the main two groups of the parametric methods: discreet choice models based on the Multinomial Logit (MNL) and regression methods using generalized linear models (GLM). The latter includes log-linear, Poisson, and Negative Binomial regressions. In both groups, the prediction is based on a linear function of several attributes, including price, seasonality or seasonal time shocks, promotion lifts, and post-promotion fatigue or pantry loading. The MNL-based methods consider this linear function as the product utility and predict demand as a market share. Their common disadvantage is the dependency on the estimation of the so-called no-purchase option coefficient, which is usually an unobservable variable. On the other hand, these methods account for the demand transference among similar products and have superior performance for the categories of products with high substitutability. GLM-based methods usually do not explicitly model the demand transference. However, recently in marketing science literature there were reports of models that account for the presence of similar products and their demand cannibalization effects[13] using the similarities of their customer attributes such as brand, color, size, etc.

The main hurdle in applying these methods to predict the sales of a particular item at a particular store or to a specific customer group is that most of these sales are very low volume and thus have a very low signal-to-noise ratio. In addition, the price changes may be very infrequent and in a very small range, which makes the estimation of the price sensitivity even more difficult. Furthermore, the sales history of an individual item may contain a number of observations too low to provide sufficient statistical power for the estimation of several parameters. All these factors make parameter estimation very unreliable when it is based on the data from the sales of an isolated item. It can, however, be mitigated by considering multiple items sharing similar parameters or the same item sold at different locations since locations and merchandise items usually form a hierarchy starting from the entire chain level to price zones and individual stores for the location hierarchy and to departments, categories, classes, and individual items for the merchandise hierarchy. This hierarchy, coupled with clustering the items at lower levels of merchandise classification, provides a convenient tool for estimating the demand model parameters at the levels of the hierarchy with sufficient statistical power. Cohen et al. (2022) provide a methodology to determine at which level each parameter is estimated in addition to building clusters of similar items for the parameter estimation.

We use these ideas to build estimation methods taking advantage of the existing hierarchical structure as well as the clusters built for estimation purposes. The output of the methods is the probability distribution of some of the parameter estimates.

3.1. The Demand Model

3.1.1. ASSUMPTIONS

We assume the availability of the general sales data aggregated over a short time period such as a day or week rather than transaction-level data reflecting individual purchases. That is, we assume that for each item i there are observations from historic sales data that consist of triples $\left(s_{it}, p_{it}, r_{it}\right)$ representing, respectively, sales, price, and a binary promotion flag for the dated time period t. In many cases, zero sales are not part of the data and in addition to that the out-of-stock (OOS) periods are not clearly flagged. The combination of these two factors makes it impossible to distinguish between the zero-demand and OOS observations. In addition, sometimes promotions are not clearly marked either, or there could be several types of promotions with different promotion lifts marked by the same flag. In the next section we propose a simple heuristic to distinguish among these cases.

We also assume that the merchandise hierarchy is known and adequately reflects the similarity between the retail items. In the next section we describe how multiple items with varying magnitudes of demand and prices can be pooled together.

3.1.2. ATTRIBUTES OF THE DEMAND MODEL

In this section we describe the attributes together with the demand output variable and how they are used by the model. We also describe some preprocessing procedures that are carried out to form an observation pool at higher levels of the hierarchy. Below, we use the notation $x_i(t)$ to denote the value of explanatory variable x observed for product i at time t.

Demand: Since multiple items that are pooled together may exhibit similar behavior but have different mean demand (e.g., for the same item at different stores), it is necessary to estimate the so-called base demand, which can be either approximated by the mean demand if the item price changes are not significant or estimated as an intercept-type constant.

Since for slow-moving products it is not possible to distinguish between zero-demand periods and unavailability of the product when the zero-inventory periods are not reliably identified in the data or appear as missing data, we consider the sufficiently long sequences of the missing or zero-sales periods as OOS. The length threshold is determined by the probability threshold of encountering a certain number of consecutive zero-demand periods, which is computed as $N_{thresh} = -\dfrac{\log p_{thresh}}{\lambda}$ where λ is the parameter of the Poisson distribution. Since the observed demand $d_i(t)$ is effectively zero-truncated, the maximum likelihood estimator of the parameter λ is obtained from solving the following equation:

$$\frac{\lambda}{1-e^{-\lambda}} = \bar{d}_i$$

where $\bar{d}_i$ is the sample mean of the observed demand for product i.[14] The threshold probability value is usually selected to be in the order of 0.01, meaning that the probability that a sequence of zero-demand periods with the length exceeding the threshold due to zero demand does not exceed 1 percent. For example, if the sample mean of the observed zero-truncated demand is 2.3, then the estimated mean demand is about 2, which means that the probability of zero demand in three or more consecutive periods is below 1 percent. Therefore, it is reasonable to assume that these would be the OOS periods.

Price: In order to pool together similar merchandise items with different prices such as different size packages of the same product, we replace their price values with relative deviation from the average or initial non-discounted price: $\tilde{p}_i(t) = \frac{p}{p_0} - 1$. The estimated coefficient of this variable is the price elasticity of demand when the demand is modeled as exponentially dependent on price.

Promotion flag: As promotions come in various kinds and flavors, there should ideally be a vector of promotion flags reflecting which campaigns were run and which promotion tools were used in each case. However, very few retailers keep historical records of the promotions. Sometimes, there are no promotion indicators at all. In this case, promotion and regular sales can be separated by running a clustering algorithm in price-demand space. We denote the promotion flag variable as $r_i(t)$.

Post-promotion: This well-known effect caused by the so-called promotion fatigue and pantry loading leads to a sales dip following the promotion period. We define this variable as 0–1, or Boolean, indicating whether there was a promotion in the previous week.

Similarity: This is the set of variables reflecting how much demand for this item is cannibalized by other item and their prices in the current assortment. Following Rooderkerk et al. (2013), we define two variables here, one for the total of the assortment item similarity, the other for the total of item prices weighted by their similarity. The latter reflects the competitive effect of the prices of the other items. The similarity between the items is computed based on the item attributes extracted from their textual descriptions. We denote the similarity and price similarity variables as $u_i(t)$ and $v_i(t)$, respectively.

Seasonality: As the timing of the most peak sales periods is determined by annual holidays, some of which follow the lunar rather than solar calendar (e.g., Easter) and others fall on different days of each year (e.g., Thanksgiving), we mark the corresponding periods by the holiday occurrence rather than calendar dates. In addition, in most cases the peak sales happen in the weeks preceding the holidays, and the holiday and post-holiday periods are characterized by drops in sales. Therefore, we define seasonality variables for three weeks per holiday. Assuming each holiday-related week is indexed by its index h, we define a set of dummy variables $w_h(t)$ indicating whether period t is the time period associated with the holiday.

We denote the vector of the explanatory variables as

$$\vec{x}_i(t) = \left(1, \tilde{p}_i(t), r_i(t), r_i(t-1), u_i(t), v_i(t), \{w_h(t) \mid h \in H\}\right) \tag{20}$$

and the vector of the coefficients as

$$\vec{\beta}_i = \left(\beta_i^0, \beta^{price}, \beta^{promo}, \beta^{postPromo}, \beta^{sim}, \beta^{priceSim}, \{\beta_h^{holiday}(t) \mid h \in H\}\right).$$

Note that only base demand coefficient β^0 is specific to product i. If the demand is modeled as Poisson distribution with the mean:

$$\lambda_i(t) = E\left(d_i(t) \mid x_i(t)\right) = e^{\vec{\beta}_i'\vec{x}_i(t)} \tag{22}$$

then the probability mass function becomes:

$$p\left(d_i(t) \mid \vec{x}_i(t); \vec{\beta}_i\right) = \frac{\lambda_i(t)^{d_i(t)}}{d_i(t)!} e^{-\lambda_i(t)}.$$ Given a series of T observations

$\left(d_i(t), x_i(t)\right)$, $t = 1, \ldots, T$, for product set M, we use the regularized regression to find the estimate of the β coefficients by maximizing the difference between the logarithm of the likelihood and the regularization term:

$$l\left(\vec{\beta}\right) = \sum_{i \in M} \sum_{t=1}^{T} \left(d_i(t) \overline{\vec{\beta}_i' \vec{x}}_i(t) - e^{\vec{\beta}_i' \vec{x}_i(t)}\right) - \frac{T|M|}{2} \alpha \parallel \vec{\beta}_i \parallel_2^2 \tag{23}$$

where α is the regularization penalty parameter estimated via cross-validation. This technique, similar to ridge regression, can reduce overfitting.

Since the log-likelihood function is concave, the Newton-Raphson or a Quasi-Newton method can be applied to find the maximum likelihood estimator (MLE) of $\vec{\beta}_i$.

In the cases when the mean demand $\bar{d}_i$ is easy to estimate for each product from the sales data, it can be entered into the equation (22) as exposure:

$$\lambda_i(t) = E\left(d_i(t) \mid x_i(t)\right) = \bar{d}_i e^{\vec{\beta}\vec{x}_i(t)} \tag{24}$$

In this case, the estimated coefficient vector β defined in (21) becomes:

$$\vec{\beta} = \left(\beta^{price}, \beta^{promo}, \beta^{postPromo}, \beta^{sim}, \beta^{priceSim}, \{\beta_h^{holiday}(t) \mid h \in H\}\right) \tag{25}$$

and becomes the same for all products.

The variable vector defined in (20) becomes:

$$\vec{x}_i(t) = \left(\tilde{p}_i(t), r_i(t), r_i(t-1), u_i(t), v_i(t), w_h(t) \mid h \in H\right). \tag{26}$$

Therefore, the number of estimated parameters is reduced by $\mid M \mid$.

3.2. Hierarchical Estimation

In this section, we describe the hierarchical approach to estimating the coefficients of the demand model defined in the previous section. We assume there are at least three levels of the hierarchy that we call category (about 100–1,000 individual SKU/UPC items), class (about 10–100 items), and individual items that may include several SKU/UPC of varying size/color of the same style. The terminology may differ among retailers, but this hierarchy is almost always present. Most of the demand model coefficients are estimated at the class or category level except for the base demand β^0, which is estimated at the item level.

3.2.1 UNCERTAINTY ESTIMATION

We propose two methods to estimate the parameter uncertainty based on Hessian at the maximum of the log-likelihood function and using the MCMC method.

Hessian-based: Since the Newton-Raphson method effectively approximates the log-likelihood function as a paraboloid with its shape determined by the Hessian of the function, the variance of the parameter estimations can be computed as the negative of their diagonal elements in the inverse of the Hessian, which provides the means for building the confidence interval by assuming the normal distribution around the estimation. For example, the 95 percent-confidence intervals can be found as

$$\hat{\beta}^j \pm 1.96\sqrt{-H_{jj}^{-1}}$$

where $\hat{\beta}^j$ is the MLE for the jth parameter and H_{jj} is the jth diagonal element of the Hessian. After that, the probability distribution can be modeled as normal with $\left(\hat{\beta}^j, \sqrt{-H_{jj}^{-1}}\right)$ parameters or uniform distribution for better tractability.

MCMC-based: In MCMC sampling, the samples are drawn from a prior distribution with the distribution of the next sample dependent on the last sample to form a Markov chain that converges to the posterior distribution $g\left(\vec{\beta} \mid d_i(t), \vec{x}_i(t), t = 1, \ldots, T, i \in M\right)$.[15] Here instead of using a common vector of regression coefficients β estimated at the higher level by pooling the data at the lower-level groups, the hierarchical model implements a solution where the degree of pooling is determined by the data and estimated parameters of the prior. Using the example of the Poisson regression, we model the posterior as

$$y_i \sim Poisson\left(e^{\vec{\beta}_j \vec{x}_i(t)}, i \in I_j\right)$$

where group-specific parameter vectors $\vec{\beta}_j$ are estimated individually for each group I_j but drawn from the priors that are common for all groups. For example,

$$\beta_j^k \sim N\left(\mu^k, \sigma^k\right).$$

All μ^k and σ^k are estimated parameters of the prior distribution with index k specifying the type of the parameter. These parameters are also drawn from their own priors ("priors of the prior"), which are set as non-informative:

$$\mu^k \sim N(0,100)$$
$$\sigma^k \sim \Gamma(2,1).$$

The uncertainty interval is computed as α-level credibility interval $[a,b]$ by determining its limits from the tails of the posterior distribution as $\int_{-\infty}^{a} f(\beta)d\beta = \frac{1-\alpha}{2}$ and $\int_{b}^{\infty} f(\beta)d\beta = \frac{1-\alpha}{2}$.

From the practical implementation perspective, these two methods have their advantages and disadvantages. MLE-based methods may be relatively fast but computationally unstable whereas MCMC-type methods are usually stable but may be computationally slow especially for large samples. In some practical implementations it may be beneficial to use a hybrid approach by applying Newton-Raphson methods at the higher hierarchy levels and MCMC at the item level with Gaussian prior obtained from the resulting Hessian at the higher level.

4. SUMMARY AND FUTURE WORK

Parameter uncertainty is an important issue to consider in order to develop a practically applicable prescriptive solution based on a parametric predictive model since in most applications it is impossible to obtain a sufficiently precise estimator of the model parameters. Together with a new formulation of joint markdown and the distribution optimization problem based on accounting for the uncertainty of the demand parameters rather than stochastic demand fluctuations, this chapter presents a novel solution approach that can be readily implemented by a wide variety of retail chain operators offering products of a limited life span.

The network flow optimization model laid out in the paper can be used as a decision-making tool to provide additional managerial insight in the situations when the retailer can benefit from additional one-time actions like load balancing between the FCs by transporting large quantities of inventory at fixed cost or improving the fault-tolerance of the supply chain between the FCs and the retail locations by increasing the density of the connections.

Other areas of future research could be development of the algorithms for alternative types of demand parameter distribution and demand models using simulation-based methods to find the optimal markdown price policy and compute the derivative of the optimal revenue as a function of the allocated inventory.

NOTES

1 Harsha, P., Subramanian, S., & Uichanco, J. (2019). Dynamic pricing of omnichannel inventories. *Manufacturing & Service Operations Management, 21*(1), 47–65. https://doi.org/10.1287/msom.2018.0737.

2 Vakhutinsky, A., Kushkuley, A., & Gupte, M. (2012). Markdown optimization with an inventory-depletion effect. *Journal of Revenue and Pricing Management, 11*(6), 632–44. https://doi.org/10.1057/rpm.2012.39.

3 Smith, S.A., & Achabal, D.D. (1998). Clearance pricing and inventory policies for retail chains. *Management Science, 44*(3), 285–300. https://www.jstor.org/stable/2634668.

4 Lei, Y.M., Jasin, S., Uichanco, J., & Vakhutinsky, A. (2018). Joint product framing (display, ranking, pricing) and order fulfillment under the MNL model for e-commerce retailers. https://dx.doi.org/10.2139/ssrn.3282019.

5 Gallego, G., & Van Ryzin, G. (1997). A multiproduct dynamic pricing problem and its applications to network yield management. *Operations Research, 45*(1), 24–41. https://doi.org/10.1287/opre.45.1.24.

6 Mai, T., & Jaillet, P. (2019). Robust multi-product pricing under general extreme value models. *ArXiv*, 1912.09552. https://doi.org/10.48550/arXiv.1912.09552.

7 Caro, F., & Gallien, J. (2012). Clearance pricing optimization for a fast-fashion retailer. *Operations Research, 60*(6), 1404–22. https://dx.doi.org/10.2139/ssrn.1731402

8 Ito, S., & Fujimaki, R. (2017). *Optimization beyond prediction: Prescriptive price optimization*. Proceedings of the 23rd ACM SIGKDD International Conference on Knowledge Discovery and Data Mining, 1833–41. https://doi.org/10.48550/arXiv.1605.05422.

9 Vakhutinsky, A., Mihic, K., & Wu, S.-M. (2019). A prescriptive analytics approach to markdown pricing for an e-commerce retailer. *Journal of Pattern Recognition Research, 14*(1), 1–20. http://dx.doi.org/10.13140/RG.2.2.35292.69767.

10 Cohen, M.C., Zhang, R.P., & Jiao, K. (2022). Data aggregation and demand prediction. *Operations Research, 70*(5), 2597–618. https://doi.org/10.1287/opre.2022.2301.

11 Cho, S., Ferguson, M., Pekgun, P., & Vakhutinsky, A. (2022). *Estimating personalized demand with unobserved no-purchases using a mixture model: An application in the hotel industry. Manufacturing & Service Operations Management, 25*(4), 1245–62. https://doi.org/10.1287/msom.2022.1094.

12 Cohen, M., & Perakis, G. (2018). *Promotion optimization in retail.* https://dx.doi.org/10.2139/ssrn.3194640.

13 Rooderkerk, R.P., Van Heerde, H.J., & Bijmolt, T.H. (2013). Optimizing retail assortments. *Marketing Science, 32*(5), 699–715. https://www.jstor.org/stable/24544773.

14 Johnson, N.L., Kemp, A.W., & Kotz, S. (2005). *Univariate discrete distributions.* John Wiley & Sons.

15 Gelman, A., Carlin, J.B., Stern, H.S., & Rubin, D.B. (2013). *Bayesian data analysis.* Chapman and Hall/CRC.

CHAPTER TWELVE

Censored Demand Estimation of Choice Models for Omnichannel Pricing

Pavithra Harsha and Shivaram Subramanian

SUMMARY OF CHAPTER

This chapter discusses the advances in retail demand forecasting and the downstream price optimization for an omnichannel retailer by modeling the multichannel shopping path of today's customers and fulfillment strategies to enhance the business impact of omnichannel retailing.

MANAGERIAL IMPLICATIONS (GENERAL)

- This chapter is of the utmost importance to every retail manager as it combines a transparent and explainable demand forecast model with an optimization strategy for pricing.
- Retail managers are urged to revise their demand forecast models as well as their pricing and promotion policies and procedures. This chapter is challenging but all the more important for the extremely rich techniques described.

MANAGERIAL IMPLICATIONS (ORGANIZATIONAL)

- The implementation and operationalization of these models requires the cooperation between different departments inside the retail company: marketing, sales, finance, procurement, and logistics, including inventory, transportation, and IT.

- This also requires the integration of various IT systems supporting different stakeholders in the retail company.
- Interdepartmental cooperation could be implemented in the form of a multidisciplinary center of excellence inside the retail company, grouping representatives of the main stakeholders, with the responsibility of designing, developing, deploying, and monitoring such types of advanced analytics and optimization models.

MANAGERIAL IMPLICATIONS (STRATEGIC, TACTICAL, AND OPERATIONAL)

- The omnichannel mode of operation is a strategic decision for a retailer that requires the fusion and reorganization of its sales channels.
- From a strategic perspective, the demand estimation models for omnichannel and pricing optimization projects have to be mapped to other projects in the context of the strategic plan. The roadmap of projects should take into consideration the dependency between projects, the availability of data, and the complexity of integration with the different IT systems in place.
- From a tactical perspective, the implementation of such a project requires the provisioning of a data and advanced analytics platform as well as sourcing the required skills. Luckily, these platforms are becoming affordable with all major cloud providers.
- Also from a tactical perspective, it might require sourcing additional external data if the internal data is not sufficient or requires additional capabilities to collect data internally (such as cameras inside bricks-and-mortar stores to capture heat map locations, customers visits, and sales/no-sales decisions).
- From an operational perspective, implementing these methods might require a partial revision of the operational model currently in place as we believe that the concepts and ideas expressed are disruptive.

MANAGERIAL IMPLICATIONS (RISK ASSESSMENT)
- Implementing the demand estimation models for omnichannel and pricing optimization project must be a mitigated risk project. The main risk is that the cost to implement and operationalize a full-scale omnichannel solution are high for a small business. To mitigate the risk, managers could proceed with a proof of concept project or a proof of value project before proceeding with a full rollout.

1. INTRODUCTION

Omnichannel retailing is a fast-growing industry trend that rapidly accelerated during the COVID-19 pandemic. An omnichannel retailer (OCR) enables a seamless customer shopping experience across multiple sales channels including e-commerce, in-store, mobile, and catalog, among others. Many OCRs employ advanced order fulfillment methods such as initiating ship-from-store fulfillment for e-commerce orders and offering a buy-online-pick-up-in-store option to enhance the convenience of receiving a product. This chapter discusses the advances in retail demand forecasting and the downstream price optimization for an OCR by modeling the multichannel shopping path of today's customers and fulfillment strategies to enhance the business impact of omnichannel retailing.

Fine-grained demand forecasts by SKU, channel, and location are the fundamental inputs that drive an OCR's downstream decision-making operations such as inventory planning and pricing. The proliferation of price-transparent, recommendation-driven omnichannel shopping platforms across the industry has spurred the need to develop forecasting solutions that (1) provide a deeper understanding of customer preferences and willingness-to-pay to estimate the proportion of customers that will substitute across products, switch channels, or buy from competitors and (2) achieve the best forecast accuracy and prediction intervals while being transparent and explainable. Forecast quality can be enhanced by identifying the demand influencers present in a wide variety of internal and external data sources such as point-of-sales data by product, channel, and location, product attributes, price and promotion data, supply chain factors, competitor prices, and market signals. The hierarchical censored demand modeling framework we discuss in this chapter is a practical means of employing high dimensional training data to achieve the aforementioned forecasting goals and obtaining a 360-degree view of future demands.

An OCR uses calibrated demand models for price optimization to identify the right prices for products and assortments across multiple channels and locations. Demand substitution across channels or competitor products are often ignored in traditional revenue management solutions, which assume that prices only affect demand in the same channel. This leads to a potential cannibalization of demand across the OCR's own channels and lost sales to competitors. Thus, the pricing problem requires a joint optimization across assortments, channels, and locations to manage correlated price-sensitive demands and satisfy price coordination constraints across all locations. We refer to this as the omnichannel pricing (OCP) problem. The presence of short life-cycle items with long lead times and limited supply and the pooling of inventories across channels for omnichannel fulfillment add an additional layer of complexity that requires synchronization of pricing with fulfilment strategies. The latter is particularly relevant in retail sectors such as fashion, luxury, seasonal products, and consumer electronics under clearance,[1] among others, where sharing of limited inventory across locations and channels is common.

Given the challenging nature of downstream pricing problems, the right choice of demand models can go a long way in ensuring that the resultant OCP problem is computationally tractable and scalable to achieve (near) optimal prices. The pricing engine should be agile enough to support rapid demand-driven reoptimization of prices across channels, locations, and assortments in a competitive and dynamic omnichannel marketplace. We formulate canonical versions of the OCP problem and discuss how the calibrated censored demand model meets these business requirements. Operationally, all these application features combine to provide a comfortable and intuitive user experience to end users. User acceptance often determines the shelf-life of an application in an organization.

In this chapter we consider an OCR selling an assortment of products in multiple channels and locations. Different products or product upgrades in this assortment periodically enter and exit the system. Assortments can vary by channel, and products can be restricted for sale in specific channels and locations. For example, packaged multiples of a product may be sold exclusively in the e-commerce channel while individual units can only be purchased in stores. In section 2, we will see how the OCR can use historical sales data, including product attributes, price changes, and promotion information, to calibrate demand models and generate demand forecasts for existing and newly introduced products for a specified granularity and time horizon depending on the requirements of the downstream business application (e.g., weekly forecasts for the next month at the product, channel, and location level). We introduce the hierarchical discrete choice demand model, explain how it is calibrated in the absence of lost sales data, and provide some implementation recommendations. Next in section 3, we will discuss how the OCR can use these forecasts to price different products subject to a variety of practical business rules and pricing constraints. We formulate a generalized omnichannel price optimization problem and discuss the transformations that can be employed to derive a tractable, scalable reformulation that works well in practice. We reference multiple case studies throughout the chapter.

This chapter provides a practice-based consolidated adaptation and generalization of the authors' academic papers on (1) estimation,[2] (2) omnichannel pricing of non-perishables,[3] and (3) dynamic omnichannel pricing of short life-cycle items,[4] combined with the authors' insights and lessons learned while implementing such demand estimation and OCP models in a variety of real-world retail settings. Interested readers can refer to the aforementioned references for additional pointers in the literature on related forecasting and pricing topics.

2. HIERARCHICAL DISCRETE CHOICE DEMAND MODELS AND CENSORED ESTIMATION

In the omnichannel setting, we want to predict demands for different purchase choices available to a customer across channels and products. We employ a hierarchy of models to predict these demands: (1) an upper-level arrival-rate model to predict the market size of interested customers and (2) a lower-level discrete customer choice model to predict the purchase probability of each available omnichannel choice. The choices also include the no-purchase option that in combination with the upper-level model provides an additional estimate of the number of customers who walk away without making a purchase.

Discrete choice demand models anchored in random utility theory are one of the commonly used demand functions to model consumer choice.[5,6] They generalize the well-known *multinomial logit* (MNL) and the *multiplicative competitive interaction* (MCI) demand models. Suppose M is the set of purchasing choices indexed by m and $\emptyset$ denotes the no-purchase choice. The demand for a choice $m \in M$ or the choice $\emptyset$ at time t in a location l is given by:

$$D_{mlt}(\mathbf{Y}_{lt}, \mathbf{X}_{lt}, S_{lt}) = \begin{matrix} \text{Arrivals at location } l \\ \text{and time } t \end{matrix} * \begin{matrix} \text{Purchase Probability of choice } m \\ \text{at time } t \text{ and location } l \end{matrix} \qquad (2.1)$$

$$= \tau_l(\mathbf{Y}_{lt}) \frac{A_{ml}(\mathbf{X}_{mlt})}{1 + \sum_{m' \in S_{lt}} A_{m'l}(\mathbf{X}_{m'lt})}, \qquad m \in S_{lt}, \qquad (2.2)$$

$$D_{mlt}(\mathbf{Y}_{lt}, \mathbf{X}_{lt}, S_{lt}) = 0, \qquad m \in M \setminus S_{lt}, \text{ and} \qquad (2.3)$$

$$D_{\emptyset lt}(\mathbf{Y}_{lt}, \mathbf{X}_{lt}, S_{lt}) = \tau_l(\mathbf{Y}_{lt}) \frac{1}{1 + \sum_{m' \in S_{lt}} A_{m'l}(\mathbf{X}_{m'lt})} \qquad (2.4)$$

where

- $\tau_l(\mathbf{Y}_{lt})$ is the model for arrivals or market size that is a measure of consumers interested in any of the choices, including the no-purchase option, as a function of a vector of the market-size attributes $\mathbf{Y}_{lt}$ at location l and time t,
- $A_{ml}(\mathbf{X}_{mlt})$ is the attraction model of choice m as a function of the vector of attributes $\mathbf{X}_{mlt}$ for choice m at location l and time t,

- $\mathbf{X}_{lt}$ is the matrix of attributes where row m corresponds to $\mathbf{X}_{mlt}$, and
- $S_{lt} \subset M$ is the set of purchasing choices that are available at location l and time t.

Equations (2.2–2.4) simply state that the demand for a product is obtained by multiplying the market size and the product's relative attractiveness within the available alternatives. In continuous time settings, market size is measured and referred to also as an arrival rate. The mean arrival rate is often assumed to be a constant in the literature, but in practice the average market size can be a function of one or more attributes. The size function aims to capture the impact of aggregate assortment level attributes that influence the arriving traffic (e.g., temporal and marketing effects such as holiday, seasonality, assortment popularity or freshness, life cycle effects, trends, local events or weather, and campaign) and is assumed to be independent of factors that influence the preference for a specific choice over another. We model the market size function as a linear, exponential, or a power function of the attributes $\mathbf{Y}_{lt}$, whose prediction coefficients have to be estimated (for example, using an exponential function, $\tau_l(\mathbf{Y}_{lt}) = e^{\gamma_l^T \mathbf{Y}_{lt}}$, the prediction coefficients are γ_l).

Purchase/choice probability models predict how consumers choose between alternatives and are defined by the relative attractiveness of alternatives (including no-purchase with a default attraction of 1.0). Attractiveness captures the true utility of a choice and is influenced by a variety of attributes including its price and product design features such as style and color. Different attraction models can be derived depending on the assumptions of the utility structure from observable components $\mathbf{X}_{mlt}$ and unobservable random distribution of a choice. The attraction function $A_{ml}(\mathbf{X}_{mlt})$ in the case of the MNL model is $e^{\beta_{ml}^T \mathbf{X}_{mlt}}$, while for the MCI model it is $\Pi_k X_{mltk}^{\beta_{mlk}}$, and the for linear model it is $\beta_{ml}^T \mathbf{X}_{mlt}$, where β_{ml} are the prediction coefficients that need to be estimated. Note that we refer to the choice probabilities as the predicted quantities from a model, while market shares are the empirical revealed preference data used to estimate choice probabilities.

A hierarchical discrete choice model is an integrated top-down method to model substitution across a large number of choices. Such a model offers a scalable alternative to a complete cross-choice feature-based bottom-up approach (potentially in combination with a top-down forecast reconciliation option). These hierarchical models enable efficient information sharing across choices, particularly in sparse data settings. A live field experiment on Alibaba's recommendation engine[7] observed that discrete choice functions that accurately model product substitution effects can yield a significantly higher revenue compared to sophisticated machine-learning models that are agnostic to substitution effects, despite the lower prediction accuracy of the former. Note that forecast accuracy is an important intermediate output in revenue management applications, and what ultimately matters are the prices recommended to the customer and their effectiveness in live testing. Interestingly, discrete choice models can also be used in a "data pooling" mode in non-substitutive hierarchical settings (e.g., estimating the demands for different sizes of a t-shirt of the same style and color, and even complementary items) where the absence of features in the lower level induces a static spread down as opposed to a substitution (which happens when features like price vary over time).

Note that even with hierarchical models, it is important to account for assortment changes that can naturally occur due to stockouts. Conlon and Mortimer[8] analyze the cascading effects of ignoring the effect of product availability on demand forecasts. They discuss how demands are underestimated due to nonavailability and, the resultant forced substitution can also overstate demands for the available alternatives conditional on the full product assortment being available. This bias can exaggerate the degree of product substitutability in the training data.

Although we restrict the discussion in this chapter to the commonly used choice model described above, several alternative choice models have been used in price optimization such as (a) the nested choice models (see Harsha et al. [2019b] for more details on definition, censored calibration, and use in the context of omnichannel pricing); (b) the hybrid discrete choice demand model[9] (see Subramanian and Sherali [2010][10] and discussion in Harsha et al. [2019a, b] on the non-convexity of the resultant pricing problem); (c) the mixed choice models;[11] and (d) non-parametric methods.[12]

The standard methods to estimate discrete choice models require at least some historical information about every choice, which in our setting, would also include the no-purchase option.[13,14] OCRs rarely have complete information about lost sales and must calibrate their demand models using incomplete data. We employ the integrated MIP based loss-minimization method proposed in Subramanian and Harsha (2021) to jointly calibrate the market size and choice probability parameters when the lost sales data is censored. This method does not require assumptions about external information on market shares and performs imputations endogenously within the MIP by estimating optimal values for the probabilities of the unobserved censored choices and minimizing the loss between the observed/imputed and predicted quantities. Compared to its iterative MLE (maximum likelihood estimator) based counterparts like the Expectation Maximization (EM) method[15] and other recent approaches,[16,17] this is a computationally fast single-step method that can simultaneously calibrate market-size covariates (e.g., with temporal causals), which is a critical requirement in practical settings. This section complements Ferguson (2020),[18] which offers a detailed technical discussion of the censored demand estimation methods for substitutable products by presenting real-world examples and insights as well as a novel method that extends the ratio-based choice model demand estimation method,[19] an alternative to MLE approaches,[20] to censored data settings. From a machine learning perspective, the censored demand estimation method we discuss below can be viewed as jointly calibrating an upper-level regression model and lower-level classification model by minimizing an integrated loss function.

We present the mathematical formulation of the multilocation hierarchical censored data demand estimation (CDE) model below for an assortment of choices which are product-channel combinations when both $A_{ml}(.)$ and $\tau_l(.)$ are exponential functions. Since the lost share proportions are unobserved in the training data, they are modeled as continuous, piecewise linear (SOS-2) decision variables bounded between 0 and 1. Doing so allows us to impute unobserved quantities such as market size and lost sales. The resultant parameter estimation problem is a computationally tractable MIP that can be quickly solved to (near) optimality using commercial optimization software packages. To deal with the issue of limited feature variations in the training data (something we often encounter in practice), we incorporate model enhancements such as variable selection using LASSO penalties and sign constraints on coefficients (e.g., negative price effect coefficients) to enable an automated machine-learning environment required for operational deployment. This MIP also includes a knapsack constraint to identify the top N competitors whose prices have the most influence on channel demands. We summarize our notation in Table 12.1.

$$\min_{\beta,\gamma,z,w} \sum_{l \in L} \sum_{t \in T} \sum_{m \in S_{lt}} \left[\mathcal{L}\left(\ln(\overline{s}_{mlt}) - \sum_{k \in K} \ln(\overline{\lambda}_{klt}) z_{klt} - \beta_{ml}^T \overline{X}_{mlt} \right) \right]$$

$$+ \mathcal{L}\left(\sum_{k \in K} \ln(\overline{\theta}_{klt}) z_{klt} - \gamma_l^T \overline{Y}_{lt} \right) \qquad \text{(CDE)}$$

$$+ \sum_{l \in L} \sum_{m \in M} \rho_m^T |\beta_{ml}| + \sum_{l \in L} \rho^T |\gamma_l|$$

$$\sum_{k \in K} z_{klt} = 1 \qquad\qquad \forall l \in L, t \in T \qquad\qquad (2.5)$$

$$\sum_{c \in C} w_c \leq N \qquad\qquad\qquad\qquad\qquad\qquad (2.6)$$

$$0 \leq \beta_{mlc} \leq u_{mc} w_c \qquad \forall c \in C, m \in M, l \in L \qquad (2.7)$$

$$\underline{u}_m \leq \beta_{ml} \leq \overline{u}_m \qquad \forall m \in M, l \in L \qquad\qquad (2.8)$$

$$\underline{u} \leq \gamma_l \leq \mathbf{u} \qquad\qquad \forall l \in L \qquad\qquad\qquad (2.9)$$

$$\beta_{mlj} = \beta_{m'l'j} \qquad \forall \{m, m', l, l', j\} \in F^{share} \qquad (2.10)$$

$$\gamma_{lj} = \gamma_{l'j} \qquad\qquad \forall \{l, l', j\} \in F^{size} \qquad\qquad (2.11)$$

$$w_c \in \{0, 1\} \qquad\qquad \forall c \in C \qquad\qquad\qquad (2.12)$$

$$\{z_{klt} \forall k \in K\} \in SOS2 \qquad \forall l \in L, t \in T \qquad\qquad (2.13)$$

Table 12.1. Summary of Notation and Description for the CDE Model

Indices

$t, m, l, k, c,$	a period, a choice, a location, a lost share value, a competitor index

Sets

$T, M, L, C,$	All training weeks, all customer purchase choices, all locations, all competitors
S_{lt}	All choices available to a customer in location l at time t
$K,$	All lost market share values chosen between $[\varepsilon, 1 - \varepsilon]$, where ε is a small number greater than 0
$F^{share},$	a user defined fixed effect set with element $\{m, m', l, l', j\}$ implying $\beta_{mlj} = \beta_{m'l'j}$
$F^{size},$	a user defined fixed effect set with element $\{l, l', j\}$ implying $\gamma_{lj} = \gamma_{l'j}$

Parameters

$\bar{s}_{mlt},$	observed sales for location l, choice m in period t
$\bar{X}_{mlt},$	row vector of attribute values for location l, choice m in period t, including observable competitor prices
$\bar{Y}_{lt},$	vector of attribute values for market size for location l in period t
$f_k,$	Lost market share value corresponding to index k
$\bar{\lambda}_{lkt},$	lost sales due to no-purchase at location l, in period t, and equals $\dfrac{f_k}{1-f_k} \sum_{m \in S_{lt}} \bar{s}_{mlt}$
$\bar{\theta}_{klt},$	Market size at location l in period t, and equals $\dfrac{1}{1-f_k} \sum_{m \in S_{lt}} \bar{s}_{mlt}$
$N,$	maximum number of competitors the retailer aims to index against
ρ_m, ρ	L1 penalty corresponding to β_{ml} and γ_l coefficients respectively
$u_m, u,$	Lower bounds corresponding β_{ml} and γ_l coefficients respectively
$\bar{u}_m, \bar{u},$	Upper bounds corresponding β_{ml} and γ_l coefficients respectively

Decision Variables

$\beta_{ml},$	row vector of coefficients for the attributes $\bar{X}_{mlt}$ of channel m, modeled as continuous variables
$\gamma_l,$	row vector of coefficients for attributes $\bar{Y}_{lt}$ of market size, modeled as continuous variables
$z_{klt},$	Probability that the lost market share at location l in period t is f_k. These auxiliary decision variables are modeled as a Special-Ordered-Set Type 2 (SOS2) variables wherein at most two adjacent members (assuming the f_k's are ordered) can be nonzero.
$w_c,$	auxiliary binary variable that is 1 if competitor c is a key competitor and 0 otherwise

This canonical model gives rise to several special cases that can be implemented to model cross-channel substitutions such as (1) single location, single-product multichannel setting; (2) single location multiproduct multichannel setting that models cross-product and channel substitution; and (3) the general multilocation setting. The machine learning framework naturally lends itself to multitask learning across choices, locations, and even other segments where coefficients can be shared across prediction tasks, allowing for a relatively easy way to handle new products as well as a means of increasing the data size in sparse data settings. For example, forecasts for newly offered choices (products) can be obtained by including them in an assortment after mapping them to a nearest calibrated choice or a best-fit combination of previously offered choices. The measure of "nearness" can be estimated using attribute-driven machine-learning approaches, for example, nearness based on the similarity of features. Also, depending on the choice of the loss function $Y(.)$ a mean or a median or quantile point forecast of the size and share can be obtained with the latter being useful in the context of demand distribution modeling.

There are practical enhancements that can be leveraged in modeling and solving CDE discussed in Subramanian and Harsha (2021) to improve performance and solution run times such as (1) use of weighted loss function across observations (e.g., sales-weighted terms), ridge penalties, and tuning of these hyper-parameters, (2) alternative attraction or size models to logarithm or linear, (3) the use of partial information of market share that can be gainfully applied to tighten the bounds on the imputed lost sales across time, (4) a heuristic to handle zero sales (note that when we work with aggregated data, for example weekly sales within a price zone, zero sales observations are infrequent but are not uncommon at a granular level), (5) an extension to disambiguate competitor market shares from lost sales using competitor attributes such as prices, and last (6) an efficient nonconvex-convex alternating heuristic for very large instances (thousands of observations) where an out-of-the-box MIP solver may not be practical. Note that the scalability of the CDE is less affected by the number of choices and features. Typically, the solution quality measured in terms of the achieved optimality gap improves as the number of choices increase, while adding more features only increases the number of continuous variables in the CDE parameter estimation and can therefore be efficiently managed in practice.

Commonly used metrics to evaluate model performance across observations and fine tune the model as part of cross-validation include, for example, bias, mean absolute percentage error, weighted or symmetric mean absolute percentage error, and mean squared error. To obtain an overall performance number across observed choices, these metrics are often weighted by their sales-rate, revenue, or margin to direct attention to relevant products and channels for an in-depth evaluation and measurement of the cost of forecast inaccuracy to the OCR.

Transparency and explainability are important aspects of forecasting, and some retailers may prefer models that score well in these aspects over opaque methods that produce marginally better forecasts. An important aspect of CDE is its ability to decompose sales into an arrival-rate model and purchase probability model. This enables CDE to differentiate and explain sales shifts driven by arrival pattern variations from those caused by changing product preferences, unlike machine learning models that do not account for lost sales. Visualization of forecasts at various levels of the product and location hierarchy can greatly enhance our understanding of such demand response patterns. The hierarchical modeling structure is transparent and represented using relatively simple generalized linear functional forms. The upper and lower model coefficients can be directly used to identify the top demand influencers and calculate key pricing parameters such as own-price and cross-product price elasticity. In contrast, opaque ML models cannot easily handle such user-acceptance constraints and require additional post hoc models to distill, explain, and interpret their predictions. Such a post-processing approach comes with its own complications.

Besides modeling and explainability, good data quality, efficient data management processes, automated hyper-parameter optimization, data visualization, secure infrastructure, and scalable deployment are essential to managing and automating the entire forecasting pipeline, which are the core aspects of leading Auto AI/ ML offerings.

2.1. Example: Estimating Cross-Product Substitution Using CDE

We explain how the CDE model predicts substitution effects and censored market shares using a publicly available illustrative data set of a tire retailer that was published in a Harvard Business Review article by Fisher and Vaidyanathan.[21] The article uses the data set to reveal how customers shop for product feature combinations within an assortment that maximizes their utility, and a fraction of these customers switch to their next preferred alternative if their first choice is unavailable. It explains how ignoring such effects can lead to incorrect demand models that result in poor assortment and pricing decisions which have bigger profitability implications. We highlight the same using the CDE model.

The original article employs a nine-parameter model and discusses an iterative estimation method when not all product choices are offered in the assortment to obtain the relative market shares when all product choices are made available. This sales data is reproduced in Table 12.2 below and consists of fifteen sales observations, corresponding to different tire sizes, for six brand-warranty product choices in decreasing order of quality (purchase price): NH (National High), NM (National Medium), H1 (House 1 High), H2 (House 2 High), M2 (House 2 Medium), and L3 (House 3 Low).

Each observation row (A-O) reports the sales values for each brand included in the corresponding assortment offered to the customer. Brands not offered within an assortment are represented by a dash. For example, in Observation A, the offered assortment set is {NH, H2, M2, L3}. Choices H2 and M2 are available in all but one assortment while the cheapest product (L3) is offered only in 20 per cent of the tire sizes or observations. Note that for any observation, the market size is unknown because the number of customers who walk away without purchasing is not available in the data. Observing that customers interested in different tire sizes express their preferences for products in terms of the attributes they offer,[22] it is not unreasonable to assume that the purchase probabilities are consistent across tire sizes for the same offer sets.

Table 12.2. Tire Sales Data Published in Fisher and Vaidyanathan (2012) for six product choices.

Tire Sizes	NH	NM	H1	H2	M2	L3
A	100	–	–	29	28	190
B	282	21	–	30	203	–
C	–	–	–	11	12	86
D	–	–	–	53	50	284
E	72	64	20	172	570	–
F	59	–	97	285	763	–
G	10	–	16	14	76	–
H	–	7	33	157	377	–
I	–	10	–	183	524	–
J	–	39	–	225	568	–
K	–	–	8	10	73	–
L	–	–	8	47	223	–
M	–	–	–	43	298	–
N	–	–	–	72	221	–
O	8	–	–	–	–	200

Source: Harvard Business Review.

An illustrative CDE model having seven parameters (intercept terms for market-size and the six brand choices) was calibrated using these fifteen observations as training data to estimate the purchase probability for each brand and the no-purchase probability accounting for cross-product substitution effects. The estimated purchase probability for each brand when all choices are offered is shown in Figure 12.1. We also plot the observed and estimated market shares (when all choices are offered) in the article for comparison and discussion. We see that M2 has the highest observed market share in the data where L3 is seldom offered. The CDE values are close to the values estimated in the original article using a different methodology. Note that this simple CDE model employs two fewer parameters compared to the latter, which uses a one-up or one-down substitution model while we assume substitution across all products.

Barring the highest quality brand (NH), the predicted purchase probability increases as the price decreases. The observed market shares and the predicted probabilities are relatively close for the three highest quality brands (NH, NM, H1) but differ sharply for the

Figure 12.1. Purchase Probabilities by choice

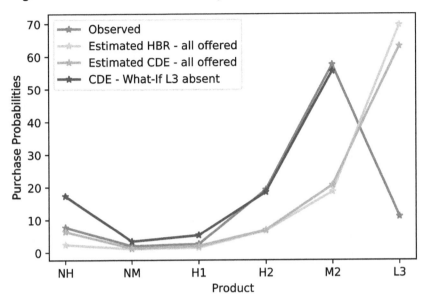

cheaper brands. Here, customers were found to be more price sensitive and willing to accept cheaper substitutes on offer. As a "what-if" analysis, Figure 12.1 also plots the CDE purchase probabilities when the cheapest choice (L3) is withdrawn from the assortment and can be seen to closely follow the observed market-shares. As explained by Fisher and Vaidyanathan (2012), we see that when brand L3 is not offered, M2's propensity increases and vice versa, indicating the degree of cross-product substitution between these two choices. The CDE model predicts that 34.9 per cent more customers switch to M2 when L3 is unavailable, suggesting that a significant fraction of customers who couldn't find the cheapest brand (L3) in the assortment would be willing to trade up to M2.

As an additional output, the CDE model estimates an average no-buy rate of 39 per cent across the fifteen observations. This predicted lost share probability drops to less than 7 per cent when all choices are offered, highlighting the impact of not offering the cheapest and most popular L3 option in 80 per cent of the assortments. Any incremental gain in revenue by upselling to higher-priced brands must be assessed in conjunction with this accompanying increase in lost sales.

Finally, note that this illustrative CDE model is simplistic in that it allows substitution across all choices. For example, the NH purchase probability increases significantly when option L3 is not offered. In practice, substitution is more likely across products having similar attributes. For example, CDE prediction accuracy can be improved by dividing the six brands into "premium" (NH, NM, H1) and "economy" customer segments (H2, M2, L3) and calibrating separate models for each segment. In practice, sophisticated segmentation methods are employed to improve solution quality and user acceptance. This estimated price sensitivity and cross-product substitutive effects can be employed within a pricing model to jointly optimize prices across the choices and segments to preserve market share and increase revenue.

2.2. Channel Switching during COVID-19

Figure 12.2 depicts the channel level daily sales of an OCR aggregated across departments during the first wave of the COVID-19 pandemic across its dominant sales channels: in-store/walk-in, and e-commerce. The channel-level market shares prior to COVID-19 closures (January to early March) were 78 per cent walk-in and 22 per cent e-commerce; after the store closures (early March to July) they were 13 per cent and 87 per cent respectively. As can be seen in the figure, prior to the start of the COVID-19 pandemic, the walk-in sales show a steady temporal pattern relative to the e-commerce channel. After the lockdown in March there was a shift in channel sales to online followed by a switch back to walk-in sales in June.

We illustrate how the CDE model can be used to forecast this channel switching using COVID-19 data.

A preliminary chain-level CDE model was calibrated for each product category using January to (early) June 2020 daily sales values by channel as training data to predict the chain-level channel switching behavior of customers and estimate the potential increase or decrease in lost sales during a fifteen-day forecast period of June 8–22, 2020. The market-size model included day-of-week, number

Figure 12.2. Daily channel sales for an OCR at chain level with partial training and test data. Scale on y-axis and holiday sales are hidden for proprietary reasons.

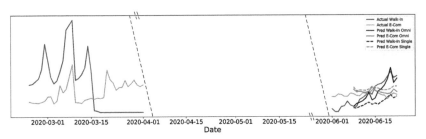

of SKUs with inventory, available inventory per SKU, and aggregate chain-level seasonality features in addition to an intercept term. The lower-level channel-share model consisted of an intercept, day-of-week, chain-level seasonality by channel,[23] lagged effects of channel sales, and smoothed COVID-19 lag features including the normalized rates of confirmed cases and their outcomes. The walk-in channel was unavailable during the temporary store closures from March through May 2020 (and modeled as a change in assortment). A single channel CDE model was also calibrated to generate baseline forecasts for comparison.

Figure 12.2 depicts the omnichannel and single channel chain-level predictions (rolled-up from the category-level) for the walk-in and e-commerce channels. When compared to the fifteen-day forecasts generated by the single channel version, the omnichannel CDE model improved the mean absolute percentage error (MAPE) for the walk-in and e-commerce channels by more than seventeen and five percentage points respectively on average across categories.[24] As Figure 12.2 shows, the single channel model significantly under predicts in-store demand while over predicting e-commerce demand. In contrast, the omnichannel CDE model predicts an increase in walk-in shopping in June along with a slight drop in e-commerce sales, closely following the actuals. This is because the single channel model predictions do not account for customers who switched back from online to in-store shopping as local stores reopened in June for walk-in shopping (resulting from the lagged time series trending upward and the lagged COVID cases dropping slightly). This example highlights the efficacy of using models like CDE in an omnichannel environment to capture substitution, which can then be used by the OCR for downstream planning.

In the following section, we discuss the use of CDE at a more granular assortment level to estimate cross-channel price substitution that we then leverage for omnichannel assortment pricing.

3. OMNICHANNEL PRICING

OCRs pursue different pricing goals to drive their market, product, and channel strategies. For example, while it may be suboptimal to always match the prices offered by e-commerce giants, OCRs can coordinate their in-store and online prices to maximize the revenue or margin based on their unique omnichannel capabilities, such as transparency, price-matching, buy-online-pickup-in-store (BOPUS), and ship-from-store (SFS). The demand forecasts must be generated at the required granularity and include features that reflect these capabilities to support this pricing goal. Some OCRs may benefit from dynamic pricing where frequent price-sensitive demand forecast refreshes are required to support rapid price changes. Other retailers may periodically offer steep channel-specific markdown or promotional discounts in order to clear excess inventory for certain product categories. In this section, we discuss a canonical pricing model for integrated omnichannel optimization across channels and locations and discuss some variations using real-life case studies.

Figure 12.3 (left) illustrates the multiple purchase options for customers of an OCR. The product assortment in each channel, the available fulfillment options, and shipping costs also influence a customer's decision to buy or walk away. The customer base is often not homogeneous, and their channel preferences vary significantly by location, demographics, and the OCR's competitive strength. A forecasting model like the CDE can learn these customer substitution preferences from the location level historical sales data for in-store and online shoppers along with market size to predict future

Figure 12.3. Proposed Omnichannel Retail Analytics Framework.

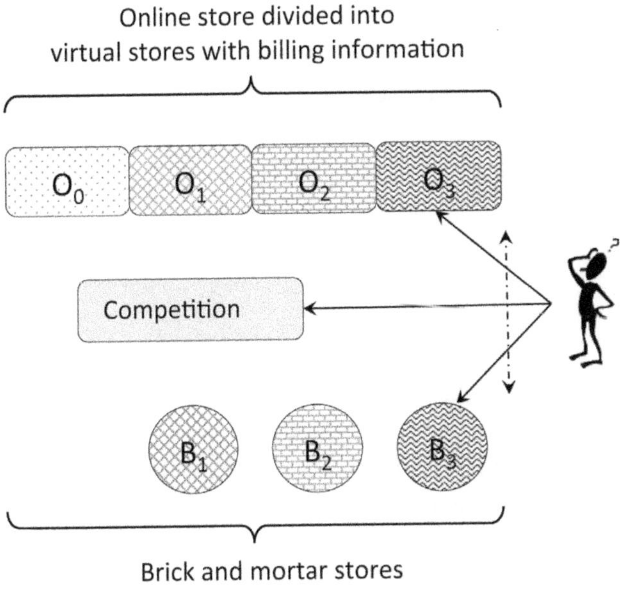

Online store divided into
virtual stores with billing information

Brick and mortar stores

demand. Figure 12.3 illustrates how the pricing formulation uses these omnichannel forecasts as input to jointly optimize prices across channels and locations to (a) manage the correlated price-sensitive demands across channels and (b) satisfy price coordination constraints across locations such as enforcing a uniform price in the e-commerce channel.

We formulate the canonical multiperiod omnichannel pricing (OCP) model with deterministic demand to identify the most profitable prices across products, locations, channels, and time periods subject to OCR's sales goals, capacity constraints, and other pricing business rules, along the lines discussed in Harsha et al. (2019a). Let $\mathbf{p}_{lt}, \mathbf{c}_l, \mathbf{D}_{lt}(\mathbf{p}_l)$ denote the prices, selling cost, and forecasted mean demand vectors across the different purchasing choices, denoted by $S_t \subset M$, offered at location $l \in L$ in time $t \in T$. Note that the notation $\mathbf{D}_{lt}(\mathbf{p}_{lt})$ assumes that all demand modeling attribute values, corresponding to $\mathbf{X}, Y$ in the prior section, except prices are known or can be predicted (e.g., competitor prices), and that the demand can be evaluated once all the prices are specified. Also, let $V_t \subset S_{lt}$ be the set of choices in the virtual channels such as e-commerce or mobile channel at time t.

$$\max_{\mathbf{p}_{lt}} \sum_{t \in T} \sum_{l \in L} (\mathbf{p}_{lt} - \mathbf{c}_l)^T \mathbf{D}_{lt}(\mathbf{p}_{lt}) \qquad \text{(OCP)}$$

$$\sum_{l,t} \mathbf{A}_{ilt} \mathbf{D}_{lt}(\mathbf{p}_{lt}) \geq g_i \qquad \forall i = 1,\dots,G \qquad (3.1)$$

$$\sum_{l,t} \mathbf{B}_{jlt} \mathbf{p}_{lt} \leq \upsilon_j \qquad \forall j = 1,\dots,J \qquad (3.2)$$

$$p_{mlt} = p_{ml't} \qquad \forall m \in V_t, l, l' \in L, t \in T \qquad (3.3)$$

$$p_{mlt} \in \Omega_{ml} \qquad \forall m \in S_{lt}, l \in L, t \in T. \qquad (3.4)$$

In this profit-maximizing canonical model, constraints (3.1–3.2) are generic polyhedral constraints on demands and prices to encapsulate the retailer's goals (such as volume goals or inventory constraints) and critical pricing business rules (such as price bounds, generalized monotonicity across products, channels and time periods, and even volume discounts) that are required for operations. Uniform pricing across the virtual channel choices and discrete prices are enforced using constraints (3.3) and (3.4) respectively. We assume that sales equal demand in this formulation. When they differ (e.g., with limited inventory or pricing rules, or when there is an exogenous fulfillment engine as in the e-commerce channel), fulfillment variables can be employed to reformulate the model while ensuring that they are feasible and representative of how fulfillment is actually implemented by the OCR.

The complicating features of the OCP model are the nonlinear and correlated demand terms in the objective and in constraint (3.1). The tractable special structure of the CDE model can exploited to eliminate the nonlinearities in the OCP model and is briefly summarized below. In the CDE model, if all demand modeling attribute values except prices are known, the market size model is price independent while the attraction model and hence the purchase probabilities continue to be functions of prices across all choices at a location. The purchase probability term can be linearized using the fractional programming transformation[25] and the resultant bi-linearities with continuous and binary discrete pricing variables can be linearized exactly using a reformulation-linearization technique (RLT) as shown in Subramanian and Sherali (2010). This procedure yields a linear mixed integer optimization model that has exactly the same number of binary variables as the number of discrete prices to be identified, that is, $O(|M|)$ per location and period. For additional details on the reformulation and the resultant model, we refer the reader to Proposition 3 in Harsha et al. (2019a).

This resultant reformulation operates in the space of both the purchase probability and the discrete pricing variables. This capability is critical in practice as it allows us to satisfy a variety of business constraints on prices as well as sales volume goals. The number of binary variables required by a general correlated demand model, in contrast to the CDE model, in this case is combinatorial, specifically $O(|\Omega|^{|M|})$ per location and period, and specialized constraints have to be added to limit the combinatorial explosion. On the other hand, the reformulated OCP model based on CDE is tractable for realistic problem instances.

Different omnichannel price optimization models can be derived from the canonical model, and we discuss and summarize the main results from two practical applications: regular or baseline pricing described in Harsha et al. (2019b) and dynamic pricing described in Harsha et al. (2019a).

3.1. Regular Pricing

In the case of basic or hardline items, products are regularly replenished and usually never go out of stock. A key question is to determine the regular or baseline prices of products by channel within a product category that are set for the next few weeks. Harsha et al. (2019a) discuss this inventory-unconstrained problem employing an MNL and nested logit (NL) extensions of CDE to predict price-sensitive demands across assortments and channels and solve the resultant omnichannel base price optimization formulation. The OCRs the authors engaged with in this study were setting baseline prices for each channel independently or simply matching the prices of competitors. In the absence of precise coordination of channel prices, the revenue performance was suboptimal. The hardline products in the analyzed categories were weakly elastic products (price elasticity is between -1 and 0), which meant that a naive pricing approach would myopically raise prices in all locations and channels. The OCP approach discussed in this chapter was implemented to increase revenue without reducing sales volume or raising prices everywhere.

An integrated data processing and machine learning framework was implemented to estimate location-specific, omnichannel price elasticities and produce point forecasts for the duration of the base pricing planning horizon. The calibrated demand model was embedded within an integrated OCP optimization engine to optimize prices across channels and store locations while satisfying additional constraints to preserve sales volume and ensure that the recommended prices were feasible to the business rules imposed. The single-product multichannel version of this formulation resembles the canonical OCP form while the multiproduct version employed a nested logit optimization model extension. These OCP models were reformulated into tractable MIPs using the transformation steps discussed previously and solved to near optimality.

An OCP implementation in two product categories for a major US retailer used a location-specific CDE model for demand calibration with temporal variables (seasonality and holidays) for market-size, price, and promotion variables for market share, projecting a 7 per cent increase in profitability by coordinating prices across channels that also preserved their market share. This gain was achieved by reducing online prices and selectively raising or lowering store prices at different locations in coordination with the recommended online price. An additional benefit of this low-high channel price strategy was that it allowed the retailer to be more competitive with e-tail giants without aggressively matching their low prices. This work also discusses how and when to match prices across the OCR's own channels.

3.2. Dynamic Pricing of Omnichannel Inventories

In the case of short life-cycle or "softline" items, products are typically seasonal goods that are available in limited quantities across the retail network. The key question here is to determine a dynamic pricing policy to maximize the retailer's revenue over a horizon with the limited inventory while also satisfying certain sell-through goals. This dynamic pricing solution is also commonly referred to as markdown price optimization (MDO) when it is used for products at the end of their life cycle when there are no more replenishments. Traditionally in such markdown solutions, inventory at a location is assumed to be an exogenous input to price optimization. This assumption does not hold with omnichannel fulfillment practices such as SFS or BOPUS, where inventory is pooled across channels to meet demand. Harsha et al. (2019b) describe a novel case of a major OCR that uses SFS extensively and employs a traditional markdown pricing solution that recommends overly steep markdowns in stores, leading to significant margin losses (see Figure 12.4). The situation motivated a need for an automated solution given the sizable number of retail store locations managed by that retailer. The authors addressed the problem by developing two practical pricing policies, a deterministic and a robust version that performs well in practice and jointly optimizes channel prices for a single product in coordination with a SFS fulfillment policy. Specifically, this work recommends prices in presence of correlated demands and shared inventory systems. We briefly summarize the results of that paper here.

The presence of shared limited inventories across channels requires additional fulfillment variables for each channel in the OCP model that are constrained to be less than the demand and the shared inventory pool from which the demands are fulfilled. This modified model, referred to as OCPX, has additional objective function terms that record the shipping costs arising from SFS fulfillment. For a deterministic hierarchical demand model, the resultant large-scale price-and-fulfillment optimization model can be reformulated into tractable MIPs as discussed in the previous example and solved to near optimality. It is important to note that we must jointly optimize prices and fulfillment patterns to identify the best partition of store inventory used to satisfy walk-in customer purchases as well as e-commerce orders. Doing so enables us to better manage the cross-channel substitutive demands and rebalance the store inventories across the network.

Figure 12.4. An illustration of an OCR's margin loss problem arising from traditional pricing solutions that ignore store inventories used for ship-from-store fulfillment.

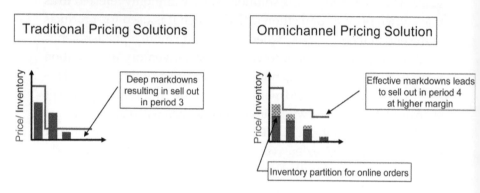

A tractable robust optimization (RO) version of OCPX was also developed to better manage the impact of uncertain demand. Towards this, we also obtained the forecast prediction intervals at the channel and chain level to set up realistic budgets of uncertainty at multiple levels that drive the RO formulation. This approach allows us to avoid overly pessimistic "worst-case" recommendations. Simulation studies showed that when we find a robust optimal solution within a small neighborhood of the prices recommended by the deterministic demand revenue model, we not only improve the worst-case but also outperform the deterministic solution in 75 per cent of the instances tested.

A proprietary version of the above methods with a CDE demand calibration method was commercially deployed for the major US retailer discussed above. The CDE calibration additionally included product life-cycle temporal features that are important in this setting. To actively relearn the customer responses to the recommended prices, the CDE was recalibrated every period with the latest demand realization prior to the price optimization, which was in turn implemented in a rolling horizon fashion wherein only the current period prices were finally executed. A causal analysis from the results of a live pilot estimated a 13.7 per cent increase in clearance-period revenue during the pilot implementation.

An important aspect of the overall OCP solution is its consistency. For typical weekly sales predictions in the omnichannel context, the CDE model, as well as the resulting OCP optimization model, can be tuned to generate near-optimal and persistent solutions. Solution persistence and optimality are critical to producing consistent responses. For small changes in input data, the CDE and OCP optimization models in combination usually produced proportionally small changes in the forecast and pricing outputs. In interactive applications where users execute a "steering" sequence of "what-ifs" by changing different dimensions or varying the values of the inputs, a consistent sequence of pricing responses is critical to a positive user experience. Consistency builds trust with the users and increases the acceptance percentage of automated OCP price recommendations.

4. CONCLUSIONS AND KEY TAKEAWAYS

Omnichannel retailing is a digital era innovation that has become a necessity in a competitive industry. While blackbox AI/ML models can enable retailers to move to data-driven forecasting relatively quickly, it does not necessarily follow that the downstream prescriptive pricing or inventory decisions will be effective.[26] Censored data in the form of unobserved lost sales, partial or complete stockouts along with other assortment changes, and cross-channel and cross-product substitutive effects are issues that have to be additionally modeled during the demand estimation process so that the demand impact of downstream decisions are accurately predicted. In tandem, downstream pricing problems can themselves be nontrivial with short life-cycle products presenting additional challenges as omnichannel fulfillment decisions are entangled with pricing. Consequently, the choice of demand models can significantly impact the effectiveness and tractability of the pricing problems in such omnichannel settings.

Combining advanced ML and behavioral models can be valuable in this context by boosting forecast accuracy without sacrificing the underlying demand modeling structure that produces efficient omnichannel pricing formulations. In this chapter, we discuss hierarchical demand modeling techniques in conjunction with integrated pricing models across sales channels that enable retail chains to accurately predict substitutable demand shifts and perform top-down reconciliation of forecasts across the product and location hierarchy. The demand estimation techniques can be augmented with attention models of external demand influencers such as events, weather, and social media signals that trigger sales surges. These demand predictions along with their uncertainty intervals can be subsequently embedded within enterprise-scale price optimization systems to precisely adjust prices of substitutable products across the physical and virtual network to maximize revenue and preserve brand and market share. Pooled inventory across channels can be synchronized with pricing to maximize product availability for walk-in customers and order fulfilment for e-commerce shoppers.

The methods described in this chapter are widely applicable not only across retail sectors; they have also been successfully employed in solving practical problems in other areas including travel and transportation, energy, and B2B pricing among others. The examples and case studies presented in this chapter provide but a small flavor of the challenges involved in omnichannel retail. We expect omnichannel retailing to accelerate along its path of innovation driven by an increasingly unified marketplace and advancements in AI and optimization methodologies.

ACKNOWLEDGMENTS

We thank and acknowledge the efforts of our co-authors, Dr. Markus Ettl and Dr. Joline Uichanco, who were key contributors to the pricing papers (Harsha et al. 2019b; 2019a respectively), that we summarize in this chapter. We also thank Dr. Brian Quanz, Dhruv Shah, and Mahesh Ramakrishna at IBM Research, who were part of the broader effort around understanding the impact of COVID-19 on retail sales data, and without whose efforts the example around channel switching during COVID-19 would not have been possible.

NOTES

1 Harsha, P., Subramanian, S., & Uichanco, J. (2019a). Dynamic pricing of omnichannel inventories. *Manufacturing & Service Operations Management, 21*(1), 47–65. https://doi.org/10.1287/msom.2018.0737.

2 Subramanian, S., & Harsha, P. (2021). Demand modeling in the presence of unobserved lost sales. *Management Science, 67*(6), 3803–33. https://doi.org/10.1287/mnsc.2020.3667.

3 Harsha, P., Subramanian, S., & Ettl, M. (2019b). A practical price optimization approach for omnichannel retailing. *INFORMS Journal on Optimization, 1*(3), 241–64. https://doi.org/10.1287/ijoo.2019.0018.

4 Harsha et al. (2019a).

5 McFadden, D. (1974). Conditional logit analysis of qualitative choice behavior. *Frontiers in Econometrics*, 105–42.

6 Berry, S.T. (1994). Estimating discrete-choice models of product differentiation. *The RAND Journal of Economics, 25*(2), 242–62. https://doi.org/10.2307/2555829.

7 Feldman, J., Zhang, D., Liu, X., & Zhang, N. (2022). Customer choice models versus machine learning: Finding optimal product displays on Alibaba. *Operations Research, 70*(1), 309–28. https://doi.org/10.1287/opre.2021.2158.

8 Conlon, C.T., & Mortimer, J.H. (2013). Demand estimation under incomplete product availability. *American Economic Journal: Microeconomics, 5*(4), 1–30. https://doi.org/10.3386/w14315.

9 Here, the total sales (instead of market size) is spread down to the purchase choices *excluding* the no-purchase option. This can induce nonintuitive cross-price elasticities (e.g., positive price elasticity for substitutive items) as the total sales depends on the prices of all the choices.

10 Subramanian, S., & Sherali, H.D. (2010). A fractional programming approach for retail category price optimization. *Journal of Global Optimization, 48*(2), 263–77. https://doi.org/10.1007/s10898-009-9491-2.

11 Cho, S., Ferguson, M., Pekgun, P., & Vakhutinsky, A. (2022). Estimating personalized demand with unobserved no-purchases using a mixture model: An application in the hotel industry. *Manufacturing & Service Operations Management, 25*(4). https://doi.org/10.1287/msom.2022.1094.

12 Jagabathula, S., & Rusmevichientong, P. (2017). A nonparametric joint assortment and price choice model. *Management Science, 63*(9), 3128–45. https://doi.org/10.1287/mnsc.2016.2491.

13 Domencich, T.A., & McFadden, D. (1975). *Urban travel demand: A behavioral analysis.* North-Holland.

14 Berkson, J. (1953). A statistically precise and relatively simple method of estimating the bio-assay with quantal response, based on the logistic function. *Journal of the American Statistical Association, 48*(263), 565–99. https://doi.org/10.1080/01621459.1953.10483494.

15 Talluri, K., & Van Ryzin, G. (2004). Revenue management under a general discrete choice model of consumer behavior. *Management Science, 50*(1), 15–33. https://doi.org/doi/10.1287/mnsc.1030.0147.

16 Newman, J.P., Ferguson, ME., Garrow, L.A., & Jacobs, T.L. (2014). Estimation of choice-based models using sales data from a single firm. *Manufacturing and Service Operations Management, 16*(2), 184–97. https://doi.org/10.1287/msom.2014.0475.

17 Abdallah, T., & Vulcano, G. (2021). Demand estimation under the multinomial logit model from sales transaction data. *Manufacturing & Service Operations Management, 23*(5), 1196–216. https://doi.org/10.1287/msom.2020.0878.

18 Ferguson, M.E. (2020). Estimating demand with constrained data and product substitutions. In S. Ray & S. Yin (Eds.), *Channel strategies and marketing mix in a connected world* (pp. 1–27). Springer.

19 Berkson (1953). Berry (1994).

20 McFadden (1974).

21 Fisher, M., & Vaidyanathan, R. (2012). Which products should you stock? A new approach to assortment planning turns an art into a science. *Harvard Business Review*, 108. https://hbr.org/2012/11/which-products-should-you-stock.

22 Subramanian & Sherali (2010).

23 Seasonalities are normalized average weekly sales in a year computed across multiple years of data at chain and channel level across multiple categories.

24 Accuracy can be improved by training the model at a more fine-grained level and using a wider set of location-specific COVID features and other external data sources that track customer response to the COVID regulatory policies on partial or complete business closures, vaccination progress, lockdowns, etc.

25 Subramanian & Sherali (2010).

26 Feldman et al. (2022).

CHAPTER THIRTEEN

Customer Lifetime Value (CLV) and Fund Transfer Pricing (FTP)

Meisam Soltani-koopa, Hootan Kamran Habibkhani, Mikhail Nediak, and Anton Ovchinnikov, with Moiz Ali and Henry Martinez

SUMMARY OF CHAPTER
The goal of this chapter is to illustrate customer lifetime value (CLV) methodologies in two international financial institutions and explain the way we can make them more precise by connecting CLV to fund transfer pricing (FTP).

MANAGERIAL IMPLICATIONS (GENERAL)
- The concepts of CLV methodologies connected to FTP are of interest to managers in financial services, and they need to be explored and analyzed even if they are not fully adopted as per this chapter.

MANAGERIAL IMPLICATIONS (ORGANIZATIONAL)
- To drive such projects successfully, there must be a form of internal excellence center for data, analytics and AI in the financial institution.
- This internal excellence center should be composed of multidisciplinary teams, including technology experts, financial experts, sales & marketing agents, legal experts, communication experts, and others.

- This internal excellence center (or any equivalent organizational entity) has the responsibility of design, development, implementation & integration, training & support, and operationalization & monitoring of these models.
- Organizations should consider having a chief data officer role (CDO) in addition to the existing CIO.

MANAGERIAL IMPLICATIONS (STRATEGIC, TACTICAL, AND OPERATIONAL)

- It is definitely a strategic decision to adopt CLV methodologies in connection with FTP to evaluate customers' profitability as it will have a profound impact on how the financial service company will market its products and services. If adopted, managers need to develop a road map for this adoption.
- From the tactical perspective, managers need to build the internal capabilities to address such types of initiatives. They need to build a data & analytics platform as well as staff for a center of excellence or an equivalent organizational structure.

MANAGERIAL IMPLICATIONS (RISK ASSESSMENT)

- One of the risks of adopting the CLV methodologies in connection with FTP is a change in how customers perceive the financial institution. Old customers might feel themselves losing the interest of their financial service provider. Other customers might feel the recommendations of products and services by the financial service provider to be geared towards the provider's interest and not their own interest, and thus they might lose trust.
- There is a brand and marketing risk associated with this adoption and operationalization.

1. INTRODUCTION

Understanding customer profitability is paramount for precision retailing (PR). An accurate view of future rather than past profitability helps companies offer products and services to best satisfy customers' needs, which in turn lead to growth in sales volumes and margins. A popular measure of such forward-looking profitability is customer lifetime value (CLV). We worked on CLV-related projects with several international financial services firms and observed that implementing the CLV methodology in a financial institution is non-trivial because of the nuanced[1] nature of both revenues and costs, which are critical for calculating value, yet are different from those in other industries as studied in the existing literature. In particular, both the revenues and costs of a financial institution depend on rates, which the institution charges or pays for providing or accessing the funds. These rates are determined through the fund transfer pricing (FTP) system. Therefore, understanding how FTP and CLV can be connected is critical for PR in financial services.

Economic crises and recession periods have stimulated companies to find ways to determine their highest-value and most profitable customers.[2] Identifying profitable customers allows companies to increase their resource allocation efficiency and improve resilience during difficult economic situations as we have seen during the 2008 recession and the 2020 pandemic. These events demonstrated that high-value customers are not only those who generate profit in the present but also those who have the potential to generate profit in the future.

In order to identify these high-value customers, companies need to use forward-looking measures, such as CLV. As Dahana et al. (2019)[3] stated, CLV "is a core metric in customer relationship management." Additionally, CLV is considered the best metric for managing customer profitability and provides greater insight than traditional, backward-looking metrics such as RFM,[4] past customer contribution, and share of wallet (SOW).[5] Customers selected based on the CLV metric are more profitable than those selected based on other widely used customer relationship management (CRM) metrics, such as previous-period customer revenue, past customer value, and customer lifetime duration, among others.[6] CLV can also be useful for improving market segmentation and resource allocation, customizing marketing communication, optimizing the timing of product offerings, and determining a firm's market value.[7,8]

The CLV metric helps a company understand how a customer will generate value for them in their future relationship. CLV is defined in many different ways. Pfeifer, Haskins, and Conroy (2005)[9] define CLV as the present value of the future cash flow attributed to a customer. Other researchers consider CLV to be the present value of future profit[10,11] or earnings[12] from a customer. Abdolvand, Albadvi, and Koosha (2014)[13] presented a collection of CLV definitions from different researchers, demonstrating how CLV has been calculated in different horizons. In this chapter, we define CLV as the discounted future revenue generated by the customer during one year of his/her relationship with the company.

A variety of methods have been proposed for calculating CLV. These methods include the Markov decision process,[14,15] approximate dynamic programming,[16] reinforcement learning,[17,18] data mining and regression,[19] RFM and Pareto/NBD,[20] RFM and Markov chain,[21] and deterministic models.[22] For a well-structured summary of the different methodologies used in CLV research, see AboEl-Hamd, Shamma, and Saleh (2020).[23] Based on the above, we identify two main categories of methods that employ CLV: CLV prediction and CLV optimization.[24] Prediction methods focus on determining the expected profitability of customers in a determined horizon while optimization methods focus on interaction marketing aimed at providing recommendations and a path for the customer journey to be more profitable.[25,26]

CLV has also become more commonly used in financial services. Haenlein, Kaplan, and Beeser (2007) proposed a customer valuation model based on a combination of Markov chains and a classification and regression tree (CART) applied to a German retail bank database. They determined the CLV of each customer as being the discounted sum of state-dependent contribution margins, weighted by their corresponding transition probabilities. Here, states are defined as homogeneous subgroups according to selected variables. Aeron et al. (2008)[27] presented a conceptual model for the CLV of credit card customers. They defined the state space based on the credit card customers' behaviors. By assigning a revenue and cost to each state, they calculated the CLV for the customers in each state.

Ekinci et al. (2014) examined the difference between the least square estimation technique and the artificial neural network technique, by comparing the predicted CLV with the actual CLV over one year. Ekinci et al. (2014) provided decision support for marketing via Markov decision processes (MDPs) for a company that offers several types of products. The states for the MDPs were generated using the predicted customer lifetime values, where the prediction was realized using a regression-based model. They provided a real-world application of their proposed model in the banking sector to show the empirical validity of the model.

Theocharous and Hallak (2013)[28] and Theocharous, Thomas, and Ghavamzadeh (2015) worked on interaction marketing optimization through reinforcement learning (RL) and MDPs.

Estrella-Ramón et al. (2016)[29] used a panel dataset from a Spanish bank to calculate the customer potential value multi-product model using the probit method. They found the influence of a set of behavioral variables on the ownership of different banking products and identified which customer's value was higher, and which was lower, by calculating the customer potential value. Lycett and Marshan (2017) developed a connected customer lifetime value (CCLV) model based on an empirical analysis of transactions in the financial services domain. They reflected the dynamic networks of business transactions in their CLV model.

Predictors in the CLV models can include all the relevant variables in a company's database. Some of the predictor variables presented in the literature have been mentioned by Ekinci et al. (2014). These variables include demographic, product ownership, intensity of usage, customer state related, risk related, and customer engagement variables.

Cost and profit information is often not clearly allocated at a customer level.[30] Considering the structure of revenue in the banking industry, revenue is generated mostly through the spread rates as the net interest income (NII). As such, FTP, which defines the cost of funds (COF) for lending products (and customer revenue for deposit products), has a critical role in calculating the revenue obtained from each customer. Providing a mechanism to calculate an accurate FTP will help provide a more realistic view of customer profitability. This mechanism includes the contribution of the wholesale rate, the yield curve, and the inherent risks and fees.

FTP is used by bankers to evaluate the profitability of deposits and loans, and for pricing.[31] FTP has been an important tool for financial institutions for several decades. This methodology was introduced to banks in the early 1980s to help allocate corporate costs and risks among business lines: for instance, what portion of the risk is driven by fee lines, loans, and deposits? The fund transfer price is a profitability-related parameter that tends to receive more attention during economic recession periods, as we observe in 2008. That is, in response to the financial crisis of 2007–8, financial service industry regulators commonly requested that the financial service industry implement FTP mechanisms.[32]

The FTP measures the contribution by each source of funding to the overall profitability in a financial institution.[33] FTP consists of both the internal management information system and methodology designed to allocate the net interest margin between funds users – such as lenders and investment officers – and funds providers, including branch deposit gathers and the treasury function.[34]

The FTP offers a critical path to enlightened risk and return net interest margin (NIM) analytics and is the key to optimizing the margin.[35] When a loan is originated, the transfer rate is established by locating on the selected transfer curve the corresponding term point, or points in the case of the recommended strip funded approach.[36]

These two financial institutions measures – CLV and FTP – give us a good view of the value of both customers and products. With the combination presented here, we can understand the customer's role in the institution's profitability while determining the institution's profit margin through spreads and the FTP. CLV is a recommended metric for customer selection, marketing programs design, and decision-making in a structured framework.[37]

As discussed above, by implementing an accurate CLV model, we can determine customers' future potential value. This information can help us segment customers based on their future versus their current value in the framework presented by Kumar and Rajan (2009) in Figure 13.1. Of note, the company may have different strategies for each segment, as mentioned in Figure 13.1.

The channel used to acquire customers depends on the customers' CLV, with a costly channel for high CLV customers and a

Figure 13.1. CLV base segmentation

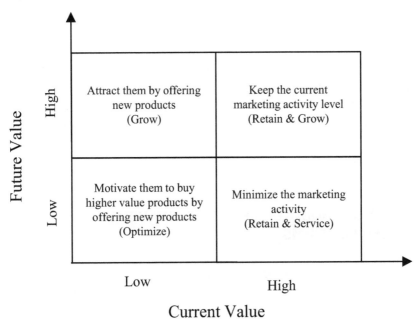

cheaper channel for low CLV customers.[38] Several studies have used the CLV base segmentation to analyze marketing strategies, acquisition/retention allocation resources, and benefit segmentation.[39,40] The potential value of the customers can also affect benefits such as fee waivers, credit limits,[41] and marketing channels.

In marketing, there is a need to develop models that focus on maximizing the CLV rather than just measuring it.[42] Considering the applications of CLV models in cross-selling and recommending new products, there are opportunities for maximizing the lifetime value of customers by recommending the right products to them.[43] A decreasing customer CLV provides the opportunity to recommend the right product and direct the customer to a more profitable path. Desirena et al. (2019)[44] implemented an insurance product recommender system based on a two-stage neural network architecture that maximized CLV. Theocharous and Hallak (2013) worked on marketing recommendations through RL and MDPs. Theocharous,

Thomas, and Ghavamzadeh (2015) also presented a framework to use RL in an ad recommendation system to optimize a customer's lifetime value.

The goal of this chapter is to illustrate CLV methodologies in two international financial institutions and explain the way we can make them more precise by connecting CLV to FTP. In the next section, the CLV methodologies are presented. In section 3, we provide a brief explanation of how FTP is determined for different financial products. In section 4, we present the impact of FTP on the CLV methodology.

2. CLV METHODOLOGIES IN TWO FINANCIAL SERVICE FIRMS

We use machine learning tools to predict the expected revenue from each customer during one year of his/her relationship with the institution. The type of tools and the models depend on the data. The predictors can be all the relevant information we have for each customer. This data can contain demographic, product, balance, risk, geographic, and segmentation information. It can be in categorical and numerical format.

We define the CLV as the discounted revenue received from customers during one year of his/her relationship with the company. The revenue is calculated by considering the provision, which is the cost of possible default. The target variable is the revenue after provision.

The approach is implemented using two data sets of 10 percent sample from a population of retail customers comprising around 500,000 from the first, and 2,500,000 from the second of two international financial institutions. We refer to these two financial institutions as Institution A and Institution B, respectively, for the rest of this article.

In order to make sure that the sample is a good representation of the population, we ran the Kolmogorov-Smirnov test and the Wilcoxon signed-rank test. The data included more than three years of transaction history on a monthly basis. The model developed on the sample data from Institution B was also implemented on its whole population of retail customers, which included around 74 million observations. The dataset from Institution A contained 427 variables and the dataset from Institution B contained 220 variables. Some of these variables were calculated based on the transaction history.

The cleaning and preparation of the data were implemented carefully to keep as much of the information as possible. Several imputation techniques were reviewed to select the methods most compatible with the variables. Segmentation, marital status, location, product ownership flags, age, and tenure variables all had missing values. We imputed the missing values by the last observation carried forward, 1-nearest neighbor, or random samples generated according to the empirical distribution of the variables. Missing values in age and tenure variables were imputed by calculation using the available data or other variables, such as date of birth and available tenure data.

In order to improve the prediction power of the model, other feature engineering techniques in addition to imputation were applied. We used log transformation for the discounted revenue generated by customers as the target variable because of its skewed distribution and outliers with high revenue. This method decreased the effect of the outliers, due to the normalization of magnitude differences, making the model more robust. We considered other normalization and scaling approaches, such as the Box-Cox transformation (of which the log-transform is a special case) but did not observe noticeable improvements. One-hot encoding was also implemented for categorical variables. This method changed the categorical variables to a numerical format, which enabled us to group the categorical data without losing any information. Same as with normalization, we also considered other more general encoding approaches (ordinal, count, credibility, etc.), but did not observe noticeable improvements in model performance either.

Data extraction is another feature engineering technique that we used to extract months/periods of transactions from the date variable. We used two extracted variables from the date variable: month number (which can be useful for capturing seasonality) and month order starting from the first month in the data. We also extracted several new variables, including averages, variances, frequencies, and recencies of customers' transactions during the past three, six, and twelve months, based on customers' transaction history. Correlation and variance inflation analysis were also implemented to determine and select the variables likely to be related to the target variable. Principal components can be used as an effective tool for finding orthogonal (i.e., uncorrelated by design) variables. Variables with very low information or variance were dropped.

In terms of the model training and validation, we split the data into two sets: One set included 80 percent of the customers for training; the other set included the remaining 20 percent for testing the model. Splitting the data based on customers prevented an information leak between the training and test sets. The model was also tested on the new month of data that we received after finishing the project. Several machine learning models – including random forest (RF), neural network, gradient boosting machines (GBM), and generalized linear model (GLM) – were implemented on the datasets in three stages, including classification and then regression.[45] Because of the characteristics of the data, which included many observations with zero value for the target variables, we decided to use a classifier in the first stage and then run the regression models. Hon and Bellotti (2016)[46] also used the first stage classifier to detect customers with nonzero credit balances.

To increase the accuracy of our models, we used two stages of regressors for Institution A. The first stage regression model was used to predict each customer's revenue. Then, we allocated each customer to one of the six intervals of revenue, or bins, such that the number of customers in each bin was equal. This allocation helped us train regression models on more homogeneous datasets. Arguably, the model performance could have been improved further by binning differently; the current approach was motivated by the business rules at Institution A.

For Institution B, we used a multi-class classification model in the second stage to assign the customers to each of the revenue intervals, as shown in Figure 13.2. However, since the three-stage model did not show an improvement in the final results, we used a two-stage model of classification and regression for Institution B.

Figure 13.2. The three-stage model for the CLV project in Institution B

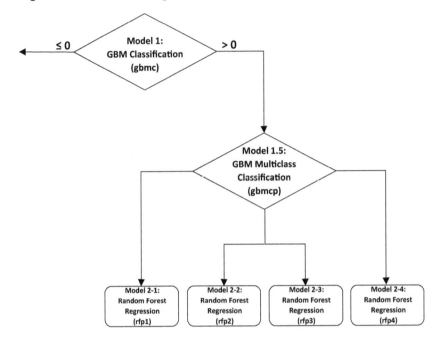

H2O package in R can be a good option for running such models. Model selection and tuning of the hyperparameters were done by optimizing the performance metrics. We looked at different metrics, depending on the model. In the classification models, we used the area under the ROC curve (AUC) as the metric for selecting the best model and for tuning the hyperparameters. The receiver operating characteristic (ROC) curve is the graph of the true positive rate (TPR) versus the false positive rate (FPR) when the decision threshold is changing in the logistic regression model. The AUC can be interpreted as the probability that the model ranks a random positive example more highly than a random negative example. The value of the AUC is between zero and one; however, an AUC of 0.5 is considered a poor classification since it is the same as a random classification. AUC is a scale-invariant and classification-threshold-invariant metric.

Since incorrectly classifying the customers with positive revenue has the cost of losing them, false negative ratio (FNR) is also an important metric. We therefore tracked the FNR while maximizing the AUC. The selected model for the first stage in Institution A was a neural network model and for Institution B was a GBM model, with maximum AUC and minimum FNR among the analyzed models.

The Gini coefficient, which ranks examples based on the likelihood of being in the positive class, was also presented for the binary classification model. Given that it can be presented in percentage, this was an interesting metric for demonstrating to managers how well the model works. The following equation shows the relation between the Gini coefficient and the AUC: $Gini = 2 * AUC - 1$. Note that, for an imbalanced binary target, using the area under the precision-recall curve (AUC-PR) is recommended.[47]

In the machine learning regression models, we used mean absolute error (MAE) to find the best model and to tune the models. The MAE presents the average deviation of each predicted point from the actual. Since it sums over all the absolute errors, positive and negative errors do not cancel each other out. Minimizing the MAE, neural network models for Institution A and RF models for Institution B were selected for regression stages. In order to have an appropriate metric with which to compare results with other prediction models, we also looked at mean absolute scaled error (MASE). Note, that a popular mean absolute percentage error (MAPE) metric could not be readily used in this context, since due to the errors made by the first stage classifier, some of the customers for whom we predict revenue in the second stage still have a zero actual revenue.

Running the finalized models on the population in Institution B presented a long running time challenge. To overcome this issue, we simplified some imputation methods and also eliminated some predictors, based on the variable importance report of each model. Running the models with the main drivers led to a small drop in the performance metrics of the models. The trade-off was acceptable and the modified models were trained and run on the whole population resulting in a much more reasonable running time of a few hours instead of several days.

The steps and process of the project in Institution B, as well as our strategy for splitting the data, are presented in the appendix at the end of this chapter.

3. FTP METHODOLOGIES

The funds transfer price is an important concept in how financial institutions determine their internal prices when allocating funds across different business units.[48] Appropriate identification of the FTP is fundamental for the pricing of commercial products, performance evaluation, bank strategy design, and hedging interest-rate risk.[49] The FTP is used to calculate the spread rates for loan and deposit products.[50] Credit spread rate is earned by the lenders for assuming credit risk, and it must be adequate to compensate for the following: credit losses, direct operating costs related to the lending operations and loan servicing, and general allocated financial service institution (FSI) overhead. This net credit spread must also make an acceptable profitability return.[51] The deposit spread must be adequate to compensate for the direct operating costs of the branch and retail delivery systems, as well as for the general allocated credit FSI overhead. This net deposit spread must also generate an adequate profitability return. Having the spread rates for each product, we can determine the NII based on the total balance of that product. NII is the main portion of the revenue in financial institutions. In the next section, we will first look at FTP from a product-centric point of view and discuss the ideas on loan and deposit products, as well as on termed and non-termed products. Next, we will discuss customer-centric FTP.

3.1. Product-centric FTP

Funds allocated to lending products are charged to asset-generating businesses whereas funds made by deposit and other funding products are credited to liability-generating businesses. Each source of funds, such as a deposit or borrowing, and each expenditure of funds, such as a loan or investment, is valued at the time of origination.[52]

Table 13.1. Components of Pricing for Loan and Deposit Products

Components of Pricing	Loan Specific	Deposit Specific
FTP	FTP cost of funds used associated with the loan	FTP value of funds used associated with the deposit
Fixed and variable lifetime costs		
Cost of assigned capital based upon all imbedded risks related to the loan as well as specific to the customer	credit, interest rate, market, liquidity, and operational risk	interest rate, market, liquidity, and operational risk
Strategic return expected		

This valuation is accomplished by assigning each financial instrument an associated transfer rate from an appropriate yield curve.[53,54]

Hanselman (2009) presented the following components for the optimal pricing of loan and deposit products as per Table 13.1.

The components presented in the last three rows of the above table should be added or subtracted from FTP to have a conceptual framework of the optimal pricing for loans or deposits, respectively (Hanselman, 2009):

FTP ± Fixed and variable lifetime costs
± Cost of assigned capital based upon all imbedded risks related to the loan as well as specific to the customer
± Strategic return expected.

In addition to the type of the financial products, another important parameter in determining FTP is the length of term or maturity of the product. Dermine (2016) presented two fundamental methods: the FTP of fixed maturity/termed products and the FTP of undefined maturity/non-termed products.

3.1.1. FTP FOR TERMED PRODUCTS

Mortgages and GICs are examples of termed products from loan and deposit type financial products, respectively. Dermine (2016) explained that the optimal volume of loans and deposits can be extracted from Figure 13.3. The horizontal line is the market

Figure 13.3.

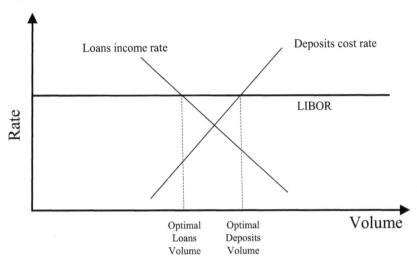

rate – the London interbank offered rate (LIBOR). The other two crossed lines show that the higher the interest rate, the less loan volume and the more deposit volume the bank will have. The optimal volume of loans and deposits can be obtained from the intersection of the lines where the marginal income of the loan products or the marginal cost of the deposit products are the same as the market rate. Dermine (2016) stated that "the maturity of the market rate used for FTP should correspond to the maturity of the fixed-term product. For short maturities of up to one year, one frequently uses the interbank market rates, and for longer fixed-rate maturities, one uses the swap rates."[55] Based on Irving Fisher's separation theorem, Dermine (2016) identified a separation between the lending and the funding decisions. Fisher's separation theorem states that loans and deposits must be priced with reference to the market rate and these decisions are independent of one another.

The FTP for mortgage products is fairly complicated and depends on many factors beyond the contractual decay of balances. These factors include prepayments, rate changes, and even macroeconomic situations. Variable rate contracts have little exposure to rate risks, but fixed rates expose the bank to interest-rate change risks and must be hedged appropriately. Other risks, such as defaults, must also be considered in FTP calculations.

3.1.2. FTP FOR NON-TERMED PRODUCTS

The following are examples of non-termed/undefined maturity products:

- Assets/Loan products: loans, lines of credit, credit cards
- Liabilities/Deposit Products: chequing, savings

Dermine (2016) explained that, for banks, a standard practice when dealing with retail deposits with undefined maturity is to split them into two categories: volatile "transient" deposits, and stable "core" deposits that are equivalent to long-term fixed-rate maturity deposits. The fund transfer price is the weighted sum of the short-term and long-term interest rates, the weights being the volume of volatile and stable deposits. Dermine (2016) worked on converting the cases of undefined maturity to fixed maturity under some conditions; however, the author identified many circumstances under which the practice of conversion into a single effective maturity is not warranted.

Considering the above discussion, it is critical to have an accurate estimation/prediction of the stable core deposit volume for each length of maturity. Having this information, the bank will have a good foundation with which to determine the FTP based on the yield curve. The above discussion applies to loan products with undefined maturity as well.

3.1.3. ADVANCED FTP METHODS

After the economic crisis in 2008, new considerations were added to the FTP system. Dermine (2013) presented the following five cases, which need to be considered for an advanced FTP method:

Rationing on the interbank market. The interbank market rate is volatile. This volatility affects the optimum volume of loans and deposits as the horizontal line in Figure 13.3 changes. Therefore, financial institutions should understand their portfolios to maximize their profit by determining product prices. Rationing on the interbank market means that, by changing the interbank market rate, the product prices need to be updated. However, the volume of loans should not exceed the volume of deposits even if the market rate horizontal line in Figure 13.3 is below the intersection of the marginal income on loans and marginal cost of deposit lines. This loans and deposits volume balance can be managed by arranging the product prices to make more profit.

Basel III contingency liquidity buffer. Interbank market liquidity dried up during the economic crisis in 2008. As a result, the Basel III committee decided to implement a new regulation to ensure sufficient liquidity in the next crisis. This liquidity buffer has a cost for banks, which in turn impacts transfer pricing.

Specific asset risk. Risk adjustment of the FTP is an important step, especially in long-term funds. It is advisable to conduct two evaluations of the economic profit of a transaction: a short-term evaluation, based on foundation economic profit and current average COF, and a long-term evaluation, based on advanced economic profit that recognizes the marginal risk of the new transaction.

Long-term funding constraint. Because of the new Basel III regulation, a long-term loan can no longer be funded with short-term market funding – with the resulting impact on the contingency liquidity buffer – and will have to be funded with long-term funding, such as a long-term bond. The cost is likely to be higher as it could incorporate a liquidity spread, which should be considered in the FTP.

Credit spread on bank's own debt. The risk of the bank default appears as a credit spread on the bank's funding. Previously, the Organization for Economic Cooperation and Development (OECD) has ignored the consequence of the risk of bank default for FTP and the cost of equity since the risk of bank default was low. Currently, bank default risk is considered in the cost of funding, debt, and equity in a number of countries, as the credit spreads are much higher.

3.2. Customer-centric FTP

The emergence of data and computing power has enabled banks to profile customers and refine their policies to infer different actions for specific clients. Having this capability, we can move from product-centric methods towards customer-centric methods. In other words, we can use the customer or segment data to predict maturity of non-termed products for each customer or segment. Then, we can use this information for a specific FTP for each customer or segment. Implementing this method, we can have personalized FTP or at least an FTP for each segment. This customer-centric approach will help present more realistic rates to customers, based on the actual resources and customer or segment predicted behaviors, rather than only looking at competitors. As a result, the institution may experience a more stable increase in sales.

4. THE WAY WE CONNECT CLV AND FTP

In this section, we explain how we can improve the CLV model described in section 2 by combining it with an FTP system. Doing so requires some modification of the CLV model, and it offers a more realistic view of customer profitability.

Looking at the CLV model in more detail and understanding how the revenue after provision is calculated, it becomes necessary to combine the CLV model and the FTP system.

The following formulation gives a better view of revenue generated by each customer:

$$Net\ Revenue = \sum_{product\ i} \left(NII_i + NIR_i \right) = \sum_{product\ i} \left[\left(InterestRate_i - COF_i \right) \times TotalBalance_i + NIR_i \right],$$

where NII is the net interest income, NIR is the non-interest income, and COF is the cost of funds.

A critical omission in the above formula is that it does not consider the liquidity and market risk.[56] By replacing the COF with the FTP (as explained in section 3), the above formulation provides a more realistic value for the net revenue. Provision for credit losses (PCL) – an estimated cost for the possible loss in case of a loan borrower default – is another type of risk cost which is calculated by the credit risk department. By subtracting PCL from the above formula, we have the revenue after provision as presented in the following formula:

$$Revenue\ after\ Provision = \Sigma_{product\ i}\ [(InterestRate_i - FTP_i) \times TotalBalance_i + NIR_i] - PCL.$$

Having the trajectory of the total balance for each customer's product, the forecast of the interest rate and FTP of each product, and forecast of the PCL for each customer, we can find the trajectory of net revenue before tax (NIBT) for each. The sum of the discounted value of such net revenues is the CLV.

We can use different statistical and machine learning models to predict the trajectory of the products' balances and PCL. The classification and regression prediction model presented in section 2 is a useful method for balance prediction, as Hon and Bellotti (2016) also discussed a two-stage method in the credit card balance prediction. The reason is the high number of accounts with zero balance. Hon and Bellotti (2016) implemented an ordinary regression, a mixture regression, and a random effect panel model in the regression stage for the credit card balance prediction. By training and tuning a classification and regression model with "Provision" as the target variable, we can predict PCL. A vast amount of literature applies machine learning models to predict probability of default.[57,58,59] Note that the dataset here is the same as that used in section 2, which includes all demographic and balance data.

Predicting interest rates is the next step. Hybrid models have worked properly in forecasting the interest rates as we implemented on the dataset of four international financial institutions. The hybrid models are trained on the training part of the data to set the optimal weights for each of the time series forecasting models. The hybrid model can include auto arima, exponential smoothing (ets), the theta model (thetam), neural network time series forecasts (nnetar), stlm, and TBATS.[60] We can use the same method to forecast the FTP for the determined horizon. Since the interest rates are affected by the economic situation, we can use the macroeconomic variables as the intervention variables. These variables include the Central Bank rate, GDP annual changes, consumer price annual changes, currency, and unemployment rate. The "forecastHybrid" package in R is one option for implementing these forecasts. The time series cross-validation method is available in R to calculate the accuracy metric in a more realistic way, in order to either accept the model or try a different one.

Having the trajectory of the product balances and the forecast of the interest rates and the FTP, we can use the above formulation to predict the trajectory of the revenue/profit. Using these results, we can calculate the discounted values of the trajectory of the revenue/profit as the CLV of each customer. The above method is more applicable to non-termed products.

Because of their contractual structure, the future balance for termed products is more predictable than for non-termed products. Therefore, with the interest rate and FTP forecasts in hand, the CLV can be determined.

5. SUMMARY

Current and future customer profitability are important concerns for companies striving to keep themselves on a growth path. Customer lifetime value models provide a forward-looking measure for understanding how the profitability of customers is changing.

To have a reliable profitability measurement in financial institutions, we need to understand the COF for each financial product, the risk involved, as well as any relevant fees and expenses. Financial institutions need an accurate FTP system to provide the costs involved with each product. Combining the CLV and the FTP creates an accurate understanding of both current and future customer profitability in financial institutions. In this chapter, we provided an illustration for this combination to use historical data, computing power, and modeling technologies to trade homogeneity for a heterogeneity that is both customer- and product-centric.

First, we reviewed the various definitions and methodologies associated with the CLV metric, studies on the CLV in the banking industry, the predictor variables used in the literature, some applications of CLV, and the importance of the FTP in profitability. Next, we outlined approaches that we used for two international financial services firms for calculating CLV by using several stacked machine learning models utilizing random forest, gradient boosting, and neural networks for classification and regression sub-problems. We used different feature engineering techniques to improve the predictability power of the models. The hyperparameters of the models have been set up through the optimization of the accuracy metrics.

We then provided a brief explanation of the FTP for loans and deposit products, in both termed and non-termed format in financial institutions. Some other concerns were discussed to present the considerations of an advanced FTP system. These concerns include rationing on the interbank market, the Basel III contingency liquidity buffer, specific asset risk, long-term funding constraint, and credit spread on a bank's own debt.

Finally, by looking at the revenue structure of financial institutions in more detail, we presented the idea of predicting revenue components in order to have a more accurate CLV for each customer. In order to do so, predicting methodologies for product balances and forecasting the interest rates and the FTP were discussed.

APPENDIX

Figure 13.4.

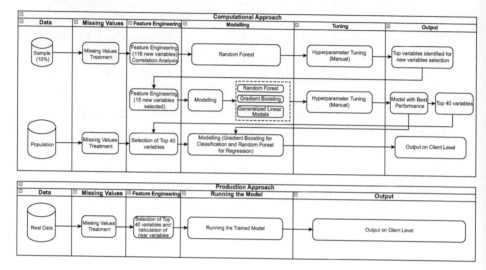

Figure 13.5.

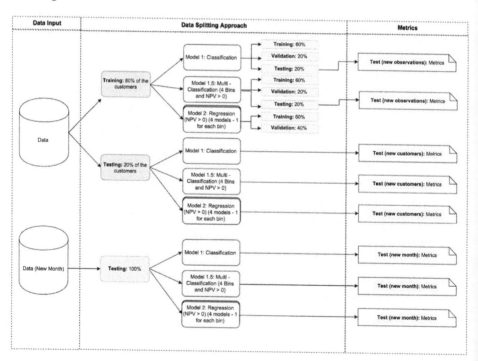

NOTES

1 Financial services is not the only industry where a rethink of CLV calculations is required. Ovchinnikov and Wang (2019), for example, show how dynamic pricing, used in the airline industry, could introduce a substantial bias into the traditional approaches for calculating CLV. Ovchinnikov, A., & Wang, J. (2019). Which customers are more valuable in dynamic pricing situations? https://dx.doi.org/10.2139/ssrn.3406526.

2 Lycett, M., & Marshan, A. (2017). *Modeling connected customer lifetime value (CCLV) in the banking domain.* 23rd Americas Conference on Information Systems, Boston, United States. https://www.researchgate.net/publication/319130658_Modeling_Connected_Customer_Lifetime_Value_Modeling_Connected_Customer_Lifetime_Value_CCLV_in_the_Banking_Domain_Full_Paper.

3 Dahana, W.D., Miwa, Y., & Morisada, M. (2019). Linking lifestyle to customer lifetime value: An exploratory study in an online fashion retail market. *Journal of Business Research, 99,* 319–31. https://doi.org/10.1016/j.jbusres.2019.02.049.

4 Recency-Frequency-Monetary value: recency is the date of the customer's last purchase, frequency value is the number of purchases a customer makes in a given time period, and the monetary value is the amount of money spent by the customer in that period.

5 Kumar, V., & Rajan, B. (2009). Profitable customer management: Measuring and maximizing customer lifetime value. *Management Accounting Quarterly, 10*(3), 1–18.

6 Venkatesan, R., & Kumar, V. (2004). A customer lifetime value framework for customer selection and resource allocation strategy. *Journal of Marketing, 68*(4), 106–25. https://doi.org/10.1509/jmkg.68.4.106.42728.

7 Gupta, S., Lehmann, D.R., & Stuart, J.A. (2004). Valuing customers. *Journal of Marketing Research, 41*(1), 7–18. https://doi.org/10.1509/jmkr.41.1.7.25084.

8 Kumar, V., Lemon, K.N., & Parasuraman, A. (2006). Managing customers for value: An overview and research agenda. *Journal of Service Research, 9*(2), 87–94. https://doi.org/10.1177/1094670506293558.

9 Pfeifer, P.E., Haskins, M.E., & Conroy, R.M. (2005). Customer lifetime value, customer profitability, and the treatment of acquisition spending. *Journal of Managerial Issues, 17*(1), 11–25. https://www.jstor.org/stable/40604472.

10 Gupta, S., Hanssens, D., Hardie, B., Kahn, W., Kumar, V., Lin, N., Ravishanker, N., & Sriram, S. (2006). Modeling customer lifetime value. *Journal of Service Research, 9*(2), 139–55. https://doi.org/10.1177/1094670506293810.

11 Haenlein, M., Kaplan, A.M., & Beeser, A.J. (2007). A model to determine customer lifetime value in a retail banking context. *European Management Journal, 25*(3), 221–34. https://doi.org/10.1016/j.emj.2007.01.004.

12 Hidalgo, P., Manzur, E., Olavarrieta, S., & Farias, P. (2008). Customer retention and price matching: The AFPs case. *Journal of Business Research, 61*(6), 691–96. https://doi.org/10.1016/j.jbusres.2007.06.046.

13 Abdolvand, N., Albadvi, A., & Koosha, H. (2014). Customer lifetime value: Literature scoping map, and an agenda for future research. *International Journal of Management Perspective.* https://ssrn.com/abstract=3926592.

14 Hanlein et al. (2007).

15 Ekinci, Y., Uray, N., & Ülengin, F. (2014). A customer lifetime value model for the banking industry: A guide to marketing actions. *European Journal of Marketing, 48*(3/4), 761–84. https://doi.org/10.1108/EJM-12-2011-0714.

16 Esteban-Bravo, M., Vidal-Sanz, J.M., & Yildirim, G. (2014). Valuing customer portfolios with endogenous mass and direct marketing interventions using a stochastic dynamic programming decomposition. *Marketing Science, 33*(5), 621–40. https://doi.org/10.1287/mksc.2014.0848.

17 Chen, P.P., Guitart, A., del Río, A.F., & Periánez, A. (2018). *Customer lifetime value in video games using deep learning and parametric models.* 2018 IEEE International Conference on Big Data (Big Data), Seattle, USA, 2134–40.

18 Theocharous, G., Thomas, P.S., & Ghavamzadeh, M. (2015). *Personalized ad recommendation systems for life-time value optimization with guarantees.* 24th International Joint Conference on Artificial Intelligence, Buenos Aires, Argentina, 1806–12.

19 Hwang, H., Jung, T., & Suh, E. (2004). An LTV model and customer segmentation based on customer value: A case study on the wireless telecommunication industry. *Expert Systems with Applications, 26*(2), 181–8. https://doi.org/10.1016/S0957 -4174(03)00133-7.

20 Fader, P.S., Hardie, B.G., & Lee, K.L. (2005). RFM and CLV: Using iso-value curves for customer base analysis. *Journal of Marketing Research, 42*(4), 415–30. https://doi .org/10.1509/jmkr.2005.42.4.415.

21 Etzion, O., Fisher, A., & Wasserkrug, S. (2004). *e-CLV: A modelling approach for customer lifetime evaluation in e-commerce domains, with an application and case study for online auctions.* IEEE International Conference on E-Technology, e-Commerce and e-Service, 2004, Taipei, Taiwan, 149–56. https://doi.ieeecomputersociety. org/10.1109/EEE.2004.1287301.

22 Berger, P.D., Eechambadi, N., George, M., Lehmann, D.R., Rizley, R., & Venkatesan, R. (2006). From customer lifetime value to shareholder value: Theory, empirical evidence, and issues for future research. *Journal of Service Research, 9*(2), 156–67. https://doi.org/10.1177/1094670506293569.

23 AboElHamd, E., Shamma, H.M., & Saleh, M. (2020). Maximizing customer lifetime value using dynamic programming: Theoretical and practical implications. *Academy of Marketing Studies Journal, 24*(1), 1–25. https://www.abacademies.org /articles/Maximizing-customer-lifetime-value-using-dynamic-programming -theoreticalandpractical-implications-1528-2678-24-1-250.pdf.

24 Ekinci et al. (2014).

25 Blattberg, R.C., & Deighton, J. (1996). Manage marketing by the customer equity test. *Harvard Business Review, 74*(4), 136–44. https://hbr.org/1996/07/manage -marketing-by-the-customer-equity-test.

26 Ovchinnikov, A., Blass, V., & Raz, G. (2014). Economic and environmental assessment of remanufacturing strategies for product+ service firms. *Production and Operations Management, 23*(5), 744–61. https://doi.org/10.1111/poms.12070.

27 Aeron, H., Bhaskar, T., Sundararajan, R., Kumar, A., & Moorthy, J. (2008). A metric for customer lifetime value of credit card customers. *Journal of Database Marketing & Customer Strategy Management, 15*(3), 153–68. https://doi.org/10.1057 /dbm.2008.13.

28 Theocharous, G., & Hallak, A. (2013). *Lifetime value marketing using reinforcement learning.* 1st Multidisciplinary Conference on Reinforcement Learning and Decision Making (RLDM) 2013, 19. https://citeseerx.ist.psu.edu/document?repid=rep1&type =pdf&doi=29027a8e55e3de3dfacb698572dd1bfe12128cda#page=19.

29 Estrella-Ramón, A., Sánchez-Pérez, M., Swinnen, G., & Vanhoof, K. (2016). Estimating customer potential value using panel data of a Spanish bank. *Journal of Business Economics and Management, 17*(4), 580–97. https://doi.org/10.3846/16111699.2014 .970571.

30 Gupta et al. (2006).

31 Dermine, J. (2016). *Fund transfer pricing for bank deposits. The case of products with undefined maturity.* INSEAD Working Paper No. 2016/06/FIN. https://dx.doi .org/10.2139/ssrn.2722392.

32 de Castroa, V.B., Leoteb, T., & Safaric, M. (2019). Using fund transfer pricing as a performance measurement system in the financial service industry. *Management Accounting Frontiers, 2*, 13–30. http://dx.doi.org/10.52153/prj0404003.

33 Dermine, J. (2013). Fund transfer pricing for deposits and loans, foundation and advanced. *Journal of Financial Perspectives, 1*(1). https://ssrn.com/abstract=3077913.

34 Hanselman, O.B. (2009). Best practices & strategic value of funds transfer pricing. *Journal of Performance Management, 22*(2), 3–16. https://www.proquest.com/docview /214033517.

35 Hanselman (2009).

36 Hanselman (2009).

37 Aeron et al. (2008).

38 Aeron et al. (2008).

39 Kahreh, M.S., Tive, M., Babania, A., & Hesan, M. (2014). Analyzing the applications of customer lifetime value (CLV) based on benefit segmentation for the banking sector. *Procedia-Social and Behavioral Sciences, 109*, 590–4. https://doi.org/10.1016 /j.sbspro.2013.12.511.

40 Gupta et al. (2006); Venkatesan & Kumar (2004).

41 Kostiv, M. (2019). Customer lifetime value for credit limit optimization. [Master's thesis, Ukrainian Catholic University]. https://er.ucu.edu.ua/bitstream/handle /1/1330/Kostiv_%20Customer%20Lifetime%20Value.pdf?sequence=1.

42 Hidalgo et al. (2008).

43 Gupta et al. (2006).

44 Desirena, G., Diaz, A., Desirena, J., Moreno, I., & Garcia, D. (2019, December). *Maximizing customer lifetime value using stacked neural networks: An insurance industry application.* 2019 18th IEEE International Conference on Machine Learning and Applications (ICMLA), Boca Raton, Florida, USA, 541–4. http://dx.doi.org/10.1109/ ICMLA.2019.00101.

45 H2O package in R can be a good option for running such models.

46 Hon, P.S., & Bellotti, T. (2016). Models and forecasts of credit card balance. *European Journal of Operational Research, 249*(2), 498–505. https://doi.org/10.1016 /j.ejor.2014.12.014.

47 Jeni, L.A., Cohn, J.F., & De La Torre, F. (2013). *Facing imbalanced data–recommendations for the use of performance metrics.* 2013 Humaine Association Conference on Affective Computing and Intelligent Interaction, Geneva, Switzerland, 245–51. https://doi.org /10.1109/acii.2013.47

48 De Castroa (2019).

49 Dermine (2016).

50 Hanselman (2009).

51 Hanselman (2009).

52 Hanselman (2009).

53 The yield curve provides fundamental information for the FTP system, necessary for understanding how rates change with respect to the financial product terms.

54 Hanselman (2009).

55 Rates from the yield curve.

56 Liquidity Risk: the risk that the bank's depositors withdraw their money before the debtors pay back. Market Risk: the risk a change in market conditions will impact the profitability of the bank operations.

57 Louzada, F., Ara, A., & Fernandes, G.B. (2016). Classification methods applied to credit scoring: Systematic review and overall comparison. *Surveys in Operations Research and Management Science, 21*(2), 117–34. https://doi.org/10.1016/j.sorms .2016.10.001.

58 Papouskova, M., & Hajek, P. (2019). Two-stage consumer credit risk modelling using heterogeneous ensemble learning. *Decision Support Systems, 118*, 33–45. https://doi.org/10.1016/J.DSS.2019.01.002.

59 Serrano-Cinca, C., Gutiérrez-Nieto, B., & López-Palacios, L. (2015). Determinants of default in P2P lending. *PloS One, 10*(10), e0139427. https://doi.org/10.1371/journal.pone.0139427.

60 Draboo, A. (2020, January 16). *Hybrid model in R*. Medium. https://medium.com/@anzardraboo/hybrid-model-in-r-bcc77914eedf.

PART FOUR

Retail Channels as Part of Business and Society Ecosystem in Moving towards Adaptive Behavior and Context

Risk, Reward, and Uncertainty in Buyer-Seller Transactions: The Seller's View on Combining Posted Prices and Auctions

Radosveta Ivanova-Stenzel and Sabine Kröger

SUMMARY OF CHAPTER

The chapter provides insights into seller behavior in the context of selling mechanisms involving a combination of posted prices and auctions. It explores how sellers deal with uncertainty, complexity, risk, reward, and bargaining power.

MANAGERIAL IMPLICATIONS (GENERAL)

- Managers in the B2C retail business should take note of the key finding based on the results from the theoretical and empirical research presented in this chapter: combining posted prices and auctions may generate higher sale prices than each of the two selling formats alone.
- Managers developing C2C platforms have strong interest in including combined mechanisms of selling formats to attract more participants.

MANAGERIAL IMPLICATIONS (ORGANIZATIONAL)

- From an organizational perspective, B2C retail managers need to ensure coherent and seamless information sharing between the different teams participating in the business processes

(marketing, sales, finance, procurement, inventory, and supply chain teams).
- IT and analytics teams must be aligned and provide the right information to support the business needs when using combined selling mechanisms.

MANAGERIAL IMPLICATIONS (STRATEGIC, TACTICAL, AND OPERATIONAL)

- From a strategic perspective, B2C retail managers need to decide whether to employ combined mechanisms, taking into account the types of products for sale, the targeted customers, and the market context.
- From a tactical perspective, managers need to adapt their business sales processes and implement the needed IT infrastructure and solutions to support the combined mechanisms. They might also proceed through an external marketplace platform supporting the combined mechanisms.
- From an operational perspective, managers need to constantly monitor the outcomes and have appropriate analytics based on product types, customers, and price tags (among others).

MANAGERIAL IMPLICATIONS (RISK ASSESSMENT)

- Financials risks are expected to be limited when adopting a combined mechanism.

1. INTRODUCTION

An essential but often neglected part of retailing is the choice of the selling format. Posted prices and auctions are the most commonly known and used formats. The key difference between the two formats is the way the price is determined: whereas posted prices are set by the retailers, prices in auctions are determined by the competition between buyers.

Posted prices and auctions have mostly been studied in isolation, even though, in reality, they are often combined in sequential order.

For example, in real estate markets, house owners who did not succeed in selling their house for an announced price might try to sell it in an auction. Producers who failed to buy at their standard vendors might call a procurement auction to acquire the missing pieces. Retailers who auction off used cars offer the owners of the cars the opportunity to post a price at which they are willing to sell the car before the auction.

Such concatenation of trading mechanisms had been largely ignored by the literature in the past, probably because of lacking empirical evidence. The increased use of combined mechanisms on online market platforms has filled part of this void and now provides ample empirical evidence. In order to attract traders, C2C and B2C platforms offer a combination of auctions and posted prices in the form of a single sequential trading mechanism, in addition to each of the two selling formats separately. For example, eBay offers the so-called "Buy-It-Now Auction," a combined mechanism allowing sellers to post pre-auction price offers before their auction starts.[1] Under the name "Best Offer," eBay also allows buyers to make a price offer to the seller before the auction. Combined mechanisms in online markets have attracted the attention of numerous scholars leading to an emerging and rapidly growing literature (see, e.g., the overview in Hasker & Sickles [2010]).[2] This literature demonstrates that combined mechanisms affect the strategic behavior of transaction partners and have important implications for their expected outcomes. A notable aspect of combined mechanisms is that their dynamic structure increases the complexity of the decision environment. The increased complexity can result in judgment failures and sub-optimal decisions.[3]

The existing surveys on combined mechanisms in private value environments[4] have mainly paid attention to buyer behavior (see, e.g., Hasker & Sickles [2010]; Kagel & Levin [2016]).[5] The present chapter offers insights into the seller's view and behavior. More precisely, it is organized around three questions that originate from the nature of combined mechanisms: (i) do sellers account for the adverse selection problem inherent to the environment; (ii) does experience with the market institution enable traders to better deal with the complexity of combined mechanisms, and (iii) does it matter who makes the pre-auction price offer? In section 2, we describe briefly the strategic aspects of transaction environments, where the seller has no information on the value that buyers attach to the item for sale. Section 3 summarizes the results of the experimental research on seller behavior in combined mechanisms. Finally, section 4 concludes and offers takeaways.

2. BUYER-SELLER TRANSACTIONS UNDER UNCERTAINTY

Buyer-seller transactions are generally subject to risk and strategic uncertainty. For example, the seller might be uncertain about the buyer's maximum willingness to pay. Buyers, on the other hand, might be uncertain about the quality of the item and the production costs for the seller. And for strategic reasons, it might be either not in the interest of the informed party to truthfully reveal the relevant information or the information cannot be credibly communicated.

These information asymmetries have strategic implications for the behavior of market participants and negatively affect market outcomes. Strategic behavior requires that market participants consider the behavior of their opponents and understand its informational content. For example, the economic literature documents that (human) buyers often ignore the effect of their price offers on the sellers: only sellers who value their item less than the offered price will accept the offer, leading to a selection of lower average quality items for sale at the offered price.[6] This ignorance results in buyers paying prices that are too high compared to the quality of the item, a judgmental failure that has been referred to in the bargaining literature as the "winner's curse."[7] Buyers might also suffer from the winner's curse when they compete against each other for an item with unknown quality. Kagel and Levin (2016, 2002)[8] report empirical evidence that buyers who win such competitions are very likely to have overestimated the item's value.

On the other side of the market, a seller faces strategic uncertainty, too. The seller's information on the buyers' maximum willingness to pay for the item is usually incomplete. This complicates the seller's choice of the "right" posted price. When asking for a price that is too high, a seller cannot sell the item. And when the price is too low, the seller leaves money on the table. From a seller's point of view, auctions have the advantage of exploiting the competition between buyers to sell the item to the buyer who values it most. Auctions have thus the potential to extract the most profit given the information asymmetry. This result holds in expectation for all auction types, and in particular for second-price auctions, one of the most commonly used auction formats in real-world online auctions (e.g., eBay) as well as offline auctions (e.g., public English art auctions).

In second-price auctions, the bidder with the highest bid wins the auction and pays the second-highest bid as a price. Therefore, it is not the winning buyer's bid that determines the price, but the highest bid of the losing bidders. Consequently, bidding one's own maximum willingness to pay is optimal in second-price auctions.[9,10] Besides, this bidding strategy is not affected by buyers' risk tolerance.

In the real world, however, sellers not only rely on one price mechanism but combine auctions and posted prices to ensure a sale. This real-world evidence is at odds with results in economic theory demonstrating that combined mechanisms are inferior to auctions when both market sides are tolerant or neutral to the risk they face. In that case, it does not matter who makes the pre-auction price offer, the seller or a buyer: the optimal pre-auction price offer is always rejected, and sales take place in the auction.[11,12,13]

The assumption of risk neutrality is restrictive as traders are often willing to pay a premium and give up part of their profit to reduce the uncertainty in buyer-seller transactions. Results from theoretical research suggest that risk aversion of sellers, or buyers, or both market sides can explain why it may be beneficial for sellers to use combined mechanisms (see, e.g., Ivanova-Stenzel & Kröger [2008]; Grebe et al. [2016][14]; Shunda [2009][15] and references therein).[16] For example, risk-averse buyers would prefer to reach an agreement at the pre-auction price instead of going to the auction. In the auction, they face competition, uncertainty about the auction price, and the risk of not winning the item. Hence, risk-averse buyers would accept paying a premium compared to the price they expect to pay in the auction. Similarly, risk-averse sellers might be willing to post a lower pre-auction price to avoid the more volatile outcome of the auction.

Consider the following combined mechanism as discussed in Ivanova-Stenzel & Kröger (2008) and Grebe et al. (2016, 2021).[17] A seller wants to sell an item and offers it first at a certain price to one of the potential buyers. If the buyer rejects this offer, a second-price auction takes place with this buyer and one additional buyer as bidders.[18] In this setting, the seller needs to form expectations about the auction price when deciding on the pre-auction price offer. In particular, the seller needs to account for the adverse selection into the auction caused by low pre-auction prices. Low pre-auction price offers will be accepted by buyers with a high willingness to pay but cannot be afforded by buyers with a low willingness to pay, who will select into the auction more often. Thus, low pre-auction price offers not only generate low profits when they are accepted, but also lead to low auction profits.

Figure 14.1 illustrates the theoretical predictions in this setting for two scenarios that differ regarding the traders' risk tolerance. The left-hand column presents the outcomes when all traders are risk neutral. The right-hand column presents the outcomes when buyers and sellers have different levels of risk tolerance.[19] The two top panels present the relation between posted pre-auction price offers and the expected seller profit in the combined mechanism. The dashed line indicates the expected seller profit in an auction without a posted price offer. The two bottom panels show the distribution of the pre-auction price offers posted by the seller.

The scenario with risk-neutral traders serves as a benchmark. Risk-neutral traders will always reach an agreement in the auction. When offered a pre-auction price at or above a certain threshold,[20] a risk-neutral buyer prefers the auction outcome and will reject such an offer. As illustrated in the top left panel

Figure 14.1. Simulated relation of profit and pre-auction price offers (top panels), distribution of predicted pre-auction price offers (bottom panels) for the case of risk-neutral traders (left-hand side) and traders with heterogeneous risk preferences (right-hand side) (Grebe et al., 2021). The horizontal dashed lines in the top panels indicate the expected profit from auctions without pre-auction price offers.

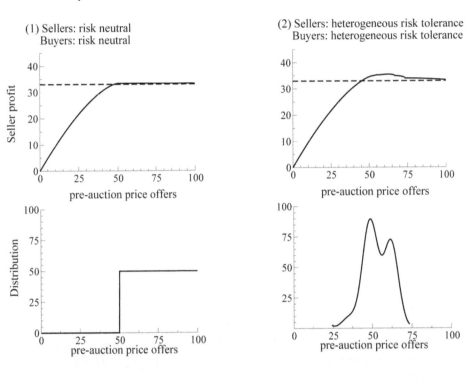

of Figure 14.1, it is indeed optimal for the seller to sell in the auction: the seller's expected profit rises with the posted pre-auction price offer and reaches its maximum at and above this threshold. Taking the behavior of the buyer into account, the seller can achieve selling in the auction with any pre-auction price offer at or above this threshold, as shown in the bottom left panel.

When traders vary in their risk tolerance, transactions will also take place at the pre-auction price offer. Sellers who are less tolerant towards risk are willing to offer pre-auction prices below this threshold to avoid the volatile outcome in the auction. Contrary to the risk-neutral case, risk-averse buyers are willing to accept pre-auction price offers at or above the threshold to avoid the auction. Thus, it is profitable for sellers to offer pre-auction prices that are high yet affordable for risk-averse buyers. Both effects are illustrated in the bottom right panel in Figure 14.1. A comparison between the expected seller profit in the combined mechanism (solid line in the top right panel) and in an auction without a pre-auction price offer (dashed line) reveals that posting a price before the auction might be beneficial for the seller. Thus, the theory predicts that if buyers are risk-averse, there is a window of opportunity for sellers to improve their profit when they offer a pre-auction price.

3. COMBINING POSTED PRICES AND AUCTIONS: EXPERIMENTAL EVIDENCE ON SELLER BEHAVIOR

This section provides insights into seller behavior in combined mechanisms based on results from laboratory experiments. The main advantage of laboratory experiments is the control the researcher has over the market environment and the information that traders possess. This allows the researcher to conduct a reliable test of the validity of the theoretical predictions and to observe aspects of behavior that are not easily available in data collected in the field.[21,22]

In experimental investigations of combined mechanisms, human participants trade fictitious items either in the role of a seller or a buyer. Sellers' costs and buyers' maximum willingness to pay for the fictitious items are numerical values drawn from a known distribution. In the case of a sale, sellers receive as profit the difference between the final price and their costs for the item, buyers receive the difference between their induced maximum willingness to pay and the final price. At the end of the experiment, all participants are paid their experimental profits in their real local currency.

3.1. The Seller's Curse

Ivanova-Stenzel and Kröger (2008) offer experimental evidence on how sellers and buyers behave in such an environment. In the experiment, the seller posts a price before a second-price sealed-bid auction. One of two potential buyers observes and then accepts or rejects this price. In case of a rejection, the auction takes place with both potential buyers as bidders.

The left-hand column of Figure 14.2 summarizes the behavior observed in the experiment.[23] The top left panel in Figure 14.2 shows the relation between the average posted pre-auction price offer and a non-parametric estimate of the realized seller profits. The horizontal dashed line indicates the auction profit without a pre-auction price offer.[24] In the combined mechanism, the seller profit increases with the posted pre-auction price offer up to a certain price and then converges to the profit in the auction without a pre-auction price offer. Ivanova-Stenzel and Kröger observe substantial variation in seller behavior, as shown in the bottom left panel in Figure 14.2, which displays the distribution of the observed posted pre-auction price offers. A majority of sellers post below-average pre-auction prices and make below-average profits. The dotted vertical line in the bottom left panel in Figure 14.2 indicates the lower bound of the interval within which posted pre-auction prices can be rationalized by relaxing the assumption of risk-neutrality. Only a fraction of the low pre-auction price offers are above this line and can thus be explained by sellers' risk aversion.

The sizable number of pre-auction price offers that are too low, that is, below this line, suggests that sellers forgo profit-making opportunities more than any risk premium could explain.

Inspired by the well-documented "winner's curse" observed in the bargaining literature, Ivanova-Stenzel and Kröger (2008) conjecture that sellers in the combined mechanism might fall prey to a "seller's curse." Similar to the winner's curse, the seller's curse happens if the (uninformed) seller does not condition their behavior on the strategic reaction of the (informed) buyer when posting their pre-auction price. More precisely, the seller's curse refers to the judgmental failure resulting in forgone profit opportunities for the

Figure 14.2. Relation of seller profit and pre-auction price offers (top panels), distributions of price offers posted before the auction (bottom panels) for data from experiments in Ivanova-Stenzel and Kröger (2008) (left-hand side) and in Grebe et al. (2021) (right-hand side). The horizontal dashed lines in the top panels indicate the expected profit from auctions without pre-auction price offers. The vertical dotted line indicates the lower bound of the range of pre-auction price offers that can be explained with heterogeneous risk preferences.

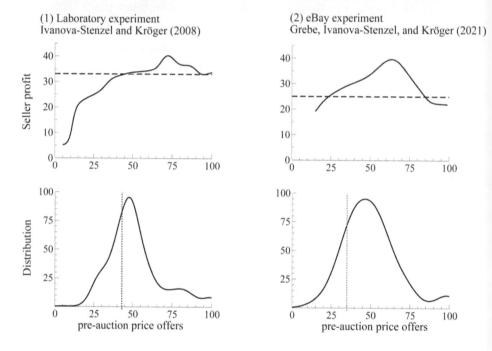

(1) Laboratory experiment
Ivanova-Stenzel and Kröger (2008)

(2) eBay experiment
Grebe, Ivanova-Stenzel, and Kröger (2021)

seller. This failure results from a seller ignoring the adverse selection effect that the posted pre-auction price imposes on the auction price. Posting too low pre-auction prices leads to low final profits from the combined mechanism for the seller. This happens for two reasons: first, buyers with a high valuation for the item accept such low pre-auction prices, and second, buyers with low valuations, who cannot afford even these low pre-auction prices, select into the auction, resulting in low auction prices.

The observed pre-auction price offers, displayed in the bottom left panel in Figure 14.2, suggest that the effect of pre-auction price offers on auction prices seems to be ignored by a substantial part of the sellers. Ivanova-Stenzel and Kröger (2008) note that sellers do not seem to learn to set higher pre-auction prices in the course of the laboratory experiment. Indeed, this is not surprising as it is difficult for those sellers who suffer from the seller's curse to learn from their mistake: low auction prices just reinforce the decision to post low pre-auction prices. Sellers can neither learn nor update their beliefs about the true relation between pre-auction price offers and final profits in the combined mechanism if they continue to offer pre-auction prices that are too low or do not vary enough.

3.2. Does Traders' Experience Matter?

In order to form correct, experience-based beliefs, sellers need to learn about the relation between pre-auction price offers and final profits. If sellers invested their resources (e.g., time, several items for sale, or money) in experimenting with various pre-auction price offers, they would realize that higher posted pre-auction prices imply higher expected final profits in the combined mechanism, even if the sale takes place in the auction.[25,26] Another way for sellers to learn is by observing the behavior of other traders and the resulting market outcomes. Both approaches are possible on online market platforms.

Based on these considerations, Grebe et al. (2021) conjecture that experience matters, and that sellers who offered their goods on online market platforms had more opportunities to learn about the relation between pre-auction prices and profits. Thus, they might be less prone to the seller's curse. In order to test this conjecture, they conducted a "field-in-the-lab" experiment. In the experiment, Grebe et al. (2021) used the same setup as in Ivanova-Stenzel & Kröger (2008), but the experiment was conducted on eBay with eBay traders. The use of the eBay platform and eBay traders allows studying behavior in an online market that is very popular among traders and ensures that participants in the experiment possess sufficient experience with the market institution.

The right-hand column in Figure 14.2 summarizes the behavior observed in the eBay experiment. The combined mechanism generates profits (black solid line, top right panel) that are substantially above those of a standard eBay auction, that is, where sellers cannot post a price before the auction (horizontal dashed line, top right panel).[27] The distribution of the pre-auction price offers is displayed in the bottom right panel. The vertical dotted line indicates the lower bound of the range of pre-auction price offers that can be explained with risk aversion. A large majority of pre-auction price offers in the eBay experiment are above this line. The considerable number of pre-auction price offers below this line provides empirical support for the seller's curse.

To investigate whether experience matters for the seller's decisions on their pre-auction price offers, Grebe et al. (2021) relate the observed pre-auction price offers to the information on traders' characteristics and their behavior available on the eBay platform. As discussed in sections 2 and 3.1, the sellers need to form expectations about the auction price when deciding on their pre-auction price offer. Sellers on eBay can form their expectations based on their understanding of the combined mechanism and their own experience, but also by observing the behavior of the buyers they interact with. If sellers use the publicly available information on eBay to update their beliefs, an empirical analysis could detect the determinants of seller behavior and shed light on how sellers set their pre-auction price offers.[28] The results of such an analysis reveal that, first, the information available on eBay about the buyers' experience and their bidding behavior correlates with the auction price and, second, the sellers consider this information strategically when deciding on their pre-auction price offers. For example, the sellers increase their pre-auction price offers when they deal with buyers who have completed more sales on eBay or when they observe in their past transactions a higher number of bids or less last-minute bidding from at least one bidder. Furthermore, sellers who have completed more sales on eBay post higher pre-auction prices before the auction. Taken together, these results indicate that sellers respond in a sophisticated way to the strategic uncertainty. They also highlight two aspects that are important to overcome judgmental failures in combined mechanisms: strategical response to information collected in markets as well as experience based on accumulated knowledge from own past transactions.

Results from both studies (Ivanova-Stenzel & Kröger [2008]; Grebe et al. [2021]) suggest that combined mechanisms can be beneficial for sellers. Pre-auction price offers that are not too low, avoiding the seller's curse, and not too high, enabling buyers to conclude a sale at the posted pre-auction price, lead to profits above those from auctions or posted prices alone.

3.3. Does Bargaining Power Matter?

The discussion of seller behavior so far considers combined mechanisms, where the seller makes the pre-auction price offer and thus has the bargaining power. The economic bargaining literature acknowledges the strategic advantage of bargaining power under complete information (e.g., Ståhl [1972]).[29] However, as discussed above, sellers do not always have complete information on buyers' willingness to pay. Thus, when there is uncertainty about the stakes in bargaining, the question arises whether having the bargaining power benefits sellers in combined mechanisms. This is an important question, as sellers can choose the market platform for their transactions and often the details of the combined mechanism, in particular, who should make the pre-auction price offer. Indeed, while in many real-world markets, sellers can post pre-auction price offers, in some markets, sellers can allow buyers to offer posted prices before an auction, for example on online trading platforms (e.g., eBay and Hood.de), but also in real estate and car markets as well as in forced sales (e.g., in Germany).[30]

Grebe et al. (2016) study whether a seller can benefit from giving up bargaining power. The study reports the results from an experimental comparison between two combined mechanisms: one where the pre-auction price is offered by the seller, and another one, where the pre-auction price is offered by a buyer. The strategic considerations in combined mechanisms conditional on who makes the pre-auction price offer are straightforward. The seller who has the bargaining power needs to form beliefs about the auction price and to take into account the adverse selection effect of the pre-auction price offer (see sections 2 and 3.1). When a buyer makes the pre-auction price offer, the interaction becomes a signaling game. The seller can use this pre-auction price offer to make inferences about the buyer's willingness to pay.

Despite very different strategic implications for sellers depending on who has the bargaining power, the experimental results suggest no effects of bargaining power on average seller profits.[31] The analysis of individual behavior reveals, however, that only sellers who demand high pre-auction prices benefit from having the bargaining power. Bargaining power is irrelevant for sellers who post or who accept low pre-auction prices, that is, who suffer from the seller's curse and fail to adjust their expectations about the auction price.[32] Indeed, Grebe (2009) reports that elicited sellers' beliefs about the buyers' maximum willingness to pay are systematically biased when the buyer makes the pre-auction price offer. This suggests that sellers fail to condition their beliefs on the buyer's pre-auction price offer.

4. SUMMARY AND TAKEAWAYS

Sequentially combining posted prices and auctions provides sellers with two chances for a sale. If the first chance fails, that is, the posted pre-auction price is not accepted, they have a second chance to achieve the sale in the auction. Along with posted prices and auctions, such combined mechanisms are commonly adopted selling formats in the (online) retail sector. The results from the theoretical and experimental research on seller behavior in private value environments so far point out why retailers might be interested in using such mechanisms.

In the following, we summarize the main takeaways from this chapter:

- Combining posted prices and auctions may generate higher sale prices than each of the two selling formats alone when sellers face uncertainty about buyers' willingness to pay.
- The complexity of the decision problem in combined mechanisms augments the probability that traders make mistakes. When sellers decide on their pre-auction price offer, they might fall prey

to the seller's curse, a judgmental failure that results in forgone profit opportunities.

- Sellers suffer from the seller's curse if they ignore the adverse selection effect that the posted pre-auction price has on buyers with different valuations and thus on the auction price.
- Information available on online market platforms helps sellers to adjust their pre-auction price offers. Experienced sellers seem to better account for the adverse selection effect of their pre-auction price offer and to avoid the seller's curse.
- Possessing the bargaining power in combined mechanisms benefits only sellers who demand high prices.

ACKNOWLEDGMENTS

We thank John J. Han and the co-editors Laurette Dubé and Bassem Monla for helpful comments that improved this chapter. We gratefully acknowledge financial support from the *Social Sciences and Humanities Research Council, Canada*, through 435-2015-1622, *Deutsche Forschungsgemeinschaft*, through CRC TRR 190 "Rationality and Competition," as well as support from the Berlin Centre for Consumer Policies (BCCP). The authors declare that they have no relevant or material financial interests that relate to the research described in this chapter.

NOTES

1 Other online auction platforms that offer the option to post a pre-auction price are, for example, Yahoo! Japan and the South African auction platform, bobshop.co.za.
2 Hasker, K., & Sickles, R. (2010). eBay in the economic literature: Analysis of an auction marketplace. *Review of Industrial Organization, 37*(1), 3–42. https://www.jstor.org/stable/41799476.
3 Decisions are "optimal" according to a particular goal, which includes, but is not limited to, profit maximization, risk minimization, and generating fast or fair sales.
4 In a "private value environment," the value of the item for sale is completely unrelated between potential buyers. In the opposite case, referred to as "common value environment," the item for sale has the same value for each buyer, which, however, is unknown before the transaction.

5 Kagel, J. & Levin, D. (2016). Auctions: A survey of experimental research. In J.H. Kagel & A.E. Roth (Eds.), *The Handbook of Experimental Economics, Volume 2* (pp. 563–629). Princeton University Press.

6 Akerlof, G.A. (1970). The market for "lemons": Quality uncertainty and the market mechanism. *The Quarterly Journal of Economics, 84*(3), 488–500. https://doi.org/10.2307/1879431.

7 Samuelson, W., & Bazerman, M.H. (1985). The winner's curse in bilateral negotiations. In V. Smith (Ed.), *Research in Experimental Economics* (pp. 105–37). JAI Press.

8 Kagel, J., & Levin, D. (2002). *Common value auctions and the winner's curse.* Princeton University Press.

9 Submitting a bid below one's own maximum willingness to pay is not advantageous because of the possibility of being outbid by another bidder and thus missing a profitable opportunity. It is also not beneficial to the buyer to submit a bid higher than their own maximum willingness to pay, because the winning buyer might end up paying a price above this amount, and thus making a loss. See Vickrey (1961), who provides the first theoretic analysis of the second-price auction. True value bidding in second-price auctions is not only theoretically an optimal strategy but also recommended to bidders by platforms offering auctions with this pricing rule, such as eBay (http://pages.ebay.com/help/buy/outbid-ov.html).

10 Vickrey, W. (1961). Counterspeculation, auctions, and competitive sealed tenders. *The Journal of Finance, 16*(1), 8–37. https://doi.org/10.1111/j.1540-6261.1961.tb02789.x.

11 Bulow, J., & Klemperer, P. (1996). Auctions versus negotiations. *American Eco- nomic Review, 86*(1), 180–94. https://www.jstor.org/stable/2118262.

12 Ivanova-Stenzel, R., & Kröger, S. (2008). Price formation in a sequential selling mechanism. *Journal of Economic Behavior & Organization, 67*(3–4), 832–43. https://doi.org/10.1016/j.jebo.2008.02.003.

13 Grebe, T. (2009). The "Sell-It-Now" option: A theoretical investigation. In *Four Essays on Auction Mechanisms* (pp. 52–76). Shaker Verlag.

14 Grebe, T., Ivanova-Stenzel, R., & Kröger, S. (2016). "Buy-It-Now" or "Sell-It-Now" auctions: Effects of changing bargaining power in sequential trading mechanism. *Economics Letters, 142*, 27–30. https://doi.org/10.1016/j.econlet.2015.12.025.

15 Shunda, N. (2009). Auctions with a buy price: The case of reference-dependent preferences. *Games and Economic Behavior, 67*(2), 645–64. https://doi.org/10.1016/j.geb.2009.04.013.

16 Other explanations include, for example, impatience and reference dependence (see Hasker & Sickles [2010]; Shunda [2009] and references therein).

17 Grebe, T., Ivanova-Stenzel, R., & Kröger, S. (2021). How do sellers benefit from Buy-It-Now prices in eBay auctions? *Journal of Economic Behavior & Organization, 183*, 189–205. https://doi.org/10.1016/j.jebo.2020.12.015.

18 This setting captures the main features of the combined mechanism offered on eBay, the "Buy-It-Now" auction, where the pre-auction price offer is temporary and disappears once a bid is submitted.

19 For illustration purposes, the graphs present a situation in which the seller's valuation for the item is commonly known to be 0. Each buyer's maximum willingness to pay for the item is private information and can be between 0 and 100 with all values drawn independently and being equally likely. The simulations in the right-hand column are based on the elicited levels of risk tolerance of eBay traders, see Ivanova-Stenzel & Kröger (2008) for details.

20 The threshold equals 50, given the assumptions about the distribution of the buyers' willingness to pay in our simulation example.

21 As an alternative to experimental studies, empirical studies on combined mechanisms collect data, mainly on outcomes, such as the number of bidders and sales as well as

final prices. They relate these data to other observable variables such as the posted pre-auction prices and traders' background characteristics (e.g., Einav et al. [2018]). The advantage of those studies is that they observe the real behavior of traders with real consequences. The main drawback is the lack of control, for example, on the variation of certain characteristics, and on how much sellers and buyers value the item.

22 Einav, L., Farronato, C., Levin, J., & Sundaresan, N. (2018). Auctions versus posted prices in online markets. *Journal of Political Economy, 126*(1), 178–215. https://doi .org/10.1086/695529.

23 For the theoretical predictions, see Figure 14.1 and the discussion in the previous section.

24 The profit from an auction without a pre-auction price offer is simulated based on the behavior of buyers in the auction.

25 The psychology literature highlights the importance of experimenting for optimal decision-making, for example Einhorn & Hogarth (1981).

26 Einhorn, H.J., & Hogarth, R.M. (1981). Behavioral decision theory: Processes of judgment and choice. *Journal of Accounting Research, 19*(1), 1–31. https://doi.org /10.2307/2490959.

27 In the eBay experiment, standard eBay auction prices (horizontal dashed line, top right panel) are substantially below those expected in second-price auctions. The empirical analysis reveals that the observed price deviations can be explained by the specific features of the eBay auction format that trigger the use of certain bidding strategies such as multiple and last-minute bidding, see Grebe et al. (2021) for more details.

28 The information of the eBay traders in the experiment contains past bidding histories, such as the number of bids, the presence of last-minute bids, auction prices, and the experience that traders have with the eBay platform.

29 Ståhl, I. (1972). *Bargaining theory.* Stockholm School of Economics.

30 See, e.g., www.adesa.com.

31 Theoretically, when both market sides are risk-neutral, it does not matter who has the bargaining power in the combined mechanism. In any case, as shown in Grebe (2009), all transactions are completed in the auction because all pre-auction price offers will be rejected – they will be either too high in the case when the seller makes the offer, or too low in the case when the buyer makes the offer.

32 One possible explanation is that those sellers simply compare the ex-ante expected profit from an auction without a pre-auction price offer to the profit they would realize if their pre-auction price offer is accepted or if they accept the buyer's pre-auction price offer.

CHAPTER FIFTEEN

Participative Pricing in B2B Markets

John J. Han and Ernan Haruvy

SUMMARY OF CHAPTER

The chapter discusses participative pricing in business-to-business markets, with a focus on auctions and bargaining, and with analysis of empirical findings in these two areas.

MANAGERIAL IMPLICATIONS (GENERAL)
- As this chapter describes in a good level of detail the participative pricing in B2B markets, managers need to understand and evaluate the integration of an automated system that implements these pricing algorithms. One of the main questions is whether managers can rely on a fully automated process or rather consider a "human in the loop" type of systems.

MANAGERIAL IMPLICATIONS (ORGANIZATIONAL)
- The procurement department is the main organizational entity concerned by this process, but it is extremely important to link this enterprise function with other enterprise functions such as marketing, sales, promotions, inventory, logistics, and even fulfillment. The main reason is that procurement, especially when coupled with participative pricing, is time-consuming and

can be inefficient. Therefore, they should evaluate whether the automation of the participative pricing process favors the enterprise's bottom line.

MANAGERIAL IMPLICATIONS (STRATEGIC, TACTICAL, AND OPERATIONAL)

- From the strategic perspective, it is critical for an enterprise to be able to automate its bidding and procurement process in order to be resilient to changes and to market disruptions. At the same time, enterprises need to have "strategic partners" and not have an entirely open bidding process. The balance between these two factors is an important strategic decision and it might be specific to the type of product to consider in the procurement.
- From a tactical perspective it is important to connect to B2B marketplaces and to implement automated systems that can interact with these markets.
- From an operational perspective, as the amounts of B2B deals are relatively high, it is essential to be able to detect fraud or anomalies automatically. The B2B platform should be auditable and trustable, ideally it would be a blockchain-based collaborative platform.

MANAGERIAL IMPLICATIONS (RISK ASSESSMENT)

- The implementation of such systems is not a high-risk initiative in itself. Rather, it is the business impact that introduces the major risk factors.
- Managers need to address and mitigate the risks associated with the adoption. Examples of such risks include the quality of products and consistency, eventual loss of strategic partners, internal fraud, and auditing capabilities.

1. INTRODUCTION

In this chapter, we discuss participative pricing in business-to-business (hereafter B2B) markets, with a focus on auctions and bargaining, and with some analysis of empirical findings in these two areas. *Participative pricing* is a term that refers to pricing mechanisms in which buyers and sellers both have a say (i.e., inputs) in determining the price of each transaction. This type of pricing stands in contrast to a *posted price format*, a format in which the seller posts a price (known as posted price or list price), and the consumer buys the item if the price is lower than the consumer's reservation value.

The term *participative pricing* applies to auctions, buyer-seller bargaining, and other innovative pricing methods.[1] Following the advent of the internet, it is relatively costless in terms of transaction costs for sellers to implement such pricing formats. That said, inertia and preferences for traditional retail shopping formats have made such advanced pricing methods slow to spread in consumer markets and confined to niche consumer markets. This is despite evidence that both auctions and bargaining can produce higher revenues for sellers.[2]

In sharp contrast to consumer markets, in B2B markets, participative pricing, such as bargaining and auctions, has long been the norm. Advances in technology did not make such methods more prevalent (as they have always been prevalent), but they most certainly made them more structured. Specifically, *B2B auctions* – more commonly known as *procurement auctions* – can now incorporate and automate a sophisticated scoring system which evaluates numerous critical dimensions (in the case of, Google Ads, hundreds of factors). Likewise, *bargaining* can now be automated to deal individually with each of tens of thousands of consumers.

In this chapter, we describe recent findings on automated processes for both auctions and bargaining at a large scale. We also discuss how to estimate key parameters using readily available data for these transaction formats.

2. B2B (PROCUREMENT) AUCTIONS

Auctions refer to pricing formats where buyers (or sellers) submit multiple bids for a contract, and the buyer with the highest (or the lowest, in the case of the seller) bid wins. Auctions are a ubiquitous format in consumer retail. For example, eBay is the dominant force in consumer auctions, offering consumers a wide range of products at bargain prices while offering small sellers a market for used products and collector items that they might otherwise dispose of. Many formats have been proposed for consumer auctions. While describing all these formats is outside the scope of this chapter, they can generally be divided along two dimensions. First, auctions can be divided into an open-bid or a sealed-bid auction. In open-bid auctions, bidders can revise their bids continually and observe something about other bidders' actions in the course of the auction. In sealed-bid auctions, bidders submit a single bid and observe nothing about others until all bids have been received. The second dimension is first vs. second price, where in first-price auctions, the winning bidder pays its own bid, and in second-price auctions, the winning bidder pays the bid of the next highest bidder.

While eBay and other consumer auctions have been researched extensively and documented thoroughly in the literature,[3,4] they may not have much resemblance to B2B auctions. For one, the contracts under B2B auctions tend to be multi-unit and/or multi-attribute.[5] In the case of multi-unit, the auction accounts for a market clearing price that involves multiple winners at different quantity amounts. In the case of a multi-attribute auction, the winner-selection rule accommodates for non-price quality-related features.[6,7,8]

The distinction between consumer auctions and B2B auctions is most pronounced in their respective purpose, as well as in the downstream consequences following the auctions. The purpose of consumer auctions is generally understood as maximizing the seller's revenue, while in contrast, auctions in B2B markets aim to maximize market thickness – that is, to attract a large number of buyers and sellers.[9] Moreover, unlike consumer auctions, which tend to be one-time events, B2B auctions often lead to more complex relationships involving repeated buyer-seller interactions in the future. Hence, enterprises enjoy repeated interactions in a B2B procurement context, for data accumulated from these interactions offer a natural automated process for price discovery.[10]

B2B auctions can be forward auctions, where a seller receives offers from multiple buyers and the highest bidder wins, or they can be reverse auctions, where a buyer receives offers from multiple sellers and the lowest bidder wins. At least in theory, forward auctions and reverse auctions are isomorphic.[11] That is, in a structured formal setting, to transform a forward auction to a reverse auction, one needs to substitute sellers for buyers and buyers for sellers and then reverse the direction of bids, such that bids go down instead of up, and the winner is the lowest bid. Theoretically, this reversal allows a forward auction format to be translated to an isomorphic reverse auction format without loss of generality.

In reality, because bidders are differentiated in B2B auctions, the flexibility for buyers to choose the winning bidders is of great importance in B2B auctions, making this a primary distinction between B2B auctions and other auctions. One consequence of differentiated bidders is that bidders adjust their bids to account for their non-price qualities. Thus, in many B2B reverse auctions we observe many bids above the lowest bid over the course of the auction (see Figure 15.1).[12] Hence, buyers need a way to assess whether a supplier has bid aggressively or cautiously held back. To this end, Jap and Naik (2008)[13] developed *BidAnalyzer*, an optimization algorithm using state-space models and a Kalman filtering technique not only to predict the ending bids of an auction (based on initial bid activity), but also to give insight into whether the supplier has held back in its bidding (implying that there is still money to be gained from post-auction negotiations), or has bid too aggressively (and is perhaps in danger of a winner's curse).

While bid data from procurement auctions, along the lines of the format in Figure 15.1, is available, analyzing it empirically is far from trivial. This is because unlike consumer auctions, prices are not the primary variable of interest. In many cases, relationship variables matter greatly as well. Combining point-by-point bid data of online buyer-determined reverse auction lots from an industrial buyer with pre- and post-surveys of bidder relationship states (i.e., propensity for a relationship with the buyer, willingness to make investments, relationship satisfaction, etc.) in online reverse auctions, Jap and Haruvy (2008) find that bidders with higher relationship propensity (both past and future) and a greater willingness to make specific investments with the buyer prior to the auction bid less aggressively during the course of the auction, while bidders who bid aggressively during the auction reduce

Figure 15.1. Bidding Activity in Online Reverse Auctions. The horizontal axis denotes time over the course of the auction. Diamonds represent bids received over the course of the auction. The black line traces the lowest bid at any point in time. Reproduced from Jap (2002).

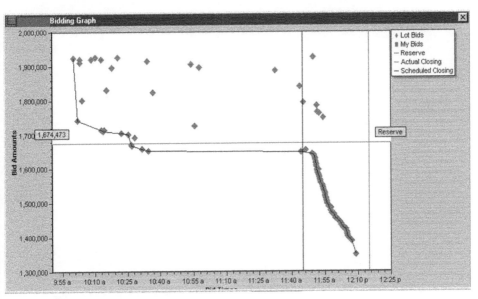

their propensity for a relationship and sour incumbent satisfaction with the buyer post-auction (cf., Carter & Stevens [2006]).[14] This research was the first to use field data to examine bidding behavior during the auction with factors *outside* of the auction mechanism (both before and after), but more importantly, it suggests that bidders systematically intertwine and trade-off bid prices and non-price attributes against each other as part of their strategic bidding behavior.

Haruvy and Jap (2013) propose that quality differentiated bidders would systematically impact bidding behavior. They propose a model in which a bidder's beliefs and observations of competitive bids jointly feed into a dynamic loop with updating to result in bid revisions (see Figure 15.2). Using bid-by-bid data from an industrial buyer, they find that differentiated, anonymous bidders appear to make inferences about their own implied

Figure 15.2. Dynamic Updating Process for Differentiated Bidders

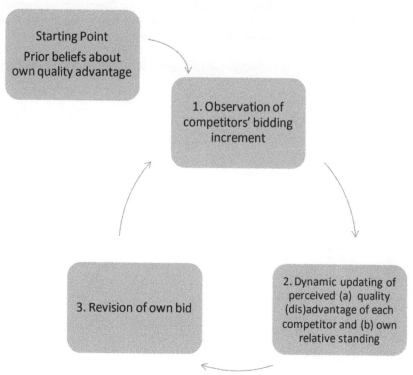

quality differentials and adjust their bidding strategies and bidding aggression accordingly. Specifically, high quality bidders tend to be more aggressive in bidding against potentially higher quality competition and less aggressive when bidding against potentially lower quality competition. In contrast, low-quality bidders compete fiercely regardless of their relative quality compared to the competition.

In summary, empirical research on B2B auctions should first identify the primary purpose of the auction, rather than assume it to be revenue maximization, as the purpose is likely to be more evolved than in consumer auctions. Second, the relationship variables need to be mapped out and incorporated into the equilibrium solution. Third, dynamic adjustment methods need to account for bidders' responses to each other.

3. B2B BARGAINING

As demonstrated in the previous section, auctions can prove productive for arriving at a price point as long as they are sensitive to the relationships and allow a participatory role for both buyers and sellers. In this regard, there is literature that explores how the typical bidding process in auctions can be integrated, sequenced, or can potentially replace negotiation efforts to provide increased flexibility and viable options for procurement efforts.

Bargaining is obviously a time-consuming process, and it is particularly cumbersome for suppliers that deal with thousands of customers and tens of thousands of negotiation occasions, as is the case in the data we study. That is, whereas an effective, autonomous sales force dealing with customers works well in many procurement settings,[15] the existing autonomous sales-force model is not expected to extend to bargaining settings with a large number of transactions with smaller buyers, especially if sales-force pricing decisions must be automated.

4. COMBINING AUCTIONS AND BARGAINING

Research has explored mechanisms that combine auction elements with negotiation processes. Haruvy et al. (2020)[16] compares a bargaining protocol that allows sellers to make concessions dynamically to one where sellers receive a take-it-or-leave-it offer. The dynamic concession protocol is like a dynamic auction, except that buyers can accept the offer and end the process at any time, and bargaining is done bilaterally with no competition. Lab studies have tested the impact of different contract formats (e.g., a wholesale price, two-part tariff contracts) on bargaining, and have shown that contracts are more efficient when sellers can make concessions dynamically. In other words, concessions matter, and starting with a final ultimatum offer at the beginning of a procurement is not optimal for the seller.

We use the insights gained from these studies in the present design with three consecutive alternating offers, where the last one is a take-it-or-leave-it ultimatum offer. We propose automated price adjustments in our sequential alternating-offer setting where the negotiation environment suggests customized prices to individual buyers based on the predicted reserve price, previous counteroffers, and/or buyer-seller relationships – that is, relationships have value.[17] In the next section, we demonstrate automated price adjustments in an industrial buying setting in which a firm engages in negotiations with multiple buyers.

5. A DEMONSTRATION OF EMPIRICAL ANALYSIS OF B2B BARGAINING

Here, we demonstrate the empirical analysis of bargaining data with attention to differentiating relationship variables and a focus on the balance between the bargaining power of both a buyer and a seller.

5.1. Data Description

A dataset was obtained from a large international manufacturer of industrial components and parts. The manufactured items can be bought at the price indicated for each item on the company's website, but buyers can and do often engage in rounds of negotiations for a lower price. Each observation in the data records how a price of a product changed from the list price down to the final negotiated price through a bargaining process between a buyer and the seller. The data also include whether the negotiated price was approved after a delay, whether the negotiated price was converted to revenue, buyer information (customer loyalty level, geographical location, and industry represented), and product information (type of product, product uniqueness, and product volume).

For the purpose of the present demonstration, we look only at the data where the buyers negotiate directly with the seller, without an intermediary such as a distributor. A summary of the data cleaning process is in Table 15.1.

Table 15.1. Summary of Data Cleaning Process

Excluded	Rationale for Exclusion
Distributor Channel	We are interested in a bargaining process between an end customer and the seller.
Auto-Approved Quotes	We only investigate deals that entered a bargaining process.
Seller Loss Leaders	Sometimes sellers sell below cost as a loss-leader technique and this cannot be considered to be the outcome of negotiation.
Buyer Loss Leaders	Buyers should not buy at a price higher than the list price. That's a loss-leader proposition on the part of the buyer.
Incorrect Quote Approval	A quote should be approved without delay if a buyer did not ask for a concession.

Also excluded were transactions in which the buyer's requests were automatically approved by the computer algorithm. These transactions were automatically approved because these are likely renewals of the price approved from the previous bargaining process. Such transactions are outside of the scope of the current chapter since no current bargaining took place.

In our data, there were two lowball threshold prices – Level 1 Threshold (L_1) and Level 2 Threshold (L_2) – that determined whether the company approved a price quote immediately or after a delay. L_1 was strictly higher than L_2. The company approved the final negotiated price immediately if the price was higher than L_1. However, if the price fell between L_1 and L_2, the price quote was transferred from sales agents to regional pricing managers for further evaluation, resulting in a delay. The same was true if the price fell below L_2.

After all the exclusion criteria were applied to the dataset, data on 82,345 negotiations were entered into further analyses.

5.2. Relationship Tiers

In the dynamic concession protocol, the company applies different discount rates to each buyer. The data shows that some buyers were given a considerable discount while others were not. Furthermore, we found that the discount rates varied across the bargaining process. The company gave some buyers their discounts early in the bargaining process while it gave other buyers discounts late in the process. We theorize that the buyer-seller relationship is a crucial factor in predicting when and how much discount was given to a buyer.

The company classified each buyer into one of several relationship tiers. For the purpose of this analysis, we classify prospective buyers into one of two broad relationship tiers. We call these tiers *preferred* customers and *regular* customers. 30 percent of the buyers in the data were preferred customers either because they have repeatedly bought from the company in the past or because they are buying products in very large quantities. Presumably, the company would give more generous concessions to preferred customers than to regular customers since they are more likely to continue a long-term partnership with the company in the future.

5.3. Seller Power: Product Differentiation

The central tenet of economics is that supply and demand are negatively related. If a product is short in supply while holding the customer demand constant, sellers would have more say in the bargaining process. In our data, 25 percent of the products were unique in that they were manufactured and sold only by the company. It is assumed that the company would be less likely to offer a generous concession to buyers who wish to buy such products since there is no competition.

On the other hand, 75 percent of the products in the data were nonexclusive goods. Since the buyers could obtain these products elsewhere, the company would be more likely to offer a generous discount to maximize the chance of procuring a deal.

In the data, we found that customer relationship tiers and product differentiation were two consistently significant predictors of the amount of discount given as well as the probability of a successful procurement. We will also show the relative contribution of the two predictors, while controlling for other factors, which we describe below.

5.4. Three-Stage Bargaining Framework

Businesses are more efficient when sellers can make concessions dynamically. Our model captures that notion. In the current section, we describe a version of the dynamic concession protocol which the company uses to procure deals from multiple buyers.

The company deals primarily with buyers who buy products in large volumes. These buyers have the bargaining power to request concessions, which can come in different forms. Here, we focus on monetary discounts.

When buyers decline to pay the list price[18] and instead request a concession, the company can entice a deal by engaging in a bargaining process that consists of three stages of alternating offers. The first stage of the process in our framework (see Stage 1 in Figure 15.3) begins with the seller (the company) determining a list price. At this point, buyers can take one of three actions: they can pay that list price to obtain the target product, exit the bargaining with the company, or request a concession. If a buyer either agrees to pay the list price or exits entirely, the buyer is considered to have exited the bargaining process and does not advance to the next stage.

Buyers who request a concession in the first stage enter the second stage of the bargaining process (see Stage 2 in Figure 15.3). The second stage begins with the seller conceding and suggesting a new price for each buyer. With the new price in hand, buyers can take one of the following four actions: accept the suggested price, quit bargaining, ask for another concession, or make a counteroffer by stating how much they would like to pay. Note that none of these actions guarantees that buyers purchase the product. In other words, buyers can exit the bargaining process even after the seller incorporates additional concessions to the price. Also, in the case of buyers making a counteroffer, they can still exit later, but we consider them as having entered the third and final bargaining stage. In other words, buyers at the second stage advance to the next stage only if they make a counteroffer.

The third stage in our framework begins with buyers making a counteroffer to the seller (see Stage 3 in Figure 15.3). After a

Figure 15.3. A flow chart of the bargaining context

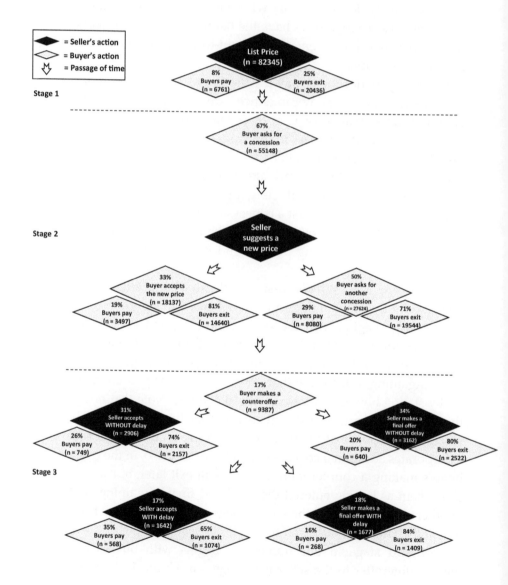

counteroffer is made, the seller can either accept it or counter-suggest a "take-it-or-leave-it" ultimatum. The seller's ultimatum determines the final price which buyers must decide to pay or forego the purchase altogether. The ultimatum offer is often made with a delay for buyers who made a particularly low counteroffer in the previous stage. In the rest of this section, we explain each stage of the bargaining process in more detail.

Stage 1: THE SELLER DETERMINES LIST PRICE AND BUYERS CAN EITHER BUY OR QUIT

Even though offers have not yet been exchanged between buying and selling parties, we consider all buyers to have entered the bargaining process at this stage. Here, the company (i.e., seller) determines the list price and buyers determine the convergence (i.e., agreement to pay) to revenue. The data showed that 33 percent of the buyers concluded the bargaining process at Stage 1 and did not request a concession of any sort. Of these buyers, 25 percent (8 percent of all buyers) bought the target product, and 75 percent (25 percent of all buyers) quit without seeking a better deal from the company (see Stage 1 in Figure 15.3).

Stage 2: THE SELLER CONCEDES WITH A SUGGESTED PRICE AND BUYERS CAN EITHER BUY OR QUIT

In our data, 67 percent of the buyers requested a concession, and they advanced to Stage 2 of our bargaining framework. At this stage, the company conceded to buyers' requests and dynamically determined a new price for each and every buyer (see Stage 2 in Figure 15.3). It is important to note that 16 percent of the buyers at this stage appeared to receive a suggested price that was higher than the list price – possibly because they asked for ancillary services in addition to their target product. However, the price was ultimately lowered after the company incorporated multiple concessions requested by the buyers. Therefore, a suggested price was always lower than a list price after incorporating buyers' request for concession.

After a suggested price was determined, the data showed that 33 percent of the buyers accepted the new price while 50 percent asked for another concession to obtain a better deal. The data also showed that more than twice the buyers ended up paying for a product when they asked for another concession than when they did not.

Stage 3: the seller determines the final price and buyers determines convergence

Unwilling to accept the company's offer at Stage 2, 17 percent of the buyers advanced to the next and final stage of the bargaining process. Buyers at Stage 3 made a counteroffer to the company by stating the price that they wished to pay. Of all the counteroffers made by the buyers, 48 percent were accepted by the company, and the rest, 52 percent, were countered with a "take-it-or-leave-it" offer.

Central to the bargaining process is strategic delay. In fact, 36 percent of all the accepted counteroffers were accepted with delay while 35 percent of all the unaccepted counteroffers were countered (with the ultimatum offer) with delay. It seems unnecessary and wasteful to introduce a delay in the bargaining process, but as a strategic device it may be effective.

The delay affected the proportion of buyers who ended up paying for the product. When the company accepted buyers' counteroffers, 26 percent of the buyers whose counteroffers were accepted without delay ended up purchasing while 35 percent of the buyers whose counteroffers were accepted with a delay ended up purchasing. On the other hand, when the company made an ultimatum in response to buyers' counteroffers, 20 percent of the buyers who received the ultimatum without delay ended up purchasing while 16 percent of the buyers who received an ultimatum with a delay ended up purchasing (see the bottom of Stage 3 in Figure 15.2).

5.5. Different Prices at Different Stages

We now turn our attention to different types of prices and other relevant variables that enabled our conceptualization of the three-stage bargaining process. There were four types of prices in the data: (1)

list price, (2) suggested price, (3) negotiated price, and (4) requested price (see Table 15.2 for description).

List price was the price that the company stated on its website. In our data, it had the highest mean price normalized by cost (M = 10.67, SE = .26)[19] compared to other types of normalized mean prices. The list price was determined prior to Stage 1 by the company, and buyers are assumed to never pay a price higher than the list price.

After the company incorporated concessions that buyers requested at Stage 2, it determined the suggested price. When it was normalized by cost, the mean suggested price was the second highest (M = 7.71, SE = .33) compared to other normalized mean prices.

Negotiated price was the final price that the company offered to its buyers. The price was determined at every stage of the bargaining process unless buyers made an early exit from the negotiation. In the data, a suggested price was equal to a negotiated price if a buyer decided not to ask for more concession and accepted the company's suggested price at Stage 2. However, if a buyer requested additional concessions past Stage 2, suggested and negotiated prices were different. On average, the negotiated price was the third highest normalized mean price (M = 6.10, SE = .13) compared to other prices.

Requested price was the price that buyers determined – as a counteroffer – at the beginning of Stage 3. The data showed that the normalized mean of the requested price was the lowest price (M = 4.91, SE = .13) compared to other prices since buyers' reservation price would be just above the cost of production, which is the lowest acceptable price by the seller.

Figure 15.4 displays different types of normalized mean prices for preferred customers and regular customers. Some concessions were given to both preferred and regular customers, but preferred customers enjoyed larger concessions than regular customers. The difference in the size of the concession is visually recognizable in the figure by comparing the differences in height between the second and the third highest bars for each customer group: the difference between the two bars is larger for the preferred customers than for

Table 15.2. Types of Prices and Other Relevant Variables

Types of Prices*	Description
List Price	List price is the price that is listed on the company's website. It is determined by the seller at the beginning of Stage 1.
Suggested Price	Suggested price is the price that the seller suggests after incorporating concessions. It is determined by the seller at Stage 2.
Negotiated Price	Negotiated price is the final price offered by the seller before buyers either pay for a product or quit the bargaining process. It is determined at every stage unless buyers make an exit from the deal.
Requested Price (i.e., counteroffer)	Requested price is the price that a buyer requests to pay for a product. It is determined by the buyer at the beginning of Stage 3.

Other Variables	Description
Level 1 Threshold (L_1)	Level 1 threshold is the lowest price that can be approved without a delay. If a negotiated price falls below this threshold, the bargaining is delayed but there is a strong chance that the price is accepted.
Level 2 Threshold (L_2)	Level 2 threshold functions much like a Level 1 threshold but an offer that falls below it is further delayed and is likely to be countered.
Cost	Cost is the seller's cost of production.

* Types of prices are presented in decreasing order of the average values.

Figure 15.4. Mean of four different types of prices normalized by cost for preferred and regular customer loyalty levels (n = 9,387)

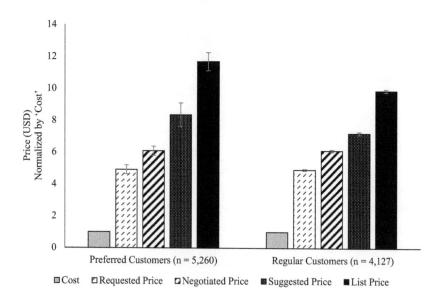

regular customers, indicating the seller's giving more generous concessions to the preferred group.

6. CONCLUSIONS

We began by covering the literature extolling the virtues of participative pricing. While such a strong pitch may be called for to convince retailers to adopt participative pricing more widely with consumer pricing, in the B2B space, participative pricing has long been a widely accepted mode of transaction, either through auctions[20] or through bargaining and negotiations. Our review of the literature and our data reveal several regularities present in both auctions and bargaining in the B2B sphere.

Differentiated sellers and differentiated buyers. The auctions we reported on were reverse auctions, with multiple sellers bidding over each contract. In these auctions, we noted that buyers strongly differentiate between sellers and that sellers differentiate among themselves in the manner they bid relative to one another. While a sizable literature has emerged to try to formalize this process, especially via scoring auctions, which quantify each possible dimension,[21] it is our experience and observation that such formal quantification of consideration attributes is either not workable or not practiced. Instead, we find a seemingly more informal yet strong differentiation.

A more informal and bargaining-oriented auction structure. The differentiation between bidders in B2B auctions allows for bargaining power before and after the auctions, whether in a prequalification phase or in a post-auction subsequent negotiation phase. Thus, everything we see in practice and in trends going forward is a movement to make auctions more flexible, and in doing so, to move auctions away from the rigid market structure and more towards a bargaining-like structure, albeit bargaining between one and many (as in one buyer and many sellers).

A more formal and auction-like bargaining structure. Just as auctions gravitate towards a more bargaining-like structure, bargaining practices appear to gravitate towards a more formal auction-like structure. That is, the entire description of the bargaining process in the previous section revolved around the organization replacing its autonomous pricing decision-makers with automated pricing rules that have strict thresholds and preset response functions for every eventuality. In essence, these rules constitute a single-bidder auction against an internal privately known (to the seller) set of reservation prices. This movement towards a more rigid set of bargaining responses is enabled with advances in computation powers and AI tools. It constitutes a potential for greatly increased efficiencies. It also means that in the near future, we may see a convergence of auctions and bargaining formats to a common space of hybrid formats.

Relationship tiers. Both our auction data and our bargaining data suggest that relationships matter, and so buyers and sellers move towards quantifying and formalizing these relationships as their key attributes. That is, while we dismissed the possibility of quantifying every possible dimension that matters, that dismissal does not extend to relationship tiers. They appear to be one of the primary considerations in both auctions and bargaining, and the movement appears to be towards formalizing that measure.

Successive concessions. In both auctions and bargaining, it seems that it was not solely the attributes of the contract that mattered, but the incidence and magnitude of concession relative to the last price considered. This is consistent with findings by Haruvy et al. (2020) that show that concessions in supply-chain bargaining are the driving force in the agreement ultimately reached. The Kalman filter proposed by Jap and Naik (2008) suggested exactly that notion, as did the data reported on in the bargaining analysis we presented.

Strategic delay. The last major reveal in the data is the importance of delay. It has long been known that strategic delay can be advantageous to one or both parties in bargaining.[22] However, our presentation here is the first demonstration that strategic delay can be structured and formalized in the field in B2B settings, and that it is widely practiced for bargaining advantage.

NOTES

1 Spann, M., Zeithammer, R., Bertini, M., Haruvy, E., Jap, S.D., Koenigsberg, O., Mak, V., Popkowski Leszczyc, P.T.L., Skiera, B., & Thomas, M. (2018). Beyond posted prices: The past, present, and future of participative pricing mechanisms. *Customer Needs and Solutions*, 5(1), 121–36. https://doi.org/10.1007/s40547-017-0082-y.

2 Cason, T.N., Friedman, D., & Milam, G.H. (2003). Bargaining versus posted price competition in customer markets. *International Journal of Industrial Organization*, *21*(2), 223–51. https://doi.org/10.1016/S0167-7187%2802%2900056-5.

3 Haruvy, E., & Popkowski Leszczyc, P.T.L. (2010a). The impact of online auction duration. *Decision Analysis*, *7*(1), 99–106. https://dx.doi.org/10.2139/ssrn. 1420304

4 Haruvy, E., & Popkowski Leszczyc, P.T.L. (2010b). Search and choice in online consumer auctions. *Marketing Science*, *29*(6), 1152–64. https://www.jstor.org/stable /40959557.

5 Xu, S.X., & Huang, G.Q. (2017). Efficient multi-attribute multi-unit auctions for B2B E-commerce logistics. *Production and Operations Management*, *26*(2), 292–304. https:// doi.org/10.1111/poms.12638.

6 Jap, S.D., & Haruvy, E. (2008). Interorganizational relationships and bidding behavior in industrial online reverse auctions. *Journal of Marketing Research*, *45*(5), 550–61. https://doi.org/10.1509/jmkr.45.5.550.

7 Haruvy, E., & Jap, S.D. (2013). Differentiated bidders and bidding behavior in procurement auctions. *Journal of Marketing Research*, *50*(2), 241–58. https://doi.org /10.1509/jmr.10.0036.

8 Engelbrecht-Wiggans, R., Haruvy, E., & Katok, E. (2007). A comparison of buyer-determined and price-based multiattribute mechanisms. *Marketing Science*, *26*(5), 629–41. https://doi.org/10.1287/mksc.1070.0281.

9 Bimpikis, K., Elmaghraby, W.J., Moon, K., & Zhang, W. (2020). Managing market thickness in online business-to-business markets. *Management Science*, *66*(12), 5783–822. https://dx.doi.org/10.2139/ssrn.3442379.

10 Tunca, T.I., Wu, D.J., & Zhong, F. (2014). An empirical analysis of price, quality, and incumbency in procurement auctions. *Manufacturing & Service Operations Management*, *16*(3), 346–64. https://dx.doi.org/10.2139/ssrn.2332533.

11 Engelbrecht-Wiggans et al. (2007).

12 Jap, S.D. (2002). Online reverse auctions: Issues, themes, and prospects for the future. *Journal of the Academy of Marketing Science*, *30*(4), 506–25. https://doi.org /10.1177/009207002236925.

13 Jap, S.D., & Naik, P.A. (2008). Bidanalyzer: A method for estimation and selection of dynamic bidding models. *Marketing Science*, *27*(6), 949–60. https://www.jstor.org /stable/40057156.

14 Carter, C.R., & Stevens, C.K. (2006). Electronic reverse auction configuration and its impact on buyer price and supplier perceptions of opportunism: A laboratory experiment. *Journal of Operations Management*, *25*(5), 1035–54. https://doi.org/10.1016 /j.jom.2006.10.005.

15 Bimpikis et al. (2020).

16 Haruvy, E., Katok, E., & Pavlov, V. (2020). Bargaining process and channel efficiency. *Management Science*, *66*(7), 2845–60. https://doi.org/10.1287/mnsc.2019.3360.

17 Zhang, J.Z., Netzer, O., & Ansari, A. (2014). Dynamic targeted pricing in B2B relationships. *Marketing Science*, *33*(3), 317–37. https://www.jstor.org/stable /24544972.

18 In the current chapter, the terms "posted price," "list price," "MSRP," and "Internet price" are interchangeable.

19 For the sake of meaningful comparisons, the means for list price, suggested price, negotiated price, and requested price reported in this section were calculated from the observations that contained no missing data in any of the prices (n = 9,387). In other words, buyers who concluded the bargaining process before Stage 3 were excluded from the calculation. Also, instead of the standard deviations, +/- 1 standard errors are reported.

20 To be clear, here we classify the standard RFP process as a degenerate form of auction. An RFP, or request for proposal, is generally mandated by most organizations for substantial contracts. That is, even if the organization has a preferred supplier, it should solicit competitive offers for sizable contracts. Whether formal, informal, structured, or unstructured, such a process of soliciting competing offers is within the definition of an auction.

21 Asker, J., & Cantillon, E. (2008). Properties of scoring auctions. *The RAND Journal of Economics, 39*(1), 69–85. https://doi.org/10.1111/j.1756-2171.2008.00004.x.

22 Admati, A.R., & Perry, M. (1987). Strategic delay in bargaining. *The Review of Economic Studies, 54*(3), 345–64. https://doi.org/10.2307/2297563.

CHAPTER SIXTEEN

Retail Supply Chains: The Growing Importance of Technology and Supply Chain Standards for Enhancing Efficiency, Visibility, Transparency, and Trust at the Digital-Physical B2B Systems Interface

John G. Keogh, Ricardo Filipe Ramos, Juan Marcelo Gómez, and Abderahman Rejeb

SUMMARY OF CHAPTER

The chapter provides an overview of existing challenges encountered by retail firms and their global supply chains. These include the possibilities of end-to-end visibility, industry standards and traceability data, and technology to increase efficiency, transparency, and trust. The importance of these elements is highlighted for businesses and consumers, and vital recommendations for practitioners are provided.

MANAGERIAL IMPLICATIONS (GENERAL)
- This chapter provides managers in retail business with a very rich, coherent, and comprehensive overview of the most important challenges that the sector is facing. It can be used as one of the main inputs for a design thinking strategy workshop.

MANAGERIAL IMPLICATIONS (ORGANIZATIONAL)

- The strategy development must go hand in hand with organizational change for a stronger integration between the processes of different functions of the enterprise such as brand building, marketing, sales, pricing, promotion, procurement, sourcing, and logistics.
- The organizational change must avoid creating internal barriers for information. Additionally, the new organization must properly address the need for a collaborative B2B supply chain network information by allocating the necessary human resources.

MANAGERIAL IMPLICATIONS (STRATEGIC, TACTICAL, AND OPERATIONAL)

- From the strategic perspective, managers in retail business need to integrate the recommendations and thoughts included in this chapter in their strategic thinking to reframe their new strategy. The resulting strategic road map has to incorporate not only internal but also external initiatives related to their partners in the supply chain, as well as the adoption of innovative technologies and standards.
- From the tactical perspective, one of the main questions that managers need to answer is how much technology resource or investment they need to undertake in order to have a balanced operation. If lack of technology is a real operational constraint and constitutes a bottleneck, then they need to consider how much of the technology investment is optimal from a financial perspective, especially since overinvesting in technology could be counterproductive.
- From the transformation operational perspective, managers need to source external skills to complement their internal capabilities.

MANAGERIAL IMPLICATIONS (RISK ASSESSMENT)

- Many initiatives can be derived from this rich overview. These new initiatives will complement existing ones. In designing the final road map of initiatives, a careful study of dependencies, complexities, quick return on investments, and associated

risks must be carried out in order to create a transformation program that is adaptable.
- Managers need to mitigate the risk of any of these initiatives as well as the risks related to the whole transformation program with its overlapping and parallel initiatives.

1. INTRODUCTION

Retailing is a critical sector of the economy, with global in-store revenues estimated at $22.1 trillion and rising e-commerce revenues estimated at $4.1 trillion for 2020. The COVID-19 pandemic caused severe disruptions in retail business operations and global supply chains. Some nonessential bricks-and-mortar retailers faced an existential threat due to the stringent lockdown measures imposed by public health authorities, forcing them to rapidly pivot to e-commerce for survival. While many notable retailers would suffer economic losses, firms providing essential services, such as groceries, achieved record revenues, and e-commerce giant Amazon reported 38 percent year-on-year growth for 2020.[1]

Before the pandemic, traditional bricks-and-mortar retailers experienced growing pressure from fast-changing consumer dynamics and e-commerce. Firms needed to be more agile and flexible while continuously adjusting product lines, managing their transactional efficiencies, and understanding omnichannel retailing and personalization. Moreover, the transformative force of digitization and digitalization affected B2B relationships, and firms were forced to adapt. These relationships are dependent on market and consumer behavior dynamics. However, many digital trends can affect the dynamics of a B2B system, such as big data analytics, Internet of Things, blockchain, or artificial intelligence. These technologies can have profound impacts by changing the digital-physical interface of B2B systems. A digital-physical interface entails integrating the organizations that make up part of a trading or exchange (eco)system.

Regarding digitization and digitalization, consumers can benefit significantly from implementing technologies that enable efficient product selection, provide product recommendations, facilitate quick reordering, and help the scheduling of "click and collect" or curbside pickup and home delivery. The adoption of new technologies in fulfillment operations and e-commerce has the potential to influence today's highly competitive business environment. Both digitization and digitalization benefit the way organizations create value and how they interact and develop intimacy with their customers as part of an overall digital transformation journey. Moreover, e-commerce compliments loyalty programs and facilitates advanced product traceability and enhanced consumer safety, as many in-store purchases are anonymous and product traceability stops at retail. The combination of loyalty membership and e-commerce purchases from non-loyalty customers increases the retailer's ability to warn consumers directly if a product they purchased is unsafe and recalled.

Beyond optimizing global supply chain processes, retailing firms are concerned with increasing supply chain efficiencies and investing in distribution centers and delivery fleets. These challenges have created opportunities for firms to integrate technologies in their operations proactively. The digitalization of retailing is important due to the inherent complexity of supply chain functions, including global sourcing and supplier management, inventory and fulfillment, transportation, warehousing, distribution, and returns. This implies the need for cross-functional collaboration to create sales and profits. Firms are required to ensure enterprise-wide information visibility and make complex trade-offs between delivery responsiveness, product variety, and convenience. Strategic cohesiveness is essential, and a lack of integration in supply chain processes between pricing, promotion, brand building, and marketing can create barriers for effective omnichannel strategy development (e.g., the seamless experience for consumers across all buying methods). Collaboration across supply chain firms and internal functions is fundamental to success.

Over the last two decades, retailing has continuously evolved through technological advances to meet changing consumer behaviors and increased competition. Although the importance of a digital-physical interface is recognized, there are many challenges associated with this process – particularly those related to achieving efficiency, usability, transparency, and trust. Moreover, addressing the omnichannel experience has been one of the most challenging hurdles for retailers. The reasons for this are that retailers have faced numerous challenges such as increased fulfillment and reverse logistics costs. Retailers are also challenged with complex product assortments, demand uncertainty, and difficulty integrating aspects of the physical and digital worlds at each customer experience stage.

Moreover, growing consumer segments have raised concerns about product quality, product safety, factory or farm worker safety, the environment, and overall supply chain transparency. Due to these pressures, retailers need to ensure consistent, integrated, and transparent information to consumers while continuously evolving their modus operandi and efficiently managing their global supply chain processes. Supply chain management (SCM) governance is of strategic importance for retailers to guarantee that the right product is in the right place at the right time and in the right quantity. Advancements in technology enhance SCM governance, which is a mechanism for enhanced product information transparency and increased trust in business-to-business exchanges. Subsequently, technology-enabled SCM governance leads to better consumer protection by improving product traceability, reducing the risks associated with counterfeits, and making product recall processes more efficient.

It is understood that every organization has different objectives. Still, if a cross-alignment exists, their combined purpose will increase performance and grow revenue for all the firms that make part of the system. The outcome will lead to an effective interdependence. The digital-physical interface will help clarify the firms' processes, strategies, and goals, leading to a less time-consuming process and better focus on the overall objective. The real challenge is to develop a conjoined effort between the stakeholders. Understanding the benefits of a digital-physical interface is fundamental to facing this challenge and creating a fully operational system.

2. SUPPLY CHAIN RISK MANAGEMENT (SCRM)

Organizations procuring goods and services as inputs into their businesses make sourcing decisions under conditions of uncertainty. Goods and services can be procured and delivered locally, regionally, nationally, or globally, and each method carries varying levels of risk. For example, a US-based organization may procure goods or services in Vietnam for local delivery under conditions where the agent (e.g., the supplier) undergoes in-market surveillance and inspection by the principal (e.g., the buyer), which reduces the risk of opportunism. The principal may procure goods or services from overseas agents with third-country delivery. Global monitoring of agents is costly to manage from a surveillance and inspection perspective. The resulting unobservability of the agents' actions and behaviors may increase the risk of opportunism and lead to reputation damage and increased transactional costs (i.e., opportunism can include compromised quality or safety, unapproved raw material or ingredient sourcing, unapproved outsourcing to a third party, slave or child labor, bribery, or corrupt practices). Product failures or product safety incidents can have a detrimental impact on a business's operational, tactical, or strategic levels. Adversarial relationships or goal conflicts can develop between principals and their agents and cause the parties to act in their self-interest, limiting information transparency and increasing the risk of moral hazard. Supply chain risk can be managed by building trusting and collaborative relationships and enhancing information transparency between the trading partners through enabling technology. The control and prevention of opportunism is crucial for mitigating the adverse effects of relationship destabilization or contract termination leading to supplier switching costs.

3. SUPPLY CHAIN TRANSPARENCY

Retail supply chain transparency is vital for firms to continuously improve their efficiency and effectiveness, and to reduce risk. The lack of transparency in the supply process obfuscates responsibility and accountability when unexpected events happen (e.g., product quality failures leading to a recall, allegations of deforestation, forced labor, or child labor). The management of organizational activities and supply chain risk will require additional investment because any of the aforementioned unexpected events can tarnish the firm's reputation and competitiveness. Sustainable and effective governance solutions reflect a supply chain system's core purpose to support a firm's revenue growth, contain sourcing and supply-related costs, enable competitive advantage, and reduce the risk of reputation damage. On the last point, continued pressure from institutional investors and regulators is forcing organizations to strengthen their supply chain transparency on environmental, sustainability, and governance factors.

Technological initiatives have emerged and are receiving considerable support to counter evolving retail and SCM landscape challenges. Global organizations have recognized the digital-physical system interface as an increasingly important strategic goal. The use of advanced technology to support organizational decision-making is a critical enabler for SCM transformation. Technologies that capture, store, analyze, and share data create unique opportunities to mitigate business risks facing managers. Advanced technologies promise a revolution in supply chain digitalization and contribute to real-time insights, predictive capabilities, and faster decision-making.

While digitalization can help new and established organizations seize emerging opportunities, adopting advanced technologies is a demanding task. Considering fast-changing customer preferences and retail fulfillment formats, managers must continuously review and adjust their competitive strategies. Managers can look at challenges through different lenses and acquire an understanding of the following key areas:

1. End-to-end business-to-business (B2B) visibility (e.g., supply chain visibility refers to the accurate and timely access to information that stakeholders have throughout the entire supply chain)
2. Full chain adoption of industry standards (e.g., GS1 standards) for data governance, traceability, efficiency, and interoperability between trading partners
3. Product information transparency and improved trust at the digital-physical (B2B system interface)

We begin by providing an overview of existing challenges encountered by retail firms and their global supply chains. Next, the possibilities of end-to-end visibility, industry standards and traceability data, and technology to increase efficiency, transparency, and trust are discussed in detail. The importance of these elements is highlighted for businesses and consumers. We provide vital recommendations for practitioners.

4. CHALLENGES FOR RETAIL ORGANIZATIONS

The premise that customers are uncertain about the real value of products, their usage condition, and whether they match their preferences has increasingly been investigated. With the proliferation of new technologies, customers become well-informed and able to exercise purchase preferences more conveniently. Some retail firms are shifting their business practices by using technology to attract sales (e.g., food delivery apps), maintain a competitive advantage, and serve several consumer segments. While these objectives are desirable, market share acquisition is still a managerial challenge (see Figure 16.1). As a central question in retailing, modern-day pricing challenges have forced retailers to focus on state-of-the-art pricing practices rooted in behavioral economics and psychology. Retailers increasingly rely on exaggerated price discount advertisements with nebulous price claims (e.g., save up to 70 percent) to promote a line of merchandise. While these pricing strategies enable them to provide salient communication and an attractive level of discounts on particular products, they make imprecise and ambiguous price promotional claims. The different discounts for multiple products can create ambiguity about the retailer's precise level of discounts. The uncertainty associated with these ambiguous claims can influence customer attitudes, responses, and decision-making. Retail organizations also face uncertainty regarding choices on two critical margins: when to change the prices of products and what new prices to set. However, dynamic price setting and adjustment may negatively impact their competitive supply chain stability and lead to

Figure 16.1. Challenges for digital-physical B2B systems interface for retail organizations.

complexity characteristics. While highly profit-oriented systems encourage manufacturers to set high prices,[2] doing so may considerably shrink the demand from loyal consumers. The authors conclude that this system may negatively influence the manufacturers and retailers if not sufficiently precise.

Strategic planners and managers strive for a significant market share for their organizations. A larger market share is a cynosure for businesses, and the focus on realizing this goal can have diverse impacts on the different aspects of the retail industry. Retail organizations' efforts to achieve a large market share can potentially affect product quality, pricing, new product developments, and releases. Retailers face high competition for market share due to supply chain dynamics such as demand amplification, ineffective decision-making, and opportunistic behavior. The different consumer expectations regarding product assortment, quantity, quality, and delivery requirements make it difficult for retailers to identify where and how much inventory to hold. Retail firms manage their inventory to ensure visibility across the supply chain and reduce stockout and overstock costs.

Compounding the difficulties of managing retail supply chains, the lack of visibility of other supply chain elements constitutes an important inhibitor for customer satisfaction and cost efficiencies. Most supply chains are managed with each section operating independently, yet striving to optimize their activities in isolation may not lead to optimizing the overall supply chain network. As a result, there is much pressure to enhance supply chain integration. Retailers need to ensure ubiquity and visibility across all channel types, stages, and agents (e.g., product information, pricing, integrated promotion, delivery, and customer service). Fulfilling these objectives may come at an expensive logistical design and realignment of multiple channels.[3]

It is imperative to obtain a sound understanding of these issues that retail organizations face in order to increase customer satisfaction, improve competitiveness, and build efficient and resilient supply chains. Under challenging conditions, resilience is a highly desirable and distinctive characteristic to maintain at the organizational and supply chain levels to handle various types of adversity. For example, resilience is a crucial asset for firms aiming to withstand a system shock like the COVID-19 pandemic. Under the operational and disruption risks posed by a pandemic, the design of robust and resilient retail networks can create substantial competitive advantage as supply chain resilience measures (e.g., risk mitigation inventories, omnichannel and data-driven business models, and real-time monitoring and visibility systems) can help organizations to survive and recover after a pandemic. The development of future retail supply chains that enable resilience and balance efficiency is essential for increasing the value propositions of organizations and solidifying consumer value and experience.

In the following sections, we discuss the pathways to these objectives, as envisioned in academic literature.

5. PATHWAYS TO INCREASED EFFICIENCY, TRUST, AND TRANSPARENCY IN DIGITAL-PHYSICAL B2B SYSTEMS

To link the previous discussions around retail organizations' challenges and the pathways to ensure efficiency and resilience at the physical-digital B2B interface, we will develop a conceptual

Figure 16.2. A conceptual framework for successful physical-digital B2B systems.

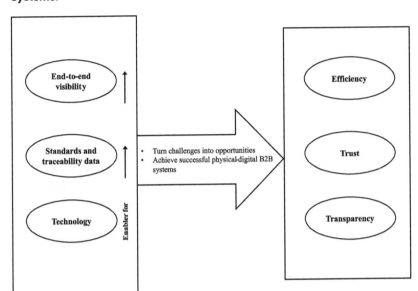

framework (Figure 16.2) and illustrate it with examples from the food supply chain. The framework highlights the potentials of end-to-end visibility, standards and traceability data, and technology to improve retail supply chains and pave the way for precision retailing as a new paradigm. Based on the results, we put forth several recommendations for managers.

6. END-TO-END B2B VISIBILITY

Supply chain visibility is considered a fundamental component in SCM. According to Barratt and Oke (2007), supply chain visibility refers to the accurate and timely access to information that stakeholders have throughout the entire supply chain.[4] Access to such information increases the accuracy of demand forecasting, permits timely adjustments to the production plan, improves delivery performance, and increases the coordination between all levels of the supply chain. Information sharing constitutes an activity, while visibility means the extent to which supply chain partners access information as the outcome of interorganizational communication behaviors. Visibility across organizational boundaries is essential for supply chain efficiency. End-to-end visibility is a critical element in any supply chain risk mitigation strategy as it builds trust and confidence throughout the supply chain.[5] Visibility supports commercial supply chains to enhance efficiency and contractual service levels, and it accelerates responses to customers.[6] End-to-end visibility allows the various levels of the supply chain to reduce the risks related to a system shock (i.e., unexpected event causing disruption) and achieve a superior level of responsiveness and resilience. B2B visibility is strongly recommended for managing risk related to supply chain failures. Moreover, it increases the exchange partner's ability to utilize data analytics for business performance and extract early or predictive insights into potential risk. The lack of visibility or the distortion of information from one end of a supply chain to the other can cause poor customer service, decreased profitability, ineffective capacity planning, and missed production schedules. Building trust and attaining better B2B visibility is imperative and especially relevant for the food industry.

Increasing the visibility of retailers' actions to other actors in the value chain enables the formation of trust in distant and indirect relationships. End-to-end visibility is far from being fully applied due to the lack of metrics, which jeopardizes its implementation in organizations. The increased visibility and transparency are also not equally distributed among supply chain partners. Firms with high visibility attract significant attention from external stakeholders, particularly from existing and prospective customers and potential employees. Consequently, they are exposed to more pressures or expectations than firms with low visibility levels.

Information access, quality, and usefulness are the three broad characteristics that should be considered when implementing supply chain visibility.[7] The business performance gain is an immediate consequence of improving the access and quality of information shared between organizations that make up a supply chain. The usefulness of information is relevant to achieve the effectiveness required in a business operation. The data must be reliable because false or manipulated data can negatively impact the entire supply chain.

The business performance gain should be automated, informational, and transformational. The automated procedure refers to using technology to conduct the entire process to accelerate all actions and mitigate possible human errors. This allows for gathering and assigning relevant data through information and communication technologies. The informational feature is related to capturing, storing, and analyzing data to manage information procedures, permitting access to pertinent information shared among all stakeholders. The outcome of the entire process is transformational. Applying the created knowledge in the business and supply chain setting should facilitate and support innovation and transformation, inducing process improvement. The use of such knowledge in the organization process to improve the targeted efficiencies will lead to a competitive advantage. For operational efficiency, information is vital. The information exchange in the supply chain process can promote flexibility to demand fluctuations, ordering operations, logistics, and delivery performance through a more accurate forecast and real-time alerts to notify managers about such changes.

End-to-end visibility is crucial for supply chain competitiveness. The exchange of relevant and timely information across the supply chain reduces conflicts in boundary-spanning or interorganizational liaison, increasing compliance and trustworthiness in the buyer-supplier relationship. A strategic element to consider is the increase in trust between all parties. The shared knowledge in the entire supply chain will strengthen network relationships, leading to trustworthy partnerships and reducing the risk of opportunism. This will reflect an asset that competitors cannot immediately copy, making the supply chain processes unique, trusted, differentiated, and a source of competitive advantage.[8] A supply chain process ought to improve responsiveness between parties, promote continuity in the network, and develop long-term, mutually-beneficial contract agreements among actors. Simultaneously, a strong and trustworthy relationship will lead to a scenario where one company can add value to another in the same supply chain by suggesting ideas through frequent contact that can improve the whole process's efficiency and future communication strategy needs for all participants. Firms have an opportunity to adapt, facilitate cooperation among partners, and understand their expectations. The positive relationship developed by the increasing bond among partners will create opportunities to learn through an exchange of information leading to further market growth opportunities. The knowledge created by end-to-end visibility will help companies quickly adapt to different circumstances such as a consumer behavior change, new competitors, new market products, or demand fluctuation, which will bring them closer to success.

7. INDUSTRY STANDARDS AND TRACEABILITY DATA IN B2B EXCHANGES

Traceability represents a complex concept that refers to sharing information about the product, its history, production, and movement along the supply chain in B2B networks. According to the global supply chain standards organization, GS1, "Traceability is the ability to trace the history, application or location of an object. When considering a product or a service, traceability can relate to: origin of materials and parts; processing history; distribution and location of the product or service after delivery."[9]

Traceability is a mechanism that necessitates coordination between the focal firm and its upstream and downstream supply chain partners. Traceability is a critical and long-term strategic investment for any supply chain channel, as companies can use it to combat fraud, improve supply chain integrity, manage complexity across supply chains, or control product safety and quality. Effective traceability creates confidence along the chain and can boost a company's image, especially when it enables rapid recall of unsafe products. Among the various benefits of using technology to track a product, determining an accurate delivery time is fundamental for internal and consumer satisfaction. A trustworthy delivery schedule is considered of utmost importance.

Firms recognize the imperative of maintaining high accuracy in inventory and end products' traceability to drive efficiencies. For instance, radio frequency identification-based traceability (RFID) allows organizations to achieve labor efficiencies by removing the need to manually scan barcodes on received products, eliminating the need to enter orders manually and record updates, increasing the capability to locate products within stores and distribution centers, and improving the accuracy of in-store inventory records. For example, Metro Group has reduced their inventory stockouts by 11 percent using RFID-based traceability.

The efficiency of a traceability system depends on the ability to know each unit that is produced (or received) and distributed, allowing continuous tracking (visibility) from the primary production to the retail point of sale. Data is vital for a successful traceability program in a supply chain. The large amount of data accumulated through recent technologies such as GPS has contributed immensely to how supply chains are managed.

The term "traceability" incorporates the ability to "track forward" in the supply chain and to "trace backward." Traceability can be observed through these two lenses, regardless of a business's point in the supply chain and depending on the type of information that is required. Backward traceability (or tracing) is the capacity to find the origin, characteristics, and history of a product. Forward traceability (or tracking) is the capacity to see the product's locality. To conduct this process, each actor must acknowledge the entire upstream and downstream chain and have an internal record-keeping system that enables tracing back and tracking forward. This is essential for product recall and to protect consumers.

As a process, traceability should enable each actor to make a record of each activity related to a product. Consequently, the record of raw material-related information, process information, product information, and accreditation or certification information will lead to a substantial amount of product information. Product data management represents a significant challenge for complex, multiparty supply chains. For example, the US Food and Drug Administration requires advanced traceability capability, posing a challenge for the food industry, which has a low rate of adoption.

Traceability stems from private and public sector requirements that are subsequently adopted by the industry. For example, the largest Italian chicken-processing company, Amadori, has established a private standard to manage the entire supply chain through traceability and centralized control of all its stages. Meanwhile, the largest Italian retailer, Coop Italia, has created the private standard "Safe Quality Coop." A private standard enables the reconstruction of each product's history, from raw material to final product.[10] The evolving consumer requirements regarding product safety, quality, and traceability make technological innovations critical to identify and characterize the product, and then capture, analyze, store, and transform data. These tools' success can only occur if a combination of internal traceability and chain traceability exists. To comply with traceability expectations, an appropriate technical implementation and a convenient operational service are needed.

8. TECHNOLOGY

The adaptation of advanced technologies characterizes the "retail 4.0" environment; they support firms in delivering improved products, services, and consumer experience, changing them from a non-sequential information processing mode to a smart and data-driven decision-making unit. The integration of visualization technology and physical-digital interaction can improve the synergy between the user and the data, enabling increased precision in omnichannel retailing. This form of contemporary retail practice aims to synchronize procedures and technologies throughout supply and sales channels.[11] Retail system research for omnichannel consumer behavior demonstrated that most manufacturers rely on diverse omnichannel strategies, which may consist of three key elements: content, data, and targeted media.[12] Big data is an essential tool for developing data-driven retailing. Sharing and analyzing big data are expected to bring significant economic value and support ubiquitous service consumers, standardization, and on-demand services through search, analysis, and visualization. Big data's value manifests in the information and actionable insights organizations can derive from it. The possibilities of leveraging big data with predictive analytics include the extraction of useful information necessary for decision-making. The exponential generation of data is associated with advances in computer storage and processing power, the critical reduction in sensors and communication costs, and the development of the Internet of Things (IoT). A growing stream of researchers has examined how the IoT can lead to more efficient, resilient, and effective physical-digital B2B systems. RFID has been a critical enabler for warehouse management and inventory control in retail management. This technology could also be used to avoid product counterfeiting and detect tampering.[13]

The IoT can increase supply chain coordination, improve operational efficiencies, and achieve cost savings. Furthermore, the advancement of artificial intelligence (AI) has made supply chains and retailing smarter. AI has been extensively used in retail environments and technologies to supply humans with additional knowledge to make better decisions.[14] AI makes physical retail stores naturally digital, creating an environment more sensitive and adaptive to the human presence. Enabling AI detection and recognition of stock-keeping units (SKUs) allows identifying the packaging of products from a raw image to facilitate smart vending or smart point of sale systems.[15] AI simplifies the integration of machine vision technology into unmanned retail systems and provides solutions in a human-like manner. For example, retail giant Amazon introduced its automated Go grocery store concept based on machine vision (i.e., image-based recognition and automation) in 2016 to record items that customers pick up. AI is gaining importance in the customer service context as the primary source for service innovation and augmentation (or replacement) of human tasks and activities within supply chains, thus becoming critical to retail.

In conjunction with AI, neuroimaging is another example of psychphysiological techniques like functional magnetic resonance imaging (fMRI) and eye-tracking within retail marketing. The applications of these neuroimaging and biometric methods enable organizations to survey the unconscious elements of customer perception. Monitoring neurological and biometric data helps uncover hidden consumer reactions linked to buying decisions.[16] These techniques can enhance the overall efficiency of retailers' marketing strategies by improving the precision of consumer segmentation, profiling, and ultimate targeting.

The complexity of implementing traceability, transparency, and trust may pose challenges for firms. The recent emergence of blockchain technology promises to enhance transparency, improve trust, and develop effective long-term relationships for organizations. Blockchain has favorable implications for consumer satisfaction.[17] For example, its traceability function can provide data provenance and minimize the perceived operational risk of paying a premium price for products with credence attributes such as halal, kosher, or organic. In reference to blockchain's ability to provide a guarantee of product provenance (e.g., geographic source or origin),[18] especially for food products, analytical science methods must be used to attain objective certainty based on ascertainable and verifiable characteristics of the product (i.e., trace elements or stable isotope analysis to link food to a particular geographic region).

Unlike centralized traceability systems, locating and detecting a product can be carried out in seconds on a blockchain, resulting in cost savings and higher precision in recalling damaged or unsafe products. With blockchain and IoT devices, retail firms have the capability to enhance SCM capabilities for real-time visibility and manage product shelf-life more efficiently. The additional benefits of blockchain also include improved marketability and increased loyalty among consumers. Yet the technology's potential depends on coordination and collaboration of information sharing processes among organizations in the supply chain.

9. CONCLUSIONS

Retail firms are continuously challenged as new technologies emerge, competition increases, and supply chain performance becomes key to competitiveness. The system shock caused by the COVID-19 pandemic forced consumers to rapidly pivot to e-commence and retailers to search for new sources of supply. Unlike previous predictions for digital transformation in the relationship with consumers, the pandemic forced ten years of digital engagement into a short three-month period, according to McKinsey.[19]

Many organizations embraced agile thinking and business practices, and the performance of their supply chains will determine the winners and losers of the new digital business ecosystem. End-to-end supply chain visibility is vital to maintain efficiency, enhance transparency, and build trust in the retail industry. A fundamental role in this effort includes information sharing, as retailers must make contingencies to deal with potential disruptions in any part of their global supply chains.

Increased visibility and real-time information sharing enable supply chain trading partners to make informed and timely decisions such as rerouting, adjusting capacities, updating production plans, and reallocating production resources. End-to-end supply chain visibility can be built with industry data and information standards (e.g., GS1) as a foundational layer. Such standards enable master data management, facilitates traceability, and promote interoperability of activities and processes within and across retail supply chains through advanced technologies.

Retail firms can link many tiers of supply chain partners, providing them with rapid knowledge of potential supply shortages and disruptions. Considering increasing consumer concerns and calls for enhanced transparency and traceability, managers may find utility in embarking on digitalization strategies and adopting new technologies to mitigate the challenges facing the retail industry. New technologies represent a tangible solution to increase efficiencies, boost trust, and enhancing transparency. Nevertheless, the adoption of new technologies represents a partial solution to some of the challenges in retail.

NOTES

1 Herrera, S. (2021, February 2). Amazon reports record sales in holiday quarter. *Wall Street Journal*. https://www.wsj.com/articles/amazon-amzn-4q-earnings-report-2020-11612221803.

2 Li, L., Chen, J., & Raghunathan, S. (2018). Recommender system rethink: Implications for an electronic marketplace with competing manufacturers. *Information Systems Research, 29*(4), 1003–23. https://doi.org/10.1287/isre.2017.0765.

3 Park, J., & Kim, R.B. (2021). The effects of integrated information & service, institutional mechanism and need for cognition (NFC) on consumer omnichannel adoption behaviour. *Asia Pacific Journal of Marketing and Logistics, 33*(6), 1386–414. https://doi.org/10.1108/APJML-06-2018-0209.

4 Barratt, M., & Oke, A. (2007). Antecedents of supply chain visibility in retail supply chains: A resource-based theory perspective. *Journal of Operations Management*, 25(6), 1217–33. https://doi.org/10.1016/j.jom.2007.01.003.

5 Christopher, M., & Lee, H. (2004). Mitigating supply chain risk through improved confidence. *International Journal of Physical Distribution & Logistics Management*, 34(5), 388–96. https://doi.org/10.1108/09600030410545436.

6 Pujawan, I.N., Kurniati, N., & Wessiani, N.A. (2009). Supply chain management for disaster relief operations: Principles and case studies. *International Journal of Logistics Systems and Management*, 5(6), 679–92. https://doi.org/10.1504/IJLSM.2009.024797.

7 Barratt & Oke (2007).

8 Barratt & Oke (2007).

9 GS1. (2017). *GS1 global traceability standard. Release 2.0. Ratified 2017.* Brussels.

10 S. Stranieri, S., Orsi, L., & Banterle, A. (2017). Traceability and risks: An extended transaction cost perspective. *Supply Chain Management*, 22(2), 145–59. https://doi.org/10.1108/SCM-07-2016-0268.

11 J. Singh, J., Goyal, G., & Gill, R. (2020). Use of neurometrics to choose optimal advertisement method for omnichannel business. *Enterprise Information Systems*, 14(2), 243–65. https://doi.org/10.1080/17517575.2019.1640392.

12 Singh et al. (2020).

13 Costa, V., Sousa, A., & Reis, A. (2018). Preventing wine counterfeiting by individual cork stopper recognition using image processing technologies. *Journal of Imaging*, 4(4), 54. https://doi.org/10.3390/jimaging4040054.

14 Paolanti, M., & Frontoni, E. (2020). Multidisciplinary pattern recognition applications: A review. *Computer Science Review*, 37(100276). https://doi.org/10.1016/j.cosrev.2020.100276.

15 Liu, L., Zhou, B., Zou, Z., Yeh, S., & Zheng, L. (2018). *A smart unstaffed retail shop based on artificial intelligence and IoT.* 2018 IEEE 23rd International Workshop on Computer Aided Modeling and Design of Communication Links and Networks (CAMAD), Barcelona, Spain, pp. 1–4. https://doi.org/10.1109/CAMAD.2018.8514988.

16 Liu et al. (2018).

17 Montecchi, M., Plangger, K., & Etter, M. (2019). It's real, trust me! Establishing supply chain provenance using blockchain. *Business Horizons*, 62(3), 283–93. https://doi.org/10.1016/j.bushor.2019.01.008.

18 Keogh, J.G., Rejeb, A., Khan, N., Dean, K., & Hand, K.J. (2020). Optimizing global food supply chains: The case for blockchain and GSI standards. In D. Detwiler (Ed.), *Building the Future of Food Safety Technology* (1st ed., pp. 171–206). Elsevier.

19 McKinsey. (2021). *Retail Reimagined.* McKinsey & Company. https://www.mckinsey.com/business-functions/marketing-and-sales/solutions/periscope/retail-reimagined.

CHAPTER SEVENTEEN

New Models in Digital-Physical Retail Processes and Systems to Create and Capture Business and Stakeholder Value

Carl Boutet

CHAPTER SUMMARY

The chapter provides highly valuable data and analysis on the recent changes in e-commerce sales, the accelerations provoked by the COVID-19 pandemic, and the shift from offline to online consumption. The purpose of tracking these changes is as much to guide operational strategies as to provoke the organizational/cultural changes needed to maintain a sustainable and resilient response to them.

MANAGERIAL IMPLICATIONS (GENERAL)

- The chapter, by itself, includes multiple valuable managerial insights as it explains the meaning and implications of the statistical charts of "Studiorx.world."
- One such insight mentioned that "Retailers need to reassess the role of their physical store and revisit their operating models to pave a new path for the future."
- It is a complete reassessment of the retail business accelerated by the COVID-19 pandemic. The implications are at all levels, from strategic to tactical and operational, with an urge for organizational changes to support these transformations.

- The economic change will put many companies out of business but will also create new opportunities for entrepreneurs. Entrepreneurially-minded people need to carefully read these charts.

MANAGERIAL IMPLICATIONS (RISK ASSESSMENT)
- The risk is considerable: with a reduction in incomes, retailers will need to invest to survive. The risk of doing nothing might be higher as it means being out of business.
- Managers need urgently to invest in e-commerce platforms. It is not an ROI-based approach but rather a class of asset that is essential to be in business.
- The competitive landscape will push managers for quick decisions on whether to be first adopters of new technology.

1. INTRODUCTION

In this chapter, I would like to focus on one key variable that has probably created the greatest impact on how we define that topic, even more so following the accelerations provoked by the COVID-19 pandemic: the shift from offline to online consumption. This graphic in Figure 17.1 below, courtesy of Vox,[1] is probably the best visual representation of the initial jolt that the first wave of pandemic lockdowns provoked in the US market. The first element noticed is how, contrary to the Great Recession of 2008–9, this "Great Acceleration" of spring 2020 provoked a diametrically opposed response in consumption behavior. Although the definition of "e-commerce" is relatively diverse and lacks uniformity of measure, the overall trends remain similar in all markets impacted by lockdowns. This acceleration created many second-order effects that provoked massive adoptions of /digital payment services and diverse last-mile logistic solutions.

For instance, in a November 2020 interview conducted by Studio Rx for The Great Acceleration book tour, a panel of e-commerce leaders in Nepal witnessed an increase for online payment from low

Figure 17.1. Changes in E-Commerce & Traditional Retail Sales since 2005

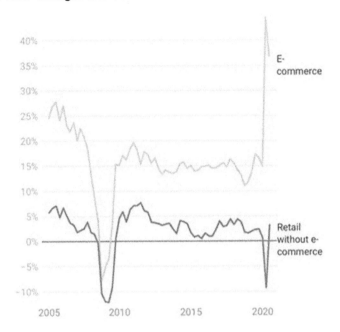

single percentages, being mostly a cash-on-delivery pre-pandemic system, to over 50 percent adoption of e-wallet payment within a couple of months. As for logistics, during an interview in September 2020 for the Canada Post Small Business Event, Charles Brewer, the new chief operating officer of Canada Post, shared how parcel volume in May 2020 reached astronomical numbers originally predicted for 2029 (based on previous 15 percent average growth of online consumption).

But focusing on these numbers doesn't tell the entire story. Looking at "in-store vs. online" misses many other changes that are somewhere between those elements, which are often considered dichotomies. For example, the massive increase in curbside/click & collect initiatives may or may not be considered as e-commerce depending on how a retailer attributes their resulting revenue.

The grocery industry is probably the most symbolic of this transformation as its adaptation to new consumption behaviors has the greatest impact due to its purchase frequency. All this is propelled by the ease for grocers and other food services to use third party solutions like Instacart & Uber Eats, not to mention massive investments in proprietary distribution and automation solutions.

Last, and the focus of many of the charts in this chapter, you'll see how regionality has played a factor as we track trends in a handful of key countries. This is a crucial step to adjusting your organization's "precision" as each region will have witnessed varying levels of acceleration depending on pre-pandemic conditions such as technology adoption and economic impacts.

The purpose of tracking these changes is as much to guide operational strategies as to provoke the organizational/cultural changes needed to maintain a sustainable and resilient response to them. For more updated information on these charts and contexts, please visit https://studiorx.world/ (subscription service) to follow their evolution.

2. DATA INSIGHTS ON GLOBAL RETAIL

All retail data and figures throughout the rest of this chapter for individual countries were obtained directly from publicly available government websites.[2,3,4,5,6,7,8,9,10,11] After visualizing the collected data, it can be clearly seen that retail sales in some countries plunged more than 25 percent from February to April 2020, with much of these declines in the clothing, accessory, and department store categories. Even after retail sales began to recover in July, the fashion and restaurant industries continued to struggle to reach pre-pandemic levels. Countries across the globe report an upper double-digit growth in e-commerce sales numbers. However, it is interesting to discuss what the term "e-commerce" actually means to different entities. To establish uniform criteria to evaluate the category, we have to ask: What sales are attributed to e-commerce by the reporting agencies? Is curbside pickup considered e-commerce or physical commerce? The answers to these questions are very subjective. Store chains that are very centralized will attribute those curbside pickup sales to e-commerce, while others might attribute them to physical sales. This report tracks official e-commerce numbers provided by each

Figure 17.2. Year-over-Year Change in Retail Sales for Canada, UK, and US

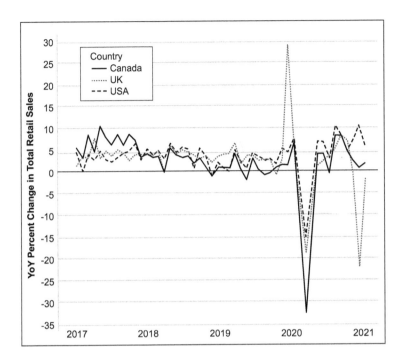

Figure 17.3. Year-over-Year Change in Retail Sales for France, Germany, and Italy

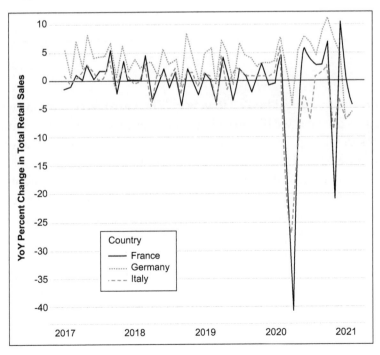

Figure 17.4. Year-over-Year Change in Retail Sales for Australia, South Africa, and South Korea

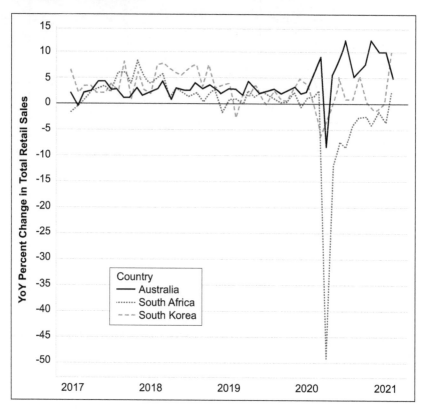

country's statistical body. However, "The Great Acceleration 2020" focuses on what we like to call "Digital Commerce," which includes curbside pickup, live shopping experiences, traditional e-commerce, and how AI facilitates the in-store shopping experience.

The purpose of the above graphics is principally to highlight the expected large dips in retail sales in March and April 2020: when COVID-19 reached across the globe and the initial panic set in. The dips are anything but surprising, however certain countries' retail sales were not affected as dramatically as others, namely Germany, Australia, and South Korea – countries who had empirically quick and effective reactions to the first wave. Canada, Italy, France, and

South Africa had very pronounced drops followed by large recoveries in retail sales, most likely due to online shopping, as will be discussed and analyzed later on in this chapter.

Looking at the right-hand side of the second graph, we can see the second wave hit Europe with another drop in retail in the final quarter of 2020. While it looks like this occurred in the UK as well, their percentage change in January 2021 can be more so attributed to an unseasonably high sales number in January of the previous year. It is quite likely that the pandemic also played a factor here, but the sudden peak of nearly 30 percent in early 2020 caused what looks like an equal and opposite reaction to the naked eye, one year later.

While the data is not yet available, we can expect to see spikes for most of the countries, if not all, at roughly April 2021 due to the previous year's shakeup. Once this is balanced out and the peaks and valleys are less intense in future years, it is hoped and expected that consistent, albeit small, retail growth patterns will re-emerge, as we saw pre-pandemic. COVID-19 was and still is the major catalyst in the upheaval of the retail industry. Companies with developed online shopping tools were able to quickly adapt and take advantage of the shift; those without were forced to create or improve this service, otherwise survival in the industry became a large source of uncertainty.

2.1. Drilling Down: Industries Affected by COVID-19 in Canada

The above charts show the volume of sales for each retail sector from early 2020, pre- coronavirus (COVID-19) lockdown in Canada. For each category, on the right is the industry weight before and during the COVID-19 pandemic, while the left simply displays growth over time. The only categories whose weight share fell were clothing, fuel, and indoor dining, explainable by stay-at-home orders. For the year-over-year changes, all industries with the exception of food showed a considerable loss during the early pandemic months, but all bounced back and had promising growth after the initial shock. Some had relatively small dips, like building materials and equipment, and general merchandising, compared to the industries that heavily suffered.

Figure 17.5. Canadian Industries Growth from before COVID-19 until Early 2021, Proportion of Total Retail in Same Time Frame

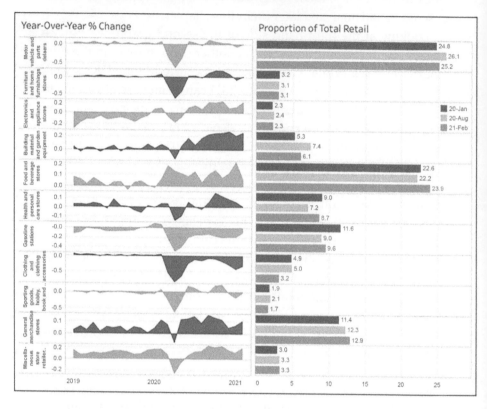

3. GLOBAL E-COMMERCE ACCELERATION

As a result of this accelerated growth in digital commerce, a complete blurring of digital and physical retail is projected by 2025, when 50 percent of retail sales will take place via physical retail outlets and 50 percent will take place digitally. This acceleration will continue to push up digital commerce, making it hard to figure out the line that differentiates between the two sales channels, leading to a complete physical/digital blur.

From the data collected, we conclude that consumers are willing to embrace new emerging digital trends, irrespective of age or

Figure 17.6. Share of Global E-Commerce Sales 2021

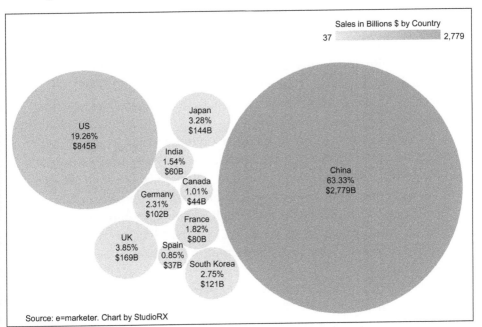

Source: e=marketer. Chart by StudioRX

gender demographics. The way forward for many retailers will require them to be more resilient and agile. Those retailers who embrace these emerging trends will come out stronger than those that resist them.

Accelerated digital shopping has been the global trend for 2020. Retailers with strong data sources and agile digital platforms succeeded in meeting consumer expectations and delivering a competitive shopping experience despite the many unavoidable challenges of operating during a pandemic. We saw a sharp increase in online grocery delivery, digital payments, in-store pickups, and AI-based retail experiences. Digital shopping journeys are the new normal of the retail industry.

Unsurprisingly, China's e-commerce market is the largest in the world with a volume of 1.94 trillion USD in 2021 (current data plus forecast for the rest of the year). According to Tenba Group and E-Marketer,[12] China's total e-commerce sales increased by 28 percent in 2020 compared to the year prior, reaching just below 45 percent of total retail. In 2021, for the first time, China's e-commerce will exceed 50 percent of total retail. As such, China's e-commerce sector is more than three times the size of the US market, which ranks second with approximately 19 percent of global share. For skeptics who do not believe e-commerce will reach a threshold of half of all retail, China is a perfect example of how this is more than possible, and even probable.

However, as we see accelerated digital growth in other markets across the globe due to the coronavirus outbreak, we do not observe similarly massive growth in Chinese market. E-commerce market penetration was already more than 30 percent in China, even before the pandemic. Such high e-commerce penetration can be attributed to the SARS pandemic in 2003, which helped Alibaba make its newly launched online platform Taobao more relevant for its users.

Figure 17.8 shows monthly e-commerce as a percentage of total retail from 2016 to early 2021 for five notable countries (members of the European Union publish the data in indices, so the calculation is not possible here). South Korea, whose data begins in 2017, leads in this statistic through virtually the entire time period. However, the United Kingdom is currently very close behind, with a large leap, the largest of any country over any time period above, occurring during the beginning of the pandemic and then later again during the second wave. There were a few months in 2020 in which the UK actually eclipsed South Korea.

The USA is in the middle of the sample, with Australia and Canada lagging behind. They have all been steadily increasing over time with similar seasonality and saw an uptick during the pandemic. However, the proportion of e-commerce to total retail is still significantly lower by comparison to the other countries. This cannot be attributed to population internet availability, as all the countries score in the high eighties (Australia is the lowest at 87 percent), to South Korea at 96 percent. One may expect the UK to be more similar to Canada and the US, but perhaps there is a cultural difference that has contributed to an increased affinity to online shopping.

Figure 17.7. Worldwide E-Commerce Retail Values (USD Billions)

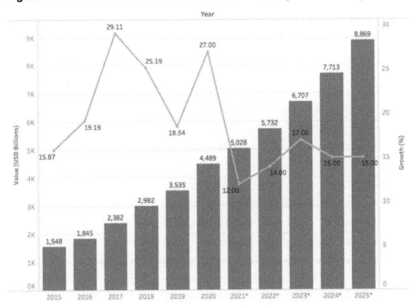

Figure 17.8. E-Commerce as a % of Total Retail Sales

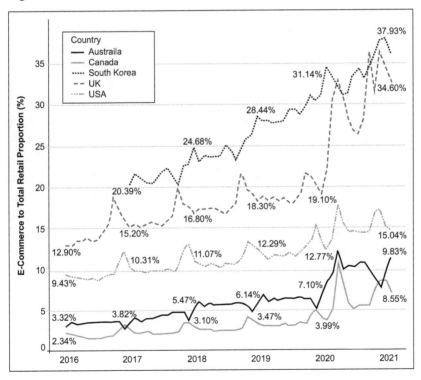

4. CLICK-AND-COLLECT INCREASING POPULARITY

There has clearly been a massive boom in e-commerce, a subset of which is click-and-collect (C&C), or curbside pickup. This section will focus on this buying method only in the US, as it is the only country with enough data. The figure below shows how in 2019, a sizable increase of 58 percent in C&C sales occurred, yet this figure is dwarfed by 2020's increase. This growth is expected to continue at a fairly consistent pace, albeit less so in magnitude compared to 2020. Curbside buying relative to total e-commerce is expected to double from 5.8 percent in 2019 to 11.6 percent 2024, with the largest increase logically also happening in 2020. This implies that C&C sales are increasing year-to-year at a slightly higher rate than traditional e-commerce. In 2020, total buyers jumped from 127.4 million to 143.8 million, a 12.9 percent growth rate.

Notably, of the over $72 billion in these sales in 2020, merely five companies, Wal-Mart, Home Depot, Best Buy, Target, and Lowes accounted for roughly $42 billion, or 58 percent. In the same year, C&C accounted for 41.9 percent of their total e-commerce sales and a staggering 50.2 percent of their combined e-commerce growth.

Digital grocery shopping is another fascinating category to consider. In 2019, 39 percent of curbside pickup users were using this service for groceries, but this number jumped to 58 percent in 2020. Nearly 90 million Americans are predicted to use this type of service to buy groceries in 2021.

Who was already using this service before the pandemic and who is using it now? There are four categories in which the proportion of new users outweighs the January 2020 C&C buyers: senior couples (index of 240), senior singles (158), large older family (104), and adult singles (101). As these are the four oldest groups of the survey, hence the groups with the highest risk of serious illness or death from the COVID-19 virus, it holds that they would be the wariest of entering a bricks-and-mortar store when complete contactless purchasing is possible.

Of the reasons listed for why people use C&C, the leading case is people simply trying to avoid stores during a pandemic when social distancing is required. Existing C&C buyers answered this at

Figure 17.9. USA Click-and-Collect Sales, % Change, % of Total E-Commerce

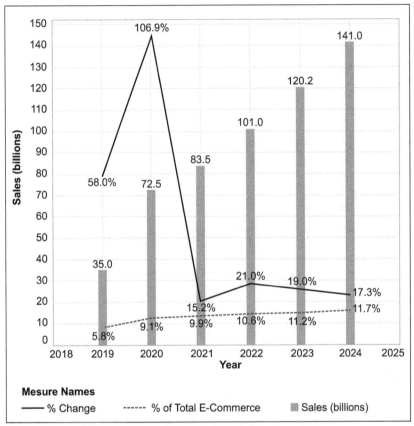

69 percent compared to 83 percent of new buyers, the only such category in which the latter is greater than the former. While people who used this method pre-COVID still list this as the most important reason, nearly 60 percent and 50 percent of these respondents also cite convenience and time-savings as factors, compared to 33 percent and 25 percent for new users. For curbside pickup to persist as a popular option past the pandemic, consumers must see the value beyond simply avoiding stores during social distancing mandates.

The below graph reinforces the idea that C&C will indeed persist. Of the existing customers surveyed in January 2020, 87 percent reported

Figure 17.10. Share of C&C Users during COVID

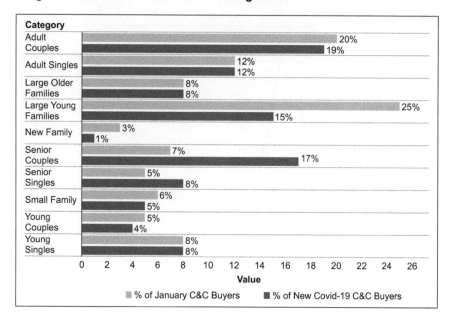

Figure 17.11. C&C Usage Drivers

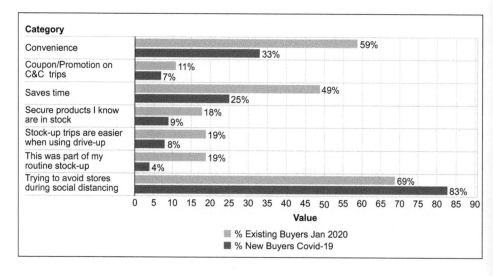

Figure 17.12. Likelihood of Using C&C Post-Pandemic

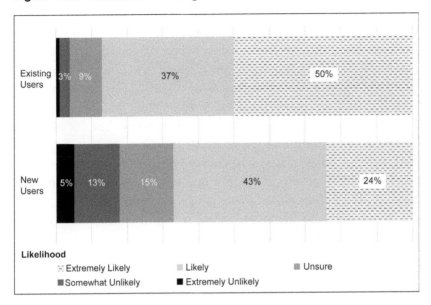

they were likely or extremely likely to continue using C&C services, compared to only 4 percent who reported they were not. While these numbers are not quite as large for the new users, they are still sizable and point to a shift in buying habits. Just about two-thirds of new customers using C&C reported they were likely to continue after the pandemic, contrasted with 18 percent who believed they would not. With a factor of roughly 3.67 between these figures, retailers should ramp up their C&C offerings as the data suggests the usage will only increase in the next decade. In the age of instant gratification and consumption at our fingertips, C&C is here to stay, across retail industries.

5. AI SHAPING THE FUTURE OF RETAIL

Recommendation Systems. "Customer who bought this also bought ..." "Other shows and movies you may like ..." "People you may know..."

The odds are that you instantly recognized the sentences seen above from different applications and services in day-to-day life.

If you don't, they are respectively from Amazon, Netflix, and Facebook. The recommendations they are making for you for products, media, and social interaction are not random; they are using artificial intelligence in their engines. As these companies collect data, they can make increasingly accurate predictions as to what an individual would like based on machine learning algorithms, a subset of AI.

There are two main branches of algorithms generally used for filtering results: content-based and collaborative. The focus of the former is on a specific shopper and their actions such as pages visited, time spent on pages, and clicks. The system learns the user's likes and dislikes, and a user profile is created to make recommendations. The latter uses a "wisdom of the crowd" technique where the actions and behaviors of similar individuals are used to make predictions for the individual.

Chatbots: Customer & Shopping Assistants. In 2016, Gartner[13] predicted that the average person would have more conversations with bots than their spouse by 2020. Whether or not that came true, the landscape of online retail is littered with chatbots that can narrow your search, personalize the experience, assist with in-store shopping, guide self-checkout, and send alerts and updates. A 2020 survey by ManageEngine[14] on remote work online behavior concluded that the majority of consumers are at ease with this technology. In fact, 76 percent of respondents said that their experience with chatbot based support was "excellent" or "satisfactory." However, this positive adoption may be somewhat age-dependent, with an inverse relationship between age groups and satisfaction level.

The beauty of this tool is that in the retail world, where speed is king, customers receive immediate support at any moment regardless of staffing. A crucial aspect, however, is that the user often still requires a feeling of engaging with someone (or something in this case) that understands their needs and concerns. The more the bot can interact in a humanlike way, the easier it will be to convert a visitor into a repeat client. Like with the algorithms employed by recommendation engines, as natural language processing and other factors are improved, chatbots will become better equipped to help the user.

Price Predictions & Adjustments. Price optimization is the practice of using data from customers and the market to find the most effective price point for a product or service that will maximize sales or profitability. There are two main objectives in price optimization:

1 Understanding how customers will react to different pricing strategies. This can help determine willingness-to-pay and price elasticity.
2 Determining the best price for a company considering its goals. These can include increased profit margins, customer growth, capture of lost sales, improved inventory turnover, etc.

Retailers are able to consider a myriad of variables present in pricing, such as consumer behavior, demographic and psychographic data, historical sales, competition, weather, season, macroeconomic variables, and special events to determine the initial price, the best price, shelf placement, and discounts. Machine learning models can analyze all aspects of the data and provide predictions of various strategies. Manual price tracking, forecasting, and adjusting are simply too time-consuming and costly. Automation removes human error that impacts sales or revenue and enables real-time analysis of current trends to adapt price points and maximize KPIs important to a specific business.

Loyalty & Customer Retention. According to a 2020 survey of CMOs of retail companies, in 2021, 73 percent of companies will be dependent on existing customers rather than trying to grow into new markets. Fortunately, AI and machine learning can be manipulated to make the most of the data and rely on existing customer relationships.

While price is still the most important factor in a consumer making a purchase, the overall journey does play a part in the user's decision-making. Based on prior interactions with a brand, an AI can automate and suggest ways to personalize the customer experience. The technology does not determine who a buyer is, but rather what they do. AI can give insights on promotion timing in order to maximize conversion or when a previous buyer might be running out of an item. By analyzing who will be a repeat buyer,

companies are better positioned to tailor offerings to improve customer retention.

6. CONCLUSION

The data included in this report clearly demonstrates emerging
digital retail trends in part provoked by the COVID-19 pandemic.
In 2020, we saw many retailers that were already facing challenges
before the pandemic being forced to close during its initial months.
Those that survived by continuing to resist the tides of change, as
opposed to adopting emerging trends, may soon find themselves in
a very critical position.

To thrive in today's environment, retailers need to overcome challenges, find new ways to interact with their customers, build trust,
and explore new opportunities. It might be the right time for retailers to assess the existing data about their physical store and rethink
its purpose. While devising strategies for the future, it is critical for
retailers to use what they have learned about their businesses in
lockdown to chart their course. Many will need to evaluate whether
it is better to continue to operate their physical store, to use it as a
fulfillment center for its digital channel, or to exit the market.

It's time for retailers to think globally and act locally. 2020 taught
us the necessity of local supply chains and our duty to support local
communities. Seamless integration between sales channels is paramount to retailers' ability to deliver a standout shopping experience.
Customers have come to expect the ability to orchestrate their shopping journey on whichever channel is the most convenient at the
moment. The same customer that buys a product online may want to
pick up the item in-store to reduce wait times. A customer may also
opt to return the product for a bigger size through postal services and
email. Seamless integration makes retailers more resilient and better
prepared for everyday black swan events. Another benefit of blurring
physical and digital channels is empowering retailers to shift to any
channel in situations when one channel is under threat. If there is a
cyberattack on a retailer's e-commerce platform, for instance, the company can lean on physical stores to fulfill its customer requirement.

The time is now. Retailers have the perfect opportunity to modify their business models to be more resilient and agile for tomorrow. The future is rife with opportunities for those who are willing to do things differently.

NOTES

1 Rey, J. (2020, December 29). *Amazon, Target, and Walmart win: In 2020, shopping changed forever*. Vox. https://www.vox.com/recode/22204578/2020-ecommerce -growth-retail-shopping-changed-forever.
2 Webstat Banque de France (2021). *Commerce de détail*. (page no longer available).
3 Gaubys, J. (2021). *Ecommerce sales by country in 2021*. Oberlo. https://www.oberlo .in/statistics/ecommerce-sales-by-country.
4 Istat. (2021, May 7). *Italy retail trade*. https://www.istat.it/en/archivio/257372.
5 KOSIS Korean Statistical Information Service. (2021). *Korea retail, wholesale services*. https://kosis.kr/eng/statisticsList/statisticsListIndex.do?menuId=M_01_01&vwcd =MT_ETITLE&parmTabId=M_01_01&statId=1988015&themaId=#J_20_1.3.
6 Statistics Canada. (2021). *Retail and wholesale*. https://www150.statcan.gc.ca/n1/en /subjects/retail_and_wholesale.
7 Office for National Statistics. (2021). *Retail industry*. https://www.ons.gov.uk /businessindustryandtrade/retailindustry.
8 Australian Bureau of Statistics. (2021, May 10). *Retail trade, Australia*. https://www .abs.gov.au/statistics/industry/retail-and-wholesale-trade/retail-trade-australia /mar-2021#data-download.
9 StatSA. (2021, March). *Retail trade sales statistical release*. http://www.statssa.gov.za /publications/P62421/P62421February2021.pdf.
10 Statista. (2021, March 26). *Global retail e-commerce sales 2014–2026*. https://www .statista.com/statistics/379046/worldwide-retail-e-commerce-sales/. Statistisches Bundesamt Deutschland. (2021, May 27). *Die Datenbankdes Statistischen Bundesamtes*. https://www-genesis.destatis.de/genesis/online?operation=find&suchanweisu ng_language=de&query=online#abreadcrumb.
11 US Census Bureau. (2021, April 29). *Monthly state retail sales*. https://www.census .gov/library/visualizations/interactive/monthly-state-retail-sales.html.
12 Cramer-Flood, E. (2021, February 10). *In global historic first, ecommerce in China will account for more than 50% of retail sales*. Insider Intelligence. https://www.emarketer. com/content/global-historic-first-ecommerce-china-will-account-more-than-50-of -retail-sales.
13 Levy, H.P. (2019, October 23). *Gartner predicts a virtual world of exponential change*. Gartner. https://www.gartner.com/smarterwithgartner/gartner-predicts-a-virtual -world-of-exponential-change/.
14 ManageEngine. (2021). *Remote Work Online Behavior Report*. https://download .manageengine.com/pdf/remote-work-online-behavior-report.pdf.

CHAPTER EIGHTEEN

The "Giant Leap Methodology": How to Chart a Course to the Moon without Being Pulled Down by the Operational, Financial, and Reputational Risks of Rapid Innovation

Melaina Vinski

SUMMARY OF CHAPTER

The chapter provides a discussion of the reputational, operational, and financial risks (and opportunities) inherent to innovations in the new world of precision retail. It explains the pressure companies face in trying to keep up with the constant innovations and the necessity for the right methodology to avoid unintended consequences.

MANAGERIAL IMPLICATIONS (GENERAL)

- Managers need to step back and make trade-off decisions across social, reputational, and operational risks of their business ambitions. This exercise is important for enabling a thriving society while keeping pace with a fast-moving market.
- This chapter is a wake-up call for managers to look at the bigger picture of the world and its challenges, and it provides a shared value framework for assessing the impact of their decisions.
- This chapter gives a best practice in innovation management by infusing a strong dimension of consequence scanning into program design.

MANAGERIAL IMPLICATIONS (ORGANIZATIONAL)
- For managers convinced of the "giant leap methodology," they need to explore the necessary organizational changes to move forward. This would be accomplished by:
  - a cultural change through awareness and training programs
  - a dedicated committee
  - the center of excellence for innovation
  - a more empowered corporate social responsibility team
  - any other organizational function

MANAGERIAL IMPLICATIONS (STRATEGIC & TACTICAL)
- From the strategic perspective, the "giant leap methodology" guides managers to:
  - rethink how company strategy is built
  - put ethics and values at the center of the strategy as they will be a part of the company mission
  - reconsider the existing road map of innovation projects
- From the tactical perspective, it might be used as a guideline for:
  - talent acquisition
  - partnership building
  - digital Infrastructure and data acquisition

MANAGERIAL IMPLICATIONS (RISK ASSESSMENT)
- Risks assessment and mitigation is an integral part of the "giant leap methodology."

1. INTRODUCTION

In a world of rapid innovation, astronauts and engineers are not the only ones seeking flight to the above and beyond. Many company war rooms around the world are scattered with paper drawings and diagrams plotting a plan to slingshot past competition by executing on the grand vision of precision retail. Strategy books are stacked along the windows, benchmarking reports and process maps are flopped open and on top of one another, and the "hooked-in" computer is projecting financial models while forty browser tabs remain open for toggling. The garbage bin is full of last night's takeout, and empty coffee cups litter the long boardroom table from the early morning rise. Coats and sweaters are slung over chairs, and outdoor shoes have been kicked to the corner. The day brings arguments and celebrations and breakthroughs in thinking, and at the end of a long day's work, some progress has been made in the launch towards the future of applied precision science.

There is a reason Google calls their big, ambitious, and often groundbreaking innovations "moonshots." In a society where innovation is moving at the speed of light and competition is fierce, breaking away from earthbound competitors and clearing the atmosphere is incredibly hard work. It also yields high returns and the prestigious status of being a visionary. Those who take care and are considerate in their approach leap forward and never look back. For those who rush the process and let pressure be the guide, the ride can be disastrous, and at worst, it can cause the project to crash and burn. The hardest problems take the most effort, and in the case of building a rocket ship to the proverbial moon – of reorienting and restructuring a business to execute on precision retail – the problem to solve is perhaps the premier corporate challenge of our time. Just as engineers comb through every assumption and calibrate for all the risks before takeoff, companies today need to comb through and mitigate risks when launching into market. What makes the calculation especially challenging is the changing nature of the risks at play. The world is changing quickly, and the expectations of business are changing even faster.

In this book, you have begun to be exposed to the beautiful world that is emerging in precision retail. You have seen how the synergy between the Internet of Things and advances in analytics, AI, and technology are creating an intelligent ecosystem in service of the Fourth Industrial Revolution. This evolution is changing how we live and work, how we build and operate our businesses, and of course, how we find and purchase the goods and services we want and need. In this chapter, I want to swing the pendulum for a moment to discuss the reputational, operational, and financial risks inherent to those operating in this new world of rapid innovation and shifting expectations. I want to tell you a story about the pressure companies face trying to keep up with the Jones's while staying between the lines, and how, without the right methodology in hand, unintended consequences can arise.

This story will introduce the "giant leap methodology" that can help those leading the way to navigate the bumpy road of high-stakes innovation. Referring to the famous line from Neil Armstrong that landing on the moon was "one small step for man, one giant leap for mankind," the methodology offers assistance for leaders to calibrate risks and recalculate value amid the whirlwind of reaching for the stars.

2. SHIFTING EXPECTATIONS OF BUSINESS ARE CHANGING THE VALUE CREATION CONVERSATION

There is no judge more critical of a system than time. She is an effective but unkind and often ruthless teacher. She shares her wisdom long after a system is built and has taken hold in society, often leaving the pupil with few tools to meaningfully change the course of history. Capitalism is not the only system that will be scolded by her in a society evolving as quickly as ours, though it is likely to be the most notorious. Capitalism was held with great expectations by society. With a foundational premise to include shareholders within the envelope of earnings and bring them into the fold through dividends and shared profits, the system offered a world where every person could participate in something bigger than themselves. Over time, however, the forceful push for profits has manifested in the court of public opinion as a push for profits *at all cost*. This is the perception, at least, and it is not difficult to understand why. Rising inequality and the slow but steady removal of human hands in favor of the machine does not sit well in the face of rising corporate returns. More and more people feel as though they are on the outside looking in and when the pressure from the outside becomes too heavy, the walls begin to crack.

Corporate giants have felt the pressure. In 2019, the Business Roundtable, a consortium of more than 180 large US companies, released a statement on the *Purpose of a Corporation* as a signal to the market that things were going to change.[1] Jamie Dimon, the CEO of JP Morgan & Chase and chair of the Roundtable, touted that they were making a commitment to shift focus from shareholder to stakeholder value. The moment was heralded as the great turning point of capitalism. The court of public opinion, however, seems less persuaded by the communiqué. According to the Edelman Trust Barometer,[2] one of the most robust and longest-running sources of trust research available to the market, over half of people surveyed believe that capitalism as it exists today does more harm than good in the world. Perhaps most importantly, the research team found that ethical behaviors are three times more potent than competence in driving trust in a company. The competitive advantage, it seems, lies in the ability to be a good corporate citizen while delivering exceptional products, goods, and experiences. The balance between the value of making good products and the value of making fair and just decisions has shifted. It is no longer a balance as much as it is a hierarchy, with competence considered table stakes. Companies, now more than ever, have an outsized potential to capture value by adhering to ethical decision-making, aligning with the greater good, and maximizing positive benefit to society. Perhaps the greatest risk for companies now is inaction to meet the moment.

Those who are able to effectively build social license to operate in lockstep with disruptive innovation will far outpace the rest – and change the world while they are at it. Those who do not, or those who push for profits at all cost, will succumb to the pressure of changing tides of public expectation and fare poorly in the grand lessons of time. Those within the retail industry are especially vulnerable.

3. WITH GREAT INNOVATION COMES GREAT RISK

Retail is a hypercompetitive industry with highly squeezed margins, dynamic omnichannel operating models, and sometimes unattainable expectations arising from a blurring of industry boundaries in the minds of customers. An excellent experience with one product or one company elevates expectations across the board. When

Starbucks began allowing customers to preorder on an app, the "efficiency bar" was raised for every other shopping experience. When Wealth Simple made signing up for complex financial savings products as easy as swiping a credit card, the "ease bar" was raised for every other onboarding experience and rendered the "complex paperwork" excuse effectively useless. When Amazon Prime customers started to receive their goods the on same day that they clicked "Purchase," seemingly regardless of which corner of the world the product was coming from, the "speed-to-access bar" was raised for every other online distributor. Retail is an industry vulnerable to disruption, and the quakes of innovation are known to knock even the sturdiest players off balance. The storied tales of Blockbuster dismissing Netflix and Kodak disregarding the digital photography movement are well-creased in business school casebooks for a reason. For those with their ears perked, however, disruption can be a good thing. Looking over your shoulder forces you to move quickly, innovate at a faster pace, and know your surroundings. In the case of retail, the tectonic plates are moving and grooving at a rapid pace, with responsive models shifting aside to make way for predictive commerce.

Predictive commerce thrives in an intelligent ecosystem with a healthy dose of human behavior expertise. Leading companies are "organizing the house" to operationalize this aspiration and allow for greater access to and integration of data in day-to-day decisionmaking. While companies are still in their infancy in applying AI and a little wobbly on its implementation, they are increasingly relying on automated and data-driven systems to learn about the cognition, emotion, and behavior of their customers and employees. Leading companies are leaning on this learning to design and evolve marketing campaigns, build human-AI hybrid engagement models, drive bottom-up and top-line growth, and optimize the capabilities, performance, and experience of employees. In retail, these companies are especially focused on enhancing the in-store experience through personalization, relying on chatbots to assist with customer service, providing real-time pricing flexibility, and improving supply chain management and logistics. These innovators – those who already report 34 percent more revenue growth and

326 percent more profitability than their peers – anticipate leveraging automated processes and self-learning software 53 percent more than other organizations.[3] The competition is fierce, and the timelines are accelerating. In the consumer shopping revolution awakened by the COVID-19 pandemic, the United States experienced 30 percent growth, and preferences for online over bricks-and-mortar shopping shifted ahead by nearly two years from initial predictions.[4]

The rush to capitalize on this demand is not without consequences. More than half of organizations have accelerated their digital transformations to meet the moment,[5] and with speed of action tends to come some sleight of hand or a slip or two of the proverbial tongue. Just as we can easily forget our grocery list when rushing to get out the door or drive over the speeding limit to get to an appointment on time, it is entirely reasonable to expect some leaders to take shortcuts to keep pace with a fast-moving market. Sometimes these shortcuts come, however, at the expense of the very people they are trying to serve. The intersection between data availability, an imbalance of information between companies and citizens, and intelligent ecosystems offered by precision retail offers a new bag of tricks for exploiting the vulnerabilities that are inherent to being human. In fact, the concern over corporate's manipulation of psychological weakness has been cautioned by some of the most prominent thinkers of our time, including the Nobel Laureates Robert Shiller, George Akerlof, and Richard Thaler. It is with this worry that while the Business Roundtable may have turned the page on traditional capitalist models, the rush to build an "intelligent empire" is bound to inspire a wave of capitalist intent to extract a newly tangible resource: the cognitive, emotional, and social capital of customers.

An intimate understanding of the ebb and flow of the human condition – an ability to map and predict the highs and lows of cognitive vulnerability and emotional fragility – offers high-minded companies the opportunity to make their way in the market while answering the call to make the world a better place. These companies or organizations enjoy a robust social license to operate and are held with great regard in the court of public opinion. They are focused on the well-being of broader society, and in most cases, their work holds tremendous promise for our future. Take, for example, a group of researchers at the Massachusetts Institute of Technology (MIT) who built a neural network model that can crunch raw text and audio data from interviews to reveal speech patterns predictive of depression.[6] As one of the most ferocious shadows plaguing our society, this model can be leveraged to monitor a citizen's text and voice for mental distress when calling into help lines, and when triggered, can send proactive alerts to provide immediate assistance and coordinate help. To meet the moment of the COVID-19 pandemic, a team at MIT also built an AI model that distinguishes asymptomatic carriers of the virus from those who are healthy with 98.5 percent accuracy. They are currently working to incorporate the model into a user-friendly app that could greatly influence how governments could design policy on economic closures amid viral surges.[7] While these AI models are relevant to diagnosing the here and now, AI models can also have a heavy hand in future outcomes. In the late months of 2020, IBM and Pfizer developed a model that uses short, noninvasive, and standardized speech tests to help predict the eventual onset of Alzheimer's disease within healthy people with 74 percent accuracy. For reference, the accuracy of clinical scales currently deployed by doctors and psychologists is 59 percent.[8] Leveraging this type of model at an annual doctor check-up could drastically change the game in preventive medicine. In each of these cases, methods of precision are leveraged to improve the well-being of the masses in service of the greater good.

Well-being is not only about physical health though. It also encompasses the emotional experience that arises from purchasing products and services from trusted brands. These brands, who operate with integrity and respect the unspoken trade-off between personalization of experience and access to personal data, leverage the understanding of customers' ebbs and flows to drive value for everyone involved. Bluecore and Nike are two good examples. Bluecore, a retail marketing technology company, teamed up with Vineyard Vines, a men's clothing retailer, to build intelligent and event-based campaigns that serve customers the products they want with the experience they need. The platform yielded a whopping 572 percent increase in revenue per email.[9] Nike, with their automated process for customer-designed sneakers known as the

"Nike Maker Experience," allows customers to use voice activation, augmented reality, object tracking, and projection systems to design a personalized and ready-to-wear shoe in two hours.[10] If there is one experience that will elevate expectations across the board, the Maker experience is likely it. Nike has long been known for setting a high standard, and their focused investments in big data and AI are meant to completely change the game, with analytics initiatives contributing to $10 billion in sales in 2018 and projected to increase by 60 percent by 2020. In an era where exceptional personalization is a dominant competitive advantage, Nike may just reign king.

Companies that innovate with integrity are able to slingshot themselves ahead of competition and land safely on the other side. For those who misstep, it can be a very bumpy ride. For the instances of good intention but poor outcome, the fault lies in loose controls more than a wobbly moral compass. In his recent book "Data and Goliath," computer security expert Bruce Schneier tells the story of how in 2000, Wells Fargo created a "community calculator" that helped keen home buyers figure out the right neighborhood for their future home.[11] The model intended to use buyers' current postal code to recommend neighborhoods that were the right fit. Unfortunately, the algorithm assumed the customers' race based on neighborhood demographics and in turn, engaged in discrimination by recommending only neighborhoods with a similar demographic spread. A class action lawsuit was filed as a result. In 2016, Microsoft launched a Twitter chatbot – an experimental AI persona named Tay – to mimic and learn the language patterns of millennial females. Unfortunately, the trolls of Twitter transformed Tay into a Nazi sympathizer (and a proud one at that) within a matter of hours.[12] Tay's launch into and removal from this world would happen in a span of twenty-four hours. In 2018, Reuters published an article recounting Amazon's attempt to streamline and automate the résumé review process for engineers and coders using an AI model. Unfortunately, the system was trained on existing software teams that were overwhelmingly male. The system therefore learned to disqualify anyone who attended a women's college or who listed women's organizations on their résumé – disproportionately excluding female candidates from the recruiting pool.[13] The difficulty with actively suing in "failure-to-hire" cases kept lawyers from knocking on Amazon's door, but the reputational damage remains in the open.

There are great stories of good companies, bad stories of great companies, and then there are the stories that make your skin crawl. These are stories of covert persuasion – companies attempting to disrupt, disregard, or damage a customer's health, wealth, or happiness in the service of their needs. These are stories of emotional capital extraction and a representation of the calling card held high by those fighting for a change in the system. Coined "sludge" by Thaler to describe the deliberate use of tactics that thwart citizens from acting in their best intentions,[14] the deployment of covert persuasion is a pervasive phenomenon in the intelligent ecosystems operating in our society today. There is likely no company more prominently on display in this category than Facebook. Famously touting to advertisers that they were able to identify when teenagers feel "insecure" or "need a confidence boost"[15] and manipulating 689,003 customers' emotions through unsolicited experiments,[16] the social media giant has since been fined $500 million for the illegal harvesting of customer data and another $5 billion for inappropriate disclaimers and sale of customer data to Cambridge Analytica in 2016 as an effort to influence the outcome of the 2016 United States presidential election. It is perhaps not surprising that Facebook is the least trusted with customer data relative to peer social media platforms.

Social media platforms like Facebook hide behind the mission of community and connectivity. Others who extract and monetize vulnerability do so behind the mission of supporting customers during their most personal endeavors. Take for example apps that track menstruation and fertility. They hold the most intimate kind of information. They know when women are ovulating, when they are menstruating, and what their plans are for starting a family. While this insight may seem relatively harmless, this data provides advertisers access to a very precise window when women are more susceptible to manipulation. To be clear, this statement is not meant to feed into the worn and dated stereotype of emotional variability that can arise for women throughout their cycle. The statement is in relation to the peer-reviewed scientific findings that show women, whether they are consciously aware or not, have evolved over thousands of years to express subtle cognitive changes in their decision-making process at different phases of their menstrual cycle.[17] These slight changes in perception, attention, memory, and cognition can make women more susceptible to targeted influence – just as teenagers who are feeling insecure are more vulnerable to the pressures of emotionally-tuned advertising. The menstruation and ovulation tracking app Flo settled with the Federal Trade Commission for just that reason, having sold sensitive health data of its users to outside companies such as Facebook and Google.[18] These sentiments are not to say that Facebook or Flo have malicious intent to harm citizens and customers. They have actually articulated quite the opposite. However, when they are unable or are unwilling to clearly show the methodology behind their decision process, guilt is often inferred by the court of public opinion through the lens of "profit at all cost."

In the race to build an intelligent empire – to innovate in service of precision retail – the extraction and sale of cognitive, emotional, and social capital of customers offers a tantalizing business model for the ambitious and able. In these models, fee structures are shifted from the end user to the advertiser, and the currency keeping revenue afloat rests almost solely on the behavioral data of customers. On the surface it is a win-win for everyone. As the citizens of the world become more aware and discerning however, and as the inequalities and challenges of our times go untamed, the calculation of value has begun to shift. The assessment and understanding of risk have shifted, too. Companies with strong moral convictions, transparent guiding values, and a competitive advantage grounded in shared value are soaring. Those who are not (whether on purpose or by accident) face increasingly steep reputational and financial costs.

4. FLY ME TO THE MOON

Precision retail offers organizations a ride to the moon. If intelligent ecosystems are the nuts and bolts that frame the rocket and data is the spark that ignites the engine, then it is the judgment of leadership that fuels the journey. It is essential that leaders do not forget this. Automation and AI may be essential tools for making decisions, but it is moral integrity and an orientation to details that separates those who land safely and those who do not. Autopilot cannot take you somewhere no one else has been. In a world shaped by artificial intelligence, human leadership matters more than ever.

Only leaders know how the organization breathes, how it bends and flexes, and where its skeletons are buried. This is especially critical when coming to terms with the fact that while the promises are tantalizing, AI does not always get it right. The case studies referenced earlier in the chapter showcase this reality. As the saying goes, you can only get out what you put in, and with only a small percentage of CEOs effectively integrating data sources to create a holistic view of the customer, models are bound to be a little wobbly. Hidden within the error margins and between the wobbles, reputational, financial, and operational risks lay in wait. Paper-thin walls and a system on trial make it very easy to misstep. So, in the push to innovate – to ride the rocket – a careful balance of grounded decision-making while reaching for the moon is necessary for survival. A "bigger picture" decision framework is needed to assist the imprecise science of precision retail. In the final pages of this chapter, I propose a risk mitigation framework called the "giant leap methodology" that sits at the nexus of Michael Porter and Mark Kramer's shared value theory, the agile methodology of consequence scanning, and the classic strategy debiasing premortem exercise. Consider it a tool to use with your teams as you work through strategy to execution and begin fleshing out your best and brightest ideas. The exercise will not only make the ride a little more comfortable, but it may also help you step into the ring and make the world a better place while you're at it.

There is perhaps no single framework better suited to meet the times than Porter and Kramer's shared value theory. In their acclaimed *Harvard Business Review* article "Creating Shared Value" which launched the idea to stardom, the authors postulate that social impact can be generated in the hunt for business value.[19] They argue that in the post-Global Recession era, a time when more and more people are looking in on the system, the companies that win will be able to drive profits while also driving positive impact for the environment and society. It is a tweak in practice that helps mollify some of the harsh lessons that time has served capitalism. It meets the "Boardroom Roundtable" moment. Indeed, there are plenty of examples where shared value shines. The global mining company Anglo-American financed and launched the first large-scale program to diagnose and treat HIV/AIDS in South Africa in an effort to protect its workforce and reduce absenteeism. They protected their human capital investments by developing a world-class (and world-changing) program to fight AIDS. That is a win-win. The payments company Mastercard expanded its operations to bring mobile-banking technology to more than 200 million people in developing countries around the world. It executed on a growth strategy to capture market share by providing access to financial services for the traditionally underserved. That is a win-win. For the purposes of this chapter, we have modified the shared value framework in a few significant ways to meet the moment of decision risk of precision retail. First, we have heightened the focus on and articulation of employee and customer well-being to the original parameters of business and social value. Think of it as breaking down the original "social value" pillar into environmental, customer, and employee impact. Forcing the articulation of intended outcomes and downstream impact across the stakeholder groups necessarily broadens the conversation (and yes, I believe mother nature and her environment is considered a "stakeholder"). As a second modification to the framework, the breakdown also serves the purpose of delineating the *unintended consequences* of the innovation on each of these stakeholders as well.

There is limited dispute over the social impact of automation and its influence on employee well-being. Machines are taking a more prominent role in the company and for those who have yet to be replaced by automation, the notion of job loss may never stray far from their minds. You don't have to read Yuval Noah Harari's *21 Lessons for the 21st Century* to understand that precision retail in practice could threaten the confidence and empowerment of employees. For example, the intended outcome of an innovation may be to make employees' jobs easier or their days more productive, but could it also hinder their psychological safety? Could it create problematic dynamics between teams? Are employees trained to handle the new type of customer complaint that innovation may inspire? It is in this spirit that customer well-being has also been included in the framework to account for how an innovation may create additional value (or consequence) above and beyond the point-in-time experience. The intended outcome may be to help their families be healthier, wealthier, or safer, but could it also discriminate against those same customers? Could it reinforce gender or racial stereotypes? Could it have an adverse impact on those who are emotionally, cognitively, or physically vulnerable? In our proposed methodology, these questions are prompted and answered using the consequence scanning tool.

Consequence scanning is a tool leveraged in agile methodology to broaden the horizon of what is possible. Originally designed by Doteveryone, a nonprofit organization with a mission to keep public interest at the heart of technology, the exercise leverages a series of prompts and a structured ideation process to help decision makers uncover both the intended and unintended consequences of product innovation.[20] It ensures innovation aligns with an organization's values and culture. In a spirit similar to Porter and Kramer in their vision of a shared value world, consequence scanning attempts to broaden the minds of those making strategic decisions and work through the greater implications of innovation. It helps uncover the risks that would have previously been hidden in the cracks but in today's new world of information superhighways are increasingly likely to emerge.

If shared value theory frames the house and consequence scanning paints the walls with color, then the premortem is the insurance policy against flood damage. The premortem was designed by Gary Klein to help solve why company projects tend to fail.[21] A celebrated psychologist and pioneer in the field of decision-making, Klein designed the premortem to tackle what he believed to be the root cause of the problem: that those making the decisions were biased and unable to properly identify implementation risks. The premise was based on a study conducted by Mitchell, Russo, and Pennington in the late 1980s that found prospective hindsight – imagining an event has already occurred – increased the ability to correctly identify the reasons for those future outcomes by 30 percent.[22] Klein flipped this notion around and crafted the premortem as a solution that is as elegant and simple as it is effective. Simply have the decision makers project themselves five years in the future to a reality where the project has *failed*. No ifs, ands, or buts. Failure is the only option. This mental shift halts the influence of overoptimism and sunk cost bias on decision-making and instead releases the valve of alternative realities. It opens the mind. Lifting and shifting this exercise to identify unintended consequences is a marriage made in heaven.

5. PUTTING THE METHODOLOGY TO USE

Frankly, the "giant leap methodology" I have proposed in this chapter is not going to be the unstoppable force needed to ride the momentum of capitalism. Nor is it meant to. It is meant to assist the mental shift that is required for companies to navigate a volatile, uncertain, and complex world where expectations are high and the cries to innovate are deafening. So, here we go.

You've got your strategy in place, and your leadership team is aligned. You've gone through the initial prioritization exercises and built the business case to choose your next big innovation. You've gathered the stickies, dot markers, and enough "brain food" snacks for a group five times the size of the one actually attending. You've got a room with whiteboard walls.

Time to start setting up the room. Starting from left to right (or right to left!) make a series of pillars with the following headers:

1. Goal of the Project
2. Alignment to the Broader Strategy
3. Business Impact
4. Direct or Indirect Impact on Customer Well-Being and Broader Society
5. Direct or Indirect Impact on the Environmental
6. Direct or Indirect Impact on Employee Well-Being

Under each header separate the space into the following four horizontal segments, from top to bottom:

1. Intended Outcomes
2. Unintended Consequences
3. Operational, Financial, or Reputational Risks (Key Risks)
4. Mitigation Strategies

In the end, it should almost resemble a six-by-four matrix spanning the four walls of a room. The multidisciplinary team has assembled, and the excitement is high. It's time to start.

Step 1: Set the Stage for Impact

- Starting with the Intended Outcomes row, have the team articulate the goal of the project in terms of how it will serve the unmet needs of customers. Make it simple and specific.
- Move onto pillar two and align the goal of the project with the overarching strategy driving the innovation. Make sure you use exact language from the strategy so that the alignment is unmistakable. Align it with the company mission and values but try not to get distracted from the task.
- Move onto pillar three and list the benefit to the business using specific metrics known to (and measurable by) the business. Measurement is key, so stick to impacts that can be tracked and monitored.

Step 2: Step into the Future and Imagine a Better World

Now take a step back from the board and think broadly about the problem. Take a breath. Imagine it is five years into the future and the project has been a smashing success. Business value has been achieved, and the project sponsors are happy.

- Staying within the Intended Outcomes row, move onto pillar four and brainstorm the additional customer value that would be directly or indirectly created by the innovation. This should include the benefits at the individual level up to the population level to reflect potential impacts for society. Think about how people's behavior will change and what that could mean for their daily lives both at work and at home, with family and friends, or when they are alone. Be as ambitious as you can but stay realistic. If your innovation has the potential to solve world hunger that is incredible, but if it doesn't, then don't put it on the board.

- Move onto pillar five and go through the same exercise for environmental impact. This pillar can include benefits that you can touch and feel like a reduction in paper use, or benefits in the atmospheric level in the form of CO_2 emission reduction and a lowering of energy consumption.
- Finally, move on to the impact on employee well-being. Think about how the change in your customer's behavior will in turn change the interaction dynamics between these two groups of people. Consider how those dynamics may shift their sense of self, confidence, or capability.

Now have the group go across the row and use one color "dot" for the outcomes they are most excited about, and another color "dot" for outcomes where data accessibility requires further consideration. For those that generate the greatest excitement (and therefore arguably the most impact) but do not clearly map to data, set them aside for further conversations to determine feasibility.

Step 3: Imagine Things Did Not Go as Planned

Time to shift to the perhaps uncomfortable part of the exercise: the Unintended Consequences row. Take a step back from the board. Imagine that it is five years into the future, and the project has failed. Not that it was a marginal success or just didn't meet the targets. Imagine that it was a spectacular flop.

- Moving to pillars one and two (collapse them together for the remaining three rows of Unintended Consequences, Key Risks, and Mitigation Strategies), brainstorm reasons why the project did not work. Stick within the particulars of the innovation. The functionality, the governance structure, the implementation, the adoption rate, or accuracy of the solution to the unmet needs you were trying to solve. Think about whether the innovation met the customer needs, or whether the customer needs were right in the first place. Consider "horror stories" you have read about in the news or issues you have experienced in innovations of the past. Do the same for pillar three. Think about how the project could have *eroded* value for the company.

- Move onto pillar four and consider the customer. Focus on how alternative channels of communication or interaction may be disrupted or how biases in the model could make things more difficult for particularly vulnerable groups in the population. Consider the internal processes and structures that govern AI models and the integrity of the data being collected and used. Consider the privacy concerns around that data, too. It will feel uncomfortable but go as deep and dark as you can.

- Then move on to pillar five and brainstorm potential consequences to the environment. Do the same for employee well-being. When considering employees, think about their emotional, social, and cognitive health. Think about issues of empowerment, confidence, and capability. Now cluster the risks into themes.

In a similar exercise to the Intended Outcomes row, now have the group go across the row and bucket the risks into "act," "influence," or "monitor." The "act" bucket reflects risks that can be directly mitigated, while the "influence" bucket reflects risks that can be directly or indirectly influenced. The "monitor" bucket reflects risks that are entirely out of your control and therefore must be watched closely. Have the team then vote by "dot" for the top three risks that they can act on, influence, and monitor – across each of the pillars (Customers/Environment/Employees). Have a discussion on why the team members chose the risks that they did and from that discussion, outline key parameters for prioritization. Outline what matters most for how you rank the risks and then perform the prioritization.

Then in the Key Risks row, identify whether the risks identified are operational, financial, or reputational. This helps clarify the mitigation strategies that will be needed.

Step 4: Tighten the Screws before Lift Off

Take a moment to shake off any leftover feelings from the consequences exercise. It can be disheartening to think about the negative, so assure the team that this is all just about making sure the innovation achieves the intended outcomes that had them so excited. You are just tightening the screws to make sure the flight is a safe one.

Moving across each of the pillars, brainstorm ways that the teams can reduce the likelihood that these unintended consequences happen. It can be through governance, controls, measurement and tracking, training and upskilling, operational model redesign, innovation design tweaks, or a communication strategy. They can be discrete initiatives, full workstreams, or a change to the way the project is run. In a similar exercise to the Intended Outcomes row, have the group go across the row and vote by "dot" for the top three mitigation tactics they think will be most effective. Discuss why the team members chose the tactics, and from that discussion, outline key parameters for prioritization. Outline what matters most for how you rank the tactics and then perform the prioritization. Assign accountabilities to each of the tactics and voila! You've got a plan.

The key insights should be integrated into a one-page document that can be passed on to leadership and used as a reminder to keep their eye on the prize.

ARE YOU READY FOR TAKEOFF?

It is not easy to build a rocket ship and fly to the moon. It is a lot of hard work and even if you do manage to take flight, there is little guarantee you will land without a bruise or two. The push and pull pressure on companies today – to accept the label of a villain while stepping forward as a humble hero – is challenging for even the most nimble and well-intentioned leaders. In the race to precision

Table 18.1 The Giant leap methodology: An illustrative example

	Goal of the project	Alignment to the broader strategy	Business impact	Direct or indirect impact on customer well-being or social impact	Direct or indirect environmental impact	Direct or indirect impact on employee well-being
	How does the AI target unmet needs of customers?	*How do those unmet needs align to our strategic pillars?*	*What is the impact on revenue, market share, market growth, or profitability?*	*Are we solving issues facing our customers or society more broadly?*	*Is there an impact on the environment?*	*If we achieve our goal, is there an impact on the social well-being of our employees?*
Intended outcomes	*An easy-to-use app that will customize the in-store experience through "smart shelves" and real-time guidance throughout the store based on history, needs, and in-store discounts*	*The project aligns to the broader strategic pillar of "delivering a seamless customer experience"*	*Increase in basket size and loyalty, reduction in profit leakage from out-of-stock instances, advertising revenue*	*Improved choices aligned to needs and goals, improved efficiency outside and in store, record of shopping history, improved family nutrition*	*Reduction in paper price tags and receipts, food waste, and carbon footprint and energy consumption from app design, hosting, and use*	*Happier customers to deal with, fewer return of items, improved efficiency of shelf stocking*
Unintended consequences	*App does not function properly and customers' experience is more arduous than before, low adoption*		*Data hacking, recommendation engine does not properly align to in-stock items*	*Discrimination in or perception of inappropriate recommendations, influence on vulnerable populations, reinforcement of gender stereotypes, long wait times for resolution*	*Increased food waste because of poor predictive engine, supply chain transparency issues*	*Feelings of uselessness or perceived threat of job loss, managing app errors real-time*
Key risks	*Operational, financial, and reputational*		*Operational and financial*	*Reputational and financial*	*Reputational*	*Operational*
Mitigation strategies	*Pilot and scale implementation methodology; robust data collection, impact measurement, and monitoring; governance committee to oversee issues management*		*Data security enhancements, clear and concise terms and conditions, opt-in engagement model*	*Appropriate controls, transparency of data, non-gender-based customer segmentation for targeted marketing*	*Robust ESG measurement and tracking, vendor management system*	*Employee engagement survey and feedback program overhaul, communications strategy, training, employee-specific app benefits*

retail, the pressure can be even more acute, and there are plenty of companies who are on the hunt. In an IBM study[23] conducted in 2020, 79 percent of retail companies planned to use intelligent automation by 2021 and project annual revenue will grow by 10 percent as a result. In the extraordinary push for competitive value and staying relevant in a world evolving as quickly as ours, it is imperative that leaders consider the parallel shifts in expectations and the costs that come with ignoring the call to action. Amid the chaos of innovation – with the late nights, crowded boardrooms, and spirited discussion – leveraging the "giant leap methodology" helps ensure the screws are tight, the trajectory is calibrated, and the flight path is clear. Are you ready for the flight?

NOTES

1 Business Roundtable. (2019). *Statement on the purpose of a corporation.* https://system
.businessroundtable.org/app/uploads/sites/5/2021/02/BRT-Statement-on-the
-Purpose-of-a-Corporation-Feburary-2021-compressed.pdf.
2 Edelman. (2023). *Edelman trust barometer: Global report.* https://www.edelman.com
/sites/g/files/aatuss191/files/2023-01/2023%20Edelman%20Trust%20Barometer
%20Global%20Report_Jan19.pdf.
3 Wright, J., & Barlow, J. (2020). *Building supply chain resiliency with AI-driven workflows.*
IBM Institute for Business Value. https://www.ibm.com/thought-leadership
/institute-business-value/report/supply-chain-resilience.
4 IBM Institute for Business Value. (2020). *Covid-19 and the future of business.* https://
www.ibm.com/thought-leadership/institute-business-value/report/covid-19
-future-business.
5 IBM Institute for Business Value (2020).
6 Matheson, R. (2018). Model can more naturally detect depression in conversation:
Neural network learns speech patterns that predict depression in clinical interview.
MIT News. https://news.mit.edu/2018/neural-network-model-detect-depression
-conversations-0830.
7 Laguarta, J., Hueto, F., & Subirana, B. (2020). COVID-19 artificial intelligence
diagnosis using only cough recordings. *IEEE Open Journal of Engineering in Medicine
and Biology, 1,* 275–81. https://doi.org/10.1109/OJEMB.2020.3026928.
8 Cecchi, G. (2020). Could AI help clinicians to predict Alzheimer's disease before it
develops? *IBM Research Blog.* https://www.ibm.com/blogs/research/2020/10/ai
-predict-alzheimers/.
9 Sutton, D. (2018, June 8). How Vineyard Vines uses analytics to win over customers.
Harvard Business Review. https://hbr.org/2018/06/how-vineyard-vines-uses
-analytics-to-win-over-customers.
10 Green, D. (2018, August 26). *Nike has unveiled a new way to try on sneakers at its
stores without talking to anyone. Here's how it works.* Business Insider. https://www
.businessinsider.com/nike-scan-to-try-tech-how-it-works-2018-8.

11 Schneier, B. (2015). *Data and Goliath: The hidden battles to collect your data and control your world.* W.W. Norton & Company.
12 Ohlheiser, A. (2016). *Trolls turn Tay, Microsoft's fun millennial AI bot, into a genocidal maniac.* The Washington Post. https://www.washingtonpost.com/news/the-intersect/wp/2016/03/24/the-internet-turned-tay-microsofts-fun-millennial-ai-bot-into-a-genocidal-maniac/.
13 Dastin, J. (2018). *Amazon scraps secret AI recruiting tool that showed bias against women.* Reuters. https://www.reuters.com/article/us-amazon-com-jobs-automation-insight/amazon-scraps-secret-ai-recruiting-tool-that-showed-biasagainst-women-idUSKCN1MK08G.
14 Thaler, R. & Sunstein, C. (2021). *Nudge: The Final Edition.* Penguin.
15 Tiku, N. (2017). *Get ready for the next big privacy backlash against Facebook.* Wired Magazine. https://www.wired.com/2017/05/welcome-next-phase-facebook-backlash/.
16 Hill, K. (2014). *Facebook manipulated 689,003 users' emotions for science.* Forbes Magazine. https://www.forbes.com/sites/kashmirhill/2014/06/28/facebook-manipulated-689003-users-emotions-for-science/?sh=64694bcc197c.
17 Sundström Poromaa, I., & Gingnell, M. (2014). Menstrual cycle influence on cognitive function and emotion processing – from a reproductive perspective. *Frontiers in neuroscience, 8,* 380. https://doi.org/10.3389/fnins.2014.00380.
18 Schiffer., Z. (2021). *Period tracking app settled charges it lied to users about privacy.* The Verge. https://www.theverge.com/2021/1/13/22229303/flo-period-tracking-app-privacy-health-data-facebook-google.
19 Porter, M., & Kramer, M. (2011). *Creating shared value.* Harvard Business Review. https://hbr.org/2011/01/the-big-idea-creating-shared-value.
20 Brown S. (2019). *Consequence scanning manual version 1.* Doteveryone.
21 Klein, G. (2007). *Performing a project premortem.* Harvard Business Review. https://hbr.org/2007/09/performing-a-project-premortem.
22 Mitchell, D.J., Russo, J.E., & Pennington, N. (1989). Back to the future: Temporal perspective in the explanation of events. *Journal of Behavioral Decision Making, 2*(1), 25–38. https://doi.org/10.1002/bdm.3960020103.
23 Chao, G., Cheung, J., Haller, K. & Lee, J. (2020). *The coming AI revolution in retail and consumer products: Intelligent automation is transforming both industries in unexpected ways.* IBV Institute for Business Value. https://cdn.nrf.com/sites/default/files/2019-01/The%20coming%20AI%20revolution.pdf.

Contributors

EDITORS

Laurette Dubé is the founding chair and scientific director of the McGill Centre for the Convergence of Health and Economics. She holds the James McGill chair of Consumer and Lifestyle Psychology and Marketing. Her work has been published in top disciplinary journals in psychology, management and medicine as well as in multidisciplinary journals. She holds an MBA in finance, and a PhD in behavioral decision-making and consumer psychology. In close collaboration with co-lead Brown and a worldwide network of scientists and action leaders, she has pioneered an approach to convergence research and innovation that is powered by digital platforms and large-scale data sets and centered around real-world projects with action partners operating at city, province, country, and global levels. During her 2020–1 sabbatical, she was a visiting scholar at the National Research Council of Canada and at the Pittsburgh Supercomputing Center, Carnegie Mellon, USA.

Maxime C. Cohen is the Scale AI chair professor of Retail and Operations Management and director of research at McGill University.

He is the chief AI officer of ELNA Medical and the scientific director of the non-profit MyOpenCourt.org. He is also a scientific advisor in AI and data science at IVADO Labs, and he is actively advising corporations, retailers, and start-ups on topics related to pricing, retail, and data science. Before joining McGill, he was an assistant professor of technology, operations, and statistics at NYU Stern and a research scientist at Google AI. He previously worked as a high-frequency trader and cofounded a real estate investment company. His core expertise lies at the intersection of data science and operations management. He has worked in retail, ride-sharing, airline, sustainability, cloud computing, online advertising, peer-to-peer lending, real estate, healthcare analytics, and conflict analytics. He has collaborated with many companies, including Google, Waze, Oracle Retail, IBM Research, Via, Spotify, Aldo Group, Couche-Tard/Circle K, L'Oréal, Cargo, and Staples, and he serves on the advisory board of several start-ups. In each project, he has worked closely with the company to develop solutions using tools such as machine learning, optimization, stochastic modeling, econometrics, and field experiments. His research and teaching have received more than thirty awards, including Poets&Quants Best 40-Under-40 MBA Professors, RETHINK Retail's Top Retail Influencers, MSOM Young Scholar Prize, and Best OM Paper in Management Science.

Nathan Yang is an assistant professor in marketing at the Cornell Dyson School of Applied Economics and Management. Previously, he was an assistant professor in marketing at McGill Desautels Faculty of Management and affiliate professor at McGill Bensadoun School of Retail Management. His main research interests are in behavioral analytics, empirical industrial organization, (mobile) health and wellness, and retail strategy. He completed his PhD in economics at the University of Toronto.

Bassem Monla has over thirty-five years of experience in IT for business and management consulting, of which twelve were in corporate and twenty-three were as a serial entrepreneur. He is currently the practice leader for the Data & Technology Transformation service line at LGS and an artificial intelligence (AI) subject matter expert at IBM. In 2021, Bassem was appointed as a professor of practice at McGill University – Desautels Faculty of Management. A technology enthusiast, Bassem believes in bridging research and practice and actively pursues knowledge in cutting-edge research in AI and applied mathematics. His deep commitment to fundamental knowledge is credited to his education at École Polytechnique-Paris, France's top institute of science and technology. He has provided professional services to different industries from telecom to finance, healthcare, government, and others.

AUTHORS

Moiz Ali has more than eight years of experience in data science, analytical engineering, and data analytics projects. His experience ranges in various domains of the financial services industry including retail customer marketing, pricing, and corporate credit risk. He loves to code, volunteer, and read books during his spare time.

Felipe Almeida is a UX and design researcher, currently employed by Microsoft in its Education team and focused on projects related to youth experiences, accessibility, equity, and inclusion. He completed his PhD at HEC's Tech3Lab with a focus on the blend of UXR, consumer psychology, and neuroscience, and has previously worked as a senior researcher in the R&D team of Immersion Corp., one of the leading companies in the development of haptic technologies. Felipe is also the adviser for the VFC project, the first Canadian neuroadaptive film experience that uses real-time brain data and generative AI models to create personalized sound experiences for the viewers. He is currently focused on using design to create positive social and environmental impact as a participant of Microsoft's Green Design V-Team, by pursuing further studies in permaculture design and volunteering to help with the design of a sustainable and educational project in Tanzania with the Maasai people.

Chloe Benaroya is the practice lead of UX and automation at GFT Group. A seasoned manager, she has led cross-functional and agile teams of designers, marketers, and engineers in Quebec, Canada and in distributed teams (US, off-shore) during digital transformation phases. She worked as an experience strategist at Manulife Innovation Lab and at Houghton Mifflin Harcourt educational publishing group as UX director, leading the Montreal studio. She has worked in different industries (media, gaming, education, financial services), in various organizations (from start-ups to international companies) and in different roles which provides her a 360-degree vision of production, service design, marketing, and product development.

Matthew Bourkas is a University of Toronto biochemistry doctoral graduate with experience in the biopharma industry and strategy consulting. He is currently working at a global strategy consulting firm with a focus on the life sciences. He previously worked as the director of insights and analytics at Q:Quest Inc., where he contributed to business strategy and market research projects with Fortune 100 companies across the food and beverage, biopharma, and healthcare services sectors.

Carl Boutet is a Montreal-based business strategist and executive adviser with over twenty-five years of hands-on operational, marketing, merchandising, and retail executive experience. He has worked across a full array of retailer environments from the very large – such as ten years with Costco Wholesale – to working as a strategy consultant for a group of eight hundred independent retailers across Canada. As the founder of StudioRx, he advises retailers, business leaders, b2c solution providers, companies, and researchers on how to tailor their solutions according to consumers' evolving needs and build effective commercial strategies. Recently named by Rethink Retail among the world's top 100 most influential retail thinkers, he's delivered major keynotes around the world including at NRF Big Show, ShopTalk, RCC STORE, Store of the Future (UK), ASEAN Retail Summit, Egyptian Retail Summit, and Economic Forum of the Americas. He is a regular contributor to CBC/Radio-Canada, BNN Bloomberg TV, CBC News, Radio-Canada Première, and CTV News. This past May, he published his first book, *The Great Acceleration: The Race to Retail Resilience*.

He holds an MBA from Queen's University and advises several start-ups, retail associations, and innovation labs including the Retail Council of Canada and is the principal adviser for the Retail Innovation Lab at McGill University. He is also lead marketing instructor at the McGill University Executive Institute and adjunct faculty at the Asian Institute of Technology.

Christopher Cannon is an assistant professor of marketing at the Shidler College of Business, University of Hawai'i at Mānoa. He received his PhD in marketing from the Kellogg School of Management at Northwestern University. He broadly studies consumer behavior from a psychological perspective. For his research, he explores consumer motivations, luxury consumption, resource scarcity, social hierarchy, and gift giving. His publications have appeared in leading academic journals, such as the *Journal of Consumer Psychology, Personality and Social Psychology Bulletin*, and *Journal of the Association for Consumer Research*.

Joanna Castellano is an international business and behavioral research leader who has worked in senior management positions across various functional areas including business and marketing strategy, new business development, behavioral research and data analytics, and brand positioning and communication strategies. Her thirty plus years of experience span a wide range of industries, including financial services, healthcare, food and beverages, and packaged goods. She has conducted work for leading Fortune 500 companies in North America, Europe, and Asia. Joanna is the founder of Q:Quest Inc., an organization whose primary focus is to offer innovative solutions to critical business issues through a comprehensive understanding of the client and the marketplace. These objectives are accomplished through the use of a unique combination of leading-edge neuro-linguistic modeling techniques, behavioral economics, and cultural archetypes. These methodologies, as qualitative and quasi quantitative tools, have delivered significant innovative insights that have been validated repeatedly through large statistical random sampling and real-life test and control experiments and KPI trackers. In addition, Q:Quest has integrated

AI to further expand our multidisciplinary convergent innovation approach. Q:Quest's strength lies in its ability to translate and help activate insights into winning strategies and tactics.

Tamar Cohen-Hillel is currently a postdoctoral research scientist at Amazon. In the fall of 2021, she joined the Operations & Logistics Division at the University of British Columbia, Sauder School of Business as an assistant professor. She is interested in research in the field of retail operations management, including retail logistics, dynamic pricing, and consumer behavior learning and modeling. Her research is influenced by her industrial collaborators, including Teva Pharmaceuticals, Marvell Technology Group, Oracle Retail Group, Zara, and Amazon. She received her PhD in operations research from the Massachusetts Institute of Technology. Her PhD supervisor was Professor Georgia Perakis, and her dissertation was titled "Past Price and Trend Effects in Promotion Planning: From Prediction to Prescription." It focused on developing new methods for learning demand and optimizing pricing and logistic decisions in order to maximize revenue. Prior to joining MIT, she received an MS degree with summa cum laude in information management engineering, and a BS degree in industrial engineering both from the Technion – Israel Institute of Technology. Her master's thesis title was "Complexity Results for Periodic Decision Problems" and was supervised by Professor Liron Yedidsion.

Remi Daviet is an assistant professor at the University of Wisconsin-Madison.

In a first stream of research, Professor Daviet works on extracting valuable insight from multiple sources of data with the help of machine learning and AI. This also leads to the development of methods to optimize and automate business processes. Applications are diverse, such as automating ad design, optimizing packaging and product pictures, selecting human models for ad campaigns, analyzing communities of social media influencers, and improving room presentations for hotels. In a second stream of research, he focuses on understanding and predicting consumer decisions by combining quantitative modeling with advanced statistics. His models of decision-making rely on insights from many fields: neuroscience, cognitive science, psychology, genomics, and economics. Before joining the Wisconsin School of Business, Professor Daviet was a postdoctoral researcher in marketing at The Wharton School, University of Pennsylvania. He completed his PhD in economics at the University of Toronto, specializing in Bayesian econometrics and decision modeling.

Tim Derksen earned a BASc (specialization in mining engineering, 2010) from the University of British Columbia and an MBA (2016) from the University of Toronto. Currently, he is pursuing a PhD in marketing at the University of Alberta, working with Dr. Kyle Murray. During his PhD studies, Tim won the best poster presentation award from the Society of Consumer Psychology 2022 conference with Dr. Murray, for their work on the value of personal information.

Before pursuing his PhD, Tim worked with a variety of companies from very large Forbes 2000 companies to very small start-ups. These companies have encompassed the oil and gas, professional services, retail, and manufacturing industries.

Bruce Doré is an assistant professor in marketing at the Desautels Faculty of Management and director of the Affective Mechanisms Lab at McGill. Prof. Doré's research focuses on understanding how ideas and emotions spread, using tools from marketing, behavioral science, and neuroscience. This work combines social-behavioral experiments with functional neuroimaging, natural language processing, and computational modeling to better understand the mechanisms that drive impactful communication and consumer word of mouth. Before joining the faculty at Desautels, Prof. Doré was a postdoctoral researcher at the University of Pennsylvania.

Kelly Goldsmith began her research program as a doctoral student in marketing at Yale University, where her research on self-regulation integrated behavioral decision theory with goal theory. After receiving her doctorate, Dr. Goldsmith joined the Kellogg School of Management as an assistant professor of marketing. At Kellogg, she received multiple honors and awards for both her research and teaching. In 2017, she joined the Owen Graduate School of Management at Vanderbilt as an associate professor of marketing. She was promoted to full professor in 2021 and awarded the E. Bronson Ingram chair in 2022. She publishes regularly in top marketing and psychology journals and is currently serving on the editorial review boards of the *Journal of Consumer Research*, the *Journal of Marketing*, and the *Journal of Consumer Psychology*. She is an area editor for the *Journal of Marketing Research* and the *Journal of the Academy of Marketing Science*.

Juan Marcelo Gómez is a trusted adviser in the private and public sector. He lectures on retail management at Toronto Metropolitan University for The Ted Rogers School of Management. He specializes in sustainable development and social change, supply chain and procurement, and risk and regulation. He participates in a wide range of projects including design and implementation of organizational programs and international business development for exclusive organizations. With a specialization in complex and multi-stakeholder supply chains, he has led projects from food waste processing to research initiatives in supply, demand, and global distribution. His past academic appointments include mentoring MBA students through the MBA Gold Mentoring programme at Manchester Business School, and he acted as an editor with the *International Journal Innovation Science* (IJIS – USA).

He holds an MBA with an engineering pathway from the University of Manchester (UK) and an MS(Dist) in business and management research from the University of Reading (UK). He is completing his doctoral research at the Henley Business School (UK) on sustainability and collaborative relationships in the disintermediated agricultural and retail value chain with particular interest in luxury products. He holds a CPIM designation with the Association of Supply Chain Management (ASCM – USA), considered a prestigious certification in supply chain. Past professional accomplishments include receipt of an international certification as a CPIM Associate Instructor (ASCM – USA), a Food Safety consultant, and ISO 22000 "Food Safety Management System" practitioner certification

(Intertek Plc – CA), and, a QMS-A "Quality Management Systems Auditor" certification (RABQSA/IATCA – USA).

Hootan Habibkhani Kamran is a machine learning scientist at Scotiabank, where he has been the principal investigator in developing and delivering multiple ML products in different sections of the bank. He also teaches part-time in the Faculty of Analytics at Northeastern University. Since 2021, he has been teaching core analytics courses in the Master's in Analytics program of the College of Professional Studies. He has publications in scientific journals including the *Journal of Physics in Medicine and Biology* and the *IEEE Journal of Biomedical and Health Informatics*.

John Han is a marketing researcher at McGill University. His research straddles quantitative modeling, consumer behavior, and behavioral economics, with emphasis on multiparty strategic interactions. He studies market design and market inefficiencies in the B2B and P2P spheres, including auctions and bargaining. In a recent study, he explored how successive concessions and strategic delays can benefit all parties involved in B2B bargaining. His econometric models provide insights on the optimal distribution of concessions at each stage of negotiation and on optimal prices that allow sellers to maximize profits while avoiding unsuccessful and unnecessarily lengthy negotiations. Another area of his research is on the decision-making of an arbiter in resolving disputes between two parties that lay proportional claims on an asset. He designed two bargaining allocation problems to investigate this issue and found that the arbiter's off-equilibrium beliefs influenced her decision, despite the known equilibria. More specifically, incentivizing the arbiter with the payoff to the lowest-paid disputant resulted in low incidence of impasse and egalitarian claims from each party. These findings provide implications for franchise property rights and shelf space allocation. In other works, he explores consumer learning with incomplete information and behavioral norms in virtual market settings.

Pravithra Harsha is a principal research staff member in the AI pillar of the IBM T.J. Watson Research Center in Yorktown Heights. She is also a visiting scientist at the MIT Sloan School of Management.

She graduated with a PhD in operations research from the Operations Research Center at the Massachusetts Institute of Technology (MIT). Her dissertation advisers were Prof. Cynthia Barnhart and Prof. David C. Parkes. She worked as a scientist in the Analytical Services division of Oracle Retail for about a year after she graduated from MIT and was a postdoctoral associate at the Laboratory for Information and Decision Systems (LIDS) at MIT for about two years after that, where she was hosted by Prof. Munther Dahleh.

Ernan Haruvy is a full professor of marketing and Cleghorn Faculty scholar at McGill University, Desautels Faculty of Management. He is chief editor of the *Review of Marketing Science*, an associate editor at *Management Science*, senior editor at *Production and Operation Management*, associate editor at the *Journal of Behavioral and Experimental Economics*, and editorial board member at the *International Journal of Research in Marketing*.

Radosveta Ivanova-Stenzel obtained her doctoral degree from Humboldt University in 2001 where she also successfully finished her habilitation in 2005. Before joining the Technische Universität Berlin in 2011 as professor of microeconomics, she was professor of economics (behavioral economics) at Helmut Schmidt University in Hamburg. Her research focuses on experimental tests of strategic behavior and the development of theoretic concepts that explain observed decision-making, taking into account the limitations of human cognition and information processing. In her research, she studies behavior in trading mechanisms, spanning from bargaining to auctions.

Her papers have been published in *European Economic Review, Games and Economic Behavior, The Economic Journal, Journal of Economic Behavior and Organization, Economic Inquiry, Experimental Economics,* and others.

Gina Kemp is a behavioral neuroscientist who specializes in the interaction between the environment and behavior. She is particularly passionate about supporting the translation and mobilization of knowledge from bench to practice. This had been fueled by her professional experiences which include developing curricula to address stress and support the resilience of students at McGill University, producing public communications on loneliness and social isolation at the Public Health Directorate of Montreal, and advancing theoretical modeling of the self in behavior at the McGill Centre for the Convergence of Health and Economics. In addition, Gina is the president of the Equity, Diversity, and Inclusion group at the Research Institute of McGill University Health Centre that focuses on the impact of systemic and societal stressors on researchers. Currently, Kemp Consultations helps businesses and non-profits identify and address the impact of social stress on their operations.

John G. Keogh is a strategist, C-level adviser, and academic researcher with twenty-five years of executive leadership roles as director, VP and SVP in global supply chain management, information technology, technology consulting, and global supply chain standards. He advises the public and private sectors worldwide and is a regular subject matter expert on TV and radio. Mr. Keogh is the managing principal at the Toronto-based, niche advisory and research firm Shantalla Inc. Mr. Keogh holds a PG diploma and an MBA in management and an MS in business and management research in transparency and trust. He is currently completing doctoral research on transparency and trust in food chains at Henley School of Business, University of Reading. He is professor of practice at the Desautels Faculty of Management, McGill Centre for the Convergence of Health and Economics.

Sabine Kröger is a professor of behavioral economics at the Department of Economics at Laval University. She studies decision-making under uncertainty and how "human traits" such as social preferences, social norms, and cognitive shortcuts affect the decision-making process.

In her research, she uses a combination of standard and innovative economic techniques. In particular, she is one of the pioneers in the use of internet web surveys to conduct economic experiments with representative samples of a population. She is the founder and acting director of the Laval Experimental Economics Laboratory and codirector of the CIRANO laboratory.

She is member of CRREP (http://www.crrep.ca/ – Centre de recherché sur les risques, les enjeux économiques et politiques publiques), the DEPPI partnership (http://deppi.org/ – Disability, Employment, and Public Policies Initiative), and the Behaviourally Informed Organisations (BiOrg https://www.biorgpartnership.com/) partnership.

Murali K. Mantrala is the Ned Fleming professor at the University of Kansas School of Business. He is a professor emeritus of marketing at the University of Missouri, Columbia, distinguished visiting faculty member at S.P. Jain Institute of Management and Research (SPJIMR), Mumbai, and senior research fellow at the Indian School of Business. His previous positions include J.C. Penney associate professor at the University of Florida, manager at ZS Associates in Evanston, Illinois, and regional sales manager at Sandoz Pharmaceuticals, Mumbai, India. Mantrala has published extensively on topics such as retail pricing, category management, advertising and sales resource allocation, sales force compensation, and two-sided platform marketing strategies. Several of his research papers have received awards, including the 1998 Frank M. Bass Best Dissertation Paper Award of Marketing Science; the 2013 Best Paper Award of *Journal of Interactive Marketing*; and honorable mentions for the 2013 and 2017 Davidson Award of *Journal of Retailing*. He also was a finalist for the 1997 and 1998 William O'Dell Award and 2018 Paul E. Green Award of *Journal of Marketing Research*. Mantrala was coeditor-in-chief of *Journal of Retailing* (2015–17) and serves on the editorial boards of multiple leading research journals of marketing. He cochaired the 43rd American Marketing Association Sheth Foundation Doctoral Consortium in 2008 and hosted the Inaugural Marketing Strategy Consortium at MU in 2018. Murali is a recipient of the Humboldt Research Award from the Alexander von Humboldt Foundation in Berlin, Germany in 2010, the Don McBane Award for his lifetime contributions from the AMA Sales SIG in 2020, and the AMA Retail and Pricing SIG's Lifetime Achievement Award in 2021.

Henry Martinez has more than twenty years of experience driving business performance improvement through advanced analytics and insights, and ideating, designing, and implementing business performance management methodologies in the financial and consulting industries in Canada and Latin America. He holds an MBA from Kellogg School of Management and a BA in sociology from Universidad Catolica Andres Bello in Caracas Venezuela.

Chris McCarthy is a seasoned innovation professional with three decades of experience advising leading brands and start-ups. While currently North America focused, Chris has over ten years of experience supporting innovation strategy for brands across Asia, LATAM, and Africa. While knowledgeable about all stages of the innovation journey, Chris's experience is most comprehensive with the innovation front end – identifying opportunities and setting innovation strategy for a diverse range of brands (CPG, financial, tech, pharma / health, B2B, foodservice, retail). This deep and diverse experience led to several R&D roles in which Chris led the creation of new research approaches and consumer behavioral models. Chris has been published and has spoken on a variety of innovation topics, with special emphasis on disruptive innovation thinking as well as the unique challenges of innovating in health and wellness markets.

Kyle Murray earned his BS (specialization psychology, 1994) and PhD (marketing and psychology, 2004) from the University of Alberta. He has been with the Alberta School of Business since 2008, serving as vice dean from 2017 to 2021 and as the director of the School of Retailing from 2008 to 2017. Kyle has held faculty appointments at the Ivey School of Business (Canada) and Monash University (Australia), as well as visiting appointments at INSEAD (France) and TU Dublin (Ireland). An expert in human decision-making, Kyle's research interests focus on innovation and behavior-change challenges in business and society. He has published several books and dozens of peer-reviewed articles in leading journals in management, marketing, information systems, and organizational behavior. Kyle's work has attracted millions in grant funding and his research and teaching have been recognized with a variety of awards, including the McCalla Professorship, Killam Professorship, Petro-Canada Young Innovators Award, and the Mackenzie Teaching Award of Excellence.

As a consultant to government and Fortune 50 companies, Kyle has advised clients that include Air Miles, the Competition Bureau of Canada, Consumers Council of Canada, General Motors, Industry Canada, Johnson and Johnson, Leger, The Research Intelligence Group, and Microsoft. He has also been involved in a variety of start-ups, as an investor and adviser, in sectors ranging from financial services to retail and from advertising to cannabis.

Prasad A. Naik develops new models and methods to improve the practice of marketing. He has published over forty articles in prestigious journals such as *Journal of Marketing Research*, *Marketing Science*, *Management Science*, *Nature Reviews*, *Journal of the American Statistical Association*, *Journal of the Royal Statistical Society*, *Biometrika*, *Journal of Econometrics*, and *The Accounting Review*. He serves on the editorial boards of *Marketing Science*, *Journal of Marketing Research*, *The International Journal of Research in Marketing*, *Quantitative Marketing and Economics*, *Marketing Letters* and *Journal of Interactive Marketing*. Naik is a recipient of the UC Davis Chancellor's Fellowship, a Frank Bass Award, *The Journal of Interactive Marketing* Best Paper Award, and an Academy of Marketing Science Doctoral Dissertation Award. He has been honored as a William O'Dell Award Finalist, a Marketing Science Institute Top Young Scholar, American Marketing Association Consortium Faculty and Professor of the Year at UC Davis for outstanding teaching. He has presented over fifty seminars at prestigious institutions such as IBM, MIT, Harvard, Yale, Columbia, Cornell, Dartmouth, Chicago, Berkeley, Rice, and Darden, as well as at global conferences in Australia, Belgium, China, Canada, France, Germany, India, New Zealand, the Netherlands, Portugal, Spain, and Singapore. Prior to doctoral studies, Naik worked for several years with Dorr-Oliver and GlaxoSmithKline, where he acquired invaluable experience in sales, distribution, and brand management. Naik holds a PhD from the University of Florida, an MBA from the Indian Institute of Management, Calcutta, and a BS in chemical engineering from the University of Bombay.

Gideon Nave studies a wide variety of technological developments, from digital footprints of online behavior and language use and information search, to emerging biomedical innovations such as magnetic resonance imaging (MRI), genotyping, and hormonal assays that quantify the building blocks of the biological processes which shapes our preferences, cognition, and decision-making. His research examines how these topics may advance efficiency, productivity, and innovation, and evaluates the ethical challenges that they give rise to. To this end, he develops theories and methods that allow businesses and policymakers to focus their efforts in a more targeted fashion, with the promise of better addressing the needs of their customers and delivering the right products, services, and messages to the right people, at the right time. He also assesses the unique threats that such technologies might impose on consumer autonomy and privacy. Nave's research was published in top academic journals such as *Science, Proceedings of the National Academy of Science, Management Science, Nature Human Behavior, Journal of Marketing* and *Journal of Marketing Research.* Nave holds a PhD in computation and neural systems from Caltech. He completed his BS and MS in electrical engineering at the Technion – Israel Institute of Technology, specializing in signal processing.

Mikhail Nediak is a tenured associate professor at Smith School of Business, Queen's University. He has received his PhD in operations research from Rutgers University, New Jersey. Mikhail Nediak has taken part in collaborative research and development in analytics with industrial partners in finance, operations, and retail. He was a member of a joint team from Smith School of Business, Toronto-based Pricing Solutions Ltd., and Molson Coors Canada that won the 2013 INFORMS Revenue Management and Pricing Practice Award.

Anton Ovchinnikov is a distinguished professor of management analytics at Smith School of Business in Kingston, Canada. His research interests include, on the theoretical side, behavioral operations, revenue management, and environmental sustainability. On the applied side, he studies data-driven applications in business, government, and nonprofit sectors.

Georgia Perakis is the William F. Pounds professor of management at the MIT Sloan School, an associate dean at the Schwarzman College of Computing and MIT Sloan, the codirector of the Operations Research Center at MIT and the editor-in-chief of the *M&SOM* journal.

She won the Graduate Student Council Teaching Award in 2002, the Jamieson Prize in 2014 for excellence in teaching and the Teacher of the Year award in 2017. She has received several awards including the CAREER Award from NSF and the PECASE Award from the Office of the President on Science and Technology. In 2016, she was elected as an INFORMS fellow, and in 2021 as a distinguished MSOM fellow. In 2012, she received the Samuel M. Seegal Award for inspiring students to achieve excellence.

Kelly Peters led the helm as the CEO of BEworks, the world's first commercial behavioral economics advisory firm, which she cofounded in 2010 with the renowned scholars Dan Ariely and Nina Mazar. She guided the sale of the firm to the international creative services agency kyu in January 2017. She pioneered the BEworks Method to build a bridge between cutting-edge science and real-world application. The method has been applied to strategy, marketing, and operations challenges at Fortune 500 companies including Unilever, Georgia Pacific, CitiBank, and Manulife. She has provided oversight for over 300 projects in the financial services, healthcare, retail, and sustainability domains. Kelly studied philosophy before starting her career with dotcom start-ups in the early 1990s where her start-up experience included leading the product development team of iMoney, a fintech start-up later acquired by Rogers Media. She spent over a decade driving strategy and innovation teams in the banking sector for BMO Bank of Montreal and then Royal Bank of Canada where, in 2009, she launched the first in-house BE practice. She has served as a faculty lecturer at the Rotman School of Business, Cornell, Columbia, and Harvard. She is a frequent international keynote speaker and has delivered three TEDx talks. Her work has been published in prestigious peer-reviewed academic journals and has also appeared in numerous media outlets such as the *New York Times*, *Globe and Mail*, CBC, and *Business Insider*. She was awarded a Lifetime Achievement Award in 2022 by the prestigious *Consulting Magazine* for her ability to innovate, deliver the highest levels of client service, and affect positive change for her peers, her teams, and the industry. Previous awards include recognition for being an Innovation leader in the dotcom sector by Meckler-Media in 1999 and Volunteer of the Year by Flare Magazine for her work as executive director of WebGrrls Toronto, then Canada, 1995–9. In 2022, she founded Trial Run, a product innovation company dedicated to bringing together the power of behavioral science with block chain technologies in order to help aspirational leaders drive their sustainability goals.

Ricardo Filipe Ramos, PhD in management with a specialization in marketing, is an assistant professor at Escola Superior de Tecnologia e Gestão de Oliveira do Hospital, Polytechnic Institute of Coimbra (ESTGOH-IPC). He conducts research in marketing, consumer behavior, and tourism and hospitality. Ricardo enjoys taking advantage of online reviews and working with text mining techniques. His work has been published in reputable journals such as the *International Journal of Hospitality Management*, *European Research on Management and Business Economics*, and *Leisure Studies*.

Abderahman Rejeb is a doctoral student and researcher at the Department of Management and Law, Faculty of Economics, University of Rome Tor Vergata. His research interests include technology applications, supply chain management and logistics, marketing, and tourism. He has published several papers in international peer-reviewed journals. Abderahman was ranked the second top student in Tunisia for the Baccalaureate (year 2013), which entitled him to be awarded with the Governor's Excellence Award and La Banque de la Tunisie's grant.

Caroline Roux is an associate professor of marketing, and she holds the Concordia University research chair in Psychology of Resource Scarcity (2018–23). Her primary area of research explores how reminders of resource scarcity affect consumers' cognitions, judgment, and behavior. More broadly, her research interests focus on better understanding how pro-social values and moral consider-ations influence consumers' decision-making. Dr. Roux's research has been published in top marketing journals, and she routinely presents her work and organizes symposia at major international marketing conferences. Dr. Roux received her PhD in marketing from Northwestern University's Kellogg School of Management.

Oliver Rubel's research examines how companies can best deter-mine and allocate resources to marketing activities when facing a realistic chance of encountering a product harm crisis such as the SUV rollover controversy faced by Ford and Firestone in 2000 or the many product recalls Mattel was forced to make in 2007. His findings point to no single, simple answer to invest less or invest more. Rather, each firm's best solution depends on the characteris-tics of the crisis, including its likelihood, its impacts on sales, and on the effectiveness of marketing instruments. Rubel has presented his work at international conferences in marketing and management science and published in *Automatica* and in the book *Advances in Dynamic Game Theory* (Springer, 2007). He authored a monograph for the French ministry of finance that explored the economic rela-tionship between Japan and China in Southeast Asia. He was previ-ously a visiting assistant professor at Purdue University. A native of France, Rubel earned his master's degree in operations research at the Université Paris–Dauphine and completed his PhD at HEC Montreal (the affiliated business school of the Université de Mon-tréal). He focused on the design of dual-marketing channels, explor-ing how to manage direct and indirect sales to consumers. He has also studied competitive online marketing.

Arun Shastri is the global leader of ZS's AI practice, which spans researching, helping clients build their capabilities, and develop-ing ZS product and platform solutions. His work on a broad range of analytics issues spans multiple industries, including travel and hospitality, pharmaceuticals, high-tech, consumer, and healthcare. He is an expert in leveraging data science and advanced analyt-ics to drive organizational effectiveness and helping clients build and transform their digital capabilities. He is a contributing writer on sales for *Harvard Business Review,* on artificial intelligence (AI) for *Forbes* and is the cohost of the "Reinventing Customer Experience" podcast. Arun Shastri was with ZS from 1995 to 2010, during which he served clients across industries on a broad range of commercial effectiveness issues. He also opened ZS's Boston office in 2001. Before rejoining ZS in 2015, he was the chief strategy officer at IntraFi, a fintech focused on providing innovative asset and liability solutions to banks. Arun holds a PhD in decision sciences from the Kellogg School of Management at Northwestern University.

Harpreet Singh is an expert in artificial intelligence and machine learning technologies for quantitative analysis of social systems including marketing, branding, pricing, consumer behavior, and product development. Harpreet has twenty-two years of experience in deploying software technology and mathematical algorithms to solve business problems for large CPG, retail, food and beverage, healthcare and financial services companies with global presence. At present, Harpreet is leading the artificial intelligence and machine learning practice at Yum Brands with a specific focus on pricing, marketing performance optimization, product development, and consumer behavior. He leads a multifunctional team of seventy people comprised of data scientists, marketing scientists, software developers, and program managers. Prior to Yum, Harpreet created a profitable, innovation driven AI & data sciences company that combined mathematics, data, and marketing expertise to drive significant growth in marketing effectiveness. Kvantum was acquired by Yum Brands for its cutting-edge innovation in analytics, and the use of data to create significant, visible improvement in business outcomes. Harpreet has also worked with Target in their data science group in a leadership position to bring real-time, GPU based compute algorithms to solve retail scale problems in forecasting and optimization. Harpreet has worked for ten years with Publicis-Sapient where he led large customer experience consulting engagements including digital marketing, social media, e-commerce, customer care, and self-service initiatives. Harpreet has an MBA degree from the University of California Davis, Graduate School of Management and undergraduate engineering degree from IIT

Delhi. Currently, Harpreet's primary area of interest and research is on establishing evolutionary, real-time, simulation-based algorithmic systems to track business performance data across all functions of an enterprise and provide real-time tracking and guidance.

Meisam Soltani-Koopa is a PhD candidate in management analytics at Smith School of Business. His research area is data science in the financial sector, customer lifetime value, trade credit in supply chain management, and stochastic processes. He has contributed in the area of data science from 2018 by developing several analytics solutions in the retail banking and finance departments of Scotiabank. He has also taught data science for business at Smith School of Business.

Shivaram Subramanian has been with IBM for more than a decade developing cognitive systems within their Services Research division. Previously, he was Oracle's lead optimization scientist for retail pricing and supply chain, and a project lead for United Airlines' crew scheduling optimization for many years. His work has led to several commercial product releases and AI intellectual property that have been acquired by a top global airline. His current research focus is on practically combining large-scale discrete optimization and machine learning. Shiva was awarded the Pritsker doctoral dissertation award by the Institute of Industrial and Systems Engineers in the year 2000 for his PhD work at Virginia Tech under the guidance of Prof. Hanif D. Sherali.

Andrew Vakhutinsky is a consulting member of technical staff in the Machine Learning Research Group at Oracle Labs. He is working on the projects in the area of demand modeling, supply chain, and price optimization using real-life customer data. Andrew's other research interests are network routing, scheduling, and online optimization algorithms. Prior to joining Oracle, he worked for a number of companies including United Airlines, Telcordia Technologies, and BAE Systems. He received his PhD in management science from the University of Maryland, College Park, and MS in applied mathematics from the Moscow Institute of Physics and Technology.

Melaina Vinski is a behavioral science and behavior change specialist with over a decade of experience in the experimental study of cognitive neuroscience and human behavior, and over eight years of experience crafting evidence-based solutions on sustainability, stakeholder management, reputation risk, issues management, operational model design, and behavior change. As the former behavioral insights lead for PwC Canada and the current lead of behavioral science at IBM, Melaina is recognized as a leading expert in weaving behavioral science within traditional problem-solving paradigms to tackle some of the toughest challenges facing business and society. She holds a degree in cognitive neuropsychology and business from the University of Guelph and a master's and PhD in cognitive neuropsychology from McMaster University.

Milton Keynes UK
Ingram Content Group UK Ltd.
UKHW040247200924
448425UK00001BA/7/J